The Federalist Papers

THE FEDERALIST PAPERS

A Collection
of
Essays
Written in Support of the Constitution of
the United States

From the Original Text of
ALEXANDER HAMILTON
JAMES MADISON
JOHN JAY

Selected and Edited by Roy P. Fairfield

SECOND EDITION

The Johns Hopkins University Press
Baltimore and London

Roy P. Fairfield's edition of *The Federalist Papers* was originally
published by Anchor Books in 1961; second edition published in
1966. Johns Hopkins Paperbacks edition, 1981, published by
arrangement with Doubleday & Company, Inc.
Second printing, 1986

The Johns Hopkins University Press, 701 West 40th Street,
Baltimore, Maryland 21211
The Johns Hopkins Press Ltd., London

Library of Congress Catalog Card Number 80-8862
ISBN-0-8018-2607-1

CONTENTS

EDITOR'S INTRODUCTION   vii
PREFACE TO SECOND EDITION   xxviii
PREFACE TO JOHNS HOPKINS EDITION   xxix

Paper No.

 1. Introduction—Purpose of the Essays   1
 2. The Utility of Union   5
 3. The Union as Safeguard against War   10
 4. On Avoiding Foreign Attack   14
10. The Source and Control of Factions   16
14. Feasibility of an Extended Republic   24
15. Lack of Sovereignty in Present Confederacy   29
16. American versus State Citizenship   36
17. National Authority Subject to State Encroachment   41
21. Major Weaknesses of the Confederacy   45
22. Further Weaknesses   50
23. Imperative Need for Energetic Government   58
24. Necessity for Having Armed Forces   63
25. Providing the Common Defense   66
26. Legislative Checks on the Military   70
31. Need for Unlimited Power of Taxation   76
32. National and State Tax Spheres   79
33. Taxation—Necessary and Proper   83
34. Financial Strength and Military Necessity   88
35. Social Classes and Tax Interests   93
37. Convention's Problems in Designing Stable
       Government   99
38. Anti-Federalist Objections: Stated and Refuted   104
39. Distinctive Character of Republican Government   111

Contents

41. Military and Tax Power for the Common Defense 118
44. State-National Power Relationships 126
45. Restrictions upon State Authority Not Serious 133
47. Montesquieu and State Constitutions on
    Separation of Power 138
48. Blending of Powers: Theory and Practice 146
49. Pros and Cons of National Referendums 151
50. Alternative Amending Techniques 155
51. Structuring Checks and Balances 158
52. House of Representatives—Length of Term 164
59. State and Congressional Control of Elections 167
60. Class Conflict and Electoral Power 172
61. Time and Place of Elections 178
62. Security Inherent in the Proposed Senate 181
64. Senate Treaty-making Authority 187
69. Presidential Powers 192
70. President: Single versus Plural Executive 198
71. President: Tenure 205
72. President: Re-election or Exclusion? 209
73. President: Compensation and Veto Power 215
75. President: Blending Treaty-making Power 221
78. Judicial Tenure and Review 226
79. Judiciary Compensation and Competence 234
80. Extent of Judicial Authority 236
81. The Function of Superior and Inferior Courts 242
82. Doctrine of Concurrent Jurisdiction 251
83. Jury Trial 255
84. Why No Bill of Rights? 259
85. Concluding Plea for Union 269
ACKNOWLEDGMENTS 277
ANNOTATIVE APPENDIX 279
NOTES ON PREFACE TO SECOND EDITION 306
BIBLIOGRAPHICAL APPENDIX, FIRST EDITION 307
BIBLIOGRAPHICAL APPENDIX, SECOND EDITION 321
SELECTED BIBLIOGRAPHY, 1981 323
INDEX 325

INTRODUCTION*

The time: October 1, 1787.
The place: New York State.
The chief protagonists: Governor George Clinton and
Alexander Hamilton.
The issue: To ratify or to reject the newly constructed
Constitution?
The fuse: Clinton's "Cato" and Hamilton's "Caesar"
letters.

The roots of the struggle were as old and deep as the
American colonies: thirteen independent states strung thinly
along a fifteen-hundred-mile coast, united by language, common-law heritage, skepticism of authority, and belief in economic opportunity—but separated by constitutional differences
and geographical perspective. Both "sunshine patriots" and
"bloodstained soldiers" had returned to their homes after defeating the British. The fighting was over, but the political
revolution continued. Proponents of strong national government observed that however significant the Articles of Confederation might be in developing an experience of "common
cause," the instrument simply was not strong enough legally,
financially, or symbolically to unify the "Disunited States."[1]
Those favoring the Articles or a modified version thereof, the
localists, did not condone Daniel Shays and his rebels, but
they were suspicious of centralized governments and the closed
doors at the Constitution Convention. Governor George Clinton of New York was especially alarmed when his two cohorts,
Robert Yates and John Lansing, returned from Philadelphia
in early July with tales about the constitutional revolution
taking place there. On September 27, ten days after the Convention adjourned, Clinton opened his attack on the proposed

* Notes on the Introduction may be found beginning on page 279.

Constitution by sending the first of several "Cato" letters to
the New York *Journal*.

Thus, New York citizens were confronted with two alternatives: to continue under a loose confederation with considerable local autonomy or to agree to the newly invented federal
system. During the next nine months they became increas-
ingly aware of their pivotal geographical location. They could
make or break the Union, even if the requisite nine states
ratified the Constitution.

On October 1, when Alexander Hamilton wrote the first
of two "Caesar" letters in response to "Cato," a new chapter
began. Much as Hamilton desired a strong, monarchical-type
government,[2] he preferred the political and economic security
which the new Constitution promised to an unstable organization permitting debtor groups like Shays' to hang themselves "from the excess of democracy."[3] So he warned that
"Cato, in his future marches, will very probably be *followed*
by . . . CAESAR."[4] Even after Clinton's second letter, Hamilton remained optimistic, informing George Washington that
"the new Constitution is as popular in this city as it is possible
for anything to be, and the prospect thus far is favorable to it
throughout the state." He warned, however, that official opposition should not be minimized.[5]

Meanwhile, James Madison, the key synthesizer at Philadelphia, was cognizant of the shaping battle. During October he
wrote Jefferson, Washington, and Edmund Randolph from
New York to convey his observations regarding the prospects
of ratification in the several states. To the latter he remarked,
"The newspapers in the Northern and Middle States begin
to team with controversial publications."[6] And "team" they
did! During the closing months of 1787 and throughout 1788,
the country's ablest men wrote thousands of vehement letters
both defending and attacking the work of the Convention.[7]
Most authors used pseudonyms to preserve their anonymity.
Some adopted the names of well-known Roman patriots;
others used homely identifications such as "A Columbian
Patriot," "Centinel," and "A Federal Farmer."[8] During his letter war with Clinton, Hamilton conceived the idea of composing a series of essays analyzing the Constitution systematically, dispassionately, and at length. Thus, writing in the cabin

of a sloop on the Hudson River, he addressed the "People of the State of New York" in the first "Publius"[9] or *Federalist* paper, which was subsequently published in *The Independent Journal* on October 27, 1787 (see list of original sources, p. 307).

> I propose . . . to discuss the following interesting particulars—*The utility of the UNION to your political prosperity—The insufficiency of the present Confederation to preserve that Union—The necessity of a government at least equally energetic with the one proposed, to the attainment of this object—The conformity of the proposed Constitution to the true principles of republican government—Its analogy to your own state constitution—* and lastly, *the additional security which its adoption will afford to the preservation of that species of government, to liberty, and to property.*

During the next seven months Hamilton fulfilled this promise. Enlisting the immediate support of his fellow New Yorker, John Jay, and the assistance of James Madison in November,[10] Hamilton engineered the construction of the most famous political commentary in American history. Illness soon forced Jay out of the project, but Hamilton and Madison continued at white heat, often turning out as many as four essays a week. Both were busy with private affairs; consequently, they sometimes completed a number while the printer waited for the manuscript. When the newspapers containing the articles came off the presses, the authors made certain that the essays reached sympathetic eyes. Madison sent the first seven numbers to Washington, remarking, ". . . perhaps the papers may be put into the hands of some of your confidential correspondents at Richmond, who would have them reprinted there."[11] Hamilton sent copies to Randolph, and young James Kent procured them for an upstate newspaper.[12] And yet the authors' identities were kept a close secret.[13] In fact, not until the appearance of the first French edition of 1792 were the three men publicly identified with the project.

Hamilton's correspondence with Randolph reveals that J. & A. M'Lean, the publishers, contemplated collecting and reprinting the essays as early as December 2.[14] But the first volume, containing *Federalist Papers 1* through 36 did not appear until March 22, 1788. The second volume came out two months later. And thus, in a stroke, Hamilton gave the Federalists a ready-made handbook for use at the New York and Virginia ratifying conventions.[15]

But neither the essays nor Hamilton's naming of the Federalist Party silenced the Clinton forces and other anti-Federalist authors. The governor continued his "Cato" letters until January. Elbridge Gerry in Massachusetts, George Mason in Virginia, and Luther Martin in Maryland, all of whom refused to sign the Constitution at Philadelphia, joined a host of others in presenting both reasoned and irrational arguments against the proposed government. Nevertheless, the ratifying conventions adopted the new instrument in rapid succession. Delaware, Pennsylvania, and New Jersey approved it in December. The next month Georgia and Connecticut voted "Yes." And by the time the New York convention opened on June 17, Massachusetts and Maryland had also agreed to join the Union, raising the total number of states to eight. This made the New York debates even more vital, though it was generally known that the New Hampshire and Virginia conventions were already in session.

When the delegates to the Poughkeepsie Convention sailed up the Hudson on two ships, one carrying Clinton's followers and the other Hamilton's, the Federalists were outnumbered two to one. During the next month, therefore, Hamilton had to compensate with political generalship for what he and his *Federalist* colleagues had apparently failed to do through the written word. Melanchthon Smith, Hamilton's most able adversary in the debates, remarked of his opponent, "[he] speaks frequently, very long and very vehemently—has, like Publius, very much to say not very applicable to the subject."[16] But this very same Smith went over to Hamilton's side after reports arrived that New Hampshire and Virginia had become the ninth and tenth states to ratify. Political jockeying ensued. And when the final vote was taken on July 26, Hamilton's group won, 30 to 27. But it was a compromise. Clinton's colleagues voted to join the Union upon the condition that a second convention would be called if their proposed amendments were not adopted.[17] Obviously the pressure for such a session was reduced when the states adopted the Bill of Rights, December 30, 1791.[18]

But what about the *Federalist?* Did it fulfill its purpose? *If* one recalls that Hamilton conceived the project as a means of swaying New Yorkers "of intelligence, patriotism, property, and independent circumstances . . ."[19] and *if* these men constituted the majority of the electorate sending the delegates to Poughkeepsie, then it would appear that the *Federalist* missed its mark. Nor are these the only qualifying "ifs." Other questions remain. Were all of the *Federalist's* readers influenced by its arguments? And did all those with pro-Constitution sympathies vote, even in an election featuring universal manhood suffrage? Evidence is far from conclusive on any of these points.[20] John B. McMaster was probably not far from the truth in remarking that, "There is no reason to suppose that the followers of Clinton gave any more heed to the writings of Publius than did the followers of Hamilton to the foolery of Brutus and the nonsense of Centinel."[21] But, at a convention in which the shift of two delegates would have defeated ratification, who can determine conclusively what subtle influences may have swayed any two of those reversing their earlier allegiance to Governor Clinton?

Although evidence is equally inconclusive about the influence the essays had in other states, one or two contemporary comments are interesting in retrospect. Archibald Maclaine, writing to James Iredell in North Carolina, remarked, "He is certainly a judicious and ingenious writer, though not well calculated for the common people."[22] Others evaluated the work in accordance with party bias. And it is said that one senator in the First Congress made a memorandum, "Get the 'Federalist,' if I can, without buying it. It isn't worth it."[23]

Distinguished contemporaries of the founders' generation reacted more kindly. Noah Webster praised the essays for their "valuable political information and precision," while John Adams pointed out in an autobiographical comment that his own writings no doubt contributed to the work. Thomas Jefferson, writing to Madison a few months after completion of the project, said it was "the best commentary on the principles of government . . . ever written."[24] And Washington's reaction was prophetic.

> *When the transient circumstances and fugitive performances which attended this Crisis shall have disappeared, That Work will merit the Notice of Posterity; because in it are candidly and ably discussed the principles of freedom and the topics of government, which will be always interesting to mankind so long as they shall be connected in Civil Society.*[25]

During the next generation Madison and Hamilton were sometimes criticized for "propagandizing" or writing a "polemic."[26] But it is a testimony to their insights that a "polemic" has become a political classic.

Since 1788 the *Federalist* has gone through more than one hundred editions and reprints. Individual essays have appeared in "countless" anthologies. It has been translated into many languages and praised by statesmen, scholars, and jurists both at home and abroad.[27] And yet the book is not closely reasoned as are other great political works, such as Plato's *Republic*, Aristotle's *Politics*, or Hobbes' *Leviathan*. It often tends toward repetition. It is sometimes inconsistent; and its localism and dated observations hardly commend it to overseas politicians. It is lengthy, and its concepts are not always defined clearly. Furthermore, it was designed to win a political campaign. Nor do Hamilton and Madison refrain from citing their opponents' arguments repeatedly, often with rhetorical flourishes rather than precise logic. And certainly the style is not modern. Thus one is entitled to ask, why the interest?

In my judgment part of the answer lies in the fact that the *Federalist* had no early competitor as an interpreter of the Constitution. The official minutes at Philadelphia were deposited with the Department of State in 1796 but not printed until 1819. Madison's now famous Convention notes did not appear until 1840, and other personal minutes were fragmentary at best. Nor did the anti-Federalist papers have a continuing impact, despite the vigor with which many of them were written. Not only were they associated with a losing cause, but they were not put into usable form until the 1880s.

In a sense, then, the *Federalist* became identified with the founders' thoughts and intentions. Jefferson referred to it in 1825 as the one book "to which appeal is habitually made by all, and rarely declined or denied by any as evidence of the general opinion of those who framed and of those who accepted the Constitution of the United States, on questions as to its genuine meaning."[28]

When Justice John Marshall began to hand down his foundation-creating decisions, he too not only appealed to the *Federalist's* arguments, but he also indicated how solidly the essays had become embodied in American political thinking. In Cohens *v*. Virginia, for example, he remarked, "It is a complete commentary on our Constitution, and it is appealed to by all parties in the questions to which that instrument gave birth." A few years later Joseph Story admitted having transferred to his *Commentaries* "all which seemed to be of permanent importance in that great work." Kent, too, composing his commentaries, which influenced several generations of lawyers, praised the *Federalist*.

> *There is no work on the subject of the constitution, and on republican and federal government generally, that deserves to be more thoroughly studied. . . . I know not, indeed, of any work on the principles of free government, that is to be compared, in instruction and intrinsic value, to this small and unpretending volume . . . not even if we resort to Aristotle, Cicero, Machiavel* [sic]*, Montesquieu, Milton, Locke, or Burke.*[29]

Also insuring its impact upon American leaders was its inclusion in college curriculums. Jefferson prescribed it for the newly founded University of Virginia. Possibly more significant, William Rawle in his widely adopted textbook, *A View on the Constitution*, quoted the *Federalist* many times and praised it for containing "the soundest principles of government." Then too, in 1865 Henry B. Dawson brought out a university edition.[30]

Not to be underestimated in any assessment of the wide appeal of the *Federalist* is consideration of other uses to which it was put in the nineteenth century. It was a commentary on American government, true, but it was also the first significant analysis of modern federalism. Overseas scholars were well aware of this fact. Alexis de Tocqueville read the book while stuck on a Mississippi River sand bar! He claimed that, along with Story and Kent, it was invaluable in clarifying our federal dualism. His distinguished countryman, François Guizot, went a step further, remarking that ". . . for all that combines a profound knowledge of the great elementary principles of human government with the wisest maxims of political administration, I do not know in the whole compass of my reading . . . so able a work." And across the Channel English intellectual giants such as Sir Henry Maine, Edward Freeman, James Bryce, and John Stuart Mill also deemed the *Federalist* a great work on the fundamental problems of government.[31]

Meanwhile, as other peoples of the world attempted to establish republican forms of government, they sought insight from the essays. As early as 1818, Henry Brackenridge found the Argentinians reading them in French translation. Before the century was over, two Portuguese and two Spanish editions were available to South Americans. When Canada, Australia, and South Africa underwent their own national birth pangs, their founders frequently cited the *Federalist*.[32]

In contemporary times, both at home and abroad, the essays have served many purposes. Recent German, Italian, and Japanese editions have emanated from intercultural exchanges. The German one, for example, grew out of the effort of the United States Information Agency, whereas the Italian one was privately initiated. The story of the latter is an arresting account of international co-operation. Dottore Negri came to Harvard on a Fulbright scholarship. When he returned to Italy, he realized that his country was a republic but that its people were ill experienced in self-government. Since he was a political-science professor, he felt a sense of responsibility for the teachers he was training. Also, he had a new awareness of the American experience of defining its philosophy and refining its laws and institutions. Why not translate the American documents so that Italians would have access to them? James D. Zellerbach, president of Crown Zellerbach, learned of Negri's concern and provided the money to launch the project under the leadership of Professor Gaspare Ambrosini. Adriano Olivetti, the Italian industrialist, also lent assistance, and the unveiling of the first book in the series, *Il Federalista*, took place at the Chigi Palace, Rome, in October 1955.[33] Upon that occasion the New York *Times* remarked, "This represents by far the most important United States–Italian cultural manifestation of the present year."[34] Within a month it had become a "best seller"; and the next year the U.S.I.A. libraries in Italy reported that "no other book is so asked for."[35] Library records reveal that high school and university students, newsmen, lawyers, priests, governmental employees, and laymen read the book.[36] The Japanese publication was similarly inspired, while the European Federalist Union sponsored the 1957 French edition.[37]

The precise extent of the book's influence on the thought and institutions of other lands is difficult to gauge. But extensive correspondence with scholars in Germany, Spain, England, India, Japan, and other countries reveals that the *Federalist* is widely utilized in classrooms and publications. And, of course, through our overseas libraries it is now available in most parts of the world. Though its circulation is not great, further translation is progressing steadily enough to assure the book's place in world literature.[38] Then too, workshops, lectures, and symposia conducted by Fulbright lecturers and cultural-affairs officers around the globe often feature the *Federalist,* thus acquainting foreign students and leaders with our Constitution-making experience.[39]

Neither foreign nor American scholars have been unanimous in their acclaim. Professor Max Beloff of Oxford University says that "it might be held that the influence of the *Federalist,* as far as American political thought is concerned, has been almost too great."[40] Many thinkers have perhaps relied too heavily upon the book both for the statement and the solution of problems. At the opposite extreme, William Crosskey is the most censorious critic. Early in his two-volume evaluation of the politics of the Constitution, he charges that the essays "contain much of sophistry; much that is merely distractive; and some things, particularly in the parts that Madison wrote, which come perilously close to falsehood." He also believes that the articles were written to fill up federal newspapers "to make less obvious the exclusion therefrom of opposing views" and that the "vogue of the *Federalist* . . .

was a vogue of a later time."[41] While it may be true that the
authors argued their cause vigorously and cleverly, it is difficult to believe, as one reviewer of Crosskey's work remarked,
that Madison "was one-third fool, one-third cheat, and one-
third Machiavelli."[42]

At still another level, many prominent historians and political commentators have given the book little or no attention.
Nor does "every schoolboy" receive exposure to its ideas in
contemporary high-school and college textbooks.[43] But many
scholars and statesmen of our day have utilized the book in a
wide variety of ways. Some have used it to probe the founding
fathers' intentions. Others have employed it as a touchstone,
putting our history up against the thought, even the predic-
tions, of Madison and Hamilton. Some public men have
found the *Federalist* a source book of plenitude—replete, as
John Foster Dulles once remarked, with "an unparalleled
wealth of political wisdom upon which we should continue
to draw."[44]

Since World War II the book has frequently been used to
highlight the analogy between the international situation and
that which the essays discuss. Between 1946 and 1949, for
example, Clarence Streit, John F. Schmidt, and Justice Owen
Roberts wrote a series of essays over the signature, "Publius
II." Upon collecting the essays for publication, they said,
". . . where *The Federalist* sought to apply federal principles
between the thirteen states, *The New Federalist* would apply
them between nations." They hoped their effort would "help
get an international federal constitution drafted."[45] Clarence
Streit also made considerable use of the essays in his two
Union Now books, while Norman Cousins, editor of the
Saturday Review, has often referred to the *Federalist* in calling for enlightened world leadership to prevent atomic catas-
trophe.[46] Then too, during the early years of its existence the
United World Federalists used the papers extensively.[47]

Interestingly enough, despite the world-wide attention
given the essays and the widely accepted American view of
their value, there is no great body of scholarship pertaining
to them. Most late-nineteenth-century editors wrote lengthy
introductions, which contained not only an analysis of the
Constitution-making period but also comments about the au-

thorship dispute. This controversy also elicited several well-reasoned essays. Although a complete survey of the argument need not concern us here, Professor Douglass Adair having recently made a brilliant analysis of the issue,[48] we might note the salient features of the topic which occupied the lion's share of *Federalist* scholarship prior to the present generation.

The dispute evolved from a note which Hamilton ostensibly left in a friend's law office prior to his fatal duel with Aaron Burr. In that hastily scribbled memo he attributed five essays to Jay, fourteen to Madison, three to the Virginian and himself written jointly, and sixty-three to himself. When Madison made his first public statement about authorship in 1818, however, his numbering disagreed with Hamilton's. He claimed a dozen essays more than Hamilton said he contributed. From that day until this, Hamilton and Madison partisans have assessed their hero's contributions differently. Today, while Hamilton's part in the *Federalist* project is not minimized, evidence weighs heavily toward the conclusion that Madison wrote the disputed essays.[49]

No survey of the uses and the abuses of the *Federalist* would be responsible without reference to Charles Beard's history-making *An Economic Interpretation of the Constitution of the United States* (1913). Beard found a pre-Marxian class argument in *Federalist, No. 10*, a view consistent with his thesis that economics motivated the construction of the Constitution. Although Beard's view has been argued and re-argued, the uncritical worshipers of the Founding Fathers have never been quite the same since 1913! Nor has *No. 10*. Virtually neglected throughout the nineteenth century, the number has been rediscovered, giving a new birth of awareness to Madison's keen insights.

Professor Gottfried Dietze, speculating upon the lack of scholarly attention given to the *Federalist*, believes that it results from three "fundamental misconceptions": 1) that there has been no general understanding that the book's thesis pivots about the concept of free government; 2) that it has been too often regarded as Jefferson saw it, a treatise on practical politics rather than theory; and 3) that it has not been widely understood as having a "split personality." Fortunately, Professor Dietze has defied tradition by writing the first full-length treatise on the essays (1960).[50] During the past two or three decades Professors A. T. Mason, Neal Riemer, Douglass Adair, and Benjamin F. Wright have also written first-rate articles analyzing particular aspects of the book.

Whatever the reasons for the seeming difference between wide acceptance and scholarly attention, I wonder whether the *Federalist* hasn't spoken most loudly for itself over the course of the generations. Possibly any analysis of intent and content may be at best a pale reflection of the original. And even the most sanguine of scholars might prefer that students and intelligent laymen come directly to grips with Hamilton's and Madison's thinking rather than risk any short-circuiting of that process. Surely this is the thought behind the Great Books and The Ford Foundation's sponsorship of recent abridged publication of the *Federalist*. With this risk in mind, it is suggested that those preferring personal exploration to reliance upon road maps go directly to the text of the essays. The next section will recapitulate some of the salient features of the book.

II

Although Hamilton's statement of purpose in *No. 1* provides a general outline, it may be helpful to take a more detailed overview.

Numbers	Subject Matter
1	Introduction to the Problem
2–14	Advantages of Union and Dangers of Disunion
15–22	Insufficiency of Confederacy under Articles
23	Need for Energetic Government
24–29	Organization and Control of Military Forces
30–36	Power of Taxation
37–46	Convention Deliberations, Republican Principles, and Classes of Powers
47–51	Separation of Powers
52–58	House of Representatives
59–61	Regulation of Elections
62–66	Senate
67–77	The Presidency
78–83	The Judiciary
84–85	Concluding Remarks

The most casual comparison of this outline with Hamilton's statement of objectives reveals that the authors managed the total project with considerable system, despite the pressure under which they often worked. Their problem in defending and explicating the Constitution was not only to prove that the Articles of Confederation were inadequate, but also that the new government would fulfill the needs of both states and individuals while providing for greater national security. Furthermore, as the project progressed and the anti-Federalists raised specific objections, Madison and Hamilton had to answer them in both theoretical and practical language. It was a tight-rope task, making the total results the more remarkable. They had to prove that the new government would be strong enough to effect unity but not so energetic that it would usurp state power. This fundamental problem of federalism arises repeatedly. Madison's argument in *No. 39* is the most skillful and sustained effort to convince readers that the Constitution would compound state and national sovereignty. Closely related to this problem was the need to allay fears that the government might become radically different from that already in existence. In *No. 40* Madison said that the "great principles . . . proposed by the convention may be considered less as absolutely new, than as the expansion of principles which are found in the articles of Confederation [sic]." Five numbers later he reassured New Yorkers that the change which the Constitution "proposes consists much less in the addition of NEW POWERS to the Union, than in the invigoration of its ORIGINAL POWERS."

However much Hamilton may be accused of compromising his own political preferences, he had the candor to admit it. And however much Madison and Hamilton may be criticized for presenting the Constitution in its best light, neither man dodged the fundamental issues which the new instrument raised. In my judgment this is a central element in the greatness of the *Federalist*. The problems they discussed were the enduring ones. Although the authors rarely mentioned their assumptions, they obviously accepted the major philosophical principles used to justify the American Revolution: belief in the state of nature, the conception of natural rights, the necessity of government, and the social compact theory.[51]

Within that framework Madison and Hamilton came to grips
with a great variety of basic political questions: Where is the
locus of power in a republic: in the people, states, or national
government? Or in a combination of these factors? What are
the objectives of government? What weighs heaviest: self-
preservation, liberty, justice, the promotion of happiness, or
the protection of property? How should these objectives be
achieved? In a federal form of government, to what extent can
the national legislature and the Executive exert an influence
upon individual citizens? Can a republic, sometimes successful in small states, survive in a large geographical area—or will
the forces of localism triumph where men regard themselves
as citizens of Massachusetts, Maryland, or Georgia, rather
than the United States? Which classes of men will benefit
most from the proposed Union—and will the new government
be threatened by factions, more concerned in promoting self-
interest than the general welfare?

And what about the army and taxes? Who should have the
power to declare war—and who should control the purse-
strings? Will the central government be strong enough to raise
a military force and moral enough to control its use? Should
military power support commercial enterprise? Is it politically
just and economically sound to permit the United States government unlimited power to raise taxes?

To what extent should man be trusted, if at all? And if not,
how should government check man's "passionate" tendencies
and channel his rational nature into creative political activity? Was Montesquieu sound in advocating separation of powers—or should these powers be blended in such a manner as to
promote the government's control of itself? Were the anti-
Federalists justified in claiming that the new Constitution
promoted too much overlapping? But then, what constitutes
a safe degree of "advise and consent" from the Senate? What
are the respective functions of the three branches of government? What constitutes a good program of rotation in office?
What are the arguments for and against a bill of rights? What
thought process did the members of the Convention at Philadelphia undergo in contemplating these problems? And, more
philosophically: would the new Constitution promote free
government?

Rarely did Hamilton and Madison (Jay being excepted here) answer these questions simple-mindedly or in a doctrinaire manner. Although both men were relatively young—thirty-three and thirty-seven, respectively—they had gained considerable experience during the previous decade. Both had read widely, though Madison was the more profound scholar.[52] They were familiar with Hobbes, Harrington, Locke, Hume, Blackstone, Montesquieu, Adam Smith, and other thinkers who had provided the Revolutionary generation with its common fund of ideas. But neither Hamilton nor Madison was a slave to authority. And rarely in the *Federalist* (*1, 37*) did they take the metaphysical leap of faith and appeal to divine authority.[53] In short, theirs was a synthesis of empiricism and rationalism. They had complex minds with which to cope with complex problems; and they usually revealed that such complex questions were "long" ones demanding complex answers.

While attempting to convince their readers that the Constitution would provide for the common defense and public peace, Madison and Hamilton repeatedly said, "Let us consult experience . . . that last best oracle of wisdom" (*52, 14*) or "history informs us" (*38, 63*); but they were not chained to the past. Madison made this clear in his second essay (*14*).

> *Is it not the glory of the people of America, that, whilst they have paid a docent regard to the opinions of former times and other nations, they have not suffered a blind veneration for antiquity, for custom, or for names to overrule the suggestions of their own good sense, the knowledge of their own situation, and the lessons of their own experience?*

Both authors repeatedly referred to the experience of Greece and Rome, but they were no doubt aware that the Constitution contained no detail taken directly from those civilizations. In *No. 63*, after discussing various ancient senates, Madison remarked that Americans should be instructed by such examples, not enslaved by them. Indeed, the Virginian, like his Philadelphia colleagues, was a creative observer and not a slavish imitator, finding in antiquity "a reservoir of wisdom, humanism, and great ideals."[54]

On the other hand, for all their appeal to experience, Hamilton and Madison often cited political "truths" with as much certainty as they might have postulated mathematical assumptions. In fact, Hamilton prefaced his discussion of political maxims in *No. 31* with a list of geometrical axioms. He then remarked

> *that there cannot be an effect without a cause; that the means ought to be proportioned to the end; that every power ought to be commensurate with its object; that there ought to be no limitation of a power destined to effect a purpose which is itself incapable of limitation. And there are other truths in the latter two sciences [ethics and politics] which, if they cannot pretend to rank in the class of axioms, are yet such direct inferences from them, and so obvious in themselves, and so agreeable to the natural and unsophisticated dictates of common sense, that they challenge the assent of a sound and unbiased mind with a degree of force and conviction almost equally irresistible.*

When Hamilton used this view as a tool of political analysis two essays later and Madison employed it in *No. 45*, they were led to the "palpable truth" (*33*) that "no part of the [Constitution's] power is unnecessary or improper for accomplishing the necessary objects of the Union." (*45*.) This was also consistent with the "plain proposition" which Madison stated in *No. 59*; namely, "that *every government ought to contain in itself the means of its own preservation*." Although the authors made other such axiomatic statements, perhaps one or two further illustrations will suffice. Beginning his discussion of the separation of powers in *No. 47*, Madison claimed that it was a "political maxim, that the legislative, executive and judiciary departments ought to be separate and distinct." It is important, of course, to bear in mind that Madison was thinking about republican government. Yet one wonders if he was justified in deriving such an axiom from Montesquieu alone. A few essays later Madison himself may have questioned his own methods in remarking that "Nothing can be more fallacious than to found our political calculations on arithematical principles." (55.)[55] And though Hamilton says in *No. 80*, "If there are such things as political axioms . . ." he rarely wrote as though he were in much doubt about their existence.

What may give Hamilton and Madison a dimension of cogency for the modern reader is their consistent consideration of alternatives in discussing the issues pertaining to the Constitution. Rarely did they introduce a topic without considering its many ramifications. In *No. 12*, for example, when urging that a tariff was the best form of tax for the proposed government, Hamilton presented the arguments both for and against other forms of taxation. Both men often discussed the various "classes of power" in their infinite variety. And, of course, in the most famous *Federalist* essay, *No. 10*, Madison moved logically from one alternative to another in considering the causes and effects of faction. Many such passages utilized anti-Federalist arguments en masse. In fact, at several points the authors so cleverly pit their opponents against one another that the latter appear ridiculously divided.[56] Sometimes, however, those sections contain rhetorical flourishes bordering on sophistry.[57] But they do afford Madison and Hamilton the opportunity to underscore the misguided efforts of their antagonists. In *No. 41* Madison remarked,

> *A bad cause seldom fails to betray itself. Of this truth, the management of the opposition to the federal government is an unvaried exemplification. But among all the blunders which have been committed, none is more striking than the attempt to enlist on that side the prudent jealousy entertained by the people, of standing armies.*

In all fairness, though, it must be observed that Hamilton and Madison were not above using imaginative horror in their own arguments. Early in the essays Hamilton frequently predicted that economic disaster, foreign attack, and political chaos would result if the states did not ratify the Constitution. And as a recent biographer notes, "Hamilton was indebted to Daniel Shays for a rare fund of propaganda with which to assail the Articles of Confederation."[58] During the course of the argument he referred to Shays' Rebellion five times; Madison mentioned it once.

Considering the fact that the *Federalist* essays were designed to win a political campaign, they are remarkably free of mudslinging, rhetorical devices, and specter psychology. In fact, this is one characteristic which distinguishes them from the anti-Federalist papers. With some exceptions the opponents of the Constitution excelled in resorting to imaginative horrors, spectral potentialities, and the fearful consequences of adopting the new form of government.[59] True, Hamilton, Madison, and especially Jay (2) occasionally flattered people by addressing them as "free and gallant citizens" (46) or referring to "the virtue and intelligence of the people of America" (49) and (57) to a "vigilant and manly spirit." On balance, however, the authors were extremely frank. Not only did they speak bluntly to their opponents, but they discussed the nature of man freely and plainly.

Professor Martin Diamond notes the difference between the eighteenth- and twentieth-century approaches to the analysis of political man.

> *Unlike modern "value-free" social scientists, the Founding Fathers believed that true knowledge of the good and bad in human conduct was possible, and that they themselves possessed sufficient knowledge to discern the really grave defects of popular government and their proper remedies. The modern relativistic . . . theories, implicitly employed by most commentators on the Founding Fathers, deny the possibility of such true knowledge and therefore deny that the Founding Fathers could have been actuated by knowledge of the good rather than by passion or interest.[60]*

But Hamilton and Madison *did* judge the good and the bad, and they relied heavily upon such judgments in discussing political behavior. In his second "Caesar" letter Hamilton bluntly stated that "the mass of the people of America . . . cannot judge with any degree of precision concerning the fitness of this New Constitution to the peculiar situation of America."[61] Nor had he changed his mind by the time he wrote *Federalist, No. 76:* "I proceed to lay it down as a rule, that one man of discernment is better fitted to analyze and estimate the peculiar qualities adapted to particular offices, than a body of men of equal or perhaps even of superior discernment." Even at the end of the papers, when he said, "I never expect to see a perfect work from imperfect man" (85), he tended to distrust both masses and individuals.

But Hamilton was not necessarily consistent. Upon two or three occasions when advocating the urgency of adopting the Constitution, he suggested that the governed were worthy of some trust. Completing *No. 22*, for example, just prior to launching into the need for an energetic government, he remarked, "The fabric of American empire ought to rest on the solid basis of The Consent of the People. The streams of national power ought to flow immediately from that pure, original foundation of all legitimate authority." Upon occasion his aristocratic bias also shone through the lines. In discussing the office of the presidency (76), he observed that "there would always be great probability of having the place supplied by a man of abilities, at least respectable." Then, of course, in *No. 78* Hamilton laid the cornerstone of the most original construction in American jurisprudence, the doctrine of judicial review. In fact, this is the only place in the *Federalist* where men seem to be trusted explicitly.[62]

Madison's view of human nature was no more exalted. "If men were angels," he remarked (51), "no government would be necessary." He believed that republican government would work if people were encouraged to participate in it; free government possible if men were permitted to associate freely (10). But he constructed no specious dichotomy. He saw *both* the better and the worse in man. "As there is a degree of depravity in mankind which requires a certain degree of circumspection and distrust, so there are other qualities in human nature which justify a certain portion of esteem and confidence." (55.) Upon this foundation Madison constructed his argument for republican government. Men's political passions should not be destroyed even if they could be. But they would serve the most creative end if channeled properly. Likewise, governments would control themselves if organized to blend and check power: institutionally, territorially, and legally. Private or economic passions would promote the general welfare if factions were controlled. And such control would result if faction were permitted to check faction. Thus, government should not inhibit man's effort to develop and exercise his talents. Such was the virtue of free government. And such was the means of reconciling liberty and authority.[63]

Contemporary scholars have called Hamilton and Madison "pessimistic naturalists" and "qualified optimists."[64] In either case it is appropriate to observe that, much as the *Federalist*'s authors might agree that the objective of government was the happiness of the people, they did not always agree upon the means to reach that end. Professors Alpheus T. Mason and Gottfried Dietze have analyzed these differences thoroughly, concluding that the *Federalist* does indeed have a "split personality." Suffice it to say here that Hamilton usually stressed the need to concentrate power, whereas Madison believed in balancing and blending it.[65]

The *Federalist* is also noteworthy for breaking several new trails in political thought. Not only was it a new synthesis in the presentation of the republican form of government, but it also opened the way for democratic modifications within the framework of the Constitution. The approach to ratification was interpreted in a democratic light (*39, 43*).[66] Then too, Hamilton pointed out that people from all walks of life would be represented in the new government, although "actual representation . . . by persons of each class is altogether visionary." (*35.*) Another departure: Madison's changing of Montesquieu's concept of the separation of powers. Whereas the Frenchman saw the branches as being relatively distinct in their functioning, the American advocated blending them (*47–51*). And how different is Hamilton's confidence in the Executive from that reflected in the Declaration of Independence! So long as the President could be checked by an intricate election system, a limited term of office, and the other two branches of government, he was a significant unifying symbol —as well as one who could get things done.

No. 10 contained two sharp breaks with the past: the advocacy of an extended republic and the legal recognition of unorthodox factions. Here Madison laid the foundation for the theory of pluralism which modern democrats have come to hold so dear. The perceptive reader of the *Federalist* will discover other new departures. Also, another fact will become evident: Madison and Hamilton were aware of their generation's pioneering effort, both in war and "in framing a government for posterity." (*34.*) Their generation, they said, "accomplished a revolution which has no parallel in the annals of human society. They reared the fabrics of governments which have no model on the face of the globe." (*14.*)

Any critical summary of the *Federalist* should include reference to the authors' avoidance of black-and-white thinking. They argued from the fullness of experience, with confidence in their method, and from the full perspective of political history and thought. For the most part they were brutally objective in facing facts squarely. They even discussed the Convention as though they had not attended it![67] Like their colleagues in Philadelphia, however, they were political realists, accepting the necessity of compromise, the inevitability of change, and the uncertainty of human behavior. Their inconsistencies no doubt resulted from genuine disagreement, hasty writing, and the lack of opportunity for fully co-ordinating the project.[68] Their misquoting the Declaration, Constitution, Montesquieu, and other sources may have stemmed from both carelessness and the desire to stress certain aspects of their authorities' work.[69] They reveal little sense of humor, but perhaps this is excusable in view of their objectives.

And theirs was no providential theory. They believed that evil days could visit Americans as well as other peoples. Hamilton once remarked that he knew "nothing to exempt this portion of the globe from the common calamities that have befallen other parts of it." (*36.*) Both Hamilton and Madison realized, too, that "parchment barriers" (*48*) would not promote liberty. They repeatedly defended the "necessary and proper" clause as the imperative means by which free government could insure its preservation.

When compared and contrasted with the anti-Federalist papers, the *Federalist* essays are urbane, rational, optimistic, and progressive.[70] Whereas the anti-Federalists were "Men of Little Faith," conservatives determined to retain the local controls which they could watch,[71] Hamilton and Madison were eager to take the step toward nationalism. "A nation without a national government," Hamilton remarked, "is . . .

an awful spectacle." (85.) Both men had confidence in the new government's promise for the future. Their essays bristle with statements having a modern ring. Their experimental utilitarianism reflects the genius of American political thought.

In its essential features the text in this edition follows that of 1788, but for easier reading omits excessive punctuation and capitalization. *No. 2*, however, is a transcription of the newspaper edition, affording the curious reader an opportunity to see how the original appeared. The controversial numbers are attributed to Madison.

In selecting the papers for this edition, the editor included those numbers of the *Federalist* most often used, groups of essays regarding particular topics rather than isolated numbers, and those numbers with most contemporary implication. The annotative materials include traditional documentation, sources from which Madison and Hamilton derived some of their insights, and comparative references leading the reader to further commentary about the topics in question.

ROY P. FAIRFIELD

Ohio University
Athens, Ohio

PREFACE TO SECOND EDITION*

During the six years since the first edition went to press,[1] there has been considerable *Federalist* scholarship. At least seven new editions have appeared. The authorship dispute has been settled. A definitive collation of texts has eliminated most ambiguity. Furthermore, schoolboys and politicians, from New York to Bangkok, continue to use *The Federalist* as a sourcebook of plenitude while critics of the contemporary American scene quote it to suit their purposes.

More specifically, the century-long authorship problem,

* For notes on this Preface, see page 306.

discussed on page xvii above, was fed to the computer by MIT and Harvard mathematicians. Using a statistical method invented in 1763 and gaining collaboration of fifty colleagues and foundation money, Frederick Mosteller and David Wallace spent four years comparing word frequencies and patterns of Madison's and Hamilton's known writings with those in the disputed essays. Result: mathematical probabilities of overwhelming proportions confirming Douglass Adair's 1944 findings, using traditional historical evidence, that Madison was the author.[2]

On the textual level: Professor Jacob Cooke completed his comparison of the newspaper and first three book texts, making readily accessible an analysis of the several forms. He confirmed Henry Dawson's view of the 1850s that most changes were relatively unimportant. Although somewhat antiquarian in concept Cooke's volume is a handsome one and worthy of exploration by those students interested in the implications of meticulous refinement.[3]

Benjamin F. Wright's former students would probably agree with this observer that his edition, published in 1961, was long overdue.[4] Those of us who had the good fortune to study with Professor Wright during the Forties heard much of what he has said in his eighty-six page introduction. But it reads as well as it sounded. No careful student of the *Federalist* can approach the American classic without spending a few hours with the mature thoughts of the former Harvard political scientist. Because I agree so much with Adrienne Koch's view that the Wright edition is "the best single edition of *The Federalist* in print,"[5] I could not disagree more with Willmoore Kendall's view that Wright's

> introduction is a *Summa* of what we may call the simplistic approach to the *Federalist* which sees in it nothing surprising, nothing exciting, above all nothing problematic. Five years hence it will seem barely credible that it should have been written at so late a moment in the development of *Federalist* criticism. But it will, for that very reason, have great value as a museum piece.[6]

But Professor Kendall's is not the only shoddy analysis. Holmes Alexander's *How to Read the Federalist*,[7] sponsored by Robert Welch and the John Birch Society, is a superb example of the "devil quoting scripture to his purpose." In "proving" the superiority of the Constitutional era over the contemporary, Mr. Alexander removes passages from context, confuses authorship (He attributes *No. 4* to Madison!), ascribes passages to the wrong essays. More seriously, he uses passages from *The Federalist* as springboards to harangue against welfare statists, free trade advocates and other such "misguided" souls. The book might properly have been entitled, *"How NOT to Read the Federalist!"*

Other monographs afford further perspective on particular aspects of *Federalist* influence.[8] Although a survey of the *Federalist's* use overseas failed to turn up any new publishing ventures, a personal check in five West African countries and fresh word from USIS librarians around the world reveal that the book continues to be used, however limitedly. Helsinki reports the book's being taken out twice in five years; Damascus: that the French edition was borrowed five times in two years, the English twice in seven; Saigon: that a reprint of the 1959 Nhu Nguyen edition is being considered; Rio de Janeiro: that the English "is limited to brief reference consultation," but the Portuguese is circulated about twice a year; Nairobi: used sixteen times in three years; Johannesburg: four editions "rarely circulate"; Abidjan: "The French version has been borrowed by members of the National Assembly, High Officials of the Ministry of Justice and the Supreme Court and by Law Students"; Baghdad: "The local book store . . . still has on hand the 1959 Arabic translation"; Singapore: "Six editions . . . loaned out 15 times since 1962; seven times to students, thrice to clerical people, twice to teachers, and once each to a librarian, film executive and salesman"; Yaoundé, Cameroon: "The French edition . . . has been borrowed ten times within the past year. The English . . . has not been borrowed"; Fort-Lamy, Chad: "six or seven times a year." Still further, we learn that the *Federalist* has not circulated at all at some of our overseas posts. But from Salisbury: ". . . presented to African leaders but no special comments have been made"; Karachi: ". . . we had copies, but the copies and all records were destroyed in the civil disturbances of September 21st [1965]"; Cairo: "There was a special demand for the book when the Government of the United Arab Republic was preparing its present charter." And from Uganda and Hong Kong we hear that "a few hundred paperback copies" and the introduction of American studies courses would no doubt lead to further use.[9] Meanwhile, back on these shores students are the primary users of the *Federalist*.

A spot check of the literature of federalism, published from London to Delhi since 1961, reveals continued reliance upon Publius' insights. And now that the authorship controversy is settled, perhaps future researchers will devote their energies to the total impact of the *Federalist* at home and abroad? Also, if we are to answer Karl Schriftgiesser's question of May 1961, "Will it in due course penetrate the Congo too?"[10] perhaps we need more study of comparative cultures? Long the source of inspiration to world federalists, the *Federalist* affords practical observations about human accommodation and political organization which *all* peoples may someday employ?

ROY P. FAIRFIELD

Putney, Vermont
March 1966

PREFACE TO JOHNS HOPKINS EDITION

Whenever issues of central vis-à-vis provincial political power become paramount for the survival of a nation, whether in the United States of America at any time, in Canada in 1980, or in the Sudan in 1981, the insights of the *Federalist* become relevant. Hence, *Federalist* "watchers" such as myself joy in finding references in the public press. While I do not tabulate the number of references each year, during the past decade I have seen such commentary in newspapers as distant as the London, Los Angeles, and New York *Times*es, the Chicago *Tribune,* and the Miami *Herald.* Meanwhile, as my updated and annotated bibliography indicates, scholars have continued to assess the value of the *Papers* for the contemporary scene.

In view of the seeming shift of American politics toward the conservative end of the continuum, confirmed perhaps by the election of Ronald Reagan in 1980, it is interesting

that the only major new edition in the recent past was published for the Conservative Book Club and coedited by
Professor Wilmoore Kendall, still exhorting conservatives to
use the *Papers* to counteract the "liberal egalitarianism" that
shifts power away from republican and toward central government. His polemic, of course, as suggested in my Preface
to the Second Edition, continues to be a polemic on the-
Papers-as-polemic.

More substantial as analysis are George Mace's and Vincent Ostrom's efforts to encourage readers to use the
Federalist as a tool for comparing other bodies of political
thought and for finding solutions to current problems.
Mace's insights are especially relevant to historians since he
reaches a conclusion quite contrary to that traditionally
held; namely, that American political foundations are more
Hobbesian than Lockean. Ostrum's efforts are valuable for
an appreciation of the complexities of *Federalist* insights
and for the perception that the complexities of current
governing, with interlocking, overlapping, and concurrent
powers in growing metropolitan areas, demand such a
paradigm as that suggested by Madison, Hamilton, and Jay.

At the time the Second Edition "went to bed" I was perhaps too optimistic in suggesting that the issue of authorship
had also been put to rest. Three more researchers, employing
still another methodology, have worked on the topic. They
compiled the number of times that twenty-four values occur
in ten papers known to be Hamilton's as well as the number
of times these same values occurred in ten papers known
to be Madison's. Their conclusions were the same as those
reached by Douglass Adair in 1944 and by Mosteller and
Wallace in 1964.

Time has precluded a formal survey of the uses of the
Papers at American libraries overseas; some enterprising
student might wish to start where I left off in 1966 to analyze
the extent to which these famous essays are used abroad.
There is no doubt whatsoever that the *Federalist* endures.

ROY P. FAIRFIELD

Bayberry Point
Biddeford, Maine
January 1981

THE FEDERALIST NO. 1

(HAMILTON)

To the People of the State of New York:

After an unequivocal experience of the inefficiency of the subsisting federal government, you are called upon to deliberate on a new Constitution for the United States of America.[1]* The subject speaks its own importance; comprehending in its consequences nothing less than the existence of the UNION, the safety and welfare of the parts of which it is composed, the fate of an empire in many respects the most interesting in the world. It has been frequently remarked that it seems to have been reserved to the people of this country, by their conduct and example, to decide the important question, whether societies of men are really capable or not of establishing good government from reflection and choice, or whether they are forever destined to depend for their political constitutions on accident and force. If there be any truth in the remark, the crisis at which we are arrived may with propriety be regarded as the era in which that decision is to be made; and a wrong election of the part we shall act may, in this view, deserve to be considered as the general misfortune of mankind.[2]

This idea will add the inducements of philanthropy to those of patriotism to heighten the solicitude which all considerate and good men must feel for the event. Happy will it be if our choice should be directed by a judicious estimate of our true interests, unperplexed and unbiased by considerations not connected with the public good. But this is a thing more ardently to be wished than seriously to be expected. The plan offered to our deliberations affects too many particular interests, innovates upon too many local institutions, not to involve in

* Notes to the text may be found beginning on page 287.

its discussion a variety of objects foreign to its merits, and of views, passions and prejudices little favorable to the discovery of truth.

Among the most formidable of the obstacles which the new Constitution will have to encounter may readily be distinguished the obvious interest of a certain class of men in every State to resist all changes which may hazard a diminution of the power, emolument, and consequence of the offices they hold under the State establishments; and the perverted ambition of another class of men, who will either hope to aggrandize themselves by the confusions of their country, or will flatter themselves with fairer prospects of elevation from the subdivision of the empire into several partial confederacies than from its union under one government.

It is not, however, my design to dwell upon observations of this nature. I am well aware that it would be disingenuous to resolve indiscriminately the opposition of any set of men (merely because their situations might subject them to suspicion) into interested or ambitious views: candor will oblige us to admit that even such men may be actuated by upright intentions; and it cannot be doubted that much of the opposition which has made its appearance, or may hereafter make its appearance, will spring from sources, blameless at least, if not respectable, the honest errors of minds led astray by preconceived jealousies and fears. So numerous indeed and so powerful are the causes which serve to give a false bias to the judgment, that we, upon many occasions, see wise and good men on the wrong as well as on the right side of questions of the first magnitude to society. This circumstance, if duly attended to, would furnish a lesson of moderation to those who are ever so thoroughly persuaded of their being in the right in any controversy. And a further reason for caution, in this respect, might be drawn from the reflection that we are not always sure that those who advocate the truth are influenced by purer principles than their antagonists. Ambition, avarice, personal animosity, party opposition, and many other motives not more laudable than these, are apt to operate as well upon those who support as those who oppose the right side of a question. Were there not even inducements to moderation, nothing could be more ill-judged than that intolerant spirit which has, at all times, characterized political parties. For in politics, as in religion, it is equally absurd to aim at making proselytes by fire and sword. Heresies in either can rarely be cured by persecution.

And yet, however just these sentiments must appear to candid men, we have already sufficient indications that it will happen in this as in all former cases of great national discussion. A torrent of angry and malignant passions will be let loose. To judge from the conduct of the opposite parties, we shall be led to conclude that they will mutually hope to evince the justness of their opinions, and to increase the number of their converts by the loudness of their declamations and the bitterness of their invectives. An enlightened zeal for the energy and efficiency of government will be stigmatized as the offspring of a temper fond of despotic power and hostile to the principles of liberty. An over-scrupulous jealousy of danger to the rights of the people, which is more commonly the fault of the head than of the heart, will be represented as mere pretence and artifice, the stale bait for popularity at the expense of the public good. It will be forgotten, on the one hand, that jealousy is the usual concomitant of love, and that the noble enthusiasm of liberty is too apt to be infected with a spirit of narrow and illiberal distrust. On the other hand, it will be equally forgotten that the vigor of government is essential to the security of liberty; that, in the contemplation of a sound and well-informed judgment, their interest can never be separated; and that a dangerous ambition more often lurks behind the specious mask of zeal for the rights of the people than under the forbidding appearance of zeal for the firmness and efficiency of government. History will teach us that the former has been found a much more certain road to the introduction of despotism than the latter, and that of those men who have overturned the liberties of republics, the greatest number have begun their career by paying an obsequious court to the people, commencing demagogues, and ending tyrants.[3]

In the course of the preceeding observations, I have had an eye, my fellow-citizens, to putting you upon your guard against all attempts, from whatever quarter, to influence your decision in a matter of the utmost moment to your welfare, by any impressions other than those which may result from the evidence of truth. You will, no doubt, at the same time, have collected from the general scope of them, that they proceed from a source not unfriendly to the new Constitution. Yes, my countrymen, I own to you that, after having given it an attentive consideration, I am clearly of opinion it is your interest to adopt it. I am convinced that this is the safest course for your liberty, your dignity, and your happiness. I affect not reserves which I do not feel. I will not amuse you with an appearance of deliberation when I have decided. I frankly acknowledge to you my convictions, and I will freely lay before you the reasons on which they are founded. The consciousness of good intentions disdains ambiguity. I shall not, however, multiply professions on this head. My motives must remain in the depository of my own breast. My arguments will be open to all, and may be judged of by all. They shall at least be offered in a spirit which will not disgrace the cause of truth.

I propose, in a series of papers, to discuss the following interesting particulars—*The utility of the UNION to your political prosperity—The insufficiency of the present Confederation to preserve that Union—The necessity of a government at least equally energetic with the one proposed, to the attainment of this object—The conformity of the proposed Constitution to the true principles of republican government—Its analogy to your own state constitution*—and lastly, *the additional security which its adoption will afford to the preservation of that species of government, to liberty, and to property.*

In the progress of this discussion I shall endeavor to give a satisfactory answer to all the objections which shall have made their appearance, that may seem to have any claim to your attention.

It may perhaps be thought superfluous to offer arguments to prove the utility of the UNION, a point, no doubt, deeply engraved on the hearts of the great body of the people in every State, and one, which it may be imagined, has no adversaries. But the fact is, that we already hear it whispered in the private circles of those who oppose the new Constitution, that the thirteen States are of too great extent for any general system, and that we must of necessity resort to separate confederacies of distinct portions of the whole. This doctrine will, in all probability, be gradually propagated, till it has votaries enough to countenance an open avowal of it. For nothing can be more evident, to those who are able to take an enlarged view of the subject, than the alternative of an adoption of the new Constitution or a dismemberment of the Union. It will therefore be of use to begin by examining the advantages of that Union, the certain evils, and the probable dangers, to which every State will be exposed from its dissolution. This shall accordingly constitute the subject of my next address.

PUBLIUS

THE FEDERALIST NO. 2

(JAY)

To the People of the State of New York:

When the people of America reflect that they are now called upon to decide a question, which, in its consequences, must prove one of the most important, that ever engaged their attention, the propriety of their taking a very comprehensive, as well as a very serious, view of it, will be evident.

Nothing is more certain than the indispensable necessity of Government, and it is equally undeniable, that whenever and however it is instituted, the people must cede to it some of their natural rights, in order to vest it with requisite powers. It is well worthy of consideration, therefore, whether it would conduce more to the interest of the people of America, that they should, to all general purposes, be one nation, under one Federal Government, or that they should divide themselves into separate confederacies, and give to the head of each, the same kind of powers which they are advised to place in one national Government.

It has until lately been a received and uncontradicted opinion, that the prosperity of the people of America depended on their continuing firmly united, and the wishes, prayers, and efforts of our best and wisest Citizens have been constantly directed to that object. But Politicians now appear, who insist that this opinion is erroneous, and that instead of looking for safety and happiness in union, we ought to seek it in a division of the States into distinct confederacies or sovereignties. However extraordinary this new doctrine may appear, it nevertheless has its advocates; and certain characters who were much opposed to it formerly, are at present of the number. Whatever may be the arguments or inducements which have wrought this change in the sentiments and declarations of these Gentlemen, it certainly would not be wise in the people at large to adopt these new political tenets without being fully convinced that they are founded in truth and sound Policy.

It has often given me pleasure to observe, that Independent America was not composed of detached and distant territories, but that one connected, fertile, wide-spreading country was the portion of our western sons of liberty. Providence has in a particular manner blessed it with a variety of soils and productions, and watered it with innumerable streams, for the delight and accommodation of its inhabitants. A succession of navigable waters forms a kind of chain round its borders, as if to bind it together; while the most noble rivers in the world, running at convenient distances, present them with highways for the easy communication of friendly aids, and the mutual transportation and exchange of their various commodities.

With equal pleasure I have as often taken notice, that Providence has been pleased to give this one connected country, to one united people; a people descended from the same ancestors, speaking the same language, professing the same religion, attached to the same principles of government, very similar in their manners and customs and who, by their joint counsels, arms and efforts, fighting side by side throughout a long and bloody war, have nobly established their general Liberty and Independence.

This country and this people seem to have been made for each other, and it appears as if it was the design of Providence, that an inheritance so proper and convenient for a band of brethren, united to each other by the strongest ties, should never be split into a number of unsocial, jealous, and alien sovereignties.

Similar sentiments have hitherto prevailed among all orders and denominations of men among us. To all general purposes we have uniformly been one people; each individual citizen everywhere enjoying the same national rights, privileges, and protection. As a nation we have made peace and war: as a nation we have vanquished our common enemies: as a nation we have formed alliances and made treaties, and entered into various compacts and conventions with foreign States.[4]

A strong sense of the value and blessings of Union induced the people, at a very early period, to institute a Federal Government to preserve and perpetuate it. They formed it almost as soon as they had a political existence; nay, at a time, when their habitations were in flames, when many of their Citizens were bleeding, and when the progress of hostility and desolation left little room for those calm and mature inquiries and reflections, which must ever precede the formation of a wise and well-balanced government for a free people. It is not to be wondered at, that a Government instituted in times so inauspicious, should on experiment be found greatly deficient and inadequate to the purpose it was intended to answer.

This intelligent people perceived and regretted these defects. Still continuing no less attached to Union, than enamored of Liberty, they observed the danger, which immediately threatened the former and more remotely the latter; and being persuaded that ample security for both, could only be found in a national Government more wisely framed, they, as with one voice, convened the late Convention at Philadelphia, to take that important subject under consideration.[5]

This Convention, composed of men who possessed the confidence of the people, and many of whom had become highly distinguished by their patriotism, virtue, and wisdom, in times which tried the minds and hearts of men, undertook the arduous task. In the mild season of peace, with minds unoccupied by other subjects, they passed many months in cool, uninterrupted, and daily consultation; and finally, without having been awed by power, or influenced by any passions except love for their Country,[6] they presented and recommended to the people the plan produced by their joint and very unanimous councils.

Admit, for so is the fact, that this plan is only *recommended*, not imposed, yet let it be remembered, that it is neither recommended to *blind* approbation, nor to *blind* reprobation; but to that sedate and candid consideration, which the magnitude and importance of the subject demand, and which it certainly ought to receive. But this, (as was remarked in the foregoing number of this Paper,) is more to be wished than expected, that it may be so considered and examined. Experience on a former occasion teaches us not to be too sanguine in such hopes. It is not yet forgotten, that well grounded apprehensions of imminent danger induced the people of America to form the Memorable Congress of 1774. That Body recommended certain measures to their Constituents, and the event proved their wisdom; yet it is fresh in our memories how soon the Press began to team with Pamphlets and weekly Papers against those very measures. Not only many of the Officers of Government, who obeyed the dictates of personal interest, but others, from a mistaken estimate of consequences, or the undue influence of former attachments, or whose ambition aimed at objects which did not correspond with the public good, were indefatigable in their endeavors to persuade the people to reject the advice of that Patriotic Congress. Many indeed were deceived and deluded, but the great majority of the people reasoned and decided judiciously; and happy they are in reflecting that they did so.

They considered that the Congress was composed of many wise and experienced men. That being convened from different parts of the country, they brought with them and communicated to each other a variety of useful information. That in the course of the time they passed together in inquiring into and discussing the true interests of their country, they must have acquired very accurate knowledge on that head. That they were individually interested in the public liberty and prosperity, and therefore that it was not less their inclination than their duty, to recommend only such measures as after the most mature deliberation they really thought prudent and advisable.

These and similar considerations then induced the people

to rely greatly on the judgment and integrity of the Congress; and they took their advice, notwithstanding the various arts and endeavors used to deter and dissuade them from it. But if the people at large had reason to confide in the men of that Congress, few of whom had then been fully tried or generally known, still greater reason have they now to respect the judgment and advice of the Convention, for it is well known that some of the most distinguished members of that Congress, who have been since tried and justly approved for patriotism and abilities, and who have grown old in acquiring political information, were also members of this Convention, and carried into it their accumulated knowledge and experience.

It is worthy of remark, that not only the first, but every succeeding Congress, as well as the late Convention, have invariably joined with the people in thinking that the prosperity of America depended on its Union. To preserve and perpetuate it, was the great object of the people in forming that Convention, and it is also the great object of the plan which the Convention has advised them to adopt. With what propriety, therefore, or for what good purposes, are attempts at this particular period, made by some men, to depreciate the importance of the Union? Or why is it suggested that three or four confederacies would be better than one? I am persuaded in my own mind, that the people have always thought right on this subject, and that their universal and uniform attachment to the cause of the Union rests on great and weighty reasons, which I shall endeavor to develop and explain in some ensuing papers. They who promote the idea of substituting a number of distinct confederacies in the room of the plan of the Convention, seem clearly to foresee that the rejection of it would put the continuance of the Union in the utmost jeopardy: that certainly would be the case, and I sincerely wish that it may be as clearly foreseen by every good Citizen, that whenever the dissolution of the Union arrives, America will have reason to exclaim in the words of the Poet, "FAREWELL! A LONG FAREWELL TO ALL MY GREATNESS."[7]   PUBLIUS

THE FEDERALIST NO. 3

(JAY)

To the People of the State of New York:

It is not a new observation that the people of any country (if, like the Americans, intelligent and well-informed) seldom adopt and steadily persevere for many years in an erroneous opinion respecting their interests. That consideration naturally tends to create great respect for the high opinion which the people of America have so long and uniformly entertained of the importance of their continuing firmly united under one federal government, vested with sufficient powers for all general and national purposes.

The more attentively I consider and investigate the reasons which appear to have given birth to this opinion, the more I become convinced that they are cogent and conclusive.

Among the many objects to which a wise and free people find it necessary to direct their attention, that of providing for their *safety* seems to be the first. The *safety* of the people doubtless has relation to a great variety of circumstances and considerations, and consequently affords great latitude to those who wish to define it precisely and comprehensively.

At present I mean only to consider it as it respects security for the preservation of peace and tranquillity, as well as against dangers from *foreign arms and influence,* as from dangers of the *like kind* arising from domestic causes. As the former of these comes first in order, it is proper it should be the first discussed. Let us therefore proceed to examine whether the people are not right in their opinion that a cordial Union, under an efficient national government, affords them the best security that can be devised against *hostilities* from abroad.

The number of wars which have happened or will happen in the world will always be found to be in proportion to the number and weight of the causes, whether *real* or *pretended,* which *provoke* or *invite* them. If this remark be just, it be-

comes useful to inquire whether so many *just* causes of war
are likely to be given by *United America* as by *disunited* America; for if it should turn out that United America will probably
give the fewest, then it will follow, that in this respect the
Union tends most to preserve the people in a state of peace
with other nations.[8]

The *just* causes of war for the most part arise either from
violations of treaties or from direct violence. America has already formed treaties with no less than six foreign nations, and
all of them, except Prussia, are maritime, and therefore able
to annoy and injure us. She has also extensive commerce with
Portugal, Spain, and Britain, and, with respect to the two latter, has, in addition, the circumstance of neighborhood to attend to.

It is of high importance to the peace of America that she
observe the laws of nations towards all these powers, and to
me it appears evident that this will be more perfectly and
punctually done by one national government than it could be
either by thirteen separate States or by three or four distinct
confederacies.

Because when once an efficient national government is established, the best men in the country will not only consent
to serve, but also will generally be appointed to manage it;
for, although town or country, or other contracted influence,
may place men in State assemblies, or senates, or courts of justice, or executive departments; yet more general and extensive
reputation for talents and other qualifications will be necessary
to recommend men to offices under the national government,
—especially as it will have the widest field for choice, and never
experience that want of proper persons which is not uncommon in some of the States. Hence, it will result that the administration, the political counsels, and the judicial decisions
of the national government will be more wise, systematical,
and judicious than those of individual States, and consequently
more satisfactory with respect to other nations, as well as
more *safe* with respect to us.

Because, under the national government, treaties and articles of treaties, as well as the laws of nations, will always be
expounded in one sense and executed in the same manner,—
whereas adjudications on the same points and questions, in

thirteen States, or in three or four confederacies, will not always accord or be consistent; and that, as well from the variety of independent courts and judges appointed by different and independent governments, as from the different local laws and interests which may affect and influence them. The wisdom of the convention, in committing such questions to the jurisdiction and judgment of courts appointed by and responsible only to one national government, cannot be too much commended.

Because the prospect of present loss or advantage may often tempt the governing party in one or two States to swerve from good faith and justice; but those temptations, not reaching the other States and consequently having little or no influence on the national government, the temptation will be fruitless, and good faith and justice be preserved. The case of the treaty of peace with Britain adds great weight to this reasoning.

Because, even if the governing party in a State should be disposed to resist such temptations, yet as such temptations may, and commonly do, result from circumstances peculiar to the State, and may affect a great number of the inhabitants, the governing party may not always be able, if willing, to prevent the injustice meditated, or to punish the aggressors. But the national government, not being affected by those local circumstances, will neither be induced to commit the wrong themselves, nor want power or inclination to prevent or punish its commission by others.

So far, therefore, as either designed or accidental violations of treaties and the laws of nations afford *just* causes of war, they are less to be apprehended under one general government than under several lesser ones, and in that respect the former most favors the *safety* of the people.

As to those just causes of war which proceed from direct and unlawful violence, it appears equally clear to me that one good national government affords vastly more security against dangers of that sort than can be derived from any other quarter.

Because such violences are more frequently caused by the passions and interests of a part than of the whole; of one or two States than of the Union. Not a single Indian war has yet been occasioned by aggressions of the present federal government, feeble as it is; but there are several instances of Indian hostilities having been provoked by the improper conduct of individual States, who, either unable or unwilling to restrain or punish offences, have given occasion to the slaughter of many innocent inhabitants.

The neighborhood of Spanish and British territories, bordering on some States and not on others, naturally confines the causes of quarrel more immediately to the borderers. The bordering States, if any, will be those who, under the impulse of sudden irritation, and a quick sense of apparent interest or injury, will be most likely, by direct violence, to excite war with these nations; and nothing can so effectually obviate that danger as a national government, whose wisdom and prudence will not be diminished by the passions which actuate the parties immediately interested.

But not only fewer just causes of war will be given by the national government, but it will also be more in their power to accommodate and settle them amicably. They will be more temperate and cool, and in that respect, as well as in others, will be more in capacity to act advisedly than the offending State. The pride of states, as well as of men, naturally disposes them to justify all their actions, and opposes their acknowledging, correcting, or repairing their errors and offences. The national government, in such cases, will not be affected by this pride, but will proceed with moderation and candor to consider and decide on the means most proper to extricate them from the difficulties which threaten them.

Besides, it is well known that acknowledgments, explanations, and compensations are often accepted as satisfactory from a strong united nation, which would be rejected as unsatisfactory if offered by a State or confederacy of little consideration or power. . . . PUBLIUS

THE FEDERALIST NO. 4

(JAY)

To the People of the State of New York:

My last paper assigned several reasons why the safety of
the people would be best secured by union against the danger
it may be exposed to by *just* causes of war given to other nations; and those reasons show that such causes would not only
be more rarely given, but would also be more easily accommodated, by a national government than either by the State
governments or the proposed little confederacies.

But the safety of the people of America against dangers
from *foreign* force depends not only on their forbearing to give
just causes of war to other nations, but also on their placing
and continuing themselves in such a situation as not to *invite*
hostility or insult; for it need not be observed that there are
pretended as well as *just* causes of war.

It is too true, however disgraceful it may be to human nature, that nations in general will make war whenever they
have a prospect of getting any thing by it . . .[9]

With France and with Britain we are rivals in the fisheries,
and can supply their markets cheaper than they can themselves, notwithstanding any efforts to prevent it by bounties
on their own or duties on foreign fish.

With them and with most other European nations we are
rivals in navigation and the carrying trade; and we shall de-
ceive ourselves if we suppose that any of them will rejoice to
see it flourish; for, as our carrying trade cannot increase without in some degree diminishing theirs, it is more their interest,
and will be more their policy, to restrain than to promote
it. . . .

The extension of our own commerce in our own vessels cannot give pleasure to any nations who possess territories on or
near this continent, because the cheapness and excellence of

our productions, added to the circumstance of vicinity, and the enterprise and address of our merchants and navigators, will give us a greater share in the advantages which those territories afford, than consists with the wishes or policy of their respective sovereigns.

Spain thinks it convenient to shut the Mississippi against us on the one side, and Britain excludes us from the Saint Lawrence on the other; nor will either of them permit the other waters which are between them and us to become the means of mutual intercourse and traffic.

From these and such like considerations, which might, if consistent with prudence, be more amplified and detailed, it is easy to see that jealousies and uneasinesses may gradually slide into the minds and cabinets of other nations, and that we are not to expect that they should regard our advancement in union, in power and consequence by land and by sea, with an eye of indifference and composure. . . .

But whatever may be our situation, whether firmly united under one national government, or split into a number of confederacies, certain it is, that foreign nations will know and view it exactly as it is; and they will act towards us accordingly. If they see that our national government is efficient and well administered, our trade prudently regulated, our militia properly organized and disciplined, our resources and finances discreetly managed, our credit re-established, our people free, contented, and united, they will be much more disposed to cultivate our friendship than provoke our resentment. If, on the other hand, they find us either destitute of an effectual government (each State doing right or wrong, as to its rulers may seem convenient), or split into three or four independent and probably discordant republics or confederacies, one inclining to Britain, another to France, and a third to Spain, and perhaps played off against each other by the three, what a poor, pitiful figure will America make in their eyes! How liable would she become not only to their contempt, but to their outrage; and how soon would dear-bought experience proclaim that when a people or family so divide, it never fails to be against themselves.   PUBLIUS

THE FEDERALIST NO. 10[10]

(MADISON)

To the People of the State of New York:

Among the numerous advantages promised by a well-constructed Union, none deserves to be more accurately developed than its tendency to break and control the violence of faction. The friend of popular governments never finds himself so much alarmed for their character and fate, as when he contemplates their propensity to this dangerous vice. He will not fail, therefore, to set a due value on any plan which, without violating the principles to which he is attached, provides a proper cure for it. The instability, injustice, and confusion introduced into the public councils, have, in truth, been the mortal diseases under which popular governments have everywhere perished; as they continue to be the favorite and fruitful topics from which the adversaries to liberty derive their most specious declamations. The valuable improvements made by the American constitutions on the popular models, both ancient and modern, cannot certainly be too much admired; but it would be an unwarrantable partiality, to contend that they have as effectually obviated the danger on this side, as was wished and expected. Complaints are everywhere heard from our most considerate and virtuous citizens, equally the friends of public and private faith, and of public and personal liberty, that our governments are too unstable; that the public good is disregarded in the conflicts of rival parties; and that measures are too often decided, not according to the rules of justice and the rights of the minor party, but by the superior force of an interested and overbearing majority.[11] However anxiously we may wish that these complaints had no foundation, the evidence of known facts will not permit us to deny that they are in some degree true. It will be found, indeed, on a candid review of our situation, that some of the distresses under which we labor have been erroneously charged on the operation of our governments; but it will be found, at the same time, that other causes will not alone account for many of our heaviest misfortunes; and, particularly, for that prevailing and increasing distrust of public engagements, and alarm for private rights, which are echoed from one end of the continent to the other. These must be chiefly, if not wholly, effects of the unsteadiness and injustice with which a factious spirit has tainted our public administrations.

By a faction, I understand a number of citizens, whether amounting to a majority or minority of the whole, who are united and actuated by some common impulse of passion, or of interest, adverse to the rights of other citizens, or to the permanent and aggregate interests of the community.[12]

There are two methods of curing the mischiefs of faction: the one, by removing its causes; the other, by controlling its effects.

There are again two methods of removing the causes of faction: the one, by destroying the liberty which is essential to its existence; the other, by giving to every citizen the same opinions, the same passions, and the same interests.

It could never be more truly said than of the first remedy, that it is worse than the disease. Liberty is to faction what air is to fire, an aliment without which it instantly expires. But it could not be less folly to abolish liberty, which is essential to political life, because it nourishes faction, than it would be to wish the annihilation of air, which is essential to animal life, because it imparts to fire its destructive agency.[13]

The second expedient is as impracticable as the first would be unwise. As long as the reason of man continues fallible, and he is at liberty to exercise it, different opinions will be formed. As long as the connection subsists between his reason and his self-love, his opinions and his passions will have a reciprocal influence on each other; and the former will be objects to which the latter will attach themselves. The diversity in the faculties of men, from which the rights of property originate, is not less an insuperable obstacle to a uniformity of interests. The protection of these faculties is the first object of government. From the protection of different and unequal faculties of acquiring property, the possession of different degrees and kinds of property immediately results; and from the influence of these on the sentiments and views of the respective proprietors, ensues a division of the society into different interests and parties.

The latent causes of faction are thus sown in the nature of man; and we see them everywhere brought into different degrees of activity, according to the different circumstances of civil society. A zeal for different opinions concerning religion, concerning government, and many other points, as well of speculation as of practice; an attachment to different leaders ambitiously contending for pre-eminence and power; or to persons of other descriptions whose fortunes have been interesting to the human passions, have, in turn, divided mankind into parties, inflamed them with mutual animosity, and rendered them much more disposed to vex and oppress each other than to co-operate for their common good.[14] So strong is this propensity of mankind to fall into mutual animosities, that where no substantial occasion presents itself, the most frivolous and fanciful distinctions have been sufficient to kindle their unfriendly passions and excite their most violent conflicts. But the most common and durable source of factions has been the various and unequal distribution of property.[15] Those who hold and those who are without property have ever formed distinct interests in society. Those who are creditors, and those who are debtors, fall under a like discrimination. A landed interest, a manufacturing interest, a mercantile interest, a moneyed interest, with many lesser interests, grow up of necessity in civilized nations, and divide them into different classes, actuated by different sentiments and views.[16] The regulation of these various and interfering interests forms the principal task of modern legislation, and involves the spirit of party and faction in the necessary and ordinary operations of the government.

No man is allowed to be a judge in his own cause, because his interest would certainly bias his judgment, and, not improbably, corrupt his integrity. With equal, nay with greater reason, a body of men are unfit to be both judges and parties at the same time; yet what are many of the most important acts of legislation, but so many judicial determinations, not indeed concerning the rights of single persons, but concerning

the rights of large bodies of citizens? and what are the different classes of legislators but advocates and parties to the causes
which they determine? Is a law proposed concerning private
debts? It is a question to which the creditors are parties on
one side and the debtors on the other. Justice ought to hold
the balance between them. Yet the parties are, and must be,
themselves the judges; and the most numerous party, or, in
other words, the most powerful faction must be expected to
prevail. Shall domestic manufactures be encouraged, and in
what degree, by restrictions on foreign manufactures? are
questions which would be differently decided by the landed
and the manufacturing classes, and probably by neither with
a sole regard to justice and the public good. The apportionment of taxes on the various descriptions of property is an act
which seems to require the most exact impartiality; yet there
is, perhaps, no legislative act in which greater opportunity and
temptation are given to a predominant party to trample on
the rules of justice. Every shilling with which they overburden
the inferior number is a shilling saved to their own pockets.

It is in vain to say that enlightened statesmen will be able
to adjust these clashing interests and render them all subservi-
ent to the public good. Enlightened statesmen will not always
be at the helm. Nor, in many cases, can such an adjustment
be made at all without taking into view indirect and remote
considerations, which will rarely prevail over the immediate
interest which one party may find in disregarding the rights
of another or the good of the whole.

The inference to which we are brought is, that the *causes*
of faction cannot be removed, and that relief is only to be
sought in the means of controlling its *effects*.

If a faction consists of less than a majority, relief is supplied
by the republican principle, which enables the majority to defeat its sinister views by regular vote. It may clog the administration, it may convulse the society; but it will be unable to
execute and mask its violence under the forms of the Constitution. When a majority is included in a faction, the form of
popular government, on the other hand, enables it to sacrifice
to its ruling passion or interest both the public good and the
rights of other citizens. To secure the public good and private
rights against the danger of such a faction, and at the same

time to preserve the spirit and the form of popular government, is then the great object to which our inquiries are directed. Let me add that it is the great desideratum by which this form of government can be rescued from the opprobrium under which it has so long labored, and be recommended to the esteem and adoption of mankind.

By what means is this object attainable? Evidently by one of two only. Either the existence of the same passion or interest in a majority at the same time must be prevented, or the majority, having such coexistent passion or interest, must be rendered by their number and local situation unable to concert and carry into effect schemes of oppression. If the impulse and the opportunity be suffered to coincide, we well know that neither moral nor religious motives can be relied on as an adequate control. They are not found to be such on the injustice and violence of individuals, and lose their efficacy in proportion to the number combined together, that is, in proportion as their efficacy becomes needful.

From this view of the subject it may be concluded that a pure democracy, by which I mean a society consisting of a small number of citizens, who assemble and administer the government in person, can admit of no cure for the mischiefs of faction.[17] A common passion or interest will, in almost every case, be felt by a majority of the whole; a communication and concert result from the form of government itself; and there is nothing to check the inducements to sacrifice the weaker party or an obnoxious individual. Hence it is that such democracies have ever been spectacles of turbulence and contention; have ever been found incompatible with personal security or the rights of property; and have in general been as short in their lives as they have been violent in their deaths. Theoretic politicians, who have patronized this species of government, have erroneously supposed that by reducing mankind to a perfect equality in their political rights, they would, at the same time, be perfectly equalized and assimilated in their possessions, their opinions, and their passions.

A republic, by which I mean a government in which the scheme of representation takes place, opens a different prospect, and promises the cure for which we are seeking. Let us examine the points in which it varies from pure democracy, and we shall comprehend both the nature of the cure and the efficacy which it must derive from the Union.

The two great points of difference between a democracy and a republic are: first, the delegation of the government in the latter to a small number of citizens elected by the rest; secondly, the greater number of citizens and greater sphere of country over which the latter may be extended.

The effect of the first difference is, on the one hand, to refine and enlarge the public views, by passing them through the medium of a chosen body of citizens,[18] whose wisdom may best discern the true interest of their country, and whose patriotism and love of justice will be least likely to sacrifice it to temporary or partial considerations. Under such a regulation, it may well happen that the public voice, pronounced by the representatives of the people, will be more consonant to the public good than if pronounced by the people themselves, convened for the purpose. On the other hand, the effect may be inverted. Men of factious tempers, of local prejudices, or of sinister designs, may by intrigue, by corruption, or by other means, first obtain the suffrages, and then betray the interests of the people. The question resulting is, whether small or extensive republics are more favorable to the election of proper guardians of the public weal; and it is clearly decided in favor of the latter by two obvious considerations.

In the first place, it is to be remarked that, however small the republic may be, the representatives must be raised to a certain number in order to guard against the cabals of a few; and that, however large it may be, they must be limited to a certain number in order to guard against the confusion of a multitude. Hence, the number of representatives in the two cases not being in proportion to that of the two constituents, and being proportionally greater in the small republic, it follows that, if the proportion of fit characters be not less in the large than in the small republic, the former will present a greater option and consequently a greater probability of a fit choice.

In the next place, as each representative will be chosen by a greater number of citizens in the large than in the small republic, it will be more difficult for unworthy candidates to practise with success the vicious arts by which elections are too often carried; and the suffrages of the people being more free, will be more likely to centre in men who possess the most attractive merit and the most diffusive and established characters.

It must be confessed that in this, as in most other cases, there is a mean, on both sides of which inconveniences will be found to lie. By enlarging too much the number of electors, you render the representative too little acquainted with all their local circumstances and lesser interests: as by reducing it too much, you render him unduly attached to these, and too little fit to comprehend and pursue great and national objects. The federal Constitution forms a happy combination in this respect; the great and aggregate interests being referred to the national, the local and particular to the State legislatures.

The other point of difference is, the greater number of citizens and extent of territory which may be brought within the compass of republican than of democratic government; and it is this circumstance principally which renders factious combinations less to be dreaded in the former than in the latter. The smaller the society, the fewer probably will be the distinct parties and interests composing it; the fewer the distinct parties and interests, the more frequently will a majority be found of the same party; and the smaller the number of individuals composing a majority, and the smaller the compass within which they are placed, the more easily will they concert and execute their plans of oppression. Extend the sphere, and you take in a greater variety of parties and interests; you make it less probable that a majority of the whole will have a common motive to invade the rights of other citizens; or if such a common motive exists, it will be more difficult for all who feel it to discover their own strength and to act in unison with each other. Besides other impediments, it may be remarked that, where there is a consciousness of unjust or dishonorable purposes, communication is always checked by distrust in proportion to the number whose concurrence is necessary.[19]

Hence, it clearly appears that the same advantage which a republic has over a democracy in controlling the effects of faction is enjoyed by a large over a small republic,—is enjoyed by the Union over the States composing it.[20] Does the advantage consist in the substitution of representatives whose enlightened views and virtuous sentiments render them superior to local prejudices and to schemes of injustice? It will not be denied that the representation of the Union will be most likely to possess these requisite endowments. Does it consist in the greater security afforded by a greater variety of parties, against the event of any one party being able to outnumber and oppress the rest? In an equal degree does the increased variety of parties comprised within the Union, increase this security. Does it, in fine, consist in the greater obstacles opposed to the concert and accomplishment of the secret wishes of an unjust and interested majority? Here, again, the extent of the Union gives it the most palpable advantage.

The influence of factious leaders may kindle a flame within their particular States, but will be unable to spread a general conflagration through the other States. A religious sect may degenerate into a political faction in a part of the Confederacy; but the variety of sects dispersed over the entire face of it must secure the national councils against any danger from that source. A rage for paper money, for an abolition of debts, for an equal division of property, or for any other improper or wicked project, will be less apt to pervade the whole body of the Union than a particular member of it; in the same proportion as such a malady is more likely to taint a particular county or district, than an entire State.

In the extent and proper structure of the Union, therefore, we behold a republican remedy for the diseases most incident to republican government. And according to the degree of pleasure and pride we feel in being republicans, ought to be our zeal in cherishing the spirit and supporting the character of Federalists.   PUBLIUS

THE FEDERALIST NO. 14

(MADISON)

To the People of the State of New York:

We have seen the necessity of the Union, as our bulwark against foreign danger, as the conservator of peace among ourselves, as the guardian of our commerce and other common interests, as the only substitute for those military establishments which have subverted the liberties of the Old World, and as the proper antidote for the diseases of faction, which have proved fatal to other popular governments, and of which alarming symptoms have been betrayed by our own. All that remains, within this branch of our inquiries, is to take notice of an objection that may be drawn from the great extent of country which the Union embraces. A few observations on this subject will be the more proper, as it is perceived that the adversaries of the new Constitution are availing themselves of the prevailing prejudice with regard to the practicable sphere of republican administration, in order to supply, by imaginary difficulties, the want of those solid objections which they endeavor in vain to find.

The error which limits republican government to a narrow district has been unfolded and refuted in preceding papers. I remark here only that it seems to owe its rise and prevalence chiefly to the confounding of a republic with a democracy, applying to the former reasonings drawn from the nature of the latter. The true distinction between these forms was also adverted to on a former occasion. It is, that in a democracy, the people meet and exercise the government in person; in a republic, they assemble and administer it by their representatives and agents. A democracy, consequently, will be confined to a small spot. A republic may be extended over a large region.

To this accidental source of the error may be added the

artifice of some celebrated authors, whose writings have had a great share in forming the modern standard of political opinions.[20] Being subjects either of an absolute or limited monarchy, they have endeavored to heighten the advantages, or palliate the evils of those forms, by placing in comparison the vices and defects of the republican, and by citing as specimens of the latter the turbulent democracies of ancient Greece and modern Italy. Under the confusion of names, it has been an easy task to transfer to a republic observations applicable to a democracy only; and among others, the observation that it can never be established but among a small number of people living within a small compass of territory.

Such a fallacy may have been the less perceived, as most of the popular governments of antiquity were of the democratic species; and even in modern Europe, to which we owe the great principle of representation, no example is seen of a government wholly popular, and founded at the same time wholly on that principle. If Europe has the merit of discovering this great mechanical power in government, by the simple agency of which the will of the largest political body may be concentred, and its force directed to any object which the public good requires, America can claim the merit of making the discovery the basis of unmixed and extensive republics. It is only to be lamented that any of her citizens should wish to deprive her of the additional merit of displaying its full efficacy in the establishment of the comprehensive system now under her consideration.

As the natural limit of a democracy is that distance from the central point which will just permit the most remote citizens to assemble as often as their public functions demand, and will include no greater number than can join in those functions; so the natural limit of a republic is that distance from the centre which will barely allow the representatives to meet as often as may be necessary for the administration of public affairs. Can it be said that the limits of the United States exceed this distance? It will not be said by those who recollect that the Atlantic coast is the longest side of the Union, that during the term of thirteen years the representatives of the States have been almost continually assembled, and that the members from the most distant States are not chargeable with greater intermissions of attendance than those from the States in the neighborhood of Congress.

That we may form a juster estimate with regard to this interesting subject, let us resort to the actual dimensions of the Union. . . .

. . . it is to be remembered that the general government is not to be charged with the whole power of making and administering laws. Its jurisdiction is limited to certain enumerated objects which concern all the members of the republic, but which are not to be attained by the separate provisions of any. The subordinate governments, which can extend their care to all those other objects which can be separately provided for, will retain their due authority and activity. Were it proposed by the plan of the convention to abolish the governments of the particular States, its adversaries would have some ground for their objection; though it would not be difficult to show that if they were abolished the general government would be compelled, by the principle of self-preservation, to reinstate them in their proper jurisdiction.

A second observation to be made is that the immediate object of the federal Constitution is to secure the union of the thirteen primitive States, which we know to be practicable; and to add to them such other States as may arise in their own bosoms or in their neighborhoods, which we cannot doubt to be equally practicable. The arrangements that may be necessary for those angles and fractions of our territory which lie on our northwestern frontier, must be left to those whom further discoveries and experience will render more equal to the task.

Let it be remarked, in the third place, that the intercourse throughout the Union will be facilitated by new improvements. Roads will everywhere be shortened and kept in better order; accommodations for travellers will be multiplied and meliorated; an interior navigation on our eastern side will be opened throughout, or nearly throughout, the whole extent of the thirteen States. The communication between the Western and Atlantic districts, and between different parts of each, will be rendered more and more easy by those numerous canals with which the beneficence of nature has intersected our country, and which art finds it so little difficult to connect and complete.

A fourth and still more important consideration is, that as almost every State will on one side or other be a frontier, and will thus find, in a regard to its safety, an inducement to make some sacrifices for the sake of the general protection; so the States which lie at the greatest distance from the heart of the Union, and which, of course, may partake least of the ordinary circulation of its benefits, will be at the same time immediately contiguous to foreign nations, and will consequently stand, on particular occasions, in greatest need of its strength and resources. It may be inconvenient for Georgia, or the States forming our western or northeastern borders, to send their representatives to the seat of government; but they would find it more so to struggle alone against an invading enemy, or even to support alone the whole expense of those precautions which may be dictated by the neighborhood of continual danger. If they should derive less benefit, therefore, from the Union in some respects than the less distant States, they will derive greater benefit from it in other respects, and thus the proper equilibrium will be maintained throughout.

I submit to you, my fellow-citizens, these considerations, in full confidence that the good sense which has so often marked your decisions will allow them their due weight and effect; and that you will never suffer difficulties, however formidable in appearance, or however fashionable the error on which they may be founded, to drive you into the gloomy and perilous scene into which the advocates for disunion would conduct you. Hearken not to the unnatural voice which tells you that the people of America, knit together as they are by so many cords of affection, can no longer live together as members of the same family; can no longer continue the mutual guardians of their mutual happiness; can no longer be fellow-citizens of one great, respectable, and flourishing empire. Hearken not to the voice which petulantly tells you that the form of government recommended for your adoption is a novelty in the political world;[21] that it has never yet had a place in the theories of the wildest projectors; that it rashly attempts what it is impossible to accomplish. No, my countrymen, shut your ears against this unhallowed language. Shut your hearts against the poison which it conveys; the kindred blood which flows in the veins of American citizens, the mingled blood which they have shed in defence of their sacred rights, consecrate their Union and excite horror at the idea of their becoming aliens, rivals, enemies. And if novelties are to be shunned, believe me, the most alarming of all novelties, the most wild of all projects, the most rash of all attempts, is that of rending us in pieces in order to preserve our liberties and promote our happiness. But why is the experiment of an extended republic to be rejected, merely because it may comprise what is new? Is it not the glory of the people of America, that, whilst they have paid a decent regard to the opinions of former times and other nations, they have not suffered a blind veneration for antiquity, for custom, or for names to overrule the suggestions of their own good sense, the knowledge of their own situation, and the lessons of their own experience? To this manly spirit posterity will be indebted for the possession, and the world for the example, of the numerous innovations displayed on the American theatre in favor of private rights and public happiness. Had no important step been taken by the leaders of the Revolution for which a precedent could not be discovered, no government established of which an exact model did not present itself, the people of the United States might at this moment have been numbered among the melancholy victims of misguided councils, must at best have been laboring under the weight of some of those forms which have crushed the liberties of the rest of mankind. Happily for America, happily, we trust, for the whole human race, they pursued a new and more noble course. They accomplished a revolution which has no parallel in the annals of human society. They reared the fabrics of governments which have no model on the face of the globe. They formed the design of a great Confederacy which it is incumbent on their successors to improve and perpetuate. If their works betray imperfections, we wonder at the fewness of them. If they erred most in the structure of the Union, this was the work most difficult to be executed; this is the work which has been new modelled by the act of your convention, and it is that act on which you are now to deliberate and to decide.

PUBLIUS

THE FEDERALIST NO. 15

(HAMILTON)

To the People of the State of New York:
. . . In pursuance of the plan which I have laid down for the discussion . . . the point next in order to be examined is the "insufficiency of the present Confederation to the preservation of the Union."[22] It may perhaps be asked what need there is of reasoning or proof to illustrate a position which is not either controverted or doubted, to which the understandings and feelings of all classes of men assent, and which in substance is admitted by the opponents as well as by the friends of the new Constitution. It must in truth be acknowledged that, however these may differ in other respects, they in general appear to harmonize in this sentiment, at least, that there are material imperfections in our national system, and that something is necessary to be done to rescue us from impending anarchy. The facts that support this opinion are no longer objects of speculation. They have forced themselves upon the sensibility of the people at large, and have at length extorted from those, whose mistaken policy has had the principal share in precipitating the extremity at which we are arrived, a reluctant confession of the reality of those defects in the scheme of our federal government, which have been long pointed out and regretted by the intelligent friends of the Union.

We may indeed with propriety be said to have reached almost the last stage of national humiliation.[23] There is scarcely any thing that can wound the pride or degrade the character of an independent nation which we do not experience. Are there engagements to the performance of which we are held by every tie respectable among men? These are the subjects of constant and unblushing violation. Do we owe debts to foreigners and to our own citizens, contracted in a time of imminent peril for the preservation of our political existence? These remain without any proper or satisfactory provision for their discharge. Have we valuable territories and important posts in the possession of a foreign power which, by express stipulations, ought long since to have been surrendered? These are still retained, to the prejudice of our interests, not less than of our rights. Are we in a condition to resent or to repel the aggression? We have neither troops, nor treasury, nor government [for the Union]. Are we even in a condition to remonstrate with dignity? The just imputations on our own faith, in respect to the same treaty, ought first to be removed. Are we entitled by nature and compact to a free participation in the navigation of the Mississippi? Spain excludes us from it. Is public credit an indispensable resource in time of public danger? We seem to have abandoned its cause as desperate and irretrievable. Is commerce of importance to national wealth? Ours is at the lowest point of declension. Is respectability in the eyes of foreign powers a safeguard against foreign encroachments? The imbecility of our government even forbids them to treat with us. Our ambassadors abroad are the mere pageants of mimic sovereignty. Is a violent and unnatural decrease in the value of land a symptom of national distress? The price of improved land in most parts of the country is much lower than can be accounted for by the quantity of waste land at market, and can only be fully explained by that want of private and public confidence, which are so alarmingly prevalent among all ranks, and which have a direct tendency to depreciate property of every kind. Is private credit the friend and patron of industry? That most useful kind which relates to borrowing and lending is reduced within the narrowest limits, and this still more from an opinion of insecurity than from the scarcity of money. To shorten an enumeration of particulars which can afford neither pleasure nor instruction, it may in general be demanded, what indication is there of national disorder, poverty, and insignificance that could befall a community so peculiarly blessed with natural advantages as we are, which does not form a part of the dark catalogue of our public misfortunes.

This is the melancholy situation to which we have been brought by those very maxims and councils which would now deter us from adopting the proposed Constitution; and which, not content with having conducted us to the brink of a precipice, seem resolved to plunge us into the abyss that awaits us below. Here, my countrymen, impelled by every motive that ought to influence an enlightened people, let us make a firm stand for our safety, our tranquillity, our dignity, our reputation. Let us at last break the fatal charm which has too long seduced us from the paths of felicity and prosperity.

It is true . . . that facts too stubborn to be resisted have produced a species of general assent to the abstract proposition that there exist material defects in our national system; but the usefulness of the concession on the part of the old adversaries of federal measures is destroyed by a strenuous opposition to a remedy, upon the only principles that can give it a chance of success. While they admit that the government of the United States is destitute of energy, they contend against conferring upon it those powers which are requisite to supply that energy. They seem still to aim at things repugnant and irreconcilable; at an augmentation of federal authority without a diminution of State authority; at sovereignty in the Union and complete independence in the members. They still, in fine, seem to cherish with blind devotion the political monster of an *imperium in imperio*. This renders a full display of the principal defects of the Confederation necessary in order to show that the evils we experience do not proceed from minute or partial imperfections, but from fundamental errors in the structure of the building, which cannot be amended otherwise than by an alteration in the first principles and main pillars of the fabric.

The great and radical vice in the construction of the existing Confederation is in the principle of LEGISLATION for STATES or GOVERNMENTS, in their CORPORATE or COLLECTIVE CAPACITIES, and as contradistinguished from the INDIVIDUALS of which they consist. Though this principle does not run through all the powers delegated to the Union, yet it pervades and governs those on which the efficacy of the rest depends. Except as to the rule of apportionment, the United States has an indefinite discretion to make requisitions for men and money; but they have no authority to raise either by regulations extending to the individual citizens of

America. The consequence of this is, that though in theory their resolutions concerning those objects are laws, constitutionally binding on the members of the Union, yet in practice they are mere recommendations which the States observe or disregard at their option.

It is a singular instance of the capriciousness of the human mind, that after all the admonitions we have had from experience on this head, there should still be found men who object to the new Constitution, for deviating from a principle which has been found the bane of the old, and which is in itself evidently incompatible with the idea of GOVERNMENT; a principle, in short, which, if it is to be executed at all, must substitute the violent and sanguinary agency of the sword to the mild influence of the magistracy.

There is nothing absurd or impracticable in the idea of a league or alliance between independent nations for certain defined purposes precisely stated in a treaty regulating all the details of time, place, circumstance, and quantity; leaving nothing to future discretion; and depending for its execution on the good faith of the parties. Compacts of this kind exist among all civilized nations, subject to the usual vicissitudes of peace and war, of observance and non-observance, as the interests or passions of the contracting powers dictate. In the early part of the present century there was an epidemical rage in Europe for this species of compacts, from which the politicians of the times fondly hoped for benefits which were never realized. With a view to establishing the equilibrium of power and the peace of that part of the world, all the resources of negotiations were exhausted, and triple and quadruple alliances were formed; but they were scarcely formed before they were broken, giving an instructive but afflicting lesson to mankind, how little dependence is to be placed on treaties which have no other sanction than the obligations of good faith, and which oppose general considerations of peace and justice to the impulse of any immediate interest or passion.

If the particular States in this country are disposed to stand in a similar relation to each other, and to drop the project of a general DISCRETIONARY SUPERINTENDENCE, the scheme would indeed be pernicious, and would entail upon us all the mischiefs which have been enumerated under the first head; but it would have the merit of being, at least, consistent and practicable. Abandoning all views towards a confederate government, this would bring us to a simple alliance offensive and defensive; and would place us in a situation to be alternate friends and enemies of each other as our mutual jealousies and rivalships, nourished by the intrigues of foreign nations, should prescribe to us.

But if we are unwilling to be placed in this perilous situation; if we still will adhere to the design of a national government . . . under the direction of a common council, we must resolve to incorporate into our plan those ingredients which may be considered as forming the characteristic difference between a league and a government; we must extend the authority of the Union to the persons of the citizens,—the only proper objects of government.[24]

Government implies the power of making laws. It is essential to the idea of a law that it be attended with a sanction; or, in other words, a penalty or punishment for disobedience. If there be no penalty annexed to disobedience, the resolutions or commands which pretend to be laws will, in fact, amount to nothing more than advice or recommendation. This penalty, whatever it may be, can only be inflicted in two ways: by the agency of the courts and ministers of justice, or by military force; by the COERCION of the magistracy, or by the COERCION of arms. The first kind can evidently apply only to men; the last kind must of necessity, be employed against bodies politic, or communities, or States. It is evident that there is no process of a court by which the observance of the laws can, in the last resort, be enforced. Sentences may be denounced against them for violations of their duty; but these sentences can only be carried into execution by the sword. In an association where the general authority is confined to the collective bodies of the communities that compose it, every breach of the laws must involve a state of war; and military execution must become the only instrument of civil obedience. Such a state of things can certainly not deserve the name of government, nor would any prudent man choose to commit his happiness to it.

There was a time when we were told that breaches by the States of the regulations of the federal authority were not to be expected; that a sense of common interest would preside over the conduct of the respective members, and would beget a full compliance with all the constitutional requisitions of the Union. This language at the present day would appear as wild as a great part of what we now hear from the same quarter will be thought, when we shall have received further lessons from that best oracle of wisdom, experience. It at all times betrayed an ignorance of the true springs by which human conduct is actuated, and belied the original inducements to the establishment of civil power. Why has government been instituted at all? Because the passions of men will not conform to the dictates of reason and justice, without constraint. Has it been found that bodies of men act with more rectitude or greater disinterestedness than individuals? The contrary of this has been inferred by all accurate observers of the conduct of mankind; and the inference is founded upon obvious reasons. Regard to reputation has a less active influence when the infamy of a bad action is to be divided among a number than when it is to fall singly upon one. A spirit of faction, which is apt to mingle its poison in the deliberations of all bodies of men, will often hurry the persons of whom they are composed into improprieties and excesses for which they would blush in a private capacity.

In addition to all this, there is, in the nature of sovereign power, an impatience of control that disposes those who are invested with the exercise of it to look with an evil eye upon all external attempts to restrain or direct its operations. From this spirit it happens, that in every political association which is formed upon the principle of uniting in a common interest a number of lesser sovereignties, there will be found a kind of eccentric tendency in the subordinate or inferior orbs, by the operation of which there will be a perpetual effort in each to fly off from the common centre. This tendency is not difficult to be accounted for. It has its origin in the love of power. Power controlled or abridged is almost always the rival and enemy of that power by which it is controlled or abridged. This simple proposition will teach us how little reason there is to expect that the persons intrusted with the administration of the affairs of the particular members of a confederacy will at all times be ready, with perfect good-humor and an unbiased regard to the public weal, to execute the resolutions or decrees of the general authority. The reverse of this results from the constitution of human nature.

If, therefore, the measures of the Confederacy cannot be executed without the intervention of the particular administrations, there will be little prospect of their being executed at all. The rulers of the respective members, whether they have a constitutional right to do it or not, will undertake to judge of the propriety of the measures themselves. They will consider the conformity of the thing proposed or required to their immediate interests or aims; the momentary conveniences or inconveniences that would attend its adoption. All this will be done; and in a spirit of interested and suspicious scrutiny, without that knowledge of national circumstances and reasons of state, which is essential to a right judgment, and with that strong predilection in favor of local objects, which can hardly fail to mislead the decision. The same process must be repeated in every member of which the body is constituted; and the execution of the plans, framed by the councils of the whole, will always fluctuate on the discretion of the ill-informed and prejudiced opinion of every part. Those who have been conversant in the proceedings of popular assemblies; who have seen how difficult it often is, where there is no exterior pressure of circumstances, to bring them to harmonious resolutions on important points, will readily conceive how impossible it must be to induce a number of such assemblies, deliberating at a distance from each other, at different times, and under different impressions, long to co-öperate in the same views and pursuits.

In our case, the concurrence of thirteen distinct sovereign wills is requisite under the Confederation to the complete execution of every important measure that proceeds from the Union. It has happened as was to have been foreseen. The measures of the Union have not been executed; the delinquencies of the States have, step by step, matured themselves to an extreme, which has, at length, arrested all the wheels of the national government, and brought them to an awful stand. Congress at this time scarcely possess the means of keeping up the forms of administration, till the States can have time to agree upon a more substantial substitute for the present shadow of a federal government. Things did not come to this desperate extremity at once. The causes which have been specified produced at first only unequal and disproportionate degrees of compliance with the requisitions of the Union. The greater deficiencies of some States furnished the pretext of example and the temptation of interest to the complying, or to the least delinquent States. Why should we do more in proportion than those who are embarked with us in the same political voyage? Why should we consent to bear more than our proper share of the common burden? These were suggestions which human selfishness could not withstand, and which even speculative men, who looked forward to remote consequences, could not, without hesitation, combat. Each State, yielding to the persuasive voice of immediate interest or convenience, has successively withdrawn its support till the frail and tottering edifice seems ready to fall upon our heads and to crush us beneath its ruins.   PUBLIUS

THE FEDERALIST NO. 16

(HAMILTON)

To the People of the State of New York:
        The tendency of the principle of legislation for States . . . in their political capacities, as it has been exemplified by the experiment we have made of it, is equally attested by the events which have befallen all other governments of the confederate kind, of which we have any account, in exact proportion to its prevalence in those systems. . . .
        This exceptionable principle may, as truly as emphatically, be styled the parent of anarchy. It has been seen that delinquencies in the members of the Union are its natural and necessary offspring; and that whenever they happen, the only constitutional remedy is force, and the immediate effect of the use of it, civil war.

It remains to inquire how far so odious an engine of government in its application to us would even be capable of answering its end. If there should not be a large army constantly at the disposal of the national government, it would either not be able to employ force at all, or, when this could be done, it would amount to a war between parts of the Confederacy concerning the infractions of a league, in which the strongest combination would be most likely to prevail, whether it consisted of those who supported or of those who resisted the general authority. It would rarely happen that the delinquency to be redressed would be confined to a single member; and if there were more than one who had neglected their duty, similarity of situation would induce them to unite for common defence. Independent of this motive of sympathy, if a large and influential State should happen to be the aggressing member, it would commonly have weight enough with its neighbors to win over some of them as associates to its cause. Specious arguments of danger to the common liberty could easily be contrived; plausible excuses for the deficiencies of the party could, without difficulty, be invented to alarm the apprehensions, inflame the passions, and conciliate the good-will even of those States which were not chargeable with any violation or omission of duty. This would be the more likely to take place, as the delinquencies of the larger members might be expected sometimes to proceed from an ambitious premeditation in their rulers, with a view to getting rid of all external control upon their designs of personal aggrandizement; the better to effect which it is presumable they would tamper beforehand with leading individuals in the adjacent States. If associates could not be found at home, recourse would be had to the aid of foreign powers, who would seldom be disinclined to encouraging the dissensions of a Confederacy, from the firm union of which they had so much to fear. When the sword is once drawn, the passions of men observe no bounds of moderation. The suggestions of wounded pride, the instigations of irritated resentment, would be apt to carry the States against which the arms of the Union were exerted, to any extremes necessary to avenge the affront or to avoid the disgrace of submission. The first war of this kind would probably terminate in a dissolution of the Union.

This may be considered as the violent death of the Confederacy. Its more natural death is what we now seem to be on the point of experiencing, if the federal system be not speedily renovated in a more substantial form. It is not probable, considering the genius of this country, that the complying States would often be inclined to support the authority of the Union by engaging in a war against the non-complying States. They would always be more ready to pursue the milder course of putting themselves upon an equal footing with the delinquent members by an imitation of their example. And the guilt of all would thus become the security of all. Our past experience has exhibited the operation of this spirit in its full light. There would, in fact, be an insuperable difficulty in ascertaining when force could with propriety be employed. In the article of pecuniary contribution, which would be the most usual source of delinquency, it would often be impossible to decide whether it had proceeded from disinclination or inability. The pretence of the latter would always be at hand. And the case must be very flagrant in which its fallacy could be detected with sufficient certainty to justify the harsh expedient of compulsion. It is easy to see that this problem alone, as often as it should occur, would open a wide field for the exercise of factious views, of partiality, and of oppression, in the majority that happened to prevail in the national council.

It seems to require no pains to prove that the States ought not to prefer a national Constitution which could only be kept in motion by the instrumentality of a large army continually on foot to execute the ordinary requisitions or decrees of the government. And yet this is the plain alternative involved by those who wish to deny it the power of extending its operations to individuals. Such a scheme, if practicable at all, would instantly degenerate into a military despotism; but it will be found in every light impracticable. The resources of the Union would not be equal to the maintenance of an army considerable enough to confine the larger States within the limits of their duty; nor would the means ever be furnished of forming such an army in the first instance. Whoever considers the populousness and strength of several of these States singly at the present juncture and looks forward to what they will become, even at the distance of half a century, will at once dismiss as idle and visionary any scheme which aims at regulating their movements by laws to operate upon them in their collective capacities, and to be executed by a coercion applicable to them in the same capacities. A project of this kind is little less romantic than the monster-taming spirit which is attributed to the fabulous heroes and demigods of antiquity.

Even in those confederacies which have been composed of members smaller than many of our counties, the principle of legislation for sovereign States, supported by military coercion, has never been found effectual. It has rarely been attempted to be employed, but against the weaker members; and in most instances attempts to coerce the refractory and disobedient have been the signals of bloody wars, in which one half of the confederacy has displayed its banners against the other half.

The result of these observations to an intelligent mind must be clearly this, that if it be possible at any rate to construct a federal government capable of regulating the common concerns and preserving the general tranquillity, it must be founded, as to the objects committed to its care, upon the reverse of the principle contended for by the opponents of the proposed Constitution. It must carry its agency to the persons of the citizens. It must stand in need of no intermediate legislations, but must itself be empowered to employ the arm of the ordinary magistrate to execute its own resolutions. The majesty of the national authority must be manifested through the medium of the courts of justice. The government of the Union, like that of each State, must be able to address itself immediately to the hopes and fears of individuals; and to attract to its support those passions which have the strongest influence upon the human heart. It must, in short, possess all the means and have a right to resort to all the methods, of executing the powers with which it is intrusted that are possessed and exercised by the governments of the particular States.

To this reasoning it may perhaps be objected that if any State should be disaffected to the authority of the Union, it could at any time obstruct the execution of its laws, and bring the matter to the same issue of force, with the necessity of which the opposite scheme is reproached.

The plausibility of this objection will vanish the moment we advert to the essential difference between a mere NON-COMPLIANCE and a DIRECT and ACTIVE RESISTANCE. If the interposition of the State legislatures be necessary to give effect to a measure of the Union, they have only NOT TO ACT, or to ACT EVASIVELY, and the measure is defeated. This neglect of duty may be disguised under affected but unsubstantial provisions, so as not to appear, and of course not to excite any alarm in the people for the safety of the Constitution. The State leaders may even make a merit of their surreptitious invasions of it on the ground of some temporary convenience, exemption, or advantage.

But if the execution of the laws of the national government should not require the intervention of the State legislatures, if they were to pass into immediate operation upon the citizens themselves, the particular governments could not interrupt their progress without an open and violent exertion of an unconstitutional power. No omissions nor evasions would answer the end. They would be obliged to act, and in such a manner as would leave no doubt that they had encroached on the national rights. An experiment of this nature would always be hazardous in the face of a constitution in any degree competent to its own defence, and of a people enlightened enough to distinguish between a legal exercise and an illegal usurpation of authority. The success of it would require not merely a factious majority in the legislature, but the concurrence of the courts of justice and of the body of the people. If the judges were not embarked in a conspiracy with the legislature, they would pronounce the resolutions of such a majority to be contrary to the supreme law of the land, unconstitutional, and void. If the people were not tainted with the spirit of their State representatives, they, as the natural guardians of the Constitution, would throw their weight into the national scale and give it a decided preponderancy in the contest. Attempts of this kind would not often be made with levity or rashness, because they could seldom be made without danger to the authors, unless in cases of a tyrannical exercise of the federal authority.

If opposition to the national government should arise from the disorderly conduct of refractory or seditious individuals, it could be overcome by the same means which are daily employed against the same evil under the State governments. The magistracy, being equally the ministers of the law of the land, from whatever source it might emanate, would doubtless be as ready to guard the national as the local regulations from the inroads of private licentiousness. As to those partial commotions and insurrections which sometimes disquiet society, from the intrigues of an inconsiderable faction or from sudden or occasional ill-humors that do not infect the great body of the community, the general government could command more extensive resources for the suppression of disturbances of that kind than would be in the power of any single member. And as to those mortal feuds which . . . spread a conflagration through a whole nation or through a very large proportion of it, proceeding either from weighty causes of discontent given by the government or from the contagion of some violent popular paroxysm, they do not fall within any ordinary rules of calculation. When they happen, they commonly amount to revolutions and dismemberments of empire. No form of government can always either avoid or control them. It is in vain to hope to guard against events too mighty for human foresight or precaution, and it would be idle to object to a government because it could not perform impossibilities. PUBLIUS

THE FEDERALIST NO. 17

(HAMILTON)

To the People of the State of New York:

An objection, of a nature different from that which has been stated and answered, in my last address, may perhaps be likewise urged against the principle of legislation for the individual citizens of America. It may be said that it would tend to render the government of the Union too powerful, and to enable it to absorb those residuary authorities which it might be judged proper to leave with the States for local purposes. Allowing the utmost latitude to the love of power which any reasonable man can require, I confess I am at a loss to discover what temptation the persons intrusted with the administration of the general government could ever feel to divest the States of the authorities of that description. The regulation of the mere domestic police of a State appears to me to hold out slender allurements to ambition. Commerce, finance, negotiation, and war seem to comprehend all the objects which have charms for minds governed by that passion; and all the powers necessary to those objects ought, in the first instance, to be lodged in the national depository. The administration of private justice between the citizens of the same State, the supervision of agriculture and of other concerns of a similar nature, all those things, in short, which are proper to be provided for by local legislation, can never be desirable cares of a general jurisdiction. It is therefore improbable that there should exist a disposition in the federal councils to usurp the powers with which they are connected; because the attempt to exercise those powers would be as troublesome as it would be nugatory; and the possession of them, for that reason, would contribute nothing to the dignity, to the importance, or to the splendor of the national government.

But let it be admitted, for argument's sake, that mere wantonness and lust of domination would be sufficient to beget that disposition; still it may be safely affirmed that the sense of the constituent body of the national representatives, or, in other words, the people of the several States, would control the indulgence of so extravagant an appetite. It will always be far more easy for the State governments to encroach upon the national authorities than for the national government to encroach upon the State authorities. The proof of this proposition turns upon the greater degree of influence which the State governments, if they administer their affairs with uprightness and prudence, will generally possess over the people; a circumstance which at the same time teaches us that there is an inherent and intrinsic weakness in all federal constitutions; and that too much pains cannot be taken in their organization to give them all the force which is compatible with the principles of liberty.

The superiority of influence in favor of the particular governments would result partly from the diffusive construction of the national government, but chiefly from the nature of the objects to which the attention of the State administrations would be directed.

It is a known fact in human nature that its affections are commonly weak in proportion to the distance or diffusiveness of the object. Upon the same principle that a man is more attached to his family than to his neighborhood, to his neighborhood than to the community at large, the people of each State would be apt to feel a stronger bias towards their local governments than towards the government of the Union; unless the force of that principle should be destroyed by a much better administration of the latter.

This strong propensity of the human heart would find powerful auxiliaries in the objects of State regulation.

The variety of more minute interests, which will necessarily fall under the superintendence of the local administrations, and which will form so many rivulets of influence running through every part of the society, cannot be particularized without involving a detail too tedious and uninteresting to compensate for the instruction it might afford.

There is one transcendent advantage belonging to the province of the State governments which alone suffices to place the matter in a clear and satisfactory light,—I mean the ordinary administration of criminal and civil justice. This, of all others, is the most powerful, most universal, and most attractive source of popular obedience and attachment. It is that which, being the immediate and visible guardian of life and property, having its benefits and its terrors in constant activity before the public eye, regulating all those personal interests and familiar concerns to which the sensibility of individuals is more immediately awake, contributes, more than any other circumstance, to impressing upon the minds of the people, affection, esteem, and reverence towards the government. This great cement of society, which will diffuse itself almost wholly through the channels of the particular governments, independent of all other causes of influence, would insure them so decided [to create] an empire over their respective citizens as to render them at all times a complete counterpoise, and, not unfrequently, dangerous rivals to the power of the Union.

The operations of the national government, on the other hand, falling less immediately under the observation of the mass of the citizens, the benefits derived from it will chiefly be perceived and attended to by speculative men. Relating to more general interests, they will be less apt to come home to the feelings of the people; and, in proportion, less likely to inspire an habitual sense of obligation and an active sentiment of attachment.

The reasoning on this head has been abundantly exemplified by the experience of all federal constitutions with which we are acquainted, and of all others which have borne the least analogy to them. . . .[25]

The separate governments in a confederacy may aptly be compared with the feudal baronies; with this advantage in their favor . . . they will generally possess the confidence and good-will of the people, and with so important a support, will be able effectually to oppose all encroachments of the national government. It will be well if they are not able to counteract its legitimate and necessary authority. The points of similitude consist in the rivalship of power, applicable to both, and in the CONCENTRATION of large portions of the strength of the community into particular DEPOSITS, in one case at the disposal of individuals, in the other case at the disposal of political bodies.

A concise review of the events that have attended confederate governments will further illustrate this important doctrine; an inattention to which has been the great source of our political mistakes, and has given our jealousy a direction to the wrong side. This review shall form the subject of some ensuing papers.   PUBLIUS

THE FEDERALIST NO. 21

(HAMILTON)

To the People of the State of New York:

. . . The next most palpable defect of the subsisting Confederation, is the total want of a SANCTION to its laws. The United States, as now composed, have no powers to exact obedience or punish disobedience to their resolutions, either by pecuniary mulcts, by a suspension or divestiture of privileges, or by any other constitutional mode. There is no express delegation of authority to them to use force against delinquent members; and if such a right should be ascribed to the federal head, as resulting from the nature of the social compact between the States, it must be by inference and construction in the face of that part of the second article by which it is declared, "that each State shall retain every power, jurisdiction, and right, not *expressly* delegated to the United States in Congress assembled" [*sic*].[26] There is, doubtless, a striking absurdity in supposing that a right of this kind does not exist, but we are reduced to the dilemma either of embracing that supposition, preposterous as it may seem, or of contravening or explaining away a provision, which has been of late a repeated theme of the eulogies of those who oppose the new Constitution; and the want of which, in that plan, has been the subject of much plausible animadversion, and severe criticism. If we are unwilling to impair the force of this applauded provision, we shall be obliged to conclude, that the United States afford the extraordinary spectacle of a government destitute even of the shadow of constitutional power to enforce the execution of its own laws. It will appear from the specimens which have been cited that the American Confederacy, in this particular, stands discriminated from every other institution of a similar kind, and exhibits a new and unexampled phenomenon in the political world.

The want of a mutual guaranty of the State governments

is another capital imperfection in the federal plan. There is nothing of this kind declared in the articles that compose it; and to imply a tacit guaranty from considerations of utility would be a still more flagrant departure from the clause which has been mentioned, than to imply a tacit power of coercion from the like considerations. The want of a guaranty, though it might in its consequences endanger the Union, does not so immediately attack its existence as the want of a constitutional sanction to its laws.

Without a guaranty the assistance to be derived from the Union in repelling those domestic dangers which may sometimes threaten the existence of the State constitutions must be renounced. Usurpation may rear its crest in each State, and trample upon the liberties of the people, while the national government could legally do nothing more than behold its encroachments with indignation and regret. A successful faction may erect a tyranny on the ruins of order and law, while no succor could constitutionally be afforded by the Union to the friends and supporters of the government. The tempestuous situation from which Massachusetts has scarcely emerged evinces that dangers of this kind are not merely speculative. Who can determine what might have been the issue of her late convulsions if the malcontents had been headed by a Cæsar or by a Cromwell? Who can predict what effect a despotism, established in Massachusetts, would have upon the liberties of New Hampshire or Rhode Island, of Connecticut or New York?[27]

The inordinate pride of State importance has suggested to some minds an objection to the principle of a guaranty in the federal government, as involving an officious interference in the domestic concerns of the members. A scruple of this kind would deprive us of one of the principal advantages to be expected from union, and can only flow from a misapprehension of the nature of the provision itself. It could be no impediment to reforms of the State constitutions by a majority of the people in a legal and peaceable mode. This right would remain undiminished. The guaranty could only operate against changes to be effected by violence. Towards the preventions of calamities of this kind, too many checks cannot be provided. The peace of society and the stability of government depend absolutely on the efficacy of the precautions adopted on this head. Where the whole power of the government is in the hands of the people, there is the less pretence for the use of violent remedies in partial or occasional distempers of the State. The natural cure for an ill-administration, in a popular or representative constitution, is a change of men. A guaranty by the national authority would be as much levelled against the usurpations of rulers as against the ferments and outrages of faction and sedition in the community.

The principle of regulating the contributions of the States to the common treasury by QUOTAS is another fundamental error in the Confederation. Its repugnancy to an adequate supply of the national exigencies has been already pointed out, and has sufficiently appeared from the trial which has been made of it. I speak of it now solely with a view to equality among the States. Those who have been accustomed to contemplate the circumstances which produce and constitute national wealth must be satisfied that there is no common standard or barometer by which the degrees of it can be ascertained. Neither the value of lands nor the numbers of the people, which have been successively proposed as the rule of State contributions, has any pretension to being a just representative. If we compare the wealth of the United Netherlands with that of Russia or Germany, or even of France, and if we at the same time compare the total value of the lands and the aggregate population of that contracted district with the total value of the lands and the aggregate population of the immense regions of either of the three last-mentioned countries, we shall at once discover that there is no comparison between the proportion of either of these two objects and that of the relative wealth of those nations. If the like parallel were to be run between several of the American States, it would furnish a like result. Let Virginia be contrasted with North Carolina, Pennsylvania with Connecticut, or Maryland with New Jersey, and we shall be convinced that the respective abilities of those States, in relation to revenue, bear little or no analogy to their comparative stock in lands or to their comparative population. The position may be equally illustrated by a similar process between the counties of the same State. No man who is acquainted with the State of New York will doubt that the active wealth of King's County bears a much greater proportion to that of Montgomery than it would appear to be if we should take either the total value of the lands or the total number of the people as a criterion!

The wealth of nations depends upon an infinite variety of causes. Situation, soil, climate, the nature of the productions, the nature of the government, the genius of the citizens, the degree of information they possess, the state of commerce, of arts, of industry,—these circumstances and many more, too complex, minute, or adventitious to admit of a particular specification, occasion differences hardly conceivable in the relative opulence and riches of different countries. The consequence clearly is that there can be no common measure of national wealth, and, of course, no general or stationary rule by which the ability of a state to pay taxes can be determined. The attempt, therefore, to regulate the contributions of the members of a confederacy by any such rule cannot fail to be productive of glaring inequality and extreme oppression.

This inequality would of itself be sufficient in America to work the eventual destruction of the Union, if any mode of enforcing a compliance with its requisitions could be devised. The suffering States would not long consent to remain associated upon a principle which distributes the public burdens with so unequal a hand, and which was calculated to impoverish and oppress the citizens of some States, while those of others would scarcely be conscious of the small proportion of the weight they were required to sustain. This, however, is an evil inseparable from the principle of quotas and requisitions.

There is no method of steering clear of this inconvenience, but by authorizing the national government to raise its own revenues in its own way. Imposts, excises, and, in general, all duties upon articles of consumption may be compared to a fluid, which will, in time, find its level with the means of paying them. The amount to be contributed by each citizen will in a degree be at his own option, and can be regulated by an attention to his resources. The rich may be extravagant, the poor can be frugal; and private oppression may always be avoided by a judicious selection of objects proper for such impositions. If inequalities should arise in some States from duties on particular objects, these will, in all probability, be counterbalanced by proportional inequalities in other States from the duties on other objects. In the course of time and things, an equilibrium, as far as it is attainable in so complicated a subject, will be established everywhere. Or, if inequalities should still exist, they would neither be so great in their degree, so uniform in their operation, nor so odious in their appearance, as those which would necessarily spring from quotas, upon any scale that can possibly be devised.

It is a signal advantage of taxes on articles of consumption that they contain in their own nature a security against excess. They prescribe their own limit; which cannot be exceeded without defeating the end proposed,—that is, an extension of the revenue. When applied to this object, the saying is as just as it is witty, that, "in political arithmetic, two and two do not always make four." If duties are too high, they lessen the consumption; the collection is eluded; and the product to the treasury is not so great as when they are confined within proper and moderate bounds. This forms a complete barrier against any material oppression of the citizens by taxes of this class, and is itself a natural limitation of the power of imposing them.

Impositions of this kind usually fall under the denomination of indirect taxes, and must for a long time constitute the chief part of the revenue raised in this country. Those of the direct kind, which principally relate to land and buildings, may admit of a rule of apportionment. Either the value of land or the number of the people may serve as a standard. The state of agriculture and the populousness of a country have been considered as nearly connected with each other. And, as a rule for the purpose intended, numbers, in the view of simplicity and certainty, are entitled to a preference. In every country it is a herculean task to obtain a valuation of the land; in a country imperfectly settled and progressive in improvement, the difficulties are increased almost to impracticability. The expense of an accurate valuation is, in all situations, a formidable objection. In a branch of taxation where no limits to the discretion of the government are to be found in the nature of things, the establishment of a fixed rule, not incompatible with the end, may be attended with fewer inconveniences than to leave that discretion altogether at large.   Publius

THE FEDERALIST NO. 22

(HAMILTON)

To the People of the State of New York:
    In addition to the defects already enumerated in the existing federal system, there are others of not less importance . . .
    The want of a power to regulate commerce is by all parties allowed to be of the number. The utility of such a power has been anticipated under the first head of our inquiries; and for this reason, as well as from the universal conviction entertained upon the subject, little need be added in this place. It is indeed evident on the most superficial view that there is no object, either as it respects the interest of trade or finance, that more strongly demands a federal superintendence. The want of it has already operated as a bar to the formation of beneficial treaties with foreign powers, and has given occasions of dissatisfaction between the States. No nation acquainted with the nature of our political association would be unwise enough to enter into stipulations with the United States, by which they conceded privileges of any importance to them, while they were apprised that the engagements on the part of the Union might at any moment be violated by its members, and while they found from experience that they might enjoy every advantage they desired in our markets without granting us any return but such as their momentary convenience might suggest. It is not, therefore, to be wondered at that Mr. Jenkinson, in ushering into the House of Commons a bill for regulating the temporary intercourse between the two countries, should preface its introduction by a declaration that similar provisions in former bills had been found to answer every purpose to the commerce of Great Britain, and that it would be prudent to persist in the plan until it should appear whether the American government was likely or not to acquire greater consistency.[28]

Several States have endeavored, by separate prohibitions, restrictions, and exclusions, to influence the conduct of that kingdom in this particular, but the want of concert, arising from the want of a general authority and from clashing and dissimilar views in the State, has hitherto frustrated every experiment of the kind, and will continue to do so as long as the same obstacles to a uniformity of measures continue to exist.

The interfering and unneighborly regulations of some States, contrary to the true spirit of the Union, have in different instances given just cause of umbrage and complaint to others, and it is to be feared that examples of this nature, if not restrained by a national control, would be multiplied and extended till they became not less serious sources of animosity and discord than injurious impediments to the intercourse between the different parts of the Confederacy. . . . We may reasonably expect, from the gradual conflicts of State regulations, that the citizens of each would at length come to be considered and treated by the others in no better light than that of foreigners and aliens.

The power of raising armies, by the most obvious construction of the articles of the Confederation, is merely a power of making requisitions upon the States for quotas of men. This practice in the course of the late war was found replete with obstructions to a vigorous and to an economical system of defence. It gave birth to a competition between the States which created a kind of auction for men. In order to furnish the quotas required of them, they outbid each other till bounties grew to an enormous and insupportable size. The hope of a still further increase afforded an inducement to those who were disposed to serve to procrastinate their enlistment, and disinclined them from engaging for any considerable periods. Hence, slow and scanty levies of men in the most critical emergencies of our affairs; short enlistments at an unparalleled expense; continual fluctuations in the troops, ruinous to their discipline and subjecting the public safety frequently to the perilous crisis of a disbanded army. Hence, also, those oppressive expedients for raising men which were upon several occasions practised, and which nothing but the enthusiasm of liberty would have induced the people to endure.

This method of raising troops is not more unfriendly to economy and vigor than it is to an equal distribution of the burden. The States near the seat of war, influenced by motives of self-preservation, made efforts to furnish their quotas, which even exceeded their abilities; while those at a distance from danger were for the most part as remiss as the others were diligent in their exertions. The immediate pressure of this inequality was not in this case, as in that of the contributions of money, alleviated by the hope of a final liquidation. The States which did not pay their proportions of money might at least be charged with their deficiencies; but no account could be formed of the deficiencies in the supplies of men. We shall not, however, see much reason to regret the want of this hope when we consider how little prospect there is that the most delinquent States will ever be able to make compensation for their pecuniary failures. The system of quotas and requisitions, whether it be applied to men or money, is, in every view, a system of imbecility in the Union, and of inequality and injustice among the members.

The right of equal suffrage among the States is another exceptionable part of the Confederation. Every idea of proportion and every rule of fair representation conspire to condemn a principle which gives to Rhode Island an equal weight in the scale of power with Massachusetts, or Connecticut, or New York; and to Delaware an equal voice in the national deliberations with Pennsylvania, or Virginia, or North Carolina. Its operation contradicts the fundamental maxim of republican government which requires that the sense of the majority should prevail. Sophistry may reply that sovereigns are equal, and that a majority of the votes of the States will be a majority of confederated America. But this kind of logical legerdemain will never counteract the plain suggestions of justice and common-sense. It may happen that this majority of States is a small minority of the people of America; and two thirds of the people of America could not long be persuaded, upon the credit of artificial distinction and syllogistic subtleties, to submit their interests to the management and disposal of one third. The larger States would after a while revolt from the idea of receiving the law from the smaller. To acquiesce in such a privation of their due importance in the political scale would be not merely to be insensible to the love of power, but even to sacrifice the desire of equality. It is neither rational to expect the first nor just to require the last. The smaller States, considering how peculiarly their safety and welfare depend on union, ought readily to renounce a pretension which, if not relinquished, would prove fatal to its duration.

It may be objected . . . that not seven but nine States, or two thirds of the whole number, must consent to the most important resolutions; and it may be thence inferred that nine States would always comprehend a majority of the Union. But this does not obviate the impropriety of an equal vote between States of the most unequal dimensions and populousness; nor is the inference accurate in point of fact; for we can enumerate nine States which contain less than a majority of the people;[29] and it is constitutionally possible that these nine may give the vote. Besides, there are matters of considerable moment determinable by a bare majority; and there are others, concerning which doubts have been entertained, which, if interpreted in favor of the sufficiency of a vote of seven States, would extend its operation to interests of the first magnitude. In addition to this, it is to be observed that there is a probability of an increase in the number of States, and no provision for a proportional augmentation of the ratio of votes.

But this is not all: what at first sight may seem a remedy, is, in reality, a poison. To give a minority a negative upon the majority is, in its tendency, to subject the sense of the greater number to that of the lesser. Congress, from the non-attendance of a few States, have been frequently in the situation of a Polish diet, where a single VOTE has been sufficient to put a stop to all their movements. A sixtieth part of the Union, which is about the proportion of Delaware and Rhode Island, has several times been able to oppose an entire bar to its operations.[30] This is one of those refinements which in practice has an effect the reverse of what is expected from it in theory. The necessity of unanimity in public bodies, or of something approaching towards it, has been founded upon a supposition that it would contribute to security. But its real operation is to embarrass the administration, to destroy the energy of the government, and to substitute the pleasure, caprice, or artifices of an insignificant, turbulent, or corrupt junto, to the regular deliberations and decisions of a respectable majority. In those emergencies of a nation in which the goodness or badness, the weakness or strength of its government is of the greatest importance, there is commonly a necessity for action. The public business must, in some way or other, go forward. If a pertinacious minority can control the opinion of a majority, respecting the best mode of conducting it, the majority, in order that something may be done, must conform to the views of the minority; and thus the sense of the smaller number will overrule that of the greater, and give a tone to the national proceedings. Hence, tedious delays; continual negotiation and intrigue; contemptible compromises of the public good. And yet, in such a system, it is even happy when such compromises can take place: for upon some occasions things will not admit of accommodation; and then the measures of government must be injuriously suspended or fatally defeated. It is often, by the impracticability of obtaining the concurrence of the necessary number of votes, kept in a state of inaction. Its situation must always savor of weakness, sometimes border upon anarchy.

It is not difficult to discover, that a principle of this kind gives greater scope to foreign corruption, as well as to domestic faction, than that which permits the sense of the majority to decide; though the contrary of this has been presumed. The mistake has proceeded from not attending with due care to the mischiefs that may be occasioned by obstructing the progress of government at certain critical seasons. When the concurrence of a large number is required by the Constitution to the doing of any national act, we are apt to rest satisfied that all is safe, because nothing improper will be likely *to be done;* but we forget how much good may be prevented, and how much ill may be produced, by the power of hindering the doing what may be necessary, and of keeping affairs in the same unfavorable posture in which they may happen to stand at particular periods.

Suppose, for instance, we were engaged in a war in conjunction with one foreign nation against another. Suppose the necessity of our situation demanded peace, and the interest or ambition of our ally led him to seek the prosecution of war with views that might justify us in making separate terms. In such a state of things, this ally of ours would evidently find it much easier, by his bribes and intrigues, to tie up the hands of government from making peace, where two thirds of all the votes were requisite to that object, than where a simple majority would suffice. In the first case, he would have to corrupt a smaller number; in the last, a greater number. Upon the same principle, it would be much easier for a foreign power with which we were at war to perplex our councils and embarrass our exertions. And, in a commercial view, we may be subjected to similar inconveniences. A nation, with which we might have a treaty of commerce, could with much greater facility prevent our forming a connection with her competitor in trade, though such a connection should be ever so beneficial to ourselves.

Evils of this description ought not to be regarded as imaginary. One of the weak sides of republics, among their numerous advantages, is that they afford too easy an inlet to foreign corruption. An hereditary monarch, though often disposed to sacrifice his subjects to his ambition, has so great a personal interest in the government and in the external glory of the nation, that it is not easy for a foreign power to give him the equivalent for what he would sacrifice by treachery to the state. The world has accordingly been witness to few examples of this species of royal prostitution, though there have been abundant specimens of every other kind.

In republics, persons elevated from the mass of the community, by the suffrages of their fellow-citizens, to stations of great pre-eminence and power, may find compensations for betraying their trust, which, to any but minds animated and guided by superior virtue, may appear to exceed the proportion of interest they have in the common stock, and to overbalance the obligations of duty. Hence it is that history furnishes us with so many mortifying examples of the prevalency of foreign corruption in republican governments. . . .

A circumstance which crowns the defects of the Confederation remains yet to be mentioned—the want of a judiciary power. Laws are a dead letter without courts to expound and define their true meaning and operation. The treaties of the United States, to have any force at all, must be considered as part of the law of the land. Their true import, as far as respects individuals, must, like all other laws, be ascertained by judicial determinations. To produce uniformity in these determinations, they ought to be submitted, in the last resort, to one SUPREME TRIBUNAL. And this tribunal ought to be instituted under the same authority which forms the treaties themselves. These ingredients are both indispensable. If there is in each State a court of final jurisdiction, there may be as many different final determinations on the same point as there are courts. There are endless diversities in the opinions of men. We often see not only different courts but the judges of the same court differing from each other. To avoid the confusion which would unavoidably result from the contradictory decisions of a number of independent judicatories, all nations have found it necessary to establish one court paramount to the rest, possessing a general superintendence, and authorized to settle and declare in the last resort a uniform rule of civil justice.

This is the more necessary where the frame of the government is so compounded that the laws of the whole are in danger of being contravened by the laws of the parts. In this case, if the particular tribunals are invested with a right of ultimate jurisdiction, besides the contradictions to be expected from differences of opinion there will be much to fear from the bias of local views and prejudices, and from the interference of local regulations. As often as such an interference was to happen, there would be reason to apprehend that the provisions of the particular laws might be preferred to those of the general laws; for nothing is more natural to men in office than to look with peculiar deference towards that authority to which they owe their official existence. The treaties of the United States, under the present Constitution, are liable to the infractions of thirteen different legislatures and as many different courts of final jurisdiction, acting under the authority of those legislatures. The faith, the reputation, the peace of the whole Union, are thus continually at the mercy of the prejudices, the passions, and the interests of every member of which it is composed. Is it possible that foreign nations can either respect or confide in such a government? Is it possible that the people of America will longer consent to trust their honor, their happiness, their safety, on so precarious a foundation?

In this review of the Confederation, I have confined myself to the exhibition of its most material defects, passing over those imperfections in its details by which even a great part of the power intended to be conferred upon it has been in a great measure rendered abortive. It must be by this time evident to all men of reflection, who can divest themselves of the prepossessions of preconceived opinions, that it is a system so radically vicious and unsound as to admit not of amendment but by an entire change in its leading features and characters.

The organization of Congress is itself utterly improper for the exercise of those powers which are necessary to be deposited in the Union. A single assembly may be a proper receptacle of those slender, or rather fettered, authorities, which have been heretofore delegated to the federal head; but it would be inconsistent with all the principles of good government to intrust it with those additional powers which, even the moderate and more rational adversaries of the proposed Constitution admit, ought to reside in the United States. If that plan should not be adopted and if the necessity of the Union should be able to withstand the ambitious aims of those men who may indulge magnificent schemes of personal aggrandizement from its dissolution, the probability would be, that we should run into the project of conferring supplementary powers upon Congress as they are now constituted; and either the machine, from the intrinsic feebleness of its structure, will moulder into pieces, in spite of our ill-judged efforts to prop it; or, by successive augmentations of its force and energy, as necessity might prompt, we shall finally accumulate in a single body all the most important prerogatives of sovereignty, and thus entail upon our posterity one of the most execrable forms of government that human infatuation ever contrived. Thus we should create in reality that very tyranny which the adversaries of the new Constitution either are, or affect to be, solicitous to avert.

It has not a little contributed to the infirmities of the existing federal system, that it never had a ratification by the PEOPLE. Resting on no better foundation than the consent of the several legislatures, it has been exposed to frequent and intricate questions concerning the validity of its powers, and has, in some instances, given birth to the enormous doctrine of a right of legislative repeal. Owing its ratification to the law of a State, it has been contended that the same authority might repeal the law by which it was ratified. However gross a heresy it may be to maintain that a *party* to a *compact* has a right to revoke that *compact,* the doctrine itself has had respectable advocates. The possibility of a question of this nature proves the necessity of laying the foundations of our national government deeper than in the mere sanction of delegated authority. The fabric of American empire ought to rest on the solid basis of THE CONSENT OF THE PEOPLE. The streams of national power ought to flow immediately from that pure, original fountain of all legitimate authority.[31]

PUBLIUS

THE FEDERALIST NO. 23

(HAMILTON)

To the People of the State of New York:
    The necessity of a Constitution, at least equally energetic with the one proposed, to the preservation of the Union, is the point at the examination of which we are now arrived.
    This inquiry will naturally divide itself into three branches —the objects to be provided for by the federal government, the quantity of power necessary to the accomplishment of those objects, the persons upon whom that power ought to operate. Its distribution and organization will more properly claim our attention under the succeeding head.
    The principal purposes to be answered by union are these— the common defence of the members; the preservation of the public peace, as well against internal convulsions as external attacks; the regulation of commerce with other nations and

between the States; the superintendence of our intercourse, political and commercial, with foreign countries.

The authorities essential to the common defence are these: to raise armies; to build and equip fleets; to prescribe rules for the government of both; to direct their operations; to provide for their support. These powers ought to exist without limitation, *because it is impossible to foresee or define the extent and variety of national exigencies, or the correspondent extent and variety of the means which may be necessary to satisfy them.* The circumstances that endanger the safety of nations are infinite, and for this reason no constitutional shackles can wisely be imposed on the power to which the care of it is committed. This power ought to be co-extensive with all the possible combinations of such circumstances; and ought to be under the direction of the same councils which are appointed to preside over the common defence.

This is one of those truths which, to a correct and unprejudiced mind, carries its own evidence along with it; and may be obscured, but cannot be made plainer by argument or reasoning. It rests upon axioms as simple as they are universal; the *means* ought to be proportioned to the *end;* the persons, from whose agency the attainment of any *end* is expected, ought to possess the *means* by which it is to be attained.[32]

Whether there ought to be a federal government intrusted with the care of the common defence is a question in the first instance open for discussion; but the moment it is decided in the affirmative, it will follow, that that government ought to be clothed with all the powers requisite to complete execution of its trust. And unless it can be shown that the circumstances which may affect the public safety are reducible within certain determinate limits; unless the contrary of this position can be fairly and rationally disputed, it must be admitted, as a necessary consequence, that there can be no limitation of that authority which is to provide for the defence and protection of the community in any matter essential to its efficacy— that is, in any matter essential to the *formation, direction,* or *support* of the NATIONAL FORCES.

Defective as the present Confederation has been proved to be, this principle appears to have been fully recognized by the framers of it; though they have not made proper or adequate provision for its exercise. Congress have an unlimited discretion to make requisitions of men and money; to govern the army and navy; to direct their operations. As their requisitions are made constitutionally binding upon the States, who are in fact under the most solemn obligations to furnish the supplies required of them, the intention evidently was, that the United States should command whatever resources were by them judged requisite to the "common defence and general welfare." It was presumed that a sense of their true interests, and a regard to the dictates of good faith, would be found sufficient pledges for the punctual performance of the duty of the members to the federal head.

The experiment has, however, demonstrated that this expectation was ill-founded and illusory; and the observations made under the last head will, I imagine, have sufficed to convince the impartial and discerning, that there is an absolute necessity for an entire change in the first principles of the system; that if we are in earnest about giving the Union energy and duration, we must abandon the vain project of legislating upon the States in their collective capacities; we must extend the laws of the federal government to the individual citizens of America; we must discard the fallacious scheme of quotas and requisitions as equally impracticable and unjust. The result from all this is that the Union ought to be invested with full power to levy troops; to build and equip fleets; and to raise the revenues which will be required for the formation and support of an army and navy, in the customary and ordinary modes practised in other governments.[33]

If the circumstances of our country are such as to demand a compound instead of a simple, a confederate instead of a sole, government, the essential point which will remain to be adjusted will be to discriminate the OBJECTS, as far as it can be done, which shall appertain to the different provinces or departments of power; allowing to each the most ample authority for fulfilling the objects committed to its charge. Shall the Union be constituted the guardian of the common safety? Are fleets and armies and revenues necessary to this purpose? The government of the Union must be empowered to pass all laws, and to make all regulations which have relation to them. The same must be the case in respect to commerce, and to every other matter to which its jurisdiction is permitted to extend. Is the administration of justice between the citizens of the same State the proper department of the local governments? These must possess all the authorities which are connected with this object, and with every other that may be allotted to their particular cognizance and direction. Not to confer in each case a degree of power commensurate to the end, would be to violate the most obvious rules of prudence and propriety, and improvidently to trust the great interests of the nation to hands which are disabled from managing them with vigor and success.

Who so likely to make suitable provisions for the public defence as that body to which the guardianship of the public safety is confided; which, as the centre of information, will best understand the extent and urgency of the dangers that threaten; as the representative of the WHOLE, will feel itself most deeply interested in the preservation of every part; which, from the responsibility implied in the duty assigned to it, will be most sensibly impressed with the necessity of proper exertions; and which, by the extension of its authority throughout the States, can alone establish uniformity and concert in the plans and measures by which the common safety is to be secured? Is there not a manifest inconsistency in devolving upon the federal government the care of the general defence, and leaving in the State governments the *effective* powers by which it is to be provided for? Is not a want of co-operation the infallible consequence of such a system? And will not weakness, disorder, and undue distribution of the burdens and calamities of war, an unnecessary and intolerable increase of expense, be its natural and inevitable concomitants? Have we not had unequivocal experience of its effects in the course of the revolution which we have just accomplished?

Every view we may take of the subject, as candid inquirers after truth, will serve to convince us, that it is both unwise and dangerous to deny the federal government an unconfined authority, as to all those objects which are intrusted to its management. It will indeed deserve the most vigilant and careful attention of the people, to see that it be modelled in such a manner as to admit of its being safely vested with the

requisite powers. If any plan which has been, or may be, offered to our consideration, should not upon a dispassionate
inspection be found to answer this description, it ought to be
rejected. A government, the constitution of which renders it
unfit to be trusted with all the powers which a free people
ought to delegate to any government, would be an unsafe and
improper depositary of the NATIONAL INTERESTS. Wherever
THESE can with propriety be confided, the coincident powers
may safely accompany them. This is the true result of all just
reasoning upon the subject. And the adversaries of the plan
promulgated by the convention ought to have confined themselves to showing, that the internal structure of the proposed
government was such as to render it unworthy of the confidence of the people. They ought not to have wandered into
inflammatory declamations and unmeaning cavils about the
extent of the powers. The POWERS are not too extensive for
the OBJECTS of federal administration, or, in other words, for
the management of our NATIONAL INTERESTS; nor can any satisfactory argument be framed to show that they are chargeable
with such an excess. If it be true, as has been insinuated by
some of the writers on the other side, that the difficulty arises
from the nature of the thing, and that the extent of the country will not permit us to form a government in which such
ample powers can safely be reposed, it would prove that we
ought to contract our views and resort to the expedient of
separate confederacies, which will move within more practicable spheres. For the absurdity must continually stare us in
the face of confiding to a government the direction of the
most essential national interests without daring to trust it to
the authorities which are indispensable to their proper and
efficient management. Let us not attempt to reconcile contradictions, but firmly embrace a rational alternative.

I trust, however, that the impracticability of one general
system cannot be shown. I am greatly mistaken if any thing
of weight has yet been advanced of this tendency; and I flatter
myself, that the observations which have been made in the
course of these papers have served to place the reverse of that
position in as clear a light as any matter still in the womb
of time and experience can be susceptible of. This, at all
events, must be evident, that the very difficulty itself, drawn

from the extent of the country, is the strongest argument in favor of an energetic government; for any other can certainly never preserve the Union of so large an empire. If we embrace the tenets of those who oppose the adoption of the proposed Constitution as the standard of our political creed, we cannot fail to verify the gloomy doctrines which predict the impracticability of a national system pervading entire limits of the present Confederacy.   PUBLIUS

THE FEDERALIST NO. 24

(HAMILTON)

To the People of the State of New York:
    To the powers proposed to be conferred upon the federal government in respect to the creation and direction of the national forces, I have met with but one specific objection . . . that proper provision has not been made against the existence of standing armies in time of peace; an objection which, I shall now endeavor to show, rests on weak and unsubstantial foundations.

    It has indeed been brought forward in the most vague and general form, supported only by bold assertions, without the appearance of argument; without even the sanction of theoretical opinions; in contradiction to the practice of other free nations, and to the general sense of America as expressed in most of the existing constitutions. The propriety of this remark will appear the moment it is recollected that the objection under consideration turns upon a supposed necessity of restraining the LEGISLATIVE authority of the nation in the article of military establishments; a principle unheard of except in one or two of our State constitutions, and rejected in all the rest.

    A stranger to our politics who was to read our newspapers at the present juncture, without having previously inspected the plan reported by the convention, would be naturally led to one of two conclusions: either that it contained a positive injunction, that standing armies should be kept up in time of peace; or that it vested in the EXECUTIVE the whole power of levying troops without subjecting his discretion, in any shape, to the control of the legislature.

If he came afterwards to peruse the plan itself, he would be surprised to discover, that neither the one nor the other was the case; that the whole power of raising armies was lodged in the *Legislature*, not in the *Executive;* that this legislature was to be a popular body consisting of the representatives of the people periodically elected; and that instead of the provision he had supposed in favor of standing armies, there was to be found . . . an important qualification even of the legislative discretion in that clause which forbids the appropriation of money for the support of an army for any longer period than two years—a precaution which, upon a nearer view of it, will appear to be a great and real security against the keeping up of troops without evident necessity. . . .

. . . From a close examination it will appear that restraints upon the discretion of the legislature in respect to military establishments in time of peace would be improper to be imposed, and if imposed, from the necessities of society, would be unlikely to be observed.

Though a wide ocean separates the United States from Europe, yet there are various considerations that warn us against an excess of confidence or security. On one side of us, and stretching far into our rear, are growing settlements subject to the dominion of Britain. On the other side, and extending to meet the British settlements, are colonies and establishments subject to the dominion of Spain. This situation and the vicinity of the West India Islands, belonging to these two powers, create between them, in respect to their American possessions and in relation to us, a common interest. The savage tribes on our Western frontier ought to be regarded as our natural enemies, their natural allies, because they have most to fear from us and most to hope from them. The improvements in the art of navigation have, as to the facility of communication, rendered distant nations, in a great measure, neighbors. Britain and Spain are among the principal maritime powers of Europe. A future concert of views between these nations ought not to be regarded as improbable. The increasing remoteness of consanguinity is every day diminishing the force of the family compact between France and Spain. And politicians have ever with great reason considered the ties of blood as feeble and precarious links of political connection. These circumstances combined, admonish us not to be too sanguine in considering ourselves as entirely out of the reach of danger.

Previous to the Revolution, and ever since the peace, there has been a constant necessity for keeping small garrisons on our Western frontier. No person can doubt that these will continue to be indispensable, if it should only be against the ravages and depredations of the Indians. These garrisons must either be furnished by occasional detachments from the militia or by permanent corps in the pay of the government. The first is impracticable; and if practicable, would be pernicious. The militia would not long, if at all, submit to be dragged from their occupations and families to perform that most disagreeable duty in times of profound peace. And if they could be prevailed upon or compelled to do it, the increased expense of a frequent rotation of service, and the loss of labor and disconcertion of the industrious pursuits of individuals, would form conclusive objections to the scheme. It would be as burdensome and injurious to the public as ruinous to private citizens. The latter resource of permanent corps in the pay of the government amounts to a standing army in time of peace; a small one, indeed, but not the less real for being small. Here is a simple view of the subject that shows us at once the impropriety of a constitutional interdiction of such establishments, and the necessity of leaving the matter to the discretion and prudence of the legislature.

In proportion to our increase in strength, it is probable, nay, it may be said certain, that Britain and Spain would augment their military establishments in our neighborhood. If we should not be willing to be exposed, in a naked and defenceless condition to their insults and encroachments, we should find it expedient to increase our frontier garrisons in some ratio to the force by which our Western settlements might be annoyed. There are, and will be, particular posts, the possession of which will include the command of large districts of territory, and facilitate future invasions of the remainder. It may be added that some of those posts will be keys to the trade with the Indian nations. Can any man think it would be wise to leave such posts in a situation to be at any instant seized by one or the other of two neighboring and formidable powers? To act this part would be to desert all the usual maxims of prudence and policy.

If we mean to be a commercial people or even to be secure on our Atlantic side, we must endeavor, as soon as possible, to have a navy. To this purpose there must be dock-yards and arsenals; and for the defence of these, fortifications, and probably garrisons. When a nation has become so powerful by sea that it can protect its dock-yards by its fleets, this supersedes the necessity of garrisons for that purpose; but where naval establishments are in their infancy, moderate garrisons will, in all likelihood, be found an indispensable security against descents for the destruction of the arsenals and dock-yards, and sometimes of the fleet itself.   Publius

THE FEDERALIST NO. 25

(HAMILTON)

To the People of the State of New York:

It may perhaps be urged that the objects enumerated in the preceding number ought to be provided for by the State governments under the direction of the Union. But this would be, in reality, an inversion of the primary principle of our political association, as it would in practice transfer the care of the common defence from the federal head to the individual members: a project oppressive to some States, dangerous to all, and baneful to the Confederacy. . . .

Reasons have been already given to induce a supposition

that the State governments will too naturally be prone to a rivalship with that of the Union, the foundation of which will be the love of power; and that in any contest between the federal head and one of its members the people will be most apt to unite with their local government. If, in addition to this immense advantage, the ambition of the members should be stimulated by the separate and independent possession of military forces, it would afford too strong a temptation and too great a facility to them to make enterprises upon, and finally to subvert, the constitutional authority of the Union. On the other hand, the liberty of the people would be less safe in this state of things than in that which left the national forces in the hands of the national government. As far as an army may be considered as a dangerous weapon of power, it had better be in those hands of which the people are most likely to be jealous than in those of which they are least likely to be jealous. For it is a truth, which the experience of ages has attested, that the people are always most in danger when the means of injuring their rights are in the possession of those of whom they entertain the least suspicion.

The framers of the existing Confederation, fully aware of the danger to the Union from the separate possession of military forces by the States, have, in express terms, prohibited them from having either ships or troops unless with the consent of Congress. The truth is, that the existence of a federal government and military establishments under State authority are not less at variance with each other than a due supply of the federal treasury and the system of quotas and requisitions.

There are other lights besides those already taken notice of, in which the impropriety of restraints on the discretion of the national legislature will be equally manifest. The design of the objection which has been mentioned is to preclude standing armies in time of peace, though we have never been informed how far it is designed the prohibition should extend: whether to raising armies as well as to *keeping them up* in a season of tranquillity or not. If it be confined to the latter it will have no precise signification, and it will be ineffectual for the purpose intended. When armies are once raised what shall be denominated "keeping them up," contrary to the sense of the Constitution? What time shall be requisite to ascertain the violation? Shall it be a week, a month, a year? Or shall we say they may be continued as long as the danger which occasioned their being raised continues? This would be to admit that they might be kept up *in time of peace,* against threatening or impending danger, which would be at once to deviate from the literal meaning of the prohibition, and to introduce an extensive latitude of construction. Who shall judge of the continuance of the danger? This must undoubtedly be submitted to the national government, and the matter would then be brought to this issue, that the national government, to provide against apprehended danger, might in the first instance raise troops, and might afterwards keep them on foot as long as they supposed the peace or safety of the community was in any degree of jeopardy. It is easy to perceive that a discretion so latitudinary as this would afford ample room for eluding the force of the provision.

The supposed utility of a provision of this kind can only be founded on the supposed probability, or at least possibility, of a combination between the executive and the legislative, in some scheme of usurpation. Should this at any time happen, how easy would it be to fabricate pretences of approaching danger! Indian hostilities, instigated by Spain or Britain, would always be at hand. Provocations to produce the desired appearances might even be given to some foreign power, and appeased again by timely concessions. If we can reasonably presume such a combination to have been formed, and that the enterprise is warranted by a sufficient prospect of success, the army, when once raised, from whatever cause or on whatever pretext, may be applied to the execution of the project.

If, to obviate this consequence, it should be resolved to extend the prohibition to the *raising* of armies in time of peace, the United States would then exhibit the most extraordinary spectacle which the world has yet seen,—that of a nation incapacitated by its Constitution to prepare for defence, before it was actually invaded. As the ceremony of a formal denunciation of war has of late fallen into disuse, the presence of an enemy within our territories must be waited for, as the legal warrant to the government to begin its levies of men for the protection of the State. We must receive the blow before we could even prepare to return it. All that kind of policy by which nations anticipate distant danger and meet the gathering storm must be abstained from, as contrary to the genuine maxims of a free government. We must expose our property and liberty to the mercy of foreign invaders, and invite them by our weakness to seize the naked and defenceless prey, because we are afraid that rulers, created by our choice, dependent on our will, might endanger that liberty by an abuse of the means necessary to its preservation.[34]

Here I expect we shall be told that the militia of the country is its natural bulwark, and would be at all times equal to the national defence. This doctrine, in substance, had like to have lost us our independence. It cost millions to the United States that might have been saved. The facts which, from our own experience, forbid a reliance of this kind, are too recent to permit us to be the dupes of such a suggestion. The steady operations of war against a regular and disciplined army can only be successfully conducted by a force of the same kind. Considerations of economy, not less than of stability and vigor, confirm this position. The American militia, in the course of the late war, have, by their valor on numerous occasions, erected eternal monuments to their fame; but the bravest of them feel and know that the liberty of their country could not have been established by their efforts alone, however great and valuable they were. War, like most other things, is a science to be acquired and perfected by diligence, by perseverance, by time, and by practice.

All violent policy, as it is contrary to the natural and experienced course of human affairs, defeats itself. . . .

. . . Nations pay little regard to rules and maxims calculated in their very nature to run counter to the necessities of society. Wise politicians will be cautious about fettering the government with restrictions that cannot be observed, because they know that every breach of the fundamental laws, though dictated by necessity, impairs that sacred reverence which ought to be maintained in the breast of rulers towards the constitution of a country, and forms a precedent for other breaches where the same plea of necessity does not exist at all, or is less urgent and palpable. PUBLIUS

THE FEDERALIST NO. 26

(HAMILTON)

To the People of the State of New York:

It was a thing hardly to be expected that in a popular revolution the minds of men should stop at that happy mean which marks the salutary boundary between POWER and PRIVILEGE, and combines the energy of government with the security of private rights. A failure in this delicate and important point is the great source of the inconveniences we experience; and if we are not cautious to avoid a repetition of the error in our future attempts to rectify and ameliorate our system, we may travel from one chimerical project to another; we may try change after change; but we shall never be likely to make any material change for the better.

The idea of restraining the legislative authority in the means of providing for the national defence is one of those refinements which owe their origin to a zeal for liberty more ardent than enlightened. We have seen, however, that it has not had thus far an extensive prevalency; that even in this country, where it made its first appearance, Pennsylvania and North Carolina are the only two States by which it has been in any degree patronized; and that all the others have refused to give it the least countenance; wisely judging that confidence must be placed somewhere; that the necessity of doing it, is implied in the very act of delegating power; and that it is better to hazard the abuse of that confidence than to embarrass the government and endanger the public safety by impolitic restrictions on the legislative authority. The opponents of the proposed Constitution combat, in this respect, the general decision of America; and instead of being taught by experience the propriety of correcting any extremes into which we may have heretofore run, they appear disposed to conduct us into others still more dangerous and more extravagant. As if the tone of government had been found too high or too rigid, the doctrines they teach are calculated to induce us to depress or to relax it by expedients which, upon other occasions, have been condemned or forborne. It may be affirmed without the imputation of invective, that if the principles they inculcate, on various points, could so far obtain as to become the popular creed, they would utterly unfit the people of this country for any species of government whatever. But a danger of this kind is not to be apprehended. The citizens of America have too much discernment to be argued into anarchy. And I am much mistaken, if experience has not wrought a deep and solemn conviction in the public mind, that greater energy of government is essential to the welfare and prosperity of the community.

It may not be amiss in this place concisely to remark the origin and progress of the idea, which aims at the exclusion of military establishments in time of peace. Though in speculative minds it may arise from a contemplation of the nature and tendency of such institutions, fortified by the events that have happened in other ages and countries; yet as a national sentiment, it must be traced to those habits of thinking which we derive from the nation from whom the inhabitants of these States have in general sprung.

In England, for a long time after the Norman Conquest, the authority of the monarch was almost unlimited. Inroads were gradually made upon the prerogative in favor of liberty, first by the barons and afterwards by the people, till the greatest part of its most formidable pretensions became extinct. But it was not till the revolution in 1688 . . . that English liberty was completely triumphant. . . . At the revolution, to abolish the exercise of so dangerous an authority, it became an article of the Bill of Rights then framed, that "the raising or keeping a standing army within the kingdom in time of peace, *unless with the consent of Parliament,* was against law."

In that kingdom, when the pulse of liberty was at its highest pitch, no security against the danger of standing armies was thought requisite beyond a prohibition of their being raised or kept up by the mere authority of the executive magistrate. The patriots, who effected that memorable revolution, were too temperate, too well-informed, to think of any restraint on the legislative discretion. They were aware that a certain number of troops for guards and garrisons were indispensable; that no precise bounds could be set to the national exigencies; that a power equal to every possible contingency must exist somewhere in the government: and that when they referred the exercise of that power to the judgment of the legislature, they had arrived at the ultimate point of precaution which was reconcilable with the safety of the community.

From the same source, the people of America may be said to have derived an hereditary impression of danger to liberty, from standing armies in time of peace. The circumstances of a revolution quickened the public sensibility on every point connected with the security of popular rights, and in some instances raised the warmth of our zeal beyond the degree which consisted with the due temperature of the body politic. The attempts of two of the States to restrict the authority of the legislature in the article of military establishments are of the number of these instances. The principles which had taught us to be jealous of the power of an hereditary monarch were by an injudicious excess extended to the representatives of the people in their popular assemblies. Even in some of the States, where this error was not adopted, we find unnecessary declarations that standing armies ought not to be kept up in time of peace WITHOUT THE CONSENT OF THE LEGISLATURE. I call them unnecessary, because the reason which had introduced a similar provision into the English Bill of Rights is not applicable to any of the State constitutions. The power of raising armies at all under those constitutions can by no construction be deemed to reside anywhere else, than in the legislatures themselves; and it was superfluous, if not absurd, to declare that a matter should not be done without the consent of a body, which alone had the power of doing it. Accordingly, in some of those constitutions, and among others, in that of this State of New York, which has been justly celebrated, both in Europe and America, as one of the best of the forms of government established in this country, there is a total silence upon the subject.

It is remarkable, that even in the two States which seem to have meditated an interdiction of military establishments in time of peace, the mode of expression made use of is rather cautionary than prohibitory. It is not said, that standing armies *shall not be* kept up, but that they *ought not* to be kept up in time of peace. This ambiguity of terms appears to have been the result of a conflict between jealousy and conviction; between the desire of excluding such establishments at all events, and the persuasion that an absolute exclusion would be unwise and unsafe.

Can it be doubted that such a provision, whenever the situation of public affairs was understood to require a departure from it, would be interpreted by the legislature into a mere admonition, and would be made to yield to the necessities or supposed necessities of the State? Let the fact already mentioned, with respect to Pennsylvania, decide. What then . . . is the use of such a provision, if it cease to operate the moment there is an inclination to disregard it?

Let us examine whether there be any comparison, in point of efficacy, between the provision alluded to and that which is contained in the new Constitution, for restraining the appropriations of money for military purposes to the period of two years. The former, by aiming at too much, is calculated to effect nothing; the latter, by steering clear of an imprudent extreme, and by being perfectly compatible with a proper provision for the exigencies of the nation, will have a salutary and powerful operation.

The legislature of the United States will be *obliged* by this provision, once at least in every two years, to deliberate upon the propriety of keeping a military force on foot; to come to a new resolution on the point; and to declare their sense of the matter by a formal vote in the face of their constituents. They are not *at liberty* to vest in the executive department permanent funds for the support of an army, if they were even incautious enough to be willing to repose in it so improper a confidence. As the spirit of party, in different degrees, must be expected to infect all political bodies, there will be, no doubt, persons in the national legislature willing enough to arraign the measures and criminate the views of the majority. The provision for the support of a military force will always be a favorable topic for declamation. As often as the question comes forward, the public attention will be roused and attracted to the subject by the party in opposition; and if the majority should be really disposed to exceed the proper limits, the community will be warned of the danger, and will have an opportunity of taking measures to guard against it. Independent of parties in the national legislature itself . . . the State legislatures, who will always be not only vigilant but suspicious and jealous guardians of the rights of the citizens against encroachments from the federal government, will constantly have their attention awake to the conduct of the national rulers; and will be ready enough, if any thing improper appears, to sound the alarm to the people, and not only to be the voice, but, if necessary, the arm of their discontent.

Schemes to subvert the liberties of a great community *require time* to mature them for execution. An army so large as seriously to menace those liberties could only be formed by progressive augmentations; which would suppose, not merely a temporary combination between the legislature and executive, but a continued conspiracy for a series of time. Is it probable that such a combination would exist at all? Is it probable that it would be persevered in, and transmitted along through all the successive variations in a representative body, which biennial elections would naturally produce in both houses? Is it presumable that every man, the instant he took his seat in the national Senate or House of Representatives, would commence a traitor to his constituents and to his country? Can it be supposed that there would not be found one man, discerning enough to detect so atrocious a conspiracy, or bold or honest enough to apprise his constituents of their danger? If such presumptions can fairly be made, there ought at once to be an end of all delegated authority. The people should resolve to recall all the powers they have heretofore parted with out of their own hands, and to divide themselves into as many States as there are counties in order that they may be able to manage their own concerns in person.

If such suppositions could even be reasonably made, still the concealment of the design for any duration would be impracticable. It would be announced by the very circumstance of augmenting the army to so great an extent in time of profound peace. What colorable reason could be assigned in a country so situated for such vast augmentations of the military force? It is impossible that the people could be long deceived;

and the destruction of the project and of the projectors would quickly follow the discovery.

It has been said that the provision which limits the appropriation of money for the support of an army to the period of two years would be unavailing, because the Executive, when once possessed of a force large enough to awe the people into submission, would find resources in that very force sufficient to enable him to dispense with supplies from the acts of the legislature. But the question again recurs, upon what pretence could he be put in possession of a force of that magnitude in time of peace? If we suppose it to have been created in consequence of some domestic insurrection or foreign war, then it becomes a case not within the principles of the objection; for this is levelled against the power of keeping up troops in time of peace. Few persons will be so visionary as seriously to contend that military forces ought not to be raised to quell a rebellion or resist an invasion; and if the defence of the community under such circumstances should make it necessary to have an army so numerous as to hazard its liberty, this is one of those calamities for which there is neither preventative nor cure. It cannot be provided against by any possible form of government; it might even result from a simple league offensive and defensive, if it should ever be necessary for the confederates or allies to form an army for common defence.

But it is an evil infinitely less likely to attend us in a united than in a disunited state; nay, it may be safely asserted that it is an evil altogether unlikely to attend us in the . . . [former] situation. It is not easy to conceive a possibility that dangers so formidable can assail the whole Union, as to demand a force considerable enough to place our liberties in the least jeopardy, especially if we take into our view the aid to be derived from the militia, which ought always to be counted upon as a valuable and powerful auxiliary. But in a state of disunion . . . the contrary of this supposition would become not only probable, but almost unavoidable.　　　PUBLIUS

THE FEDERALIST NO. 31[35]

(HAMILTON)

To the People of the State of New York:

In disquisitions of every kind, there are certain primary truths or first principles upon which all subsequent reasonings must depend. These contain an internal evidence which, antecedent to all reflection or combination, commands the assent of the mind. Where it produces not this effect, it must proceed either from some defect or disorder in the organs of perception, or from the influence of some strong interest, or passion, or prejudice. Of this nature are the maxims in geometry, that "the whole is greater than its parts; things equal to the same are equal to one another; two straight lines cannot enclose a space; and all right angles are equal to each other." Of the same nature are these other maxims in ethics and politics, that there cannot be an effect without a cause; that the means ought to be proportioned to the end; that every power ought to be commensurate with its object; that there ought to be no limitation of a power destined to effect a purpose which is itself incapable of limitation. And there are other truths in the two latter sciences which, if they cannot pretend to rank in the class of axioms, are yet such direct inferences from them, and so obvious in themselves, and so agreeable to the natural and unsophisticated dictates of common-sense, that they challenge the assent of a sound and unbiased mind with a degree of force and conviction almost equally irresistible.

The objects of geometrical inquiry are so entirely abstracted from those pursuits which stir up and put in motion the unruly passions of the human heart, that mankind, without difficulty, adopt not only the more simple theorems of the science, but even those abstruse paradoxes which, however they may appear susceptible of demonstration, are at variance with the natural conceptions which the mind, without the aid of philos-

ophy, would be led to entertain upon the subject. The IN-
FINITE DIVISIBILITY of matter, or, in other words, the INFINITE
divisibility of a FINITE thing, extending even to the minutest
atom, is a point agreed among geometricians, though not less
incomprehensible to common-sense than any of those mys-
teries in religion against which the batteries of infidelity have
been so industriously levelled.

But in the sciences of morals and politics, men are found
far less tractable. To a certain degree, it is right and useful
that this should be the case. Caution and investigation are a
necessary armor against error and imposition. But this untract-
ableness may be carried too far, and may degenerate into obstinacy, perverseness, or disingenuity. Though it cannot be
pretended that the principles of moral and political knowledge
have, in general, the same degree of certainty with those of
the mathematics, yet they have much better claims in this
respect than, to judge from the conduct of men in particular
situations, we should be disposed to allow them. The obscurity
is much oftener in the passions and prejudices of the reasoner
than in the subject. Men, upon too many occasions, do not
give their own understandings fair play; but, yielding to some
untoward bias, they entangle themselves in words and confound themselves in subtleties.

How else could it happen (if we admit the objectors to be
sincere in their opposition), that positions so clear as those
which manifest the necessity of a general power of taxation
in the government of the Union, should have to encounter any
adversaries among men of discernment? Though these positions have been elsewhere fully stated, they will perhaps not
be improperly recapitulated in this place, as introductory to
an examination of what may have been offered by way of
objection to them. They are in substance as follows:

A government ought to contain in itself every power requisite to the full accomplishment of the objects committed to
its care, and to the complete execution of the trusts for which
it is responsible, free from every other control but a regard to
the public good and to the sense of the people.

As the duties of superintending the national defence and of
securing the public peace against foreign or domestic violence
involve a provision for casualties and dangers to which no pos-

sible limits can be assigned, the power of making that provision ought to know no other bounds than the exigencies of the nation and the resources of the community.

As revenue is the essential engine by which the means of answering the national exigencies must be procured, the power of procuring that article in its full extent must necessarily be comprehended in that of providing for those exigencies.

As theory and practice conspire to prove that the power of procuring revenue is unavailing when exercised over the States in their collective capacities, the federal government must of necessity be invested with an unqualified power of taxation in the ordinary modes.

Did not experience evince the contrary, it would be natural to conclude that the propriety of a general power of taxation in the national government might safely be permitted to rest on the evidence of these propositions, unassisted by any additional arguments or illustrations. But we find, in fact, that the antagonists of the proposed Constitution, so far from acquiescing in their justness or truth, seem to make their principal and most zealous effort against this part of the plan. It may therefore be satisfactory to analyze the arguments with which they combat it.

Those of them which have been most labored with that view, seem in substance to amount to this: "It is not true, because the exigencies of the Union may not be susceptible of limitation, that its power of laying taxes ought to be unconfined. Revenue is as requisite to the purposes of the local administrations as to those of the Union; and the former are at least of equal importance with the latter to the happiness of the people. It is, therefore, as necessary that the State governments should be able to command the means of supplying their wants, as that the national government should possess the like faculty in respect to the wants of the Union. But an indefinite power of taxation in the *latter* might, and probably would in time, deprive the *former* of the means of providing for their own necessities; and would subject them entirely to the mercy of the national legislature. As the laws of the Union are to become the supreme law of the land, as it is to have power to pass all laws that may be NECESSARY for carrying into execution the authorities with which it is proposed to vest it, the national government might at any time abolish the taxes imposed for State objects upon the pretence of an interference with its own. It might allege a necessity of doing this in order to give efficacy to the national revenues. And thus all the resources of taxation might by degrees become the subjects of federal monopoly, to the entire exclusion and destruction of the State governments."[36]

This mode of reasoning appears sometimes to turn upon the supposition of usurpation in the national government; at other times it seems to be designed only as a deduction from the constitutional operation of its intended powers. It is only in the latter light that it can be admitted to have any pretensions to fairness. The moment we launch into conjectures about the usurpations of the federal government, we get into an unfathomable abyss, and fairly put ourselves out of the reach of all reasoning. Imagination may range at pleasure till it gets bewildered amidst the labyrinths of an enchanted castle, and knows not on which side to turn to extricate itself from the perplexities into which it has so rashly adventured. Whatever may be the limits or modifications of the powers of the Union, it is easy to imagine an endless train of possible dangers; and by indulging an excess of jealousy and timidity, we may bring ourselves to a state of absolute scepticism and irresolution. . . .

PUBLIUS

THE FEDERALIST NO. 32

(HAMILTON)

To the People of the State of New York:

Although I am of opinion that there would be no real danger of the consequences which seem to be apprehended to the State governments from a power in the Union to control them in the levies of money, because I am persuaded that the sense of the people, the extreme hazard of provoking the re-

sentments of the State governments, and a conviction of the
utility and necessity of local administrations for local purposes,
would be a complete barrier against the oppressive use of
such a power; yet I am willing here to allow, in its full extent,
the justness of the reasoning which requires that the individual
States should possess an independent and uncontrollable authority to raise their own revenues for the supply of their own
wants. And making this concession, I affirm that (with the
sole exception of duties on imports and exports) they would
. . . retain that authority in the most absolute and unqualified
sense; and that an attempt on the part of the national government to abridge them in the exercise of it would be a violent
assumption of power, unwarranted by any article or clause of
its Constitution.

An entire consolidation of the States into one complete national sovereignty would imply an entire subordination of the
parts; and whatever powers might remain in them would be
altogether dependent on the general will. But as the plan of
the convention aims only at a partial union or consolidation,
the State governments would clearly retain all the rights of
sovereignty which they before had, and which were not by
that act *exclusively* delegated to the United States. This exclusive delegation, or rather this alienation, of State sovereignty,
would only exist in three cases:[37] where the Constitution in
express terms granted an exclusive authority to the Union;
where it granted in one instance an authority to the Union, and
in another prohibited the States from exercising the like authority; and where it granted an authority to the Union, to
which a similar authority in the States would be absolutely
and totally *contradictory* and *repugnant*. I use these terms to
distinguish this last case from another which might appear to
resemble it, but which would, in fact, be essentially different;
I mean where the exercise of a concurrent jurisdiction might
be productive of occasional interferences in the *policy* of any
branch of administration, but would not imply any direct contradiction or repugnancy in point of constitutional authority.
These three cases of exclusive jurisdiction in the federal government may be exemplified by the following instances: The
last clause but one in the eighth section of the first article
provides expressly that Congress shall exercise *"exclusive legis-*

lation" over the district to be appropriated as the seat of government. This answers to the first case. The first clause of the same section empowers Congress "*to lay and collect taxes, duties, imposts, and excises*"; and the second clause of the tenth section of the same article declares that, "*no State shall, without the consent of Congress, lay any imposts or duties on imports or exports,* except for the purpose of executing its inspection laws" [*sic*].[38] Hence would result an exclusive power in the Union to lay duties on imports and exports, with the particular exception mentioned; but this power is abridged by another clause, which declares that no tax or duty shall be laid on articles exported from any State; in consequence of which qualification, it now only extends to the *duties on imports*. This answers to the second case. The third will be found in that clause which declares that Congress shall have power "to establish an UNIFORM RULE of naturalization throughout the United States" [*sic*].[39] This must necessarily be exclusive; because if each State had power to prescribe a DISTINCT RULE, there could not be a UNIFORM RULE.

A case which may perhaps be thought to resemble the latter, but which is in fact widely different, affects the question immediately under consideration. I mean the power of imposing taxes on all articles other than exports and imports. This, I contend, is manifestly a concurrent and coequal authority in the United States and in the individual States. There is plainly no expression in the granting clause which makes that power *exclusive* in the Union. There is no independent clause or sentence which prohibits the States from exercising it. So far is this from being the case, that a plain and conclusive argument to the contrary is to be deduced from the restraint laid upon the States in relation to duties on imports and exports. This restriction implies an admission that, if it were not inserted, the States would possess the power it excludes; and it implies a further admission, that as to all other taxes, the authority of the States remains undiminished. In any other view it would be both unnecessary and dangerous; it would be unnecessary, because if the grant to the Union of the power of laying such duties implied the exclusion of the States, or even their subordination in this particular there could be no need of such a restriction; it would be dangerous, because the introduction of it leads directly to the conclusion which has been mentioned, and which, if the reasoning of the objectors be just, could not have been intended; I mean that the States, in all cases to which the restriction did not apply, would have a concurrent power of taxation with the Union. The restriction in question amounts to what lawyers call a NEGATIVE PREGNANT—that is, a *negation* of one thing and an *affirmance* of another; a negation of the authority of the States to impose taxes on imports and exports, and an affirmance of their authority to impose them on all other articles. It would be mere sophistry to argue that it was meant to exclude them *absolutely* from the imposition of taxes of the former kind, and to leave them at liberty to lay others *subject to the control* of the national legislature. The restraining or prohibitory clause only says, that they shall not, ["]*without the consent of Congress,*["] lay such duties; and if we are to understand this in the sense last mentioned, the Constitution would then be made to introduce a formal provision for the sake of a very absurd conclusion; which is, that the States, *with the consent* of the national legislature, might tax imports and exports; and that they might tax every other article, *unless controlled* by the same body. If this was the intention, why not leave it, in the first instance, to what is alleged to be the natural operation of the original clause, conferring a general power of taxation upon the Union? It is evident that this could not have been the intention, and that it will not bear a construction of the kind.

As to a supposition of repugnancy between the power of taxation in the States and in the Union, it cannot be supported in that sense which would be requisite to work an exclusion of the States. It is, indeed, possible that a tax might be laid on a particular article by a State which might render it *inexpedient* that thus a further tax should be laid on the same article by the Union; but it would not imply a constitutional inability to impose a further tax. The quantity of the imposition, the expediency or inexpediency of an increase on either side, would be mutually questions of prudence; but there would be involved no direct contradiction of power. The particular policy of the national and of the State systems of finance might now and then not exactly coincide and might require reciprocal forbearances. It is not, however, a mere possibility of inconvenience in the exercise of powers, but an immediate constitutional repugnancy that can by implication alienate and extinguish a preëxisting right of sovereignty.

The necessity of a concurrent jurisdiction in certain cases results from the division of the sovereign power; and the rule that all authorities, of which the States are not explicitly divested in favor of the Union, remain with them in full vigor, is not a theoretical consequence of that division, but is clearly admitted by the whole tenor of the instrument which contains the articles of the proposed Constitution. We there find that, notwithstanding the affirmative grants of general authorities, there has been the most pointed care in those cases where it was deemed improper that the like authorities should reside in the States, to insert negative clauses prohibiting the exercise of them by the States. The tenth section of the first article consists altogether of such provisions. This circumstance is a clear indication of the sense of the convention, and furnishes a rule of interpretation out of the body of the act, which justifies the position I have advanced and refutes every hypothesis to the contrary.   PUBLIUS

THE FEDERALIST NO. 33

(HAMILTON)

To the People of the State of New York:
    The residue of the argument against the provisions of the Constitution in respect to taxation is ingrafted upon the following clause.[40] The last clause of the eighth section of the first article of the plan under consideration authorizes the national legislature "to make all laws which shall be *necessary* and *proper* for carrying into execution *the powers* by that Constitution vested in the government of the United States, or in any department or officer thereof"; and the second clause of the sixth article declares, "that the Constitution and the laws

of the United States made *in pursuance thereof,* and the treaties made by their authority shall be the *supreme law* of the land, any thing in the constitution or laws of any State to the contrary notwithstanding" [*sic*].[41]

These two clauses have been the source of much virulent invective and petulant declamation against the proposed Constitution. They have been held up to the people in all the exaggerated colors of misrepresentation as the pernicious engines by which their local governments were to be destroyed and their liberties exterminated; as the hideous monster whose devouring jaws would spare neither sex nor age, nor high nor low, nor sacred nor profane; and yet, strange as it may appear after all this clamor to those who may not have happened to contemplate them in the same light, it may be affirmed with perfect confidence that the constitutional operation of the intended government would be precisely the same, if these clauses were entirely obliterated,[42] as if they were repeated in every article. They are only declaratory of a truth which would have resulted by necessary and unavoidable implication from the very act of constituting a federal government, and vesting it with certain specified powers. This is so clear a proposition, that moderation itself can scarcely listen to the railings which have been so copiously vented against this part of the plan, without emotions that disturb its equanimity.

What is a power, but the ability or faculty of doing a thing? What is the ability to do a thing, but the power of employing the *means* necessary to its execution? What is a LEGISLATIVE power, but a power of making LAWS? What are the *means* to execute a LEGISLATIVE power, but LAWS? What is the power of laying and collecting taxes, but a *legislative power,* or a power of *making laws,* to lay and collect taxes? What are the proper means of executing such a power, but *necessary* and *proper* laws?

This simple train of inquiry furnishes us at once with a test by which to judge of the true nature of the clause complained of. It conducts us to this palpable truth, that a power to lay and collect taxes must be a power to pass all laws *necessary* and *proper* for the execution of that power; and what does the unfortunate and calumniated provision in question do more than declare the same truth, to wit, that the national legislature, to whom the power of laying and collecting taxes had been previously given, might in the execution of that power pass all laws *necessary* and *proper* to carry it into effect? I have applied these observations thus particularly to the power of taxation, because it is the immediate subject under consideration, and because it is the most important of the authorities proposed to be conferred upon the Union. But the same process will lead to the same result, in relation to all other powers declared in the Constitution. And it is *expressly* to execute these powers that the sweeping clause, as it has been affectedly called, authorizes the national legislature to pass all *necessary* and *proper* laws. If there is any thing exceptionable, it must be sought for in the specific powers upon which this general declaration is predicated. The declaration itself, though it may be chargeable with tautology or redundancy, is at least perfectly harmless.

But SUSPICION may ask, Why then was it introduced? The answer is, that it could only have been done for greater caution, and to guard against all cavilling refinements in those who might hereafter feel a disposition to curtail and evade the legitimate authorities of the Union. The Convention probably foresaw what it has been a principal aim of these papers to inculcate, that the danger which most threatens our political welfare is that the State governments will finally sap the foundations of the Union; and might therefore think it necessary in so cardinal a point to leave nothing to construction. Whatever may have been the inducement to it, the wisdom of the precaution is evident from the cry which has been raised against it; as that very cry betrays a disposition to question the great and essential truth which it is manifestly the object of that provision to declare.

But it may be again asked, Who is to judge of the *necessity* and *propriety* of the laws to be passed for executing the powers of the Union? I answer first, that this question arises as well and as fully upon the simple grant of those powers as upon the declaratory clause; and I answer in the second place, that the national government like every other, must judge in the first instance, of the proper exercise of its powers, and its constituents in the last. If the federal government should overpass the just bounds of its authority and make a tyrannical use of its powers, the people, whose creature it is, must appeal to the standard they have formed, and take such measures to redress the injury done to the Constitution as the exigency may suggest and prudence justify.[43] The propriety of a law in a constitutional light must always be determined by the nature of the powers upon which it is founded. Suppose, by some forced constructions of its authority . . . the Federal legislature should attempt to vary the law of descent in any State, would it not be evident that in making such an attempt, it had exceeded its jurisdiction, and infringed upon that of the State? Suppose again, that upon the pretence of an interference with its revenues, it should undertake to abrogate a land-tax imposed by the authority of a State; would it not be equally evident that this was an invasion of that concurrent jurisdiction in respect to this species of tax, which its Constitution plainly supposes to exist in the State governments? If there ever should be a doubt on this head, the credit of it will be entirely due to those reasoners who, in the imprudent zeal of their animosity to the plan of the convention, have labored to envelop it in a cloud calculated to obscure the plainest and simplest truths.

But it is said that the laws of the Union are to be the *supreme law* of the land. But what inference can be drawn from this, or what would they amount to if they were not to be supreme? It is evident they would amount to nothing. A LAW, by the very meaning of the term, includes supremacy. It is a rule which those to whom it is prescribed are bound to observe. This results from every political association. If individuals enter into a state of society, the laws of that society must be the supreme regulator of their conduct. If a number of political societies enter into a larger political society, the laws which the latter may enact, pursuant to the powers intrusted to it by its constitution, must necessarily be supreme over those societies, and the individuals of whom they are composed. It would otherwise be a mere treaty, dependent on the good faith of the parties, and not a government, which is only another word for POLITICAL POWER AND SUPREMACY. But it will not follow from this doctrine that acts of the larger society which are *not pursuant* to its constitutional powers, but which are invasions of the residuary authorities of the smaller societies, will become the supreme law of the land. These will be merely acts of usurpation, and will deserve to be treated as such. Hence we perceive that the clause which declares the supremacy of the laws of the Union, like the one we have just before considered, only declares a truth which flows immediately and necessarily from the institution of a federal government. It will not, I presume, have escaped observation, that it *expressly* confines this supremacy to laws made *pursuant to the Constitution;* which I mention merely as an instance of caution in the convention; since that limitation would have been to be understood, though it had not been expressed.

Though a law, therefore, laying a tax for the use of the United States would be supreme in its nature and could not legally be opposed or controlled, yet a law for abrogating or preventing the collection of a tax laid by the authority of the State (unless upon imports and exports), would not be the supreme law of the land, but a usurpation of power not granted by the Constitution. As far as an improper accumulation of taxes on the same object might tend to render the collection difficult or precarious, this would be a mutual inconvenience, not arising from a superiority or defect of power on either side, but from an injudicious exercise of power by one or the other, in a manner equally disadvantageous to both. It is to be hoped and presumed, however, that mutual interest would dictate a concert in this respect which would avoid any material inconvenience. The inference from the whole is, that the individual States would . . . retain an independent and uncontrollable authority to raise revenue to any extent of which they may stand in need, by every kind of taxation except duties on imports and exports. It will be shown in the next paper that this CONCURRENT JURISDICTION in the article of taxation was the only admissible substitute for an entire subordination, in respect to this branch of power, of the State authority to that of the Union.   PUBLIUS

THE FEDERALIST NO. 34

(HAMILTON)

To the People of the State of New York:

I flatter myself it has been clearly shown in my last number that the particular States, under the proposed Constitution, would have COEQUAL authority with the Union in the article of revenue except as to duties on imports. As this leaves open to the States far the greatest part of the resources of the community, there can be no color for the assertion that they would not possess means as abundant as could be desired for the supply of their own wants, independent of all external control. That the field is sufficiently wide will more fully appear when we come to advert to the inconsiderable share of the public expenses for which it will fall to the lot of the State governments to provide.

To argue upon abstract principles that this coördinate authority cannot exist, is to set up supposition and theory against fact and reality. However proper such reasonings might be to show that a thing *ought not to exist*, they are wholly to be rejected when they are made use of to prove that it does not exist contrary to the evidence of the fact itself. . . .

. . . In practice there is little reason to apprehend any inconvenience; because, in a short course of time, the wants of the States will naturally reduce themselves within *a very narrow compass;* and in the interim, the United States will in all probability find it convenient to abstain wholly from those objects to which the particular States would be inclined to resort.

To form a more precise judgment of the true merits of this question, it will be well to advert to the proportion between the objects that will require a federal provision in respect to revenue, and those which will require a State provision. We shall discover that the former are altogether unlimited, and that the latter are circumscribed within very moderate bounds.

In pursuing this inquiry, we must bear in mind that we are not to confine our view to the present period, but to look forward to remote futurity. Constitutions of civil government are not to be framed upon a calculation of existing exigencies, but upon a combination of these with the probable exigencies of ages, according to the natural and tried course of human affairs. Nothing, therefore, can be more fallacious than to infer the extent of any power, proper to be lodged in the national government, from an estimate of its immediate necessities. There ought to be a CAPACITY to provide for future contingencies as they may happen; and as these are illimitable in their nature, it is impossible safely to limit that capacity. It is true, perhaps, that a computation might be made with sufficient accuracy to answer the purpose of the quantity of revenue requisite to discharge the subsisting engagements of the Union, and to maintain those establishments which, for some time to come, would suffice in time of peace. But would it be wise, or would it not rather be the extreme of folly to stop at this point, and to leave the government intrusted with the care of the national defence in a state of absolute incapacity to provide for the protection of the community against future invasions of the public peace, by foreign war or domestic convulsions? If, on the contrary, we ought to exceed this point, where can we stop, short of an indefinite power of providing for emergencies as they may arise? Though it is easy to assert in general terms the possibility of forming a rational judgment of a due provision against probable dangers, yet we may safely challenge those who make the assertion to bring forward their data, and may affirm that they would be found as vague and uncertain as any that could be produced to establish the probable duration of the world. Observations confined to the mere prospects of internal attacks can deserve no weight; though even these will admit of no satisfactory calculation: but if we mean to be a commercial people, it must form a part of our policy to be able one day to defend that commerce. The support of a navy and of naval wars would involve contingencies that must baffle all the efforts of political arithmetic.

Admitting that we ought to try the novel and absurd experiment in politics of tying up the hands of government from offensive war founded upon reasons of state, yet certainly we ought not to disable it from guarding the community against the ambition or enmity of other nations. A cloud has been for some time hanging over the European world. If it should break forth into a storm, who can insure us that in its progress a part of its fury would not be spent upon us? No reasonable man would hastily pronounce that we are entirely out of its reach. Or if the combustible materials that now seem to be collecting should be dissipated without coming to maturity, or if a flame should be kindled without extending to us, what security can we have that our tranquillity will long remain undisturbed from some other course or from some other quarter? Let us recollect that peace or war will not always be left to our option; that however moderate or unambitious we may be, we cannot count upon the moderation, or hope to extinguish the ambition of others. Who could have imagined at the conclusion of the last war that France and Britain, wearied and exhausted as they both were, would so soon have looked with so hostile an aspect upon each other? To judge from the history of mankind, we shall be compelled to conclude that the fiery and destructive passions of war reign in the human breast with much more powerful sway than the mild and beneficent sentiments of peace; and that to model our political systems upon speculations of lasting tranquillity, is to calculate on the weaker springs of the human character.

What are the chief sources of expense in every government? What has occasioned that enormous accumulation of debts with which several of the European nations are oppressed? The answer plainly is, wars and rebellions; the support of those institutions which are necessary to guard the body politic against these two most mortal diseases of society. The expenses arising from those institutions which are relative to the mere domestic police of a state, to the support of its legislative, executive, and judicial departments, with their different appendages, and to the encouragement of agriculture and manufactures (which will comprehend almost all the objects of state expenditure), are insignificant in comparison with those which relate to the national defence.

In the kingdom of Great Britain, where all the ostentatious apparatus of monarchy is to be provided for, not above a fifteenth part of the annual income of the nation is appropriated to the class of expenses last mentioned; the other fourteen fifteenths are absorbed in the payment of the interest of debts contracted for carrying on the wars in which that country has been engaged and in the maintenance of fleets and armies. If, on the one hand, it should be observed that the expenses incurred in the prosecution of the ambitious enterprises and vainglorious pursuits of a monarchy are not a proper standard by which to judge of those which might be necessary in a republic, it ought, on the other hand, to be remarked that there should be as great a disproportion between the profusion and extravagance of a wealthy kingdom in its domestic administration and the frugality and economy which in that particular become the modest simplicity of republican government. If we balance a proper deduction from one side against that which it is supposed ought to be made from the other, the proportion may still be considered as holding good.

But let us advert to the large debt which we have ourselves contracted in a single war, and let us only calculate on a common share of the events which disturb the peace of nations, and we shall instantly perceive, without the aid of any elaborate illustration, that there must always be an immense disproportion between the objects of federal and state expenditures. It is true that several of the States, separately, are encumbered with considerable debts, which are an excrescence of the late war. But this cannot happen again if the proposed system be adopted; and when these debts are discharged, the only call for revenue of any consequence, which the State governments will continue to experience, will be for the mere support of their respective civil lists; to which, if we add all contingencies, the total amount in every State ought to fall considerably short of two hundred thousand pounds.

In framing a government for posterity as well as ourselves, we ought, in those provisions which are designed to be permanent, to calculate not on temporary but on permanent causes of expense. If this principle be a just one, our attention would be directed to a provision in favor of the State governments for an annual sum of about two hundred thousand pounds; while the exigencies of the Union could be susceptible of no limits, even in imagination. In this view of the subject, by what logic can it be maintained that the local governments ought to command, in perpetuity, an EXCLUSIVE source of revenue for any sum beyond the extent of two hundred thousand pounds? To extend its power further, in *exclusion* of the authority of the Union, would be to take the resources of the community out of those hands which stood in need of them for the public welfare, in order to put them into other hands which could have no just or proper occasion for them.

Suppose, then, the convention had been inclined to proceed upon the principle of a repartition of the objects of revenue, between the Union and its members, in *proportion* to their comparative necessities; what particular fund could have been selected for the use of the States that would not either have been too much or too little—too little for their present, too much for their future wants? As to the line of separation between external and internal taxes, this would leave to the States, at a rough computation, the command of two thirds of the resources of the community to defray from a tenth to a twentieth part of its expenses; and to the Union, one third of the resources of the community to defray from nine tenths to nineteen twentieths of its expenses. If we desert this boundary and content ourselves with leaving to the States an exclusive power of taxing houses and lands, there would still be a great disproportion between the *means* and the *end;* the possession of one third of the resources of the community to supply, at most, one tenth of its wants. If any fund could have been selected and appropriated, equal to and not greater than the object, it would have been inadequate to the discharge of the existing debts of the particular States, and would have left them dependent on the Union for a provision for this purpose.

The preceding train of observation will justify the position which has been elsewhere laid down, that "A CONCURRENT JURISDICTION in the article of taxation was the only admissible substitute for an entire subordination, in respect to this branch of power, of State authority to that of the Union."[44] Any separation of the objects of revenue that could have been fallen upon, would have amounted to a sacrifice of the great INTERESTS of the Union to the POWER of the individual States. The convention thought the concurrent jurisdiction preferable to that subordination; and it is evident that it has at least the merit of reconciling an indefinite constitutional power of taxation in the Federal government with an adequate and independent power in the States to provide for their own necessities. There remain a few other lights, in which this important subject of taxation will claim a further consideration.

PUBLIUS

THE FEDERALIST NO. 35

(HAMILTON)

To the People of the State of New York:
Before we proceed to examine any other objections to an indefinite power of taxation in the Union, I shall make one general remark; which is, that if the jurisdiction of the national government in the article of revenue should be restricted to particular objects, it would naturally occasion an undue proportion of the public burdens to fall upon those objects. Two evils would spring from this source: the oppression of particular branches of industry; and an unequal distribution of the taxes, as well among the several States as among the citizens of the same State.

Suppose, as has been contended for, the federal power of taxation were to be confined to duties on imports, it is evident that the government, for want of being able to command other resources, would frequently be tempted to extend these duties to an injurious excess. There are persons who imagine that they can never be carried to too great a length; since the higher they are, the more it is alleged they will tend to discourage an extravagant consumption, to produce a favorable balance of trade, and to promote domestic manufactures. But all extremes are pernicious in various ways. Exorbitant duties on imported articles would beget a general spirit of smuggling; which is always prejudicial to the fair trader, and eventually to the revenue itself: they tend to render other classes of the community tributary, in an improper degree, to the manufacturing classes, to whom they give a premature monopoly of the markets; they sometimes force industry out of its more natural channels into others in which it flows with less advantage; and in the last place, they oppress the merchant, who is often obliged to pay them himself without any retribution from the consumer. When the demand is equal to the quantity of goods at market, the consumer generally pays the duty; but when the markets happen to be overstocked, a great proportion falls upon the merchant, and sometimes not only exhausts his profits, but breaks in upon his capital. I am apt to think that a division of the duty, between the seller and the buyer, more often happens than is commonly imagined. It is not always possible to raise the price of a commodity in exact proportion to every additional imposition laid upon it. The merchant, especially in a country of small commercial capital, is often under a necessity of keeping prices down in order to [make] a more expeditious sale.

The maxim that the consumer is the payer is so much oftener true than the reverse of the proposition, that it is far more equitable that the duties on imports should go into a common stock, than that they should redound to the exclusive benefit of the importing States. But it is not so generally true as to render it equitable, that those duties should form the only national fund. When they are paid by the merchant, they operate as an additional tax upon the importing State, whose citizens pay their proportion of them in the character of consumers. In this view they are productive of inequality among the States; which inequality would be increased with the increased extent of the duties. The confinement of the national revenues to this species of imposts would be attended with inequality, from a different cause, between the manufacturing and the non-manufacturing States. The States which can go farthest towards the supply of their own wants by their own manufactures, will not, according to their numbers or wealth, consume so great a proportion of imported articles as those States which are not in the same favorable situation. They would not, therefore, in this mode alone contribute to the public treasury in a ratio to their abilities. To make them do this it is necessary that recourse be had to excises, the proper objects of which are particular kinds of manufactures.

New York is more deeply interested in these considerations than such of her citizens as contend for limiting the power of the Union to external taxation may be aware of. New York is an importing State and is not likely speedily to be, to any great extent, a manufacturing State. She would, of course, suffer in a double light from restraining the jurisdiction of the Union to commercial imposts.

So far as these observations tend to inculcate a danger of the import duties being extended to an injurious extreme it may be observed . . . that the interest of the revenue itself would be a sufficient guard against such an extreme. I readily admit that this would be the case as long as other resources were open; but if the avenues to them were closed, HOPE, stimulated by necessity, would beget experiments, fortified by rigorous precautions and additional penalties, which, for a time, would have the intended effect, till there had been leisure to contrive expedients to elude these new precautions. The first success would be apt to inspire false opinions, which it might require a long course of subsequent experience to correct. Necessity, especially in politics, often occasions false hopes, false reasoning, and a system of measures correspondingly erroneous. But even if this supposed excess should not be a consequence of the limitation of the federal power of taxation, the inequalities spoken of would still ensue, though not in the same degree, from the other causes that have been noticed. Let us now return to the examination of objections.

One which, if we may judge from the frequency of its repetition, seems most to be relied on, is, that the House of Representatives is not sufficiently numerous for the reception of all the different classes of citizens, in order to combine the interests and feelings of every part of the community, and to produce a due sympathy between the representative body and its constituents.[45] This argument presents itself under a very specious and seducing form; and is well calculated to lay hold of the prejudices of those to whom it is addressed. But when we come to dissect it with attention, it will appear to be made up of nothing but fair-sounding words. The object it seems to aim at is, in the first place, impracticable, and in the sense in which it is contended for, is unnecessary. I reserve for another place the discussion of the question which relates to the sufficiency of the representative body in respect to numbers, and shall content myself with examining here the particular use which has been made of a contrary supposition in reference to the immediate subject of our inquiries.

The idea of an actual representation of all classes of the people, by persons of each class, is altogether visionary. Unless it were expressly provided in the Constitution, that each different occupation should send one or more members, the thing would never take place in practice. Mechanics and manufacturers will always be inclined, with few exceptions, to give their votes to merchants in preference to persons of their own professions or trades. Those discerning citizens are well aware that the mechanic and manufacturing arts furnish the materials of mercantile enterprise and industry. Many of them, indeed, are immediately connected with the operations of commerce. They know that the merchant is their natural patron and friend; and they are aware, that however great the confidence they may justly feel in their own good sense, their interests can be more effectually promoted by the merchant than by themselves. They are sensible that their habits in life have not been such as to give them those acquired endowments without which, in a deliberative assembly, the greatest natural abilities are for the most part useless; and that the influence and weight and superior acquirements of the merchants render them more equal to a contest with any spirit which might happen to infuse itself into the public councils, unfriendly to the manufacturing and trading interests. These considerations, and many others that might be mentioned, prove, and experience confirms it, that artisans and manufacturers will commonly be disposed to bestow their votes upon merchants and those whom they recommend. We must therefore consider merchants as the natural representatives of all these classes of the community.

With regard to the learned professions, little need be observed; they truly form no distinct interest in society, and according to their situation and talents will be indiscriminately the objects of the confidence and choice of each other, and of other parts of the community.

Nothing remains but the landed interest; and this, in a political view and particularly in relation to taxes, I take to be perfectly united, from the wealthiest landlord down to the poorest tenant. No tax can be laid on land which will not affect the proprietor of millions of acres as well as the proprietor of a single acre. Every landholder will therefore have a common interest to keep the taxes on land as low as possible; and common interest may always be reckoned upon as the surest bond of sympathy. But if we even could suppose a distinction of interest between the opulent landholder and the middling farmer, what reason is there to conclude that the first would stand a better chance of being deputed to the national legislature than the last? If we take fact as our guide and look into our own senate and assembly, we shall find that moderate proprietors of land prevail in both; nor is this less the case in the senate, which consists of a smaller number, than in the assembly, which is composed of a greater number. Where the qualifications of the electors are the same, whether they have to choose a small or a large number, their votes will fall upon those in whom they have most confidence; whether these happen to be men of large fortunes, or of moderate property, or of no property at all.

It is said to be necessary, that all classes of citizens should have some of their own number in the representative body in order that their feelings and interests may be the better understood and attended to. But we have seen that this will never happen under any arrangement that leaves the votes of the people free. Where this is the case, the representative body, with too few exceptions to have any influence on the spirit of the government, will be composed of landholders, merchants, and men of the learned professions. But where is the danger that the interests and feelings of the different classes of citizens will not be understood or attended to by these three descriptions of men? Will not the landholder know and feel whatever will promote or insure the interest of landed property? And will he not, from his own interest in that species of property, be sufficiently prone to resist every attempt to prejudice or encumber it? Will not the merchant understand and be disposed to cultivate, as far as may be proper, the interests of the mechanic and manufacturing arts to which his commerce is so nearly allied? Will not the man of the learned profession, who will feel a neutrality to the rivalships between the different branches of industry, be likely to prove an impartial arbiter between them, ready to promote either so far as it shall appear to him conducive to the general interests of the society?

If we take into the account the momentary humors or dispositions which may happen to prevail in particular parts of the society and to which a wise administration will never be inattentive, is the man whose situation leads to extensive inquiry and information less likely to be a competent judge of their nature, extent, and foundation than one whose observation does not travel beyond the circle of his neighbors and acquaintances? Is it not natural that a man who is a candidate for the favor of the people and who is dependent on the suffrages of his fellow-citizens for the continuance of his public honors, should take care to inform himself of their dispositions and inclinations, and should be willing to allow them their proper degree of influence upon his conduct? This dependence, and the necessity of being bound himself, and his posterity, by the laws to which he gives his assent, are the true, and they are the strong chords of sympathy between the representative and the constituent.

There is no part of the administration of government that requires extensive information and a thorough knowledge of the principles of political economy so much as the business of taxation. The man who understands those principles best will be least likely to resort to oppressive expedients or to sacrifice any particular class of citizens to the procurement of revenue. It might be demonstrated that the most productive system of finance will always be the least burdensome. There can be no doubt that in order to [achieve] a judicious exercise of the power of taxation, it is necessary that the person in whose hands it is should be acquainted with the general genius, habits, and modes of thinking of the people at large, and with the resources of the country. And this is all that can be reasonably meant by a knowledge of the interests and feelings of the people. In any other sense the proposition has either no meaning, or an absurd one. And in that sense let every considerate citizen judge for himself where the requisite qualification is most likely to be found.   PUBLIUS

THE FEDERALIST NO. 37

(MADISON)

To the People of the State of New York:

In reviewing the defects of the existing Confederation, and showing that they cannot be supplied by a government of less energy than that before the public, several of the most important principles of the latter fell of course under consideration. But as the ultimate object of these papers is to determine clearly and fully the merits of this Constitution and the expediency of adopting it, our plan cannot be complete without taking a more critical and thorough survey of the work of the convention, without examining it on all its sides, comparing it in all its parts, and calculating its probable effects. . . .

Among the difficulties encountered by the convention a very important one must have lain in combining the requisite stability and energy in government with the inviolable attention due to liberty and to the republican form. Without substantially accomplishing this part of their undertaking, they would have very imperfectly fulfilled the object of their appointment or the expectation of the public; yet that it could not be easily accomplished will be denied by no one who is unwilling to betray his ignorance of the subject. Energy in government is essential to that security against external and internal danger, and to that prompt and salutary execution of the laws which enter into the very definition of good government. Stability in government is essential to national character and to the advantages annexed to it, as well as to that repose and confidence in the minds of the people, which are among the chief blessings of civil society. An irregular and mutable legislation is not more an evil in itself than it is odious to the people; and it may be pronounced with assurance that the people of this country, enlightened as they are with regard to the nature, and interested, as the great body of them are, in the effects of good government, will never be satisfied till some remedy be applied to the vicissitudes and uncertainties which characterize the State administrations. On comparing, however, these valuable ingredients with the vital principles of liberty, we must perceive at once the difficulty of mingling them together in their due proportions. The genius of republican liberty seems to demand on one side, not only that all power should be derived from the people, but that those intrusted with it should be kept in dependence on the people, by a short duration of their appointments; and that even during this short period the trust should be placed not in a few, but a number of hands. Stability, on the contrary, requires that the hands in which power is lodged should continue for a length of time the same. A frequent change of men will result from a frequent return of elections; and a frequent change of measures from a frequent change of men; whilst energy in government requires not only a certain duration of power, but the execution of it by a single hand.

How far the convention may have succeeded in this part of their work will better appear on a more accurate view of it. From the cursory view here taken, it must clearly appear to have been an arduous part.

Not less arduous must have been the task of marking the proper line of partition between the authority of the general and that of the State governments. . . .

When we pass from the works of nature, in which all the delineations are perfectly accurate, and appear to be otherwise only from the imperfection of the eye which surveys them, to the institutions of man, in which the obscurity arises as well from the object itself as from the organ by which it is contemplated, we must perceive the necessity of moderating still further our expectations and hopes from the efforts of human sagacity. Experience has instructed us that no skill in the science of government has yet been able to discriminate and define with sufficient certainty its three great provinces—the legislative, executive, and judiciary; or even the privileges and powers of the different legislative branches. Questions daily occur in the course of practice, which prove the obscurity which reigns in these subjects, and which puzzle the greatest adepts in political science.

The experience of ages, with the continued and combined labors of the most enlightened legislators and jurists, has been equally unsuccessful in delineating the several objects and limits of different codes of laws and different tribunals of justice. The precise extent of the common law, and the statute law, the maritime law, the ecclesiastical law, the law of corporations, and other local laws and customs, remains still to be clearly and finally established in Great Britain, where accuracy in such subjects has been more industriously pursued than in any other part of the world. The jurisdiction of her several courts, general and local, of law, of equity, of admiralty, etc., is not less a source of frequent and intricate discussions, sufficiently denoting the indeterminate limits by which they are respectively circumscribed. All new laws, though penned with the greatest technical skill, and passed on the fullest and most mature deliberation, are considered as more or less obscure and equivocal until their meaning be liquidated and ascertained by a series of particular discussions and adjudications. Besides the obscurity arising from the complexity of objects, and the imperfection of the human faculties, the medium through which the conceptions of men are conveyed to each other adds a fresh embarrassment. The use of words is to express ideas. Perspicuity, therefore, requires not only that the ideas should be distinctly formed, but that they should be expressed by words distinctly and exclusively appropriate to them. But no language is so copious as to supply words and phrases for every complex idea, or so correct as not to include many equivocally denoting different ideas. Hence it must happen that however accurately objects may be discriminated in themselves and however accurately the discrimination may be considered, the definition of them may be rendered inaccurate by the inaccuracy of the terms in which it is delivered. And this unavoidable inaccuracy must be greater or less, according to the complexity and novelty of the objects defined. When the Almighty himself condescends to address mankind in their own language, his meaning, luminous as it must be, is rendered dim and doubtful by the cloudy medium through which it is communicated.

Here, then, are three sources of vague and incorrect definitions: indistinctness of the object, imperfection of the organ of conception, inadequateness of the vehicle of ideas. Any one of these must produce a certain degree of obscurity. The convention, in delineating the boundary between the federal and State jurisdictions, must have experienced the full effect of them all.

To the difficulties already mentioned may be added the interfering pretensions of the larger and smaller States. We cannot err in supposing that the former would contend for a participation in the government, fully proportioned to their superior wealth and importance; and that the latter would not be less tenacious of the equality at present enjoyed by them. We may well suppose that neither side would entirely yield to the other, and consequently that the struggle could be terminated only by compromise. It is extremely probable, also, that after the ratio of representation had been adjusted, this very compromise must have produced a fresh struggle between the same parties, to give such a turn to the organization of the government and to the distribution of its powers, as would increase the importance of the branches, in forming which they had respectively obtained the greatest share of influence. There are features in the Constitution which warrant each of these suppositions; and as far as either of them is well founded, it shows that the convention must have been compelled to sacrifice theoretical propriety to the force of extraneous considerations.

Nor could it have been the large and small States only which would marshal themselves in opposition to each other on various points. Other combinations, resulting from a difference of local position and policy, must have created additional difficulties. As every State may be divided into different districts and its citizens into different classes, which give birth to contending interests and local jealousies, so the different parts of the United States are distinguished from each other by a variety of circumstances, which produce a like effect on a larger scale. And although this variety of interests, for reasons sufficiently explained in a former paper [*No. 10*], may have a salutary influence on the administration of the government when formed, yet every one must be sensible of the contrary influence which must have been experienced in the task of forming it.

Would it be wonderful if, under the pressure of all these difficulties, the convention should have been forced into some deviations from that artificial structure and regular symmetry which an abstract view of the subject might lead an ingenious theorist to bestow on a Constitution planned in his closet or in his imagination? The real wonder is that so many difficulties should have been surmounted, and surmounted with a unanimity almost as unprecedented as it must have been unexpected. It is impossible for any man of candor to reflect on this circumstance without partaking of the astonishment. It is impossible for the man of pious reflection not to perceive in it a finger of that Almighty hand which has been so frequently and signally extended to our relief in the critical stages of the revolution.

We had occasion, in a former paper [*No. 20*], to take notice of the repeated trials which have been unsuccessfully made in the United Netherlands for reforming the baneful and notorious vices of their constitution. The history of almost all the great councils and consultations held among mankind for reconciling their discordant opinions, assuaging their mutual jealousies, and adjusting their respective interests, is a history of factions, contentions, and disappointments, and may be classed among the most dark and degraded pictures which display the infirmities and depravities of the human character. If, in a few scattered instances, a brighter aspect is presented, they serve only as exceptions to admonish us of the general truth; and by their lustre to darken the gloom of the adverse prospect to which they are contrasted. In revolving the causes from which these exceptions result, and applying them to the particular instances before us, we are necessarily led to two important conclusions. The first is that the convention must have enjoyed, in a very singular degree, an exemption from the pestilential influence of party animosities—the disease most incident to deliberative bodies, and most apt to contaminate their proceedings. The second conclusion is that all the deputations composing the convention were satisfactorily accommodated by the final act, or were induced to accede to it by a deep conviction of the necessity of sacrificing private opinions and partial interests to the public good, and by a despair of seeing this necessity diminished by delays or by new experiments.[46]   PUBLIUS

THE FEDERALIST NO. 38

(MADISON)

To the People of the State of New York:

It is not a little remarkable that in every case reported by ancient history, in which government has been established with deliberation and consent, the task of framing it has not been committed to an assembly of men, but has been performed by some individual citizen of pre-eminent wisdom and approved integrity. . . .

Whence could it have proceeded that a people, jealous as the Greeks were of their liberty, should so far abandon the rules of caution as to place their destiny in the hands of a single citizen? Whence could it have proceeded that the Athenians, a people who would not suffer an army to be commanded by fewer than ten generals and who required no other proof of danger to their liberties than the illustrious merit of a fellow-citizen, should consider one illustrious citizen as a more eligible depositary of the fortunes of themselves and their posterity than a select body of citizens from whose common deliberations more wisdom, as well as more safety, might have been expected? These questions cannot be fully answered, without supposing that the fears of discord and disunion among a number of counsellors exceeded the apprehension of treachery or incapacity in a single individual. History informs us, likewise, of the difficulties with which these celebrated reformers had to contend, as well as the expedients which they were obliged to employ in order to carry their reforms into effect. Solon, who seems to have indulged a more temporizing policy, confessed that he had not given to his countrymen the government best suited to their happiness, but most tolerable to their prejudices. And Lycurgus, more true to his object, was under the necessity of mixing a portion of violence with the authority of superstition, and of securing his final success by a voluntary renunciation, first of his country, and then of his life.[47] If these lessons teach us, on one hand, to admire the improvement made by America on the ancient mode of preparing and establishing regular plans of government, they serve not less, on the other, to admonish us of the hazards and difficulties incident to such experiments, and of the great imprudence of unnecessarily multiplying them.

Is it an unreasonable conjecture, that the errors which may be contained in the plan of the convention are such as have resulted rather from the defect of antecedent experience on this complicated and difficult subject, than from a want of accuracy or care in the investigation of it; and, consequently, such as will not be ascertained until an actual trial shall have pointed them out? This conjecture is rendered probable, not only by many considerations of a general nature, but by the particular case of the Articles of Confederation. It is observable that among the numerous objections and amendments suggested by the several States, when these articles were submitted for their ratification, not one is found which alludes to the great and radical error which on actual trial has discovered itself. And if we except the observations which New Jersey was led to make, rather by her local situation, than by her peculiar foresight, it may be questioned whether a single suggestion was of sufficient moment to justify a revision of the system. There is abundant reason, nevertheless, to suppose that immaterial as these objections were, they would have been adhered to with a very dangerous inflexibility, in some States, had not a zeal for their opinions and supposed interests been stifled by the more powerful sentiment of self-preservation. One State [Maryland] . . . persisted for several years in refusing her concurrence, although the enemy remained the whole period at our gates, or rather in the very bowels of our country. Nor was her pliancy in the end effected by a less motive, than the fear of being chargeable with protracting the public calamities, and endangering the event of the contest. . . .

A patient who finds his disorder daily growing worse, and that an efficacious remedy can no longer be delayed without extreme danger, after coolly revolving his situation, and the characters of different physicians, selects and calls in such of them as he judges most capable of administering relief, and best entitled to his confidence. . . .

Such a patient and in such a situation is America at this moment. She has been sensible of her malady. She has obtained a regular and unanimous advice from men of her own deliberate choice. And she is warned by others against following this advice under pain of the most fatal consequences. Do the monitors deny the reality of her danger? No. Do they deny the necessity of some speedy and powerful remedy? No. Are they agreed, are any two of them agreed, in their objections to the remedy proposed, or in the proper one to be substituted? Let them speak for themselves. This one tells us that the proposed Constitution ought to be rejected, because it is not a confederation of the States, but a government over individuals. Another admits that it ought to be a government over individuals to a certain extent, but by no means to the extent proposed. A third does not object to the government over individuals, or to the extent proposed, but to the want of a bill of rights. A fourth concurs in the absolute necessity of a bill of rights, but contends that it ought to be declaratory, not of the personal rights of individuals, but of the rights reserved to the States in their political capacity. A fifth is of opinion that a bill of rights of any sort would be superfluous and misplaced, and that the plan would be unexceptionable but for the fatal power of regulating the times and places of election. An objector in a large State exclaims loudly against the unreasonable equality of representation in the Senate. An objector in a small State is equally loud against the dangerous inequality in the House of Representatives. From this quarter, we are alarmed with the amazing expense, from the number of persons who are to administer the new government. From another quarter, and sometimes from the same quarter on another occasion, the cry is that the Congress will be but a shadow of a representation, and that the government would be far less objectionable if the number and the expense were doubled. A patriot in a State that does not import or export discerns insuperable objections against the power of direct taxation. The patriotic adversary in a State of great exports and imports is not less dissatisfied that the whole burden of taxes may be thrown on consumption. This politician discovers in the Constitution a direct and irresistible tendency to monarchy; that is equally sure it will end in aristocracy.[48] Another is puzzled to say which of these shapes it will ultimately assume, but sees clearly it must be one or other of them; whilst a fourth is not wanting, who with no less confidence affirms that the Constitution is so far from having a bias towards either of these dangers, that the weight on that side will not be sufficient to keep it upright and firm against its opposite propensities. With another class of adversaries to the Constitution the language is that the legislative, executive, and judiciary departments are intermixed in such a manner as to contradict all the ideas of regular government and all the requisite precautions in favor of liberty. Whilst this objection circulates in vague and general expressions, there are but a few who lend their sanction to it. Let each one come forward with his particular explanation, and scarce any two are exactly agreed upon the subject. In the eyes of one the junction of the Senate with the President in the responsible function of appointing to offices, instead of vesting this executive power in the Executive alone, is the vicious part of the organization. To another, the exclusion of the House of Representatives, whose numbers alone could be a due security against corruption and partiality in the exercise of such a power, is equally obnoxious. With another, the admission of the President into any share of a power which must ever be a dangerous engine in the hands of the executive magistrate, is an unpardonable violation of the maxims of republican jealousy. No part of the arrangement, according to some, is more inadmissible than the trial of impeachments by the Senate, which is alternately a member both of the legislative and executive departments, when this power so evidently belonged to the judiciary department. "We concur fully," reply others, "in the objection to this part of the plan, but we can never agree that a reference of impeachments to the judiciary authority would be an amendment of the error. Our principal dislike to the organization arises from the extensive powers already lodged in that department." Even among the zealous patrons of a council of state the most irreconcilable variance is discovered concerning the mode in which it ought to be constituted. The demand of one gentleman is that the council should consist of a small number to be appointed by the most numerous branch of the legislature. Another would prefer a larger number and considers it as a fundamental condition that the appointment should be made by the President himself.

As it can give no umbrage to the writers against the plan of the federal Constitution, let us suppose, that as they are the most zealous, so they are also the most sagacious of those who think the late convention were unequal to the task assigned them, and that a wiser and better plan might and ought to be substituted. Let us further suppose that their country should concur, both in this favorable opinion of their merits, and in their unfavorable opinion of the convention; and should accordingly proceed to form them into a second convention with full powers and for the express purpose of revising and remoulding the work of the first. Were the experiment to be seriously made, though it required some effort to view it seriously even in fiction, I leave it to be decided by the sample of opinions just exhibited, whether, with all their enmity to their predecessors, they would in any one point depart so widely from their example, as in the discord and ferment that would mark their own deliberations; and whether the Constitution now before the public would not stand as fair a chance for immortality, as Lycurgus gave to that of Sparta, by making its change to depend on his own return from exile and death, if it were to be immediately adopted, and were to continue in force, not until a BETTER, but until ANOTHER should be agreed upon by this new assembly of lawgivers.

It is a matter both of wonder and regret that those who raise so many objections against the new Constitution should never call to mind the defects of that which is to be exchanged for it.[49] It is not necessary that the former should be perfect: it is sufficient that the latter is more imperfect. No man would refuse to give brass for silver or gold, because the latter had some alloy in it. No man would refuse to quit a shattered and tottering habitation for a firm and commodious building, because the latter had not a porch to it, or because some of the rooms might be a little larger or smaller, or the ceiling a little higher or lower than his fancy would have planned them. But waiving illustrations of this sort, is it not manifest that most of the capital objections urged against the new system lie with tenfold weight against the existing Confederation? Is an indefinite power to raise money dangerous in the hands of the federal government? The present Congress can make requisitions to any amount they please, and the States are constitutionally bound to furnish them; they can emit bills of credit as long as they will pay for the paper; they can borrow both abroad and at home as long as a shilling will be lent. Is an indefinite power to raise troops dangerous? The Confederation gives to Congress that power also; and they have already begun to make use of it. Is it improper and unsafe to intermix the different powers of government in the same body of men? Congress, a single body of men, are the sole depositary of all the federal powers. Is it particularly dangerous to give the keys of the treasury and the command of the army into the same hands? The Confederation places them both in the hands of Congress. Is a bill of rights essential to liberty? The Confederation has no bill of rights. Is it an objection against the new Constitution, that it empowers the Senate with the concurrence of the Executive to make treaties which are to be the laws of the land? The existing Congress without any such control can make treaties which they themselves have declared, and most of the States have recognized, to be the supreme law of the land. Is the importation of slaves permitted by the new Constitution for twenty years? By the old it is permitted forever.

I shall be told, that however dangerous this mixture of powers may be in theory, it is rendered harmless by the dependence of Congress on the States for the means of carrying them into practice; that however large the mass of powers may be, it is in fact a lifeless mass. Then, say I, in the first place, that the Confederation is chargeable with the still greater folly of declaring certain powers in the federal government to be absolutely necessary, and at the same time rendering them absolutely nugatory; and, in the next place, that

if the Union is to continue and no better government be substituted, effective powers must either be granted to, or assumed by, the existing Congress; in either of which events,
the contrast just stated will hold good. But this is not all. Out
of this lifeless mass has already grown an excrescent power,
which tends to realize all the dangers that can be apprehended
from a defective construction of the supreme government of
the Union. It is now no longer a point of speculation and hope
that the Western territory is a mine of vast wealth to the
United States; and although it is not of such a nature as to
extricate them from their present distresses, or for some time
to come to yield any regular supplies for the public expenses;
yet must it hereafter be able under proper management, both
to effect a gradual discharge of the domestic debt, and to
furnish, for a certain period, liberal tributes to the federal
treasury. A very large proportion of this fund has been already
surrendered by individual States; and it may with reason be
expected that the remaining States will not persist in with-
holding similar proofs of their equity and generosity. We may
calculate, therefore, that a rich and fertile country, of an area
equal to the inhabited extent of the United States, will soon
become a national stock. Congress have assumed the administration of this stock. They have begun to render it productive.
Congress have undertaken to do more: they have proceeded
to form new States, to erect temporary governments, to appoint officers for them, and to prescribe the conditions on
which such States shall be admitted into the Confederacy. All
this has been done; and done without the least color of constitutional authority. Yet no blame has been whispered; no
alarm has been sounded. A GREAT and INDEPENDENT fund of
revenue is passing into the hands of a SINGLE BODY of men,
who can RAISE TROOPS to an INDEFINITE NUMBER, and appropriate money to their support for an INDEFINITE PERIOD OF
TIME. And yet there are men who have not only been silent
spectators of this prospect, but who are advocates for the
system which exhibits it; and, at the same time, urge against
the new system the objections which we have heard. Would
they not act with more consistency, in urging the establishment of the latter as no less necessary to guard the Union
against the future powers and resources of a body constructed

like the existing Congress, than to save it from the dangers
threatened by the present impotency of that Assembly?

I mean not . . . to throw censure on the measures which
have been pursued by Congress. I am sensible they could not
have done otherwise. The public interest, the necessity of the
case, imposed upon them the task of overleaping their constitutional limits. But is not the fact an alarming proof of the
danger resulting from a government which does not possess
regular powers commensurate to its objects? A dissolution or
usurpation is the dreadful dilemma to which it is continually
exposed. PUBLIUS

THE FEDERALIST NO. 39

(MADISON)

To the People of the State of New York:

The last paper having concluded the observations which
were meant to introduce a candid survey of the plan of government reported by the convention, we now proceed to the
execution of that part of our undertaking.

The first question that offers itself is, whether the general
form and aspect of the government be strictly republican. It
is evident that no other form would be reconcilable with the
genius of the people of America; with the fundamental principles of the Revolution; or with that honorable determination
which animates every votary of freedom, to rest all our political
experiments on the capacity of mankind for self-government.
If the plan of the convention, therefore, be found to depart
from the republican character, its advocates must abandon it
as no longer defensible.

What, then, are the distinctive characters of the republican
form?[50] Were an answer to this question to be sought, not
by recurring to principles, but in the application of the term
by political writers, to the constitutions of different States, no

satisfactory one would ever be found. Holland, in which no particle of the supreme authority is derived from the people, has passed almost universally under the denomination of a republic. The same title has been bestowed on Venice where absolute power over the great body of the people is exercised in the most absolute manner by a small body of hereditary nobles. Poland, which is a mixture of aristocracy and of monarchy in their worst forms, has been dignified with the same appellation. The government of England, which has one republican branch only, combined with an hereditary aristocracy and monarchy, has, with equal impropriety, been frequently placed on the list of republics. These examples, which are nearly as dissimilar to each other as to a genuine republic, show the extreme inaccuracy with which the term has been used in political disquisitions.

If we resort for a criterion to the different principles on which different forms of government are established, we may define a republic to be, or at least may bestow that name on, a government which derives all its powers directly or indirectly from the great body of the people, and is administered by persons holding their offices during pleasure, for a limited period, or during good behavior. It is *essential* to such a government that it be derived from the great body of the society, not from an inconsiderable proportion, or a favored class of it; otherwise a handful of tyrannical nobles, exercising their oppressions by a delegation of their powers, might aspire to the rank of republicans and claim for their government the honorable title of republic. It is *sufficient* for such a government that the persons administering it be appointed, either directly or indirectly, by the people; and that they hold their appointments by either of the tenures just specified; otherwise every government in the United States, as well as every other popular government that has been or can be well organized or well executed, would be degraded from the republican character. According to the constitution of every State in the Union, some or other of the officers of government are appointed indirectly only by the people. According to most of them, the chief magistrate himself is so appointed. And according to one, this mode of appointment is extended to one of the coördinate branches of the legislature. According to all the constitutions, also, the tenure of the highest offices is extended to a definite period, and in many instances, both within the legislative and executive departments, to a period of years. According to the provisions of most of the constitutions, again, as well as according to the most respectable and received opinions on the subject, the members of the judiciary department are to retain their offices by the firm tenure of good behavior.

On comparing the Constitution planned by the convention with the standard here fixed, we perceive at once that it is, in the most rigid sense, conformable to it. The House of Representatives, like that of one branch at least of all the State legislatures, is elected immediately by the great body of the people. The Senate, like the present Congress, and the Senate of Maryland, derives its appointment indirectly from the people. The President is indirectly derived from the choice of the people, according to the example in most of the States. Even the judges with all other officers of the Union, will, as in the several States, be the choice, though a remote choice, of the people themselves. The duration of the appointments is equally conformable to the republican standard and to the model of State constitutions. The House of Representatives is periodically elective, as in all the States; and for the period of two years, as in the State of South Carolina. The Senate is elective for the period of six years; which is but one year more than the period of the Senate of Maryland, and but two more than that of the Senates of New York and Virginia. The President is to continue in office for the period of four years; . . . in New York and Delaware the chief magistrate is elected for three years, and in South Carolina for two years. In the other States the election is annual. In several of the States, however, no constitutional provision is made for the impeachment of the chief magistrate. And in Delaware and Virginia he is not impeachable till out of office. The President of the United States is impeachable at any time during his continuance in office. The tenure by which the judges are to hold their places is, as it unquestionably ought to be, that of good behavior. The tenure of the ministerial offices generally, will be a subject of legal regulation, conformably to the reason of the case and the example of the State constitutions.

Could any further proof be required of the republican complexion of this system, the most decisive one might be found in its absolute prohibition of titles of nobility, both under the federal and the State governments; and in its express guaranty of the republican form to each of the latter.

"But it was not sufficient," say the adversaries of the proposed Constitution, "for the convention to adhere to the republican form. They ought, with equal care, to have preserved the *federal* form, which regards the Union as a *Confederacy* of sovereign states; instead of which, they have framed a *national* government, which regards the Union as a *consolidation* of the States."[51] And it is asked by what authority this bold and radical innovation was undertaken? The handle which has been made of this objection requires that it should be examined with some precision.

Without inquiring into the accuracy of the distinction on which the objection is founded, it will be necessary to a just estimate of its force, first, to ascertain the real character of the government in question; secondly, to inquire how far the convention were authorized to propose such a government; and thirdly, how far the duty they owed to their country could supply any defect of regular authority.

First.—In order to ascertain the real character of the government, it may be considered in relation to the foundation on which it is to be established; to the sources from which its ordinary powers are to be drawn; to the operation of those powers; to the extent of them; and to the authority by which future changes in the government are to be introduced.

On examining the first relation, it appears, on one hand, that the Constitution is to be founded on the assent and ratification of the people of America, given by deputies elected for the special purpose; but, on the other, that this assent and ratification is to be given by the people, not as individuals composing one entire nation, but as composing the distinct and independent States to which they respectively belong. It is to be the assent and ratification of the several States, derived from the supreme authority in each State,—the authority of the people themselves. The act, therefore, establishing the Constitution, will not be a *national,* but a *federal* act.[52]

That it will be a federal and not a national act, as these

terms are understood by the objectors, the act of the people as forming so many independent States, not as forming one aggregate nation, is obvious from this single consideration: that it is to result neither from the decision of a *majority* of the people of the Union, nor from that of a *majority* of the States. It must result from the *unanimous* assent of the several States that are parties to it, differing no otherwise from their ordinary assent than in its being expressed, not by the legislative authority, but by that of the people themselves. Were the people regarded in this transaction as forming one nation, the will of the majority of the whole people of the United States would bind the minority in the same manner as the majority in each State must bind the minority; and the will of the majority must be determined either by a comparison of the individual votes, or by considering the will of the majority of the States as evidence of the will of a majority of the people of the United States. Neither of these rules has been adopted. Each State, in ratifying the Constitution, is considered as a sovereign body, independent of all others, and only to be bound by its own voluntary act. In this relation, then, the new Constitution will, if established, be a *federal,* and not a *national* constitution.[53]

The next relation is to the sources from which the ordinary powers of government are to be derived. The House of Representatives will derive its powers from the people of America; and the people will be represented in the same proportion, and on the same principle, as they are in the legislature of a particular State. So far the government is *national,* not *federal.* The Senate, on the other hand, will derive its powers from the States, as political and coequal societies; and these will be represented on the principle of equality in the Senate, as they now are in the existing Congress. So far the government is *federal,* not *national.* The executive power will be derived from a very compound source. The immediate election of the President is to be made by the States in their political characters. The votes allotted to them are in a compound ratio, which considers them partly as distinct and coequal societies, partly as unequal members of the same society. The eventual election, again, is to be made by that branch of the legislature which consists of the national representatives; but in this particular act they are to be thrown into the form of individual delegations, from so many distinct and coequal bodies politic. From this aspect of the government it appears to be of a mixed character, presenting at least as many *federal* as *national* features.

The difference between a federal and national government, as it relates to the *operation of the government,* is supposed to consist in this, that in the former the powers operate on the political bodies composing the Confederacy in their political capacities; in the latter, on the individual citizens composing the nation in their individual capacities. On trying the Constitution by this criterion, it falls under the *national,* not the *federal* character; though perhaps not so completely as has been understood. In several cases, and particularly in the trial of controversies to which States may be parties, they must be viewed and proceeded against in their collective and political capacities only. So far the national countenance of the government on this side seems to be disfigured by a few federal features. But this blemish is perhaps unavoidable in any plan; and the operation of the government on the people, in their individual capacities, in its ordinary and most essential proceedings, may, on the whole designate it in this relation, a *national* government.

But if the government be national with regard to the *operation* of its powers, it changes its aspect again when we contemplate it in relation to the extent of its powers. The idea of a national government involves in it, not only an authority over the individual citizens, but an indefinite supremacy over all persons and things, so far as they are objects of lawful government. Among a people consolidated into one nation, this supremacy is completely vested in the national legislature. Among communities united for particular purposes, it is vested partly in the general and partly in the municipal legislatures. In the former case, all local authorities are subordinate to the supreme; and may be controlled, directed, or abolished by it at pleasure. In the latter, the local or municipal authorities form distinct and independent portions of the supremacy, no more subject within their respective spheres to the general authority, than the general authority is subject to them within its own sphere. In this relation, then, the proposed government cannot be deemed a *national* one; since its jurisdiction extends to certain enumerated objects only, and leaves to the several States a residuary and inviolable sovereignty over all other objects. It is true that in controversies relating to the boundary between the two jurisdictions, the tribunal which is ultimately to decide, is to be established under the general government. But this does not change the principle of the case. The decision is to be impartially made, according to the rules of the Constitution; and all the usual and most effectual precautions are taken to secure this impartiality. Some such tribunal is clearly essential to prevent an appeal to the sword and a dissolution of the compact; and that it ought to be established under the general rather than under the local governments, or, to speak more properly, that it could be safely established under the first alone, is a position not likely to be combated.

If we try the Constitution by its last relation to the authority by which amendments are to be made, we find it neither wholly *national* nor wholly *federal*. Were it wholly national, the supreme and ultimate authority would reside in the *majority* of the people of the Union; and this authority would be competent at all times, like that of a majority of every national society, to alter or abolish its established government. Were it wholly federal, on the other hand, the concurrence of each State in the Union would be essential to every alteration that would be binding on all. The mode provided by the plan of the convention is not founded on either of these principles. In requiring more than a majority, and particularly in computing the proportion by *States*, not by *citizens*, it departs from the *national* and advances towards the *federal* character; in rendering the concurrence of less than the whole number of States sufficient, it loses again the *federal* and partakes of the *national* character.

The proposed Constitution, therefore, is, in strictness, neither a national nor a federal Constitution, but a composition of both. In its foundation it is federal, not national; in the sources from which the ordinary powers of the government are drawn, it is partly federal and partly national; in the operation of these powers, it is national, not federal; in the extent of them, again, it is federal, not national; and, finally, in the authoritative mode of introducing amendments, it is neither wholly federal nor wholly national.[54]   PUBLIUS

THE FEDERALIST NO. 41

(MADISON)

To the People of the State of New York:
The Constitution proposed by the convention may be considered under two general points of view. The FIRST relates to the sum or quantity of power which it vests in the government, including the restraints imposed on the States. The SECOND, to the particular structure of the government and the distribution of this power among its several branches.

Under the *first* view of the subject, two important questions arise: 1. Whether any part of the powers transferred to the general government be unnecessary or improper? 2. Whether the entire mass of them be dangerous to the portion of jurisdiction left in the several States?

Is the aggregate power of the general government greater than ought to have been vested in it? This is the *first* question. . . .

. . . In every political institution, a power to advance the public happiness involves a discretion which may be misapplied and abused; . . . in all cases where power is to be conferred, the point first to be decided is, whether such a power be necessary to the public good; . . . in case of an affirmative decision, to guard as effectually as possible against a perversion of the power to the public detriment.[55]

That we may form a correct judgment on this subject, it will be proper to review the several powers conferred on the government of the Union; and that this may be the more conveniently done they may be reduced into different classes as they relate to the following different objects: 1. Security against foreign danger; 2. Regulation of the intercourse with foreign nations; 3. Maintenance of harmony and proper intercourse among the States; 4. Certain miscellaneous objects of general utility; 5. Restraint of the States from certain injurious acts; 6. Provisions for giving due efficacy to all these powers.

The powers falling within the *first* class are those of declaring war and granting letters of marque; of providing armies and fleets; of regulating and calling forth the militia; of levying and borrowing money.

Security against foreign danger is one of the primitive objects of civil society. It is an avowed and essential object of the American Union. The powers requisite for attaining it must be effectually confided to the federal councils.

Is the power of declaring war necessary? No man will answer this question in the negative. It would be superfluous, therefore, to enter into a proof of the affirmative. The existing Confederation establishes this power in the most ample form.

Is the power of raising armies and equipping fleets necessary? This is involved in the foregoing power. It is involved in the power of self-defence.

But was it necessary to give an INDEFINITE POWER of raising TROOPS, as well as providing fleets; and of maintaining both in PEACE, as well as in war?

The answer to these questions has been too far anticipated in another place [*Nos. 24–27*] to admit an extensive discussion of them in this place. The answer indeed seems to be so obvious and conclusive as scarcely to justify such a discussion in any place. With what color of propriety could the force necessary for defence be limited by those who cannot limit the force of offence? If a federal Constitution could chain the ambition or set bounds to the exertions of all other nations, then indeed might it prudently chain the discretion of its own government, and set bounds to the exertions for its own safety.

How could a readiness for war in time of peace be safely prohibited, unless we could prohibit in like manner the preparations and establishments of every hostile nation? The means of security can only be regulated by the means and the danger of attack. They will, in fact, be ever determined by these rules and by no others. It is in vain to oppose constitutional barriers to the impulse of self-preservation. It is worse

than in vain; because it plants in the Constitution itself necessary usurpations of power, every precedent of which is a
germ of unnecessary and multiplied repetitions. If one nation
maintains constantly a disciplined army, ready for the service
of ambition or revenge, it obliges the most pacific nations who
may be within the reach of its enterprises to take corresponding precautions. . . .

A standing force, therefore, is a dangerous, at the same time
that it may be a necessary, provision. On the smallest scale it
has its inconveniences. On an extensive scale its consequences
may be fatal. On any scale it is an object of laudable circumspection and precaution. A wise nation will combine all these
considerations; and, whilst it does not rashly preclude itself
from any resource which may become essential to its safety,
will exert all its prudence in diminishing both the necessity
and the danger of resorting to one which may be inauspicious
to its liberties.

The clearest marks of this prudence are stamped on the
proposed Constitution. The Union itself, which it cements and
secures, destroys every pretext for a military establishment
which could be dangerous. America united, with a handful of
troops or without a single soldier, exhibits a more forbidding
posture to foreign ambition than America disunited, with a
hundred thousand veterans ready for combat. It was remarked,
on a former occasion, [*No. 8*] that the want of this pretext
had saved the liberties of one nation in Europe. Being rendered
by her insular situation and her maritime resources impregnable to the armies of her neighbors, the rulers of Great Britain
have never been able, by real or artificial dangers, to cheat the
public into an extensive peace establishment. The distance of
the United States from the powerful nations of the world gives
them the same happy security. A dangerous establishment can
never be necessary or plausible, so long as they continue a
united people. But let it never for a moment be forgotten that
they are indebted for this advantage to the Union alone. The
moment of its dissolution will be the date of a new order of
things. The fears of the weaker, or the ambition of the stronger
States or Confederacies, will set the same example in the New,
as Charles VII did in the Old World. The example will be
followed here from the same motives which produced univer-

sal imitation there. Instead of deriving from our situation the precious advantage which Great Britain has derived from hers, the face of America will be but a copy of that of the continent of Europe. It will present liberty everywhere crushed between standing armies and perpetual taxes. The fortunes of disunited America will be even more disastrous than those of Europe. The sources of evil in the latter are confined to her own limits. No superior powers of another quarter of the globe intrigue among her rival nations, inflame their mutual animosities, and render them the instruments of foreign ambition, jealousy, and revenge. In America the miseries springing from her internal jealousies, contentions, and wars, would form a part only of her lot. A plentiful addition of evils would have their source in that relation in which Europe stands to this quarter of the earth, and which no other quarter of the earth bears to Europe.

This picture of the consequences of disunion cannot be too highly colored or too often exhibited. Every man who loves peace, every man who loves his country, every man who loves liberty, ought to have it ever before his eyes, that he may cherish in his heart a due attachment to the Union of America, and be able to set a due value on the means of preserving it.

Next to the effectual establishment of the Union, the best possible precaution against danger from standing armies is a limitation of the term for which revenue may be appropriated to their support. This precaution the Constitution has prudently added. I will not repeat here the observations which I flatter myself have placed this subject in a just and satisfactory light [*No. 26*]. But it may not be improper to take notice of an argument against this part of the Constitution, which has been drawn from the policy and practice of Great Britain. It is said that the continuance of an army in that kingdom requires an annual vote of the legislature; whereas the American Constitution has lengthened this critical period to two years. This is the form in which the comparison is usually stated to the public, but is it a just form? Is it a fair comparison? Does the British Constitution restrain the parliamentary discretion to one year? Does the American impose on the Congress appropriations for two years? On the contrary, it cannot be unknown to the authors of the fallacy themselves, that the British Constitution fixes no limit whatever to the discretion of the legislature, and that the American ties down the legislature to two years as the longest admissible term.

Had the argument from the British example been truly stated, it would have stood thus: The term for which supplies may be appropriated to the army establishment, though unlimited by the British Constitution, has nevertheless, in practice, been limited by parliamentary discretion to a single year. Now, if in Great Britain, where the House of Commons is elected for seven years; where so great a proportion of the members are elected by so small a proportion of the people; where the electors are so corrupted by the representatives and the representatives so corrupted by the Crown, the representative body can possess a power to make appropriations to the army for an indefinite term without desiring or without daring to extend the term beyond a single year; [if true in Britain], ought not suspicion herself to blush in pretending that the representatives of the United States, elected FREELY by the WHOLE BODY of the people every SECOND YEAR, cannot be safely intrusted with the discretion over such appropriations, expressly limited to the short period of TWO YEARS?

A bad cause seldom fails to betray itself. Of this truth the management of the opposition to the federal government is an unvaried exemplification. But among all the blunders which have been committed, none is more striking than the attempt to enlist on that side the prudent jealousy entertained by the people, of standing armies. The attempt has awakened fully the public attention to that important subject; and has led to investigations which must terminate in a thorough and universal conviction, not only that the Constitution has provided the most effectual guards against danger from that quarter, but that nothing short of a Constitution fully adequate to the national defence and the preservation of the Union, can save America from as many standing armies as it may be split into States or Confederacies; and from such a progressive augmentation of these establishments in each, as will render them as burdensome to the properties and ominous to the liberties of the people, as any establishment that can become necessary, under a united and efficient government, must be tolerable to the former and safe to the latter.

The palpable necessity of the power to provide and main-

tain a navy has protected that part of the Constitution against
a spirit of censure, which has spared few other parts. It must,
indeed, be numbered among the greatest blessings of America,
that as her Union will be the only source of her maritime
strength, so this will be a principal source of her security
against danger from abroad. In this respect our situation bears
another likeness to the insular advantage of Great Britain. The
batteries most capable of repelling foreign enterprises on our
safety are happily such as can never be turned by a perfidious
government against our liberties.

The inhabitants of the Atlantic frontier are all of them
deeply interested in this provision for naval protection, and if
they have hitherto been suffered to sleep quietly in their beds;
if their property has remained safe against the predatory spirit
of licentious adventurers; if their maritime towns have not yet
been compelled to ransom themselves from the terrors of a
conflagration by yielding to the exactions of daring and sudden invaders, these instances of good fortune are not to be
ascribed to the capacity of the existing government for the
protection of those from whom it claims allegiance, but to
causes that are fugitive and fallacious. If we except perhaps
Virginia and Maryland, which are peculiarly vulnerable on
their eastern frontiers, no part of the Union ought to feel more
anxiety on this subject than New York. Her sea-coast is extensive. A very important district of the State is an island. The
State itself is penetrated by a large navigable river for more
than fifty leagues. The great emporium of its commerce . . .
lies every moment at the mercy of events, and may almost be
regarded as a hostage for ignominious compliances with the
dictates of a foreign enemy, or even with the rapacious demands of pirates and barbarians. Should a war be the result
of the precarious situation of European affairs, and all the unruly passions attending it be let loose on the ocean, our escape
from insults and depredations, not only on that element, but
every part of the other bordering on it, will be truly miraculous. In the present condition of America, the States more immediately exposed to these calamities have nothing to hope
from the phantom of a general government which now exists;
and if their single resources were equal to the task of fortifying
themselves against the danger, the object to be protected

would be almost consumed by the means of protecting them.

The power of regulating and calling forth the militia has been already sufficiently vindicated and explained [*Nos. 28–29*].

The power of levying and borrowing money, being the sinew of that which is to be exerted in the national defence, is properly thrown into the same class with it. This power, also, has been examined already with much attention . . . [*Nos. 30–35*]. I will address one additional reflection only to those who contend that the power ought to have been restrained to external taxation—by which they mean taxes on articles imported from other countries. It cannot be doubted that this will always be a valuable source of revenue; that for a considerable time it must be a principal source; that at this moment it is an essential one. But we may form very mistaken ideas on this subject if we do not call to mind in our calculations, that the extent of revenue drawn from foreign commerce must vary with the variations, both in the extent and the kind of imports; and that these variations do not correspond with the progress of population, which must be the general measure of the public wants. As long as agriculture continues the sole field of labor, the importation of manufactures must increase as the consumers multiply. As soon as domestic manufactures are begun by the hands not called for by agriculture, the imported manufactures will decrease as the numbers of people increase. In a more remote stage, the imports may consist in a considerable part of raw materials, which will be wrought into articles for exportation, and will, therefore, require rather the encouragement of bounties, than to be loaded with discouraging duties.[56] A system of government, meant for duration, ought to contemplate these revolutions and be able to accommodate itself to them.

Some, who have not denied the necessity of the power of taxation, have grounded a very fierce attack against the Constitution, on the language in which it is defined. It has been urged and echoed, that the power "to lay and collect taxes, duties, imposts, and excises, to pay the debts and provide for the common defence and general welfare of the United States," amounts to an unlimited commission to exercise every power which may be alleged to be necessary for the common defence or general welfare. No stronger proof could be given of the distress under which these writers labor for objections, than their stooping to such a misconstruction.

Had no other enumeration or definition of the powers of the Congress been found in the Constitution than the general expressions just cited, the authors of the objection might have had some color for it; though it would have been difficult to find a reason for so awkward a form of describing an authority to legislate in all possible cases. A power to destroy the freedom of the press, the trial by jury, or even to regulate the course of descents, or the forms of conveyances, must be very singularly expressed by the terms "to raise money for the general welfare."

But what color can the objection have when a specification of the objects alluded to by these general terms immediately follows, and is not even separated by a longer pause than a semicolon? If the different parts of the same instrument ought to be so expounded, as to give meaning to every part which will bear it, shall one part of the same sentence be excluded altogether from a share in the meaning; and shall the more doubtful and indefinite terms be retained in their full extent, and the clear and precise expressions be denied any signification whatsoever? For what purpose could the enumeration of particular powers be inserted if these and all others were meant to be included in the preceding general power? Nothing is more natural nor common than first to use a general phrase, and then to explain and qualify it by a recital of particulars. But the idea of an enumeration of particulars which neither explain nor qualify the general meaning, and can have no other effect than to confound and mislead, is an absurdity, which, as we are reduced to the dilemma of charging either on the authors of the objection or on the authors of the Constitution, we must take the liberty of supposing, had not its origin with the latter.

The objection here is the more extraordinary, as it appears that the language used by the convention is a copy from the articles of Confederation. The objects of the Union among the States, as described in article third, are, "their common defence, [the] security of their liberties and [their] mutual and general welfare." The terms of article eighth are still more identical: "All charges of war and all other expenses, that shall be incurred for the common defence or general welfare, and allowed by the United States in Congress [assembled], shall be defrayed out of a common treasury," etc. A similar language again occurs in article ninth. Construe either of these articles by the rules which would justify the construction put on the new Constitution, and they vest in the existing Congress a power to legislate in all cases whatsoever. But what would have been thought of that assembly, if, attaching themselves to these general expressions and disregarding the specifications which ascertain and limit their import, they had exercised an unlimited power of providing for the common defence and general welfare? I appeal to the objectors themselves, whether they would in that case have employed the same reasoning in justification of Congress as they now make use of against the convention. How difficult it is for error to escape its own condemnation!   PUBLIUS

THE FEDERALIST NO. 44

(MADISON)

To the People of the State of New York:

A *fifth* class[57] of provisions in favor of the federal authority consists of the following restrictions on the authority of the several States.

1. "No State shall enter into any treaty, alliance, or confederation; grant letters of marque and reprisal; coin money; emit bills of credit; make anything but gold and silver a legal tender in payment of debts; pass any bill of attainder, *ex-post-facto* law, or law impairing the obligation of contracts; or grant any title of nobility."

The prohibition against treaties, alliances, and confederations makes a part of the existing articles of Union; and for reasons which need no explanation, is copied into the new

Constitution. The prohibition of letters of marque is another part of the old system, but is somewhat extended in the new. According to the former, letters of marque could be granted by the States after a declaration of war; according to the latter, these licenses must be obtained, as well during war as previous to its declaration, from the government of the United States. This alteration is fully justified by the advantage of uniformity in all points which relate to foreign powers; and of immediate responsibility to the nation in all those for whose conduct the nation itself is to be responsible.

The right of coining money, which is here taken from the States, was left in their hands by the Confederation, as a concurrent right with that of Congress, under an exception in favor of the exclusive right of Congress to regulate the alloy and value. In this instance, also, the new provision is an improvement on the old. Whilst the alloy and value depended on the general authority, a right of coinage in the particular States could have no other effect than to multiply expensive mints and diversify the forms and weights of the circulating pieces. The latter inconveniency defeats one purpose for which the power was originally submitted to the federal head; and as far as the former might prevent an inconvenient remittance of gold and silver to the central mint for recoinage, the end can be as well attained by local mints established under the general authority.

The extension of the prohibition to bills of credit must give pleasure to every citizen, in proportion to his love of justice and his knowledge of the true springs of public prosperity. The loss which America has sustained since the peace, from the pestilent effects of paper money on the necessary confidence between man and man, on the necessary confidence in the public councils, on the industry and morals of the people, and on the character of republican government, constitutes an enormous debt against the States chargeable with this unadvised measure, which must long remain unsatisfied; or rather an accumulation of guilt, which can be expiated no otherwise than by a voluntary sacrifice on the altar of justice, of the power which has been the instrument of it. In addition to these persuasive considerations, it may be observed, that the same reasons which show the necessity of denying to the

States the power of regulating coin prove with equal force that they ought not to be at liberty to substitute a paper medium in the place of coin. Had every State a right to regulate the value of its coin, there might be as many different currencies as States, and thus the intercourse among them would be impeded; retrospective alterations in its value might be made, and thus the citizens of other States be injured, and animosities be kindled among the States themselves. The subjects of foreign powers might suffer from the same cause, and hence the Union be discredited and embroiled by the indiscretion of a single member. No one of these mischiefs is less incident to a power in the States to emit paper money than to coin gold or silver. The power to make anything but gold and silver a tender in payment of debts is withdrawn from the States, on the same principle with that of issuing a paper currency.

Bills of attainder, *ex-post-facto* laws, and laws impairing the obligation of contracts are contrary to the first principles of the social compact, and to every principle of sound legislation. The two former are expressly prohibited by the declarations prefixed to some of the State constitutions, and all of them are prohibited by the spirit and scope of these fundamental charters. Our own experience has taught us, nevertheless, that additional fences against these dangers ought not to be omitted. Very properly, therefore, have the convention added this constitutional bulwark in favor of personal security and private rights; and I am much deceived if they have not, in so doing, as faithfully consulted the genuine sentiments as the undoubted interests of their constituents. The sober people of America are weary of the fluctuating policy which has directed the public councils. They have seen with regret and indignation that sudden changes and legislative interferences, in cases affecting personal rights, become jobs in the hands of enterprising and influential speculators, and snares to the more-industrious and less-informed part of the community. They have seen, too, that one legislative interference is but the first link of a long chain of repetitions, every subsequent interference being naturally produced by the effects of the preceding. They very rightly infer, therefore, that some thorough reform is wanting, which will banish speculations on public measures, inspire a general prudence and industry, and give a regular course to the business of society. The prohibition with respect to titles of nobility is copied from the articles of Confederation, and needs no comment. . . .

The *sixth* and last class consists of the several powers and provisions by which efficacy is given to all the rest.

1. Of these the first is, the . . . power "To make all laws which shall be necessary and proper for carrying into execution the foregoing powers, and all other powers vested by this Constitution in the Government of the United States, or in any department or office thereof."

Few parts of the Constitution have been assailed with more intemperance than this; yet on a fair investigation of it, no part can appear more completely invulnerable. Without the *substance* of this power the whole Constitution would be a dead letter. Those who object to the article . . . can only mean that the *form* of the provision is improper. But have they considered whether a better form could have been substituted?

There are four other possible methods which the Constitution might have taken on this subject. They might have copied the second article of the existing Confederation, which would have prohibited the exercise of any power not *expressly* delegated; they might have attempted a positive enumeration of the powers comprehended under the general terms "necessary and proper"; they might have attempted a negative enumeration of them by specifying the powers excepted from the general definition; they might have been altogether silent on the subject, leaving these necessary and proper powers to construction and inference.

Had the convention taken the first method of adopting the second article of Confederation, it is evident that the new Congress would be continually exposed, as their predecessors have been, to the alternative of construing the term "*expressly*" with so much rigor as to disarm the government of all real authority whatever, or with so much latitude as to destroy altogether the force of the restriction. It would be easy to show . . . that no important power delegated by the articles of Confederation has been or can be executed by Congress without recurring more or less to the doctrine of *construction* or *implication*. As the powers delegated under the new system are more extensive, the government which is to administer it would find itself still more distressed with the alternative of betraying the public interests by doing nothing, or of violating the Constitution by exercising powers indispensably necessary and proper, but, at the same time, not *expressly* granted.

Had the convention attempted a positive enumeration of the powers necessary and proper for carrying their other powers into effect, the attempt would have involved a complete digest of laws on every subject to which the Constitution relates; accommodated too, not only to the existing state of things, but to all the possible changes which futurity may produce; for in every new application of a general power, the *particular powers*, which are the means of attaining the *object* of the general power, must always necessarily vary with that object and be often properly varied whilst the object remains the same.

Had they attempted to enumerate the particular powers or means not necessary or proper for carrying the general powers into execution, the task would have been no less chimerical; and would have been liable to this further objection, that every defect in the enumeration would have been equivalent to a positive grant of authority. If, to avoid this consequence, they had attempted a partial enumeration of the exceptions and described the residue by the general terms, *not necessary or proper*, it must have happened that the enumeration would comprehend a few of the excepted powers only; that these would be such as would be least likely to be assumed or tolerated, because the enumeration would of course select such as would be least necessary or proper; and that the unnecessary and improper powers included in the residuum, would be less forcibly excepted, than if no partial enumeration had been made.

Had the Constitution been silent on this head, there can be no doubt that all the particular powers requisite as means of executing the general powers would have resulted to the government by unavoidable implication. No axiom is more clearly established in law or in reason, than that wherever the end is required, the means are authorized; wherever a general power to do a thing is given, every particular power necessary for doing it is included. Had this last method, therefore, been pursued by the convention, every objection now urged against their plan would remain in all its plausibility; and the real inconveniency would be incurred of not removing a pretext which may be seized on critical occasions for drawing into question the essential powers of the Union.

If it be asked what is to be the consequence, in case the Congress shall misconstrue this part of the Constitution and exercise powers not warranted by its true meaning, I answer, the same as if they should misconstrue or enlarge any other power vested in them; as if the general power had been reduced to particulars, and any one of these were to be violated; the same, in short, as if the State legislatures should violate their respective constitutional authorities. In the first instance, the success of the usurpation will depend on the executive and judiciary departments, which are to expound and give effect to the legislative acts; and in the last resort a remedy must be obtained from the people, who can, by the election of more faithful representatives, annul the acts of the usurpers. The truth is that this ultimate redress may be more confided in against unconstitutional acts of the federal than of the State legislatures for this plain reason, that as every such act of the former will be an invasion of the rights of the latter, these will be ever ready to mark the innovation, to sound the alarm to the people, and to exert their local influence in effecting a change of federal representatives. There being no such intermediate body between the State legislatures and the people interested in watching the conduct of the former, violations of the State constitutions are more likely to remain unnoticed and unredressed.

2. "This Constitution and the laws of the United States which shall be made in pursuance thereof, and all treaties made, or which shall be made, under the authority of the United States, shall be the supreme law of the land, and the Judges in every State shall be bound thereby, anything in the Constitution or laws of any State to the contrary notwithstanding."

The indiscreet zeal of the adversaries to the Constitution has betrayed them into an attack on this part of it also, without which it would have been evidently and radically defective. To be fully sensible of this, we need only suppose for a moment that the supremacy of the State constitutions had been left complete by a saving clause in their favor.[58]

In the first place, as these constitutions invest the State legislatures with absolute sovereignty in all cases not excepted by the existing articles of Confederation, all the authorities contained in the proposed Constitution, so far as they exceed those enumerated in the Confederation, would have been annulled, and the new Congress would have been reduced to the same impotent condition with their predecessors.

In the next place, as the constitutions of some of the States do not even expressly and fully recognize the existing powers of the Confederacy, an express saving of the supremacy of the former would . . . have brought into question every power contained in the proposed Constitution.

In the third place, as the constitutions of the States differ much from each other, it might happen that a treaty or national law of great and equal importance to the States would interfere with some and not with other constitutions, and would consequently be valid in some of the States at the same time that it would have no effect in others.

In fine, the world would have seen for the first time a system of government founded on an inversion of the fundamental principles of all government; it would have seen the authority of the whole society everywhere subordinate to the authority of the parts; it would have seen a monster in which the head was under the direction of the members.

3. "The Senators and Representatives [. . .], and the members of the several State Legislatures, and all Executive and Judicial officers, both of the United States and [of] the several States, shall be bound by oath or affirmation, to support this Constitution."

It has been asked why it was thought necessary that the State magistracy should be bound to support the federal Constitution, and unnecessary that a like oath should be imposed on the officers of the United States in favor of the State constitutions.

Several reasons might be assigned for the distinction. I content myself with one, which is obvious and conclusive. The members of the federal government will have no agency in carrying the State constitutions into effect. The members and officers of the State governments, on the contrary, will have an essential agency in giving effect to the federal Constitution. The election of the President and Senate will depend in all cases on the legislatures of the several States. And the election of the House of Representatives will equally depend on the same authority in the first instance; and will probably forever be conducted by the officers and according to the laws of the States.

4. Among the provisions for giving efficacy to the federal powers might be added those which belong to the executive and judiciary departments; but as these are reserved for particular examination in another place [67–83], pass them over in this.

We have now reviewed in detail all the articles composing the sum or quantity of power delegated by the proposed Constitution to the federal government, and are brought to this undeniable conclusion, that no part of the power is unnecessary or improper for accomplishing the necessary objects of the Union. The question, therefore, whether this amount of power shall be granted or not resolves itself into another question, whether or not a government commensurate to the exigencies of the Union shall be established; or, in other words, whether the Union itself shall be preserved.   Publius

THE FEDERALIST NO. 45

(MADISON)

To the People of the State of New York:
Having shown that no one of the powers transferred to the federal government is unnecessary or improper, the next question to be considered is, whether the whole mass of them

will be dangerous to the portion of authority left in the several States.

The adversaries to the plan of the convention, instead of considering in the first place what degree of power was absolutely necessary for the purposes of the federal government, have exhausted themselves in a secondary inquiry into the possible consequences of the proposed degree of power to the governments of the particular States. But if the Union . . . be essential to the security of the people of America against foreign danger; if it be essential to their security against contentions and wars among the different States; if it be essential to guard them against those violent and oppressive factions which embitter the blessings of liberty, and against those military establishments which must gradually poison its very fountain; if, in a word, the Union be essential to the happiness of the people of America, is it not preposterous to urge as an objection to a government, without which the objects of the Union cannot be attained, that such a government may derogate from the importance of the governments of the individual States? Was, then, the American Revolution effected, was the American Confederacy formed, was the precious blood of thousands spilt, and the hard-earned substance of millions lavished, not that the people of America should enjoy peace, liberty, and safety, but that the government of the individual States, that particular municipal establishments, might enjoy a certain extent of power and be arrayed with certain dignities and attributes of sovereignty? We have heard of the impious doctrine in the Old World, that the people were made for kings, not kings for the people. Is the same doctrine to be revived in the New in another shape—that the solid happiness of the people is to be sacrificed to the views of political institutions of a different form? It is too early for politicians to presume on our forgetting that the public good, the real welfare of the great body of the people, is the supreme object to be pursued; and that no form of government whatever has any other value than as it may be fitted for the attainment of this object. Were the plan of the convention adverse to the public happiness, my voice would be, reject the plan. Were the Union itself inconsistent with the public happiness, it would be, abolish the Union. In like manner, as far as the sovereignty of the States cannot be reconciled to the happiness of the people, the voice of every good citizen must be, let the former be sacrificed to the latter. How far the sacrifice is necessary, has been shown. How far the unsacrificed residue will be endangered, is the question before us.

Several important considerations have been touched in the course of these papers, which discountenance the supposition that the operation of the federal government will by degrees prove fatal to the State governments. The more I revolve the subject, the more fully I am persuaded that the balance is much more likely to be disturbed by the preponderancy of the last than of the first scale. . . .

The State governments will have the advantage of the federal government, whether we compare them in respect to the immediate dependence of the one on the other; to the weight of personal influence which each side will possess; to the powers respectively vested in them; to the predilection and probable support of the people; to the disposition and faculty of resisting and frustrating the measures of each other.

The State governments may be regarded as constituent and essential parts of the federal government; whilst the latter is nowise essential to the operation or organization of the former. Without the intervention of the State legislatures, the President of the United States cannot be elected at all. They must in all cases have a great share in his appointment, and will, perhaps, in most cases, of themselves determine it. The Senate will be elected absolutely and exclusively by the State legislatures. Even the House of Representatives, though drawn immediately from the people, will be chosen very much under the influence of that class of men, whose influence over the people obtains for themselves an election into the State legislatures. Thus, each of the principal branches of the federal government will owe its existence more or less to the favor of the State governments, and must consequently feel a dependence, which is much more likely to beget a disposition too obsequious than too overbearing towards them. On the other side, the component parts of the State governments will in no instance be indebted for their appointment to the direct agency of the federal government, and very little, if at all, to the local influence of its members.

The number of individuals employed under the Constitution of the United States will be much smaller than the number employed under the particular States. There will consequently be less of personal influence on the side of the former than of the latter. The members of the legislative, executive, and judiciary departments of thirteen and more States, the justices of peace, officers of militia, ministerial officers of justice, with all the county, corporation, and town officers, for three millions and more of people, intermixed, and having particular acquaintance with every class and circle of people, must exceed, beyond all proportion, both in number and influence, those of every description who will be employed in the administration of the federal system. Compare the members of the three great departments of the thirteen States, excluding from the judiciary department the justices of peace, with the members of the corresponding departments of the single government of the Union; compare the militia officers of three millions of people with the military and marine officers of any establishment which is within the compass of probability, or . . . of possibility, and in this view alone, we may pronounce the advantage of the States to be decisive. If the federal government is to have collectors of revenue, the State governments will have theirs also. And as those of the former will be principally on the sea-coast and not very numerous, whilst those of the latter will be spread over the face of the country and will be very numerous, the advantage in this view also lies on the same side. It is true that the Confederacy is to possess and may exercise the power of collecting internal as well as external taxes throughout the States; but it is probable that this power will not be resorted to, except for supplemental purposes of revenue; that an option will then be given to the States to supply their quotas by previous collections of their own; and that the eventual collection, under the immediate authority of the Union, will generally be made by the officers, and according to the rules, appointed by the several States. Indeed it is extremely probable that in other instances, particularly in the organization of the judicial power, the officers of the States will be clothed with the correspondent authority of the Union. Should it happen, however, that separate collectors of internal revenue should be appointed under the federal government, the influence of the whole number would not bear a comparison with that of the multitude of State officers in the opposite scale. Within every district to which a federal collector would be allotted, there would not be less than thirty or forty, or even more, officers of different descriptions, and many of them persons of character and weight, whose influence would lie on the side of the State.

The powers delegated by the proposed Constitution to the federal government are few and defined. Those which are to remain in the State governments are numerous and indefinite. The former will be exercised principally on external objects, as war, peace, negotiation, and foreign commerce; with which last the power of taxation will, for the most part, be connected. The powers reserved to the several States will extend to all the objects which, in the ordinary course of affairs, concern the lives, liberties, and properties of the people, and the internal order, improvement, and prosperity of the State.

The operations of the federal government will be most extensive and important in times of war and danger, those of the State governments in times of peace and security. As the former periods will probably bear a small proportion to the latter, the State governments will here enjoy another advantage over the federal government. The more adequate, indeed, the federal powers may be rendered to the national defence, the less frequent will be those scenes of danger which might favor their ascendancy over the governments of the particular States.

If the new Constitution be examined with accuracy and candor, it will be found that the change which it proposes consists much less in the addition of NEW POWERS to the Union, than in the invigoration of its ORIGINAL POWERS. The regulation of commerce, it is true, is a new power; but that seems to be an addition which few oppose and from which no apprehensions are entertained. The powers relating to war and peace, armies and fleets, treaties and finance, with the other more considerable powers, are all vested in the existing Congress by the articles of Confederation. The proposed change does not enlarge these powers; it only substitutes a more effectual mode of administering them. The change relating to taxation may be regarded as the most important; and

yet the present Congress have as complete authority to RE-
QUIRE of the States indefinite supplies of money for the common defence and general welfare as the future Congress will
have to require them of individual citizens; and the latter will
be no more bound than the States themselves have been to
pay the quotas respectively taxed on them. Had the States
complied punctually with the articles of Confederation or
could their compliance have been enforced by as peaceable
means as may be used with success towards single persons, our
past experience is very far from countenancing an opinion,
that the State governments would have lost their constitutional powers, and have gradually undergone an entire consolidation. To maintain that such an event would have ensued,
would be to say at once, that the existence of the State governments is incompatible with any system whatever that ac-
complishes the essential purposes of the Union.   PUBLIUS

THE FEDERALIST NO. 47

(MADISON)

To the People of the State of New York:
     Having reviewed the general form of the proposed gov-
ernment and the general mass of power allotted to it, I proceed to examine the particular structure of this government
and the distribution of this mass of power among its constituent parts.
     One of the principal objections inculcated by the more re-
spectable adversaries to the Constitution, is its supposed violation of the political maxim, that the legislative, executive,
and judiciary departments ought to be separate and distinct.[59]
In the structure of the federal government, no regard, it is
said, seems to have been paid to this essential precaution in
favor of liberty. The several departments of power are distributed and blended in such a manner as at once to destroy

all symmetry and beauty of form, and to expose some of the essential parts of the edifice to the danger of being crushed by the disproportionate weight of other parts.

No political truth is certainly of greater intrinsic value or is stamped with the authority of more enlightened patrons of liberty, than that on which the objection is founded. The accumulation of all powers, legislative, executive, and judiciary, in the same hands, whether of one, a few, or many, and whether hereditary, self-appointed, or elective, may justly be pronounced the very definition of tyranny. Were the federal Constitution, therefore, really chargeable with the accumulation of power, or with a mixture of powers having a dangerous tendency to such an accumulation, no further arguments would be necessary to inspire a universal reprobation of the system. I persuade myself, however, . . . that the charge cannot be supported, and that the maxim on which it relies has been totally misconceived and misapplied. In order to form correct ideas on this important subject, it will be proper to investigate the sense in which the preservation of liberty requires that the three great departments of power should be separate and distinct.

The oracle who is always consulted and cited on this subject is the celebrated Montesquieu.[60] If he be not the author of this invaluable precept in the science of politics, he has the merit at least of displaying and recommending it most effectually to the attention of mankind. Let us endeavor . . . to ascertain his meaning on this point.

The British Constitution was to Montesquieu what Homer has been to the didactic writers on epic poetry. As the latter have considered the work of the immortal bard as the perfect model from which the principles and rules of the epic art were to be drawn and by which all similar works were to be judged, so this great political critic appears to have viewed the Constitution of England as the standard, or to use his own expression, as the mirror of political liberty; and to have delivered in the form of elementary truths the several characteristic principles of that particular system. That we may be sure, then, not to mistake his meaning in this case, let us recur to the source from which the maxim was drawn.

On the slightest view of the British Constitution, we must

perceive that the legislative, executive, and judiciary departments are by no means totally separate and distinct from each other. The executive magistrate forms an integral part of the legislative authority. He alone has the prerogative of making treaties with foreign sovereigns, which, when made, have, under certain limitations, the force of legislative acts. All the members of the judiciary department are appointed by him, can be removed by him on the address of the two Houses of Parliament, and form, when he pleases to consult them, one of his constitutional councils. One branch of the legislative department forms also a great constitutional council to the executive chief as . . . it is the sole depositary of judicial power in cases of impeachment, and is invested with the supreme appellate jurisdiction in all other cases. The judges, again, are so far connected with the legislative department as often to attend and participate in its deliberations, though not admitted to a legislative vote.

From these facts, by which Montesquieu was guided, it may clearly be inferred that, in saying "There can be no liberty where the legislative and executive powers are united in the same person, or body of magistrates," or, "if the power of judging be not separated from the legislative and executive powers" [sic], he did not mean that these departments ought to have no *partial agency* in, or no *control* over, the acts of each other.[61] His meaning . . . can amount to no more than this, that where the *whole* power of one department is exercised by the same hands which possess the *whole* power of another department, the fundamental principles of a free constitution are subverted. This would have been the case in the constitution examined by him if the king, who is the sole executive magistrate, had possessed also the complete legislative power or the supreme administration of justice; or if the entire legislative body had possessed the supreme judiciary or the supreme executive authority. This, however is not among the vices of that constitution. The magistrate in whom the whole executive power resides cannot of himself make a law, though he can put a negative on every law; nor administer justice in person, though he has the appointment of those who do administer it. The judges can exercise no executive prerogative, though they are shoots from the executive stock;

nor any legislative function, though they may be advised with by the legislative councils. The entire legislature can perform no judiciary act, though by the joint act of two of its branches the judges may be removed from their offices, and though one of its branches is possessed of the judicial power in the last resort. The entire legislature, again, can exercise no executive prerogative, though one of its branches constitutes the supreme executive magistracy, and another, on the impeachment of a third, can try and condemn all the subordinate officers in the executive department.

The reasons on which Montesquieu grounds his maxim are a further demonstration of his meaning. "When the legislative and executive powers are united in the same person or body," says he, "there can be no liberty, because apprehensions may arise lest *the same* monarch or senate should *enact* tyrannical laws to *execute* them in a tyrannical manner." Again: "Were the power of judging joined with the legislative, the life and liberty of the subject would be exposed to arbitrary control, for *the judge* would then be *the legislator.* Were it joined to the executive power, *the judge* might behave with all the violence of *an oppressor*" [*sic*].[61] Some of these reasons are more fully explained in other passages; but briefly stated as they are here, they sufficiently establish the meaning which we have put on this celebrated maxim of this celebrated author.

If we look into the constitutions of the several States, we find that, notwithstanding the emphatical and, in some instances, the unqualified terms in which this axiom has been laid down, there is not a single instance in which the several departments of power have been kept absolutely separate and distinct. New Hampshire, whose constitution was the last formed, seems to have been fully aware of the impossibility and inexpediency of avoiding any mixture whatever of these departments, and has qualified the doctrine by declaring "that the legislative, executive, and judiciary powers ought to be kept as separate from, and independent of, each other *as the nature of a free government will admit; or as is consistent with that chain of connection that binds the whole fabric of the constitution in one indissoluble bond of unity and amity*" [*sic*].[62] Her constitution accordingly mixes these departments in several respects. The Senate, which is a branch of the legislative department, is also a judicial tribunal for the trial of impeachments. The President, who is the head of the executive department, is the presiding member also of the Senate; and, besides an equal vote in all cases, has a casting vote in case of a tie. The executive head is himself eventually elective every year by the legislative department, and his council is every year chosen by and from the members of the same department. Several of the officers of state are also appointed by the legislature. And the members of the judiciary department are appointed by the executive department.

The constitution of Massachusetts has observed a sufficient though less pointed caution in expressing this fundamental article of liberty. It declares "that the legislative departments shall never exercise the executive and judicial powers, or either of them; the executive shall never exercise the legislative and judicial powers, or either of them; the judicial shall never exercise the legislative and executive powers, or either of them" [*sic*].[63] This declaration corresponds precisely with the doctrine of Montesquieu . . . and is not in a single point violated by the plan of the convention. It goes no farther than to prohibit any one of the entire departments from exercising the powers of another department. In the very Constitution to which it is prefixed, a partial mixture of powers has been admitted. The executive magistrate has a qualified negative on the legislative body, and the Senate, which is a part of the legislature, is a court of impeachment for members both of the executive and judiciary departments. The members of the judiciary department, again, are appointable by the executive department and removable by the same authority on the address of the two legislative branches. Lastly, a number of the officers of government are annually appointed by the legislative department. As the appointment to offices, particularly executive offices, is in its nature an executive function, the compilers of the Constitution have, in this last point at least, violated the rule established by themselves.

I pass over the constitutions of Rhode Island and Connecticut, because they were formed prior to the Revolution, and even before the principle under examination had become an object of political attention.

The constitution of New York contains no declaration on

this subject; but appears very clearly to have been framed with an eye to the danger of improperly blending the different departments. It gives, nevertheless, to the executive magistrate a partial control over the legislative department; and, what is more, gives a like control to the judiciary department; and even blends the executive and judiciary departments in the exercise of this control. In its council of appointment members of the legislative are associated with the executive authority in the appointment of officers, both executive and judiciary. And its court for the trial of impeachments and correction of errors is to consist of one branch of the legislature and the principal members of the judiciary department.

The constitution of New Jersey has blended the different powers of government more than any of the preceding. The governor, who is the executive magistrate, is appointed by the legislature; is chancellor and ordinary, or surrogate of the State; is a member of the Supreme Court of Appeals, and president, with a casting vote, of one of the legislative branches. The same legislative branch acts again as executive council of the governor, and with him constitutes the Court of Appeals. The members of the judiciary department are appointed by the legislative department, and removable by one branch of it on the impeachment of the other.

According to the constitution of Pennsylvania, the president, who is the head of the executive department, is annually elected by a vote in which the legislative department predominates. In conjunction with an executive council, he appoints the members of the judiciary department, and forms a court of impeachment for trial of all officers, judiciary as well as executive. The judges of the Supreme Court and justices of the peace seem also to be removable by the legislature; and the executive power of pardoning in certain cases, to be referred to the same department. The members of the executive council are made EX-OFFICIO justices of peace throughout the State.

In Delaware the chief executive magistrate is annually elected by the legislative department. The speakers of the two legislative branches are vice-presidents in the executive department. The executive chief, with six others, appointed, three by each of the legislative branches, constitutes the Supreme Court of Appeals; he is joined with the legislative department in the appointment of the other judges. Throughout the States it appears that the members of the legislature may at the same time be justices of the peace; in this State the members of one branch of it are EX-OFFICIO justices of the peace as are also the members of the executive council. The principal officers of the executive department are appointed by the legislative; and one branch of the latter forms a court of impeachments. All officers may be removed on address of the legislature.

Maryland has adopted the maxim in the most unqualified terms; declaring that the legislative, executive, and judicial powers of government ought to be forever separate and distinct from each other. Her constitution, notwithstanding, makes the executive magistrate appointable by the legislative department and the members of the judiciary by the executive department.

The language of Virginia is still more pointed on this subject. Her constitution declares, "that the legislative, executive, and judiciary departments shall be separate and distinct; so that neither exercise the powers properly belonging to the other; nor shall any person exercise the powers of more than one of them at the same time, except that the justices of [the] county courts shall be eligible to either House of Assembly" [sic].[64] Yet we find not only this express exception with respect to the members of the inferior courts, but that the chief magistrate with his executive council are appointable by the legislature; that two members of the latter are triennially displaced at the pleasure of the legislature; and that all the principal offices, both executive and judiciary, are filled by the same department. The executive prerogative of pardon, also, is in one case vested in the legislative department.

The constitution of North Carolina, which declares "that the legislative, executive, and supreme judicial powers of government ought to be forever separate and distinct from each other,"[65] refers, at the same time, to the legislative department, the appointment not only of the executive chief, but all the principal officers within both that and the judiciary department.

In South Carolina, the constitution makes the executive

magistracy eligible by the legislative department. It gives to the latter, also, the appointment of the members of the judiciary department, including even justices of the peace and sheriffs; and the appointment of officers in the executive department, down to captains in the army and navy of the State.

In the constitution of Georgia, where it is declared "that the legislative, executive, and judiciary departments shall be separate and distinct, so that neither exercise the powers properly belonging to the other,"[66] we find that the executive department is to be filled by appointments of the legislature; and the executive prerogative of pardon to be finally exercised by the same authority. Even justices of the peace are to be appointed by the legislature.

In citing these cases in which the legislative, executive, and judiciary departments have not been kept totally separate and distinct, I wish not to be regarded as an advocate for the particular organizations of the several State governments. I am fully aware that among the many excellent principles which they exemplify, they carry strong marks of the haste, and still stronger of the inexperience, under which they were framed. It is but too obvious that in some instances the fundamental principle under consideration has been violated by too great a mixture, and even an actual consolidation, of the different powers; and that in no instance has a competent provision been made for maintaining in practice the separation delineated on paper. What I have wished to evince is, that the charge brought against the proposed Constitution, of violating the sacred maxim of free government, is warranted neither by the real meaning annexed to that maxim by its author, nor by the sense in which it has hitherto been understood in America. This interesting subject will be resumed in the ensuing paper.[67]   PUBLIUS

THE FEDERALIST NO. 48

(MADISON)

To the People of the State of New York:

It was shown in the last paper that the political apothegm there examined does not require that the legislative, executive, and judiciary departments should be wholly unconnected with each other. I shall undertake, in the next place, to show that unless these departments be so far connected and blended as to give to each a constitutional control over the others, the degree of separation which the maxim requires, as essential to a free government, can never in practice be duly maintained.

It is agreed on all sides that the powers properly belonging to one of the departments ought not to be directly and completely administered by either of the other departments. It is equally evident that none of them ought to possess, directly or indirectly, an overruling influence over the others in the administration of their respective powers. It will not be denied that power is of an encroaching nature, and that it ought to be effectually restrained from passing the limits assigned to it. After discriminating . . . in theory the several classes of power as they may in their nature be legislative, executive, or judiciary, the next and most difficult task is to provide some practical security for each, against the invasion of the others. What this security ought to be is the great problem to be solved.

Will it be sufficient to mark with precision the boundaries of these departments in the constitution of the government, and to trust to these parchment barriers against the encroaching spirit of power? This is the security which appears to have been principally relied on by the compilers of most of the American constitutions. But experience assures us that the efficacy of the provision has been greatly overrated; and that some more adequate defence is indispensably necessary for the more feeble, against the more powerful, members of the government. The legislative department is everywhere extending the sphere of its activity, and drawing all power into its impetuous vortex.

The founders of our republics have so much merit for the wisdom which they have displayed that no task can be less pleasing than that of pointing out the errors into which they have fallen. A respect for truth, however, obliges us to remark that they seem never for a moment to have turned their eyes from the danger to liberty from the overgrown and all-grasping prerogative of an hereditary magistrate, supported and fortified by an hereditary branch of the legislative authority. They seem never to have recollected the danger from legislative usurpations, which, by assembling all power in the same hands, must lead to the same tyranny as is threatened by executive usurpations.

In a government where numerous and extensive prerogatives are placed in the hands of an hereditary monarch, the executive department is very justly regarded as the source of danger, and watched with all the jealousy which a zeal for liberty ought to inspire. In a democracy, where a multitude of people exercise in person the legislative functions, and are continually exposed, by their incapacity for regular deliberation and concerted measures, to the ambitious intrigues of their executive magistrates, tyranny may well be apprehended, on some favorable emergency, to start up in the same quarter. But in a representative republic, where the executive magistracy is carefully limited, both in the extent and the duration of its power; and where the legislative power is exercised by an assembly, which is inspired, by a supposed influence over the people, with an intrepid confidence in its own strength; which is sufficiently numerous to feel all the passions which actuate a multitude, yet not so numerous as to be incapable of pursuing the objects of its passions, by means which reason prescribes; it is against the enterprising ambition of this department that the people ought to indulge all their jealousy and exhaust all their precautions.

The legislative department derives a superiority in our governments from other circumstances. Its constitutional powers being at once more extensive and less susceptible of precise limits, it can with the greater facility mask under complicated and indirect measures the encroachments which it makes on the coördinate departments. It is not unfrequently a question of real nicety in legislative bodies, whether the operation of a particular measure will, or will not, extend beyond the legislative sphere. On the other side, the executive power being restrained within a narrower compass and being more simple in its nature, and the judiciary being described by landmarks still less uncertain, projects of usurpation by either of these departments would immediately betray and defeat themselves. Nor is this all; as the legislative department alone has access to the pockets of the people, and has in some constitutions full discretion, and in all a prevailing influence, over the pecuniary rewards of those who fill the other departments, a dependence is thus created in the latter, which gives still greater facility to encroachments of the former.

I have appealed to our own experience for the truth of what I advance on this subject. Were it necessary to verify this experience by particular proofs, they might be multiplied without end. I might find a witness in every citizen who has shared in, or been attentive to, the course of public administrations. I might collect vouchers in abundance from the records and archives of every State in the Union. But as a more concise, and at the same time equally satisfactory, evidence, I will refer to the example of two States, attested by two unexceptionable authorities.

The first example is that of Virginia, a State which, as we have seen, has expressly declared in its constitution, that the three great departments ought not to be intermixed. The authority in support of it is Mr. Jefferson, who, besides his other advantages for remarking the operation of the government, was himself the chief magistrate of it. In order to convey fully the ideas with which his experience had impressed him on this subject, it will be necessary to quote a passage of some length from his very interesting "Notes on the State of Virginia," p. 195. "All the powers of government, legislative, executive, and judiciary, result to the legislative body. The concentrating these in the same hands, is precisely the definition of despotic government. It will be no alleviation, that these powers will be exercised by a plurality of hands, and not by a single one. One hundred and seventy-three despots would surely be as oppressive as one. Let those who doubt it, turn their eyes on the republic of Venice. As little will it avail us, that they are chosen by ourselves. An *elective despotism* was not the government we fought for; but one which should not only be founded on free principles, but in which the powers of government should be so divided and balanced among several bodies of magistracy, as that no one could transcend their legal limits, without being effectually checked and restrained by the others. For this reason, that convention which passed the ordinance of government, laid its foundation on this basis, that the legislative, executive, and judiciary departments should be separate and distinct, so that no person should exercise the powers of more than one of them at the same time. *But no barrier was provided between these several powers.* The judiciary and the executive members were left dependent on the legislative for their subsistence in office, and some of them for their continuance in it. If, therefore, the legislature assumes executive and judiciary powers, no opposition is likely to be made; nor, if made, can be effectual; because in that case they may put their proceedings into the form of an act of Assembly, which will render them obligatory on the other branches. They have accordingly, *in many* instances, *decided rights* which should have been left to *judiciary controversy, and the direction of the executive, during the whole time of their session, is becoming habitual and familiar.*"[68]

The other State which I shall take for an example is Pennsylvania; and the other authority, the Council of Censors, which assembled in the years 1783 and 1784. A part of the duty of this body as marked out by the constitution was "to inquire whether the constitution had been preserved inviolate in every part; and whether the legislative and executive branches of government had performed their duty as guardians of the people, or assumed to themselves, or exercised, other or greater powers than they are entitled to by the constitution" [*sic*].[69] In the execution of this trust the council were necessarily led to a comparison of both the legislative and executive proceedings with the constitutional powers of these departments; and from the facts enumerated, and to the truth of most of which both sides in the council subscribed, it appears

that the constitution had been flagrantly violated by the legislature in a variety of important instances.

A great number of laws had been passed, violating, without any apparent necessity, the rule requiring that all bills of
a public nature shall be previously printed for the consideration of the people; although this is one of the precautions
chiefly relied on by the constitution against improper acts of
the legislature.

The constitutional trial by jury had been violated, and powers assumed which had not been delegated by the constitution.

Executive powers had been usurped.

The salaries of the judges, which the constitution expressly
requires to be fixed, had been occasionally varied; and cases
belonging to the judiciary department frequently drawn within
legislative cognizance and determination.

Those who wish to see the several particulars falling under
each of these heads may consult the journals of the council,
which are in print. Some of them . . . may be imputable to
peculiar circumstances connected with the war, but the greater
part of them may be considered as the spontaneous shoots of
an ill-constituted government.

It appears, also, that the executive department had not been
innocent of frequent breaches of the constitution. There are
three observations, however, which ought to be made on this
head: *first,* a great proportion of the instances were either immediately produced by the necessities of the war, or recommended by Congress or the commander-in-chief; *secondly,* in
most of the other instances, they conformed either to the declared or the known sentiments of the legislative department;
thirdly, the executive department of Pennsylvania is distinguished from that of the other States by the number of members composing it. In this respect, it has as much affinity to a
legislative assembly as to an executive council. And being at
once exempt from the restraint of an individual responsibility
for the acts of the body, and deriving confidence from mutual
example and joint influence, unauthorized measures would, of
course, be more freely hazarded than where the executive department is administered by a single hand or by a few hands.

The conclusion which I am warranted in drawing from these
observations is, that a mere demarcation on parchment of the

constitutional limits of the several departments, is not a sufficient guard against those encroachments which lead to a tyrannical concentration of all the powers of government in the same hands.   PUBLIUS

THE FEDERALIST NO. 49

(MADISON)

To the People of the State of New York:
The author of the "Notes on the State of Virginia," quoted in the last paper, has subjoined to that valuable work the draught of a constitution, which had been prepared in order to be laid before a convention expected to be called in 1783, by the legislature, for the establishment of a constitution for that commonwealth. The plan, like every thing from the same pen, marks a turn of thinking, original, comprehensive, and accurate; and is the more worthy of attention as it equally displays a fervent attachment to republican government and an enlightened view of the dangerous propensities against which it ought to be guarded. One of the precautions which he proposes, and on which he appears ultimately to rely as a palladium to the weaker departments of power against the invasions of the stronger, is perhaps altogether his own, and as it immediately relates to the subject of our present inquiry, ought not to be overlooked.

His proposition is . . . that whenever ["]any two of the three branches of government . . . [concurring] in opinion, each by the voices of two thirds of their whole [existing] number, that a convention is necessary for altering the constitution, or *correcting breaches of it,*["] a convention shall be called for the purpose. . . .[70]

As the people are the only legitimate fountain of power and it is from them that the constitutional charter, under which the several branches of government hold their power, is de-

rived, it seems strictly consonant to the republican theory to
recur to the same original authority, not only whenever it may
be necessary to enlarge, diminish, or new-model the powers of
the government, but also whenever any one of the departments
may commit encroachments on the chartered authorities of
the others. The several departments being perfectly coördinate
by the terms of their common commission, none of them . . .
can pretend to an exclusive or superior right of settling the
boundaries between their respective powers; and how are the
encroachments of the stronger to be prevented or the wrongs
of the weaker to be redressed, without an appeal to the people themselves, who, as the grantors of the commission, can
alone declare its true meaning and enforce its observance?

There is certainly great force in this reasoning, and it must
be allowed to prove that a constitutional road to the decision
of the people ought to be marked out and kept open for certain great and extraordinary occasions. But there appear to
be insuperable objections against the proposed recurrence to
the people as a provision in all cases for keeping the several
departments of power within their constitutional limits.

In the first place, the provision does not reach the case of a
combination of two of the departments against the third. If
the legislative authority, which possesses so many means of
operating on the motives of the other departments, should be
able to gain to its interest either of the others or even one
third of its members, the remaining department could derive
no advantage from its remedial provision. I do not dwell, however, on this objection, because it may be thought to be rather
against the modification of the principle than against the principle itself.

In the next place, it may be considered as an objection inherent in the principle, that as every appeal to the people
would carry an implication of some defect in the government,
frequent appeals would in a great measure deprive the government of that veneration which time bestows on every thing,
and without which perhaps the wisest and freest governments
would not possess the requisite stability. If it be true that all
governments rest on opinion, it is no less true that the strength
of opinion in each individual, and its practical influence on
his conduct, depend much on the number which he supposes

to have entertained the same opinion. The reason of man, like man himself, is timid and cautious when left alone, and acquires firmness and confidence in proportion to the number with which it is associated. When the examples which fortify opinion are *ancient* as well as *numerous*, they are known to have a double effect. In a nation of philosophers this consideration ought to be disregarded. A reverence for the laws would be sufficiently inculcated by the voice of an enlightened reason. But a nation of philosophers is as little to be expected as the philosophical race of kings wished for by Plato.[71] And in every other nation the most rational government will not find it a superfluous advantage to have the prejudices of the community on its side.

The danger of disturbing the public tranquillity by interesting too strongly the public passions, is a still more serious objection against a frequent reference of constitutional questions to the decision of the whole society. Notwithstanding the success which has attended the revisions of our established forms of government, and which does so much honor to the virtue and intelligence of the people of America, it must be confessed that the experiments are of too ticklish a nature to be unnecessarily multiplied. We are to recollect that all the existing constitutions were formed in the midst of a danger which repressed the passions most unfriendly to order and concord; of an enthusiastic confidence of the people in their patriotic leaders, which stifled the ordinary diversity of opinions on great national questions; of a universal ardor for new and opposite forms, produced by a universal resentment and indignation against the ancient government; and whilst no spirit of party connected with the changes to be made, or the abuses to be reformed, could mingle its leaven in the operation. The future situations in which we must expect to be usually placed, do not present any equivalent security against the danger which is apprehended.

But the greatest objection of all is, that the decisions which would probably result from such appeals would not answer the purpose of maintaining the constitutional equilibrium of the government. We have seen that the tendency of republican governments is to an aggrandizement of the legislative at the expense of the other departments. The appeals to the people, therefore, would usually be made by the executive and judiciary departments. But whether made by one side or the other, would each side enjoy equal advantages on the trial? Let us view their different situations. The members of the executive and judiciary departments are few in number, and can be personally known to a small part only of the people. The latter, by the mode of their appointment, as well as by the nature and permanency of it, are too far removed from the people to share much in their prepossessions. The former are generally the objects of jealousy, and their administration is always liable to be discolored and rendered unpopular. The members of the legislative department, on the other hand, are numerous. They are distributed and dwell among the people at large. Their connections of blood, of friendship, and of acquaintance embrace a great proportion of the most influential part of the society. The nature of their public trust implies a personal influence among the people, and that they are more immediately the confidential guardians of the rights and liberties of the people. With these advantages it can hardly be supposed that the adverse party would have an equal chance for a favorable issue.

But the legislative party would not only be able to plead their cause most successfully with the people. They would probably be constituted themselves the judges. The same influence which had gained them an election into the legislature, would gain them a seat in the convention. If this should not be the case with all, it would probably be the case with many, and pretty certainly with those leading characters on whom every thing depends in such bodies. The convention, in short, would be composed chiefly of men who had been, who actually were, or who expected to be, members of the department whose conduct was arraigned. They would consequently be parties to the very question to be decided by them.

It might, however, sometimes happen that appeals would be made under circumstances less adverse to the executive and judiciary departments. The usurpations of the legislature might be so flagrant and so sudden as to admit of no specious coloring. A strong party among themselves might take side with the other branches. The executive power might be in the hands of a peculiar favorite of the people. In such a posture of things, the public decision might be less swayed by prepossessions in favor of the legislative party. But still it could never be expected to turn on the true merits of the question. It would inevitably be connected with the spirit of preëxisting parties, or of parties springing out of the question itself. It would be connected with persons of distinguished character and extensive influence in the community. It would be pronounced by the very men who had been agents in, or opponents of, the measures to which the decision would relate. The *passions*, therefore, not the *reason* of the public would sit in judgment. But it is the reason, alone, of the public, that ought to control and regulate the government. The passions ought to be controlled and regulated by the government.

We found in the last paper, that mere declarations in the written constitution are not sufficient to restrain the several departments within their legal rights. It appears in this that occasional appeals to the people would be neither a proper nor an effectual provision for that purpose. How far the provisions of a different nature contained in the plan above quoted might be adequate, I do not examine. Some of them are unquestionably founded on sound political principals, and all of them are framed with singular ingenuity and precision. PUBLIUS

THE FEDERALIST NO. 50

(MADISON)

To the People of the State of New York:

It may be contended, perhaps, that instead of *occasional* appeals to the people, which are liable to the objections urged against them, *periodical* appeals are the proper and adequate means of *preventing and correcting infractions of the Constitution.*

It will be attended to, that in the examination of these expedients, I confine myself to their aptitude for *enforcing* the

Constitution, by keeping the several departments of power within their due bounds, without particularly considering them as provisions for *altering* the Constitution itself. In the first view, appeals to the people at fixed periods appear to be nearly as ineligible as appeals on particular occasions as they emerge. If the periods be separated by short intervals, the measures to be reviewed and rectified will have been of recent date, and will be connected with all the circumstances which tend to vitiate and pervert the result of occasional revisions. If the periods be distant from each other, the same remark will be applicable to all recent measures; and in proportion as the remoteness of the others may favor a dispassionate review of them, this advantage is inseparable from inconveniences which seem to counterbalance it. In the first place, a distant prospect of public censure would be a very feeble restraint on power from those excesses to which it might be urged by the force of present motives. Is it to be imagined that a legislative assembly, consisting of a hundred or two hundred members, eagerly bent on some favorite object, and breaking through the restraints of the Constitution in pursuit of it, would be arrested in their career, by considerations drawn from a censorial revision of their conduct at the future distance of ten, fifteen, or twenty years? In the next place, the abuses would often have completed their mischievous effects before the remedial provision would be applied. And in the last place, where this might not be the case, they would be of long standing, would have taken deep root, and would not easily be extirpated.

The scheme of revising the constitution, in order to correct recent breaches of it, as well as for other purposes, has been actually tried in one of the States. One of the objects of the Council of Censors which met in Pennsylvania in 1783 and 1784 was, as we have seen, to inquire, "whether the constitution had been violated, and whether the legislative and executive departments had encroached on each other."[72] This important and novel experiment in politics merits . . . very particular attention. . . .

First. It appears, from the names of the gentlemen who composed the council, that some, at least, of its most active and leading members had also been active and leading characters in the parties which preëxisted in the State.

Secondly. It appears that the same active and leading members of the council had been active and influential members of the legislative and executive branches within the period to be reviewed; and even patrons or opponents of the very measures to be thus brought to the test of the constitution. Two of the members had been vice-presidents of the State, and several others members of the executive council, within the seven preceding years. One of them had been speaker, and a number of others distinguished members, of the legislative assembly within the same period.

Thirdly. Every page of their proceedings witnesses the effect of all these circumstances on the temper of their deliberations. Throughout the continuance of the council, it was split into two fixed and violent parties. The fact is acknowledged and lamented by themselves. Had this not been the case, the face of their proceedings exhibits a proof equally satisfactory. In all questions, however unimportant in themselves or unconnected with each other, the same names stand invariably contrasted on the opposite columns. Every unbiased observer may infer, without danger of mistake, and at the same time without meaning to reflect on either party, or any individuals of either party, that unfortunately, *passion* not *reason*, must have presided over their decisions. When men exercise their reason coolly and freely on a variety of distinct questions, they inevitably fall into different opinions on some of them. When they are governed by a common passion, their opinions, if they are so to be called, will be the same.

Fourthly. It is at least problematical, whether the decisions of this body do not in several instances, misconstrue the limits prescribed for the legislative and executive departments instead of reducing and limiting them within their constitutional places.

Fifthly. I have never understood that the decisions of the council on constitutional questions, whether rightly or erroneously formed, have had any effect in varying the practice founded on legislative constructions. It even appears . . . that in one instance the contemporary legislature denied the constructions of the council and actually prevailed in the contest.

This censorial body, therefore, proves at the same time, by its researches, the existence of the disease, and by its example, the inefficacy of the remedy.

This conclusion cannot be invalidated by alleging that the State in which the experiment was made was at that crisis, and had been for a long time before, violently heated and distracted by the rage of party. Is it to be presumed that at any future septennial epoch the same State will be free from parties? Is it to be presumed that any other State, at the same or any other given period, will be exempt from them? Such an event ought to be neither presumed nor desired; because an extinction of parties necessarily implies either a universal alarm for the public safety, or an absolute extinction of liberty.

Were the precaution taken of excluding from the assemblies elected by the people, to revise the preceding administration of the government, all persons who should have been concerned with the government within the given period, the difficulties would not be obviated. The important task would probably devolve on men, who, with inferior capacities, would in other respects be little better qualified. Although they might not have been personally concerned in the administration and therefore not immediately agents in the measures to be examined, they would probably have been involved in the parties connected with these measures, and have been elected under their auspices.   PUBLIUS

THE FEDERALIST NO. 51

(MADISON)

To the People of the State of New York:

To what expedient, then, shall we finally resort for maintaining in practice the necessary partition of power among the several departments as laid down in the Constitution? The only answer that can be given is, that as all these exterior provisions are found to be inadequate, the defect must be supplied by so contriving the interior structure of the government as that its several constituent parts may, by their mutual relations, be the means of keeping each other in their proper places. Without presuming to undertake a full development of this important idea, I will hazard a few general observations, which may perhaps place it in a clearer light, and enable us to form a more correct judgment of the principles and structure of the government planned by the convention.

In order to lay a due foundation for that separate and distinct exercise of the different powers of government, which to a certain extent is admitted on all hands to be essential to the preservation of liberty, it is evident that each department should have a will of its own; and consequently should be so constituted that the members of each should have as little agency as possible in the appointment of the members of the others. Were this principle rigorously adhered to, it would require that all the appointments for the supreme executive, legislative, and judiciary magistracies should be drawn from the same fountain of authority, the people, through channels having no communication whatever with one another. Perhaps such a plan of constructing the several departments would be less difficult in practice than it may in contemplation appear. Some difficulties, however, and some additional expense would attend the execution of it. Some deviations, therefore, from the principle must be admitted. In the constitution of the judiciary department in particular, it might be inexpedient to insist rigorously on the principle: first, because peculiar qualifications being essential in the members, the primary consideration ought to be to select that mode of choice which best secures these qualifications; secondly, because the permanent tenure by which the appointments are held in that department must soon destroy all sense of dependence on the authority conferring them.

It is equally evident, that the members of each department should be as little dependent as possible on those of the others for the emoluments annexed to their offices. Were the executive magistrate or the judges not independent of the legislature in this particular, their independence in every other would be merely nominal.

But the great security against a gradual concentration of the several powers in the same department, consists in giving to those who administer each department the necessary constitutional means and personal motives to resist encroachments of the others. The provision for defence must in this, as in all other cases, be made commensurate to the danger of attack. Ambition must be made to counteract ambition. The interest of the man must be connected with the constitutional rights of the place. It may be a reflection on human nature, that such devices should be necessary to control the abuses of government. But what is government itself, but the greatest of all reflections on human nature? If men were angels, no government would be necessary. If angels were to govern men, neither external nor internal controls on government would be necessary.[73] In framing a government which is to be administered by men over men, the great difficulty lies in this: you must first enable the government to control the governed; and in the next place oblige it to control itself. A dependence on the people is, no doubt, the primary control on the government; but experience has taught mankind the necessity of auxiliary precautions.

This policy of supplying, by opposite and rival interests, the defect of better motives might be traced through the whole system of human affairs, private as well as public. We see it particularly displayed in all the subordinate distributions of power, where the constant aim is to divide and arrange the several offices in such a manner as that each may be a check on the other—that the private interest of every individual may be a sentinel over the public rights. These inventions of prudence cannot be less requisite in the distribution of the supreme powers of the State.

But it is not possible to give to each department an equal power of self-defence. In republican government the legislative authority necessarily predominates. The remedy for this inconveniency is to divide the legislature into different branches; and to render them, by different modes of election and different principles of action, as little connected with each other as the nature of their common functions and their common dependence on the society will admit. It may even be necessary to guard against dangerous encroachments by still further precautions. As the weight of the legislative authority requires that it should be thus divided, the weakness of the executive may require, on the other hand, that it should be fortified. An absolute negative on the legislature appears, at first view, to be the natural defence with which the executive magistrate should be armed. But perhaps it would be neither altogether safe nor alone sufficient. On ordinary occasions it might not be exerted with the requisite firmness, and on extraordinary occasions it might be perfidiously abused. May not this defect of an absolute negative be supplied by some qualified connection between this weaker department and the weaker branch of the stronger department, by which the latter may be led to support the constitutional rights of the former, without being too much detached from the rights of its own department?

If the principles on which these observations are founded be just . . . and they be applied as a criterion to the several State constitutions and to the federal Constitution, it will be found that if the latter does not perfectly correspond with them, the former are infinitely less able to bear such a test.

There are, moreover, two considerations particularly applicable to the federal system of America, which place that system in a very interesting point of view.

First. In a single republic, all the power surrendered by the people is submitted to the administration of a single government; and the usurpations are guarded against by a division of the government into distinct and separate departments. In the compound republic of America, the power surrendered by the people is first divided between two distinct governments, and then the portion allotted to each subdivided among distinct and separate departments. Hence a double security arises to the rights of the people. The different governments will control each other, at the same time that each will be controlled by itself.

Second. It is of great importance in a republic not only to guard the society against the oppression of its rulers, but to guard one part of the society against the injustice of the other part. Different interests necessarily exist in different classes of citizens. If a majority be united by a common interest, the rights of the minority will be insecure. There are but two methods of providing against this evil: the one by creating a will in the community independent of the majority—that is, of the society itself; the other by comprehending in the society so many separate descriptions of citizens as will render an unjust combination of a majority of the whole very improbable, if not impracticable.[74] The first method prevails in all governments possessing an hereditary or self-appointed authority. This, at best, is but a precarious security; because a power independent of the society may as well espouse the unjust views of the major, as the rightful interests of the minor party, and may possibly be turned against both parties. The second method will be exemplified in the federal republic of the United States. Whilst all authority in it will be derived from and dependent on the society, the society itself will be broken into so many parts, interests and classes of citizens, that the rights of individuals or of the minority will be in little danger from interested combinations of the majority. In a free government the security for civil rights must be the same as that for religious rights. It consists in the one case in the multiplicity of interests and in the other in the multiplicity of sects. The degree of security in both cases will depend on the number of interests and sects; and this may be presumed to depend on the extent of country and number of people comprehended under the same government. This view of the subject must particularly recommend a proper federal system to all the sincere and considerate friends of republican government, since it shows that in exact proportion as the territory of the Union may be formed into more circumscribed Confederacies or States, oppressive combinations of a majority will be facilitated; the best security under the republican forms for the rights of every class of citizens will be diminished; and consequently the stability and independence of some member of the government, the only other security, must be proportionally increased. Justice is the end of government. It is the end of civil society.[75] It ever has been and ever will be pursued until it be obtained, or until liberty be lost in the pursuit. In a society under the forms of which the stronger faction can readily unite and oppress the weaker, anarchy may as truly be said to reign as in a state of nature, where the weaker individual is not secured against the violence of the stronger; and, as in the latter state even the stronger individuals are prompted, by the uncertainty of their condition, to submit to a government which may protect the weak as well as themselves; so, in the former state will the more powerful factions or parties be gradually induced by a like motive to wish for a government which will protect all parties, the weaker as well as the more powerful. It can be little doubted that if the State of Rhode Island was separated from the Confederacy and left to itself, the insecurity of rights under the popular form of government within such narrow limits would be displayed by such reiterated oppressions of factious majorities that some power altogether independent of the people would soon be called for by the voice of the very factions whose misrule had proved the necessity of it. In the extended republic of the United States and among the great variety of interests, parties, and sects which it embraces, a coalition of a majority of the whole society could seldom take place on any other principles than those of justice and the general good; whilst there being thus less danger to a minor from the will of a major party, there must be less pretext, also, to provide for the security of the former, by introducing into the government a will not dependent on the latter, or, in other words, a will independent of the society itself. It is no less certain than it is important, notwithstanding the contrary opinions which have been entertained, that the larger the society, provided it lie within a practical sphere, the more duly capable it will be of self-government. And happily for the *republican cause*, the practicable sphere may be carried to a very great extent by a judicious modification and mixture of the *federal principle*.   Publius

THE FEDERALIST NO. 52

(MADISON)

To the People of the State of New York:

From the more general inquiries pursued in the four last papers, I pass on to a more particular examination of the several parts of the government. I shall begin with the House of Representatives.

The first view to be taken of this part of the government relates to the qualifications of the electors and the elected. Those of the former are to be the same with those of the electors of the most numerous branch of the State legislatures. The definition of the right of suffrage is very justly regarded as a fundamental article of republican government. It was incumbent on the convention, therefore, to define and establish this right in the Constitution. To have left it open for the occasional regulation of the Congress would have been improper for the reason just mentioned. To have submitted it to the legislative discretion of the States would have been improper for the same reason; and for the additional reason that it would have rendered too dependent on the State governments that branch of the federal government which ought to be dependent on the people alone. To have reduced the different qualifications in the different States to one uniform rule would probably have been as dissatisfactory to some of the States as it would have been difficult to the convention. The provision made by the convention appears, therefore, to be the best that lay within their option. It must be satisfactory to every State, because it is conformable to the standard already established, or which may be established, by the State itself. It will be safe to the United States, because, being fixed by the State constitutions, it is not alterable by the State governments, and it cannot be feared that the people of the States will alter this part of their constitutions in such a manner as to abridge the rights secured to them by the federal Constitution.

The qualifications of the elected, being less carefully and properly defined by the State constitutions, and being at the same time more susceptible of uniformity, have been very properly considered and regulated by the convention. A representative of the United States must be of the age of twenty-five years; must have been seven years a citizen of the United States; must, at the time of his election, be an inhabitant of the State he is to represent; and, during the time of his service, must be in no office under the United States. Under these reasonable limitations the door of this part of the federal government is open to merit of every description, whether native or adoptive, whether young or old, and without regard to poverty or wealth, or to any particular profession or religious faith.

The term for which the representatives are to be elected falls under a second view which may be taken of this branch. In order to decide on the propriety of this article, two questions must be considered: first, whether biennial elections will, in this case, be safe; secondly, whether they be necessary or useful.

First. As it is essential to liberty that the government in general should have a common interest with the people, so it is particularly essential that the branch of it under consideration should have an immediate dependence on, and an intimate sympathy with, the people. Frequent elections are unquestionably the only policy by which this dependence and sympathy can be effectually secured. But what particular degree of frequency may be absolutely necessary for the purpose does not appear to be susceptible of any precise calculation, and must depend on a variety of circumstances with which it may be connected. Let us consult experience, the guide that ought always to be followed whenever it can be found.

The scheme of representation as a substitute for a meeting of the citizens in person, being at most but very imperfectly known to ancient polity, it is in more modern times only that we are to expect instructive examples. And even here, in order to avoid a research too vague and diffusive, it will be proper to confine ourselves to the few examples which are best known, and which bear the greatest analogy to our particular case. The first to which this character ought to be applied, is the House of Commons in Great Britain. . . .[76]

Let us bring our inquiries nearer home. The example of these States, when British colonies, claims particular attention at the same time that it is so well known as to require little to be said on it. The principle of representation, in one branch of the legislature at least, was established in all of them. But the periods of election were different. They varied from one to seven years. Have we any reason to infer from the spirit and conduct of the representatives of the people prior to the Revolution, that biennial elections would have been dangerous to the public liberties? The spirit which everywhere displayed itself at the commencement of the struggle, and which vanquished the obstacles to independence, is the best of proofs that a sufficient portion of liberty had been everywhere enjoyed to inspire both a sense of its worth and a zeal for its proper enlargement. This remark holds good, as well with regard to the then colonies whose elections were least frequent as to those whose elections were most frequent. Virginia was the colony which stood first in resisting the parliamentary usurpations of Great Britain; it was the first also in espousing by public act the resolution of independence. In Virginia, nevertheless, if I have not been misinformed, elections under the former government were septennial. This particular example is brought into view, not as a proof of any peculiar merit, for the priority in those instances was probably accidental; and still less of any advantage in *septennial* elections, for when compared with a greater frequency they are inadmissible; but merely as a proof, and I conceive it to be a very substantial proof, that the liberties of the people can be in no danger from *biennial* elections.

The conclusion resulting from these examples will be not a little strengthened by recollecting three circumstances. The first is, that the federal legislature will possess a part only of that supreme legislative authority which is vested completely in the British Parliament; and which with a few exceptions was exercised by the colonial assemblies and the Irish legislature. It is a received and well-founded maxim, that where no other circumstances affect the case, the greater the power is, the shorter ought to be its duration; and, conversely, the smaller the power, the more safely may its duration be protracted. In the second place, . . . the federal legislature will not only be restrained by its dependence on the people, as other legislative bodies are, but . . . it will be . . . watched and controlled by the several collateral legislatures, which other legislative bodies are not. And in the third place, no comparison can be made between the means that will be possessed by the more permanent branches of the federal government for seducing, if they should be disposed to seduce, the House of Representatives from their duty to the people, and the means of influence over the popular branch possessed by the other branches of the government above cited. With less power, therefore, to abuse, the federal representatives can be less tempted on one side, and will be doubly watched on the other.   PUBLIUS

THE FEDERALIST NO. 59

(HAMILTON)

To the People of the State of New York:
The natural order of the subject leads us to consider in this place that provision of the Constitution which authorizes the national legislature to regulate, in the last resort, the election of its own members.

It is in these words: "The *times, places,* and *manner* of holding elections for senators and representatives shall be prescribed in each State by the legislature thereof; but the Congress may, at any time, by law, make or alter *such regulations,* except as to the *places* of choosing senators" [*sic*].[77] This provision has not only been declaimed against by those who condemn the Constitution in the gross; but it has been censured by those who have objected with less latitude and greater moderation; and, in one instance, it has been thought exceptionable by a gentleman who has declared himself the advocate of every other part of the system.[78]

I am greatly mistaken . . . if there be any article in the whole plan more completely defensible than this. Its propriety rests upon the evidence of this plain proposition, that *every government ought to contain in itself the means of its own preservation.* Every just reasoner will at first sight approve an adherence to this rule . . . ; and will disapprove every deviation from it which may not appear to have been dictated by the necessity of incorporating into the work some particular ingredient, with which a rigid conformity to the rule was incompatible. Even in this case, though he may acquiesce in the necessity, yet he will not cease to regard and to regret a departure from so fundamental a principle, as a portion of imperfection in the system which may prove the seed of future weakness, and perhaps anarchy.

It will not be alleged that an election law could have been framed and inserted in the Constitution, which would have been always applicable to every probable change in the situation of the country; and it will therefore not be denied that a discretionary power over elections ought to exist somewhere. It will, I presume, be as readily conceded that there were only three ways in which this power could have been reasonably modified and disposed: that it must either have been lodged wholly in the national legislature, or wholly in the State legislatures, or primarily in the latter and ultimately in the former. The last mode has, with reason, been preferred by the convention. They have submitted the regulation of elections for the federal government, in the first instance, to the local administrations; which, in ordinary cases and when no improper views prevail, may be both more convenient and more satisfactory; but they have reserved to the national authority a right to interpose whenever extraordinary circumstances might render that interposition necessary to its safety.

Nothing can be more evident, than that an exclusive power of regulating elections for the national government in the hands of the State legislatures, would leave the existence of the Union entirely at their mercy. They could at any moment annihilate it by neglecting to provide for the choice of persons to administer its affairs. It is to little purpose to say that a neglect or omission of this kind would not be likely to take place. The constitutional possibility of the thing, without an equivalent for the risk, is an unanswerable objection. Nor has any satisfactory reason been yet assigned for incurring that risk. The extravagant surmises of a distempered jealousy can never be dignified with that character. If we are in a humor to presume abuses of power, it is as fair to presume them on the part of the State governments as on the part of the general government. And as it is more consonant to the rules of a just theory to trust the Union with the care of its own existence than to transfer that care to any other hands, if abuses of power are to be hazarded on the one side or on the other, it is more rational to hazard them where the power would naturally be placed, than where it would unnaturally be placed.

Suppose an article had been introduced into the Constitution, empowering the United States to regulate the elections for the particular States, would any man have hesitated to condemn it, both as an unwarrantable transposition of power and as a premeditated engine for the destruction of the State governments? The violation of principle, in this case, would have required no comment; and, to an unbiased observer it will not be less apparent in the project of subjecting the existence of the national government, in a similar respect, to the pleasure of the State governments. An impartial view of the matter cannot fail to result in a conviction, that each, as far as possible, ought to depend on itself for its own preservation.

As an objection to this position, it may be remarked that the constitution of the national Senate would involve, in its full extent, the danger which it is suggested might flow from an exclusive power in the State legislatures to regulate the federal elections. It may be alleged, that by declining the appointment of senators, they might at any time give a fatal blow to the Union; and from this it may be inferred, that as its existence would be thus rendered dependent upon them in so essential a point, there can be no objection to intrusting them with it in the particular case under consideration. The interest of each State . . . to maintain its representation in the national councils would be a complete security against an abuse of the trust.

This argument, though specious, will not upon examination be found solid. It is certainly true that the State legislatures, by forbearing the appointment of senators, may destroy the national government. But it will not follow that, because they have the power to do this in one instance, they ought to have it in every other. There are cases in which the pernicious tendency of such a power may be far more decisive, without any motive equally cogent with that which must have regulated the conduct of the convention in respect to the formation of the Senate, to recommend their admission into the system. So far as that construction may expose the Union to the possibility of injury from the State legislatures, it is an evil; but it is an evil which could not have been avoided without excluding the States, in their political capacities, wholly from a place in the organization of the national government. If this had been done, it would doubtless have been interpreted into an entire dereliction of the federal principle; and would certainly have deprived the State governments of that absolute safeguard which they will enjoy under this provision. But however wise it may have been to have submitted in this instance to an inconvenience for the attainment of a necessary advantage or a greater good, no inference can be drawn from thence to favor an accumulation of the evil, where no necessity urges, nor any greater good invites.

It may be easily discerned also that the national government would run a much greater risk from a power in the State legislatures over the elections of its House of Representatives, than from their power of appointing the members of its Senate. The senators are to be chosen for the period of six years; there is to be a rotation by which the seats of a third part of them are to be vacated and replenished every two years; and no State is to be entitled to more than two senators; a quorum of the body is to consist of sixteen members. The joint result of these circumstances would be, that a temporary combination of a few States to intermit the appointment of senators could neither annul the existence nor impair the activity of the body; and it is not from a general and permanent combination of the States that we can have any thing to fear. The first might proceed from sinister designs in the leading members of a few of the State legislatures; the last would suppose a fixed and rooted disaffection in the great body of the people, which will either never exist at all, or will in all probability proceed from an experience of the inaptitude of the general government to the advancement of their happiness—in which event no good citizen could desire its continuance.

But with regard to the federal House of Representatives, there is intended to be a general election of members once in two years. If the State legislatures were to be invested with an exclusive power of regulating these elections, every period of making them would be a delicate crisis in the national situation, which might issue in a dissolution of the Union if the leaders of a few of the most important States should have entered into a previous conspiracy to prevent an election.

I shall not deny that there is a degree of weight in the observation, that the interests of each State to be represented in the federal councils will be a security against the abuse of a power over its elections in the hands of the State legislatures. But the security will not be considered as complete by those who attend to the force of an obvious distinction: between the interest of the people in the public felicity and the interest of their local rulers in the power and consequence of their offices. The people of America may be warmly attached to the government of the Union at times when the particular rulers of particular States, stimulated by the natural rivalship of power and by the hopes of personal aggrandizement, and supported by a strong faction in each of those States, may be in a very opposite temper. This diversity of sentiment between a majority of the people and the individuals who have the greatest credit in their councils, is exemplified in some of the States at the present moment on the present question. The scheme of separate confederacies, which will always multiply the chances of ambition, will be a never failing bait to all such influential characters in the State administrations as are capable of preferring their own emolument and advancement to the public weal. With so effectual a weapon in their hands as the exclusive power of regulating elections for the national government, a combination of a few such men in a few of the most considerable States, where the temptation will always be the strongest, might accomplish the destruction of the Union, by seizing the opportunity of some casual dissatisfaction among the people (and which perhaps they may themselves have excited), to discontinue the choice of members for the federal House of Representatives. It ought never to be forgotten that a firm union of this country, under an efficient government, will probably be an increasing object of jealousy to more than one nation of Europe; and that enterprises to subvert it will sometimes originate in the intrigues of foreign powers, and will seldom fail to be patronized and abetted by some of them. Its preservation therefore ought, in no case that can be avoided, to be committed to the guardianship of any but those whose situation will uniformly beget an immediate interest in the faithful and vigilant performance of the trust.

PUBLIUS

THE FEDERALIST NO. 60

(HAMILTON)

To the People of the State of New York:
We have seen that an uncontrollable power over the elections to the federal government could not, without hazard, be committed to the State legislatures. Let us now see what would be the danger on the other side; that is, from confiding the ultimate right of regulating its own elections to the Union itself. It is not pretended that this right would ever be used for the exclusion of any State from its share in the representation. The interest of all would, in this respect at least, be the security of all. But it is alleged that it might be employed in such a manner as to promote the election of some favorite class of men in exclusion of others, by confining the places of election to particular districts, and rendering it impracticable to the citizens at large to partake in the choice. Of all chimerical suppositions this seems to be the most chimerical. On the one hand, no rational calculation of proba-

bilities would lead us to imagine that the disposition which a conduct so violent and extraordinary would imply, could ever find its way into the national councils; and on the other, it may be concluded with certainty that if so improper a spirit should ever gain admittance into them, it would display itself in a form altogether different and far more decisive.

The improbability of the attempt may be satisfactorily inferred from this single reflection, that it could never be made without causing an immediate revolt of the great body of the people, headed and directed by the State governments. It is not difficult to conceive that this characteristic right of freedom may in certain turbulent and factious seasons be violated, in respect to a particular class of citizens, by a victorious and overbearing majority; but that so fundamental a privilege, in a country so situated and enlightened, should be invaded to the prejudice of the great mass of the people, by the deliberate policy of the government, without occasioning a popular revolution, is altogether inconceivable and incredible.

In addition to this general reflection, there are considerations of a more precise nature which forbid all apprehension on the subject. The dissimilarity in the ingredients which will compose the national government, and still more in the manner in which they will be brought into action in its various branches, must form a powerful obstacle to a concert of views in any partial scheme of elections. There is sufficient diversity in the state of property, in the genius, manners, and habits of the people of the different parts of the Union, to occasion a material diversity of disposition in their representatives towards the different ranks and conditions in society. And though an intimate intercourse under the same government will promote a gradual assimilation in some of these respects; yet there are causes, as well physical as moral, which may, in a greater or less degree, permanently nourish different propensities and inclinations in this respect. But the circumstance which will be likely to have the greatest influence in the matter will be the dissimilar modes of constituting the several component parts of the government. The House of Representatives being to be elected immediately by the people, the Senate by the State legislatures, the President by electors chosen for that purpose by the people, there would be little probability of a common interest to cement these different branches in a predilection for any particular class of electors.

As to the Senate, it is impossible that any regulation of "time and manner" . . . can affect the spirit which will direct the choice of its members. The collective sense of the State legislatures can never be influenced by extraneous circumstances of that sort, a consideration which alone ought to satisfy us that the discrimination apprehended would never be attempted. For what inducement could the Senate have to concur in a preference in which itself would not be included? Or to what purpose would it be established in reference to one branch of the legislature if it could not be extended to the other. The composition of the one would in this case counteract that of the other. And we can never suppose that it would embrace the appointments to the Senate unless we can at the same time suppose the voluntary coöperation of the State legislatures. If we make the latter supposition, it then becomes immaterial where the power in question is placed—whether in their hands or in those of the Union.

But what is to be the object of this capricious partiality in the national councils? Is it to be exercised in a discrimination between the different departments of industry, or between the different kinds of property, or between the different degrees of property? Will it lean in favor of the landed interest, or the moneyed interest, or the mercantile interest, or the manufacturing interest? Or, to speak in the fashionable language of the adversaries to the Constitution, will it court the elevation of "the wealthy and the well-born" to the exclusion and debasement of all the rest of the society?[79]

If this partiality is to be exerted in favor of those who are concerned in any particular description of industry or property, I presume it will readily be admitted that the competition for it will lie between landed men and merchants. And I scruple not to affirm that it is infinitely less likely that either of them should gain an ascendant in the national councils, than that the one or the other of them should predominate in all the local councils. The inference will be, that a conduct tending to give an undue preference to either is much less to be dreaded from the former than from the latter.

The several States are in various degrees addicted to agriculture and commerce. In most, if not all of them, agriculture is predominant. In a few of them, however, commerce nearly divides its empire, and in most of them has a considerable share of influence. In proportion as either prevails, it will be conveyed into the national representation; and, for the very reason that this will be an emanation from a greater variety of interests and in much more various proportions than are to be found in any single State, it will be much less apt to espouse either of them with a decided partiality, than the representation of any single State.

In a country consisting chiefly of the cultivators of land, where the rules of an equal representation obtain, the landed interest must . . . preponderate in the government. As long as this interest prevails in most of the State legislatures, so long it must maintain a correspondent superiority in the national Senate, which will generally be a faithful copy of the majorities of those assemblies. It cannot therefore be presumed that a sacrifice of the landed to the mercantile class will ever be a favorite object of this branch of the federal legislature. In applying thus particularly to the Senate a general observation suggested by the situation of the country, I am governed by the consideration that the credulous votaries of State power cannot, upon their own principles, suspect that the State legislatures would be warped from their duty by any external influence. But in reality the same situation must have the same effect, in the primitive composition at least of the federal House of Representatives; an improper bias towards the mercantile class is as little to be expected from this quarter as from the other.

In order, perhaps, to give countenance to the objection . . . it may be asked, is there not danger of an opposite bias in the national government, which may dispose it to endeavor to secure a monopoly of the federal administration to the landed class? As there is little likelihood that the supposition of such a bias will have any terrors for those who would be immediately injured by it, a labored answer to this question will be dispensed with. It will be sufficient to remark, first, that for the reasons elsewhere assigned, it is less likely that any decided partiality should prevail in the councils of the Union than in those of any of its members. Secondly, that there would be no temptation to violate the Constitution in favor of the landed class, because that class would, in the natural course of things, enjoy as great a preponderancy as itself could desire. And thirdly, that men accustomed to investigate the sources of public prosperity upon a large scale, must be too well convinced of the utility of commerce to be inclined to inflict upon it so deep a wound as would result from the entire exclusion of those who would best understand its interest from a share in the management of them. The importance of commerce, in the view of revenue alone, must effectually guard it against the enmity of a body which would be continually importuned in its favor by the urgent calls of public necessity.

I rather consult brevity in discussing the probability of a preference founded upon a discrimination between the different kinds of industry and property, because, as far as I understand the meaning of the objectors, they contemplate a discrimination of another kind. They appear to have in view, as the objects of the preference with which they endeavor to alarm us, those whom they designate by the description of "the wealthy and the well-born." These, it seems, are to be exalted to an odious preëminence over the rest of their fellow-citizens. At one time, however, their elevation is to be a necessary consequence of the smallness of the representative body; at another time it is to be effected by depriving the people at large of the opportunity of exercising their right of suffrage in the choice of that body.

But upon what principle is the discrimination of the places of election to be made, in order to answer the purpose of the meditated preference? Are "the wealthy and the well-born" . . . confined to particular spots in the several States? Have they by some miraculous instinct or foresight set apart in each of them a common place of residence? Are they only to be met with in the towns or cities? Or are they, on the contrary, scattered over the face of the country as avarice or chance may have happened to cast their own lot or that of their predecessors? If the latter is the case, . . . is it not evident that the policy of confining the places of election to particular districts would be as subversive of its own aim as it would be exceptionable on every other account? The truth is, that there is no method of securing to the rich the preference apprehended but by prescribing qualifications of property either for those who may elect or be elected. But this forms no part of the power to be conferred upon the national government. Its authority would be expressly restricted to the regulation of the *times*, the *places*, the *manner* of elections. The qualifications of the persons who may choose or be chosen . . . are defined and fixed in the Constitution, and are unalterable by the legislature.

Let it, however, be admitted for argument sake that the expedient suggested might be successful; and let it at the same time be equally taken for granted that all the scruples, which a sense of duty or an apprehension of the danger of the experiment might inspire, were overcome in the breasts of the national rulers; still I imagine it will hardly be pretended that they could ever hope to carry such an enterprise into execution without the aid of a military force sufficient to subdue the resistance of the great body of the people. The improbability of the existence of a force equal to that object has been discussed and demonstrated in different parts of these papers; but that the futility of the objection under consideration may appear in the strongest light, it shall be conceded for a moment that such a force might exist, and the national government shall be supposed to be in the actual possession of it. What will be the conclusion? With a disposition to invade the essential rights of the community and with the means of gratifying that disposition, is it presumable that the persons who were actuated by it would amuse themselves in the ridiculous task of fabricating election laws for securing a preference to a favorite class of men? Would they not be likely to prefer a conduct better adapted to their own immediate aggrandizement? Would they not rather boldly resolve to perpetuate themselves in office by one decisive act of usurpation, than to trust to precarious expedients which, in spite of all the precautions that might accompany them, might terminate in the dismission, disgrace, and ruin of their authors? Would they not fear that citizens, not less tenacious than conscious of their rights, would flock from the remote extremes of their respective States to the places of election, to overthrow their tyrants, and to substitute men who would be disposed to avenge the violated majesty of the people?   PUBLIUS

THE FEDERALIST NO. 61

(HAMILTON)

To the People of the State of New York:

The more candid opposers of the provision respecting elections . . . when pressed in argument will sometimes concede the propriety of that provision; with this qualification, however, that it ought to have been accompanied with a declaration, that all elections should be had in the counties where the electors resided. This, say they, was a necessary precaution against an abuse of the power. A declaration of this nature would certainly have been harmless; so far as it would have had the effect of quieting apprehensions, it might not have been undesirable. But it would, in fact, have afforded little or no additional security against the danger apprehended; and the want of it will never be considered by an impartial and judicious examiner as a serious, still less as an insuperable, objection to the plan. The different views taken of the subject in the two preceding papers must be sufficient to satisfy all dispassionate and discerning men, that if the public liberty should ever be the victim of the ambition of the national rulers, the power under examination, at least, will be guiltless of the sacrifice.

If those who are inclined to consult their jealousy only would exercise it in a careful inspection of the several State constitutions, they would find little less room for disquietude and alarm, from the latitude which most of them allow in respect to elections, than from the latitude which is proposed to be allowed to the national government in the same respect. . . .

The alarming indifference discoverable in the exercise of so invaluable a privilege under the existing laws, which afford every facility to it, furnishes a ready answer to this question. And, abstracted from any experience on the subject, we can be at no loss to determine that when the place of election is at an *inconvenient distance* from the elector, the effect upon his conduct will be the same whether that distance be twenty miles or twenty thousand miles. Hence it must appear, that objections to the particular modification of the federal power of regulating elections will, in substance, apply with equal force to the modification of the like power in the constitution of this State; and for this reason it will be impossible to acquit the one and to condemn the other. A similar comparison would lead to the same conclusion in respect to the constitutions of most of the other States.

If it should be said that defects in the State constitutions furnish no apology for those which are to be found in the plan proposed, I answer, that as the former have never been thought chargeable with inattention to the security of liberty, where the imputations thrown on the latter can be shown to be applicable to them also, the presumption is that they are rather the cavilling refinements of a predetermined opposition, than the well-founded inferences of a candid research after truth. To those who are disposed to consider as innocent omissions in the State constitutions what they regard as unpardonable blemishes in the plan of the convention, nothing can be said; or at most, they can only be asked to assign some substantial reason why the representatives of the people in a single State should be more impregnable to the lust of power or other sinister motives, than the representatives of the people of the United States? If they cannot do this, they ought at least to prove to us that it is easier to subvert the liberties of three millions of people, with the advantage of local governments to head their opposition, than of two hundred thousand people who are destitute of that advantage. And in relation to the point immediately under consideration, they ought to convince us that it is less probable that a predominant faction in a single State should, in order to maintain its superiority, incline to a preference of a particular class of electors, than that a similar spirit should take possession of the representatives of thirteen States, spread over a vast region, and in several respects distinguishable from each other by a diversity of local circumstances, prejudices, and interests.

Hitherto my observations have only aimed at a vindication of the provision in question, on the ground of theoretic propriety, on that of the danger of placing the power elsewhere, and on that of the safety of placing it in the manner proposed. But there remains to be mentioned a positive advantage which will result from this disposition, and which could not as well have been obtained from any other: I allude to the circumstance of uniformity in the time of elections for the federal House of Representatives. It is more than possible that this uniformity may be found by experience to be of great importance to the public welfare, both as a security against the perpetuation of the same spirit in the body and as a cure for the diseases of faction. If each State may choose its own time of election, it is possible there may be at least as many different periods as there are months in the year. The times of election in the several States, as they are now established for local purposes, vary between extremes as wide as March and November.[80] The consequence of this diversity would be that there could never happen a total dissolution or renovation of the body at one time. If an improper spirit of any kind should happen to prevail in it, that spirit would be apt to infuse itself into the new members as they come forward in succession. The mass would be likely to remain nearly the same, assimilating constantly to itself its gradual accretions. There is a contagion in example which few men have sufficient force of mind to resist. I am inclined to think that treble the duration in office, with the condition of a total dissolution of the body at the same time, might be less formidable to liberty than one third of that duration subject to gradual and successive alterations.

Uniformity in the time of elections seems not less requisite for executing the idea of a regular rotation in the Senate, and for conveniently assembling the legislature at a stated period in each year.

It may be asked, Why, then, could not a time have been fixed in the Constitution? As the most zealous adversaries of the plan of the convention in this State are, in general, not less zealous admirers of the constitution of the State, the question may be . . . asked, Why was not a time for the like purpose fixed in the constitution of this State? No better answer can be given than that it was a matter which might safely be entrusted to legislative discretion; and that if a time had been appointed, it might, upon experiment, have been found less convenient than some other time. The same answer may be given to the question put on the other side. And it may be added that the supposed danger of a gradual change being merely speculative, it would have been hardly advisable upon that speculation to establish as a fundamental point what would deprive several States of the convenience of having the elections for their own governments and for the national government at the same epochs.   PUBLIUS

THE FEDERALIST NO. 62

(MADISON)

To the People of the State of New York:
    Having examined the constitution of the House of Representatives, and answered such of the objections against it as seemed to merit notice, I enter next on the examination of the Senate.
    The heads into which this member of the government may be considered are: I. The qualifications of senators; II. The appointment of them by the State legislatures; III. The equality of representation in the Senate; IV. The number of senators, and the term for which they are to be elected; V. The powers vested in the Senate.
    I. The qualifications proposed for senators, as distinguished from those of representatives, consist in a more advanced age and a longer period of citizenship. A senator must be thirty years of age at least; as a representative must be twenty-five. And the former must have been a citizen nine years; as seven years are required for the latter. The propriety of these

distinctions is explained by the nature of the senatorial trust, which, requiring greater extent of information and stability of character, requires at the same time that the senator should have reached a period of life most likely to supply these advantages; and which, participating immediately in transactions with foreign nations, ought to be exercised by none who are not thoroughly weaned from the prepossessions and habits incident to foreign birth and education. The term of nine years appears to be a prudent . . . [median] between a total exclusion of adopted citizens, whose merits and talents may claim a share in the public confidence, and an indiscriminate and hasty admission of them, which might create a channel for foreign influence on the national councils.

II. It is equally unnecessary to dilate on the appointment of senators by the State legislatures. Among the various modes which might have been devised for constituting this branch of the government, that which has been proposed by the convention is probably the most congenial with the public opinion. It is recommended by the double advantage of favoring a select appointment, and of giving to the State governments such an agency in the formation of the federal government as must secure the authority of the former, and may form a convenient link between the two systems.

III. The equality of representation in the Senate is another point, which, being evidently the result of compromise between the opposite pretensions of the large and the small States, does not call for much discussion. If indeed it be right, that among a people thoroughly incorporated into one nation, every district ought to have a *proportional* share in the government; and that among independent and sovereign States, bound together by a simple league, the parties, however unequal in size, ought to have an *equal* share in the common councils; it does not appear to be without some reason that in a compound republic, partaking both of the national and federal character, the government ought to be founded on a mixture of the principles of proportional and equal representation. But it is superfluous to try by the standard of theory, a part of the Constitution which is allowed on all hands to be the result, not of theory, but "of a spirit of amity, and that mutual deference and concession which the peculiarity of our political situation rendered indispensable." A common government with powers equal to its objects is called for by the voice, and still more loudly by the political situation, of America. A government founded on principles more consonant to the wishes of the larger States is not likely to be obtained from the smaller States. The only option, then, for the former lies between the proposed government and a government still more objectionable. Under this alternative the advice of prudence must be to embrace the lesser evil; and, instead of indulging a fruitless anticipation of the possible mischiefs which may ensue, to contemplate rather the advantageous consequences which may qualify the sacrifice.

In this spirit it may be remarked, that the equal vote allowed to each State is at once a constitutional recognition of the portion of sovereignty remaining in the individual States, and an instrument for preserving that residuary sovereignty. So far the equality ought to be no less acceptable to the large than to the small States; since they are not less solicitous to guard, by every possible expedient, against an improper consolidation of the States into one simple republic.

Another advantage accruing from this ingredient in the constitution of the Senate is the additional impediment it must prove against improper acts of legislation. No law or resolution can now be passed without the concurrence, first, of a majority of the people, and then, of a majority of the States. It must be acknowledged that this complicated check on legislation may in some instances be injurious as well as beneficial; and that the peculiar defence which it involves in favor of the smaller States would be more rational, if any interests common to them, and distinct from those of the other States, would otherwise be exposed to peculiar danger. But as the larger States will always be able, by their power over the supplies, to defeat unreasonable exertions of this prerogative of the lesser States, and as the facility and excess of lawmaking seem to be the diseases to which our governments are most liable, it is not impossible that this part of the Constitution may be more convenient in practice than it appears to many in contemplation.

IV. The number of senators and the duration of their appointment come next to be considered. In order to form an accurate judgment on both these points, it will be proper to inquire into the purposes which are to be answered by a senate; and in order to ascertain these, it will be necessary to review the inconveniences which a republic must suffer from the want of such an institution.

First. It is a misfortune incident to republican government, though in a less degree than to other governments, that those who administer it may forget their obligations to their constituents and prove unfaithful to their important trust. In this point of view, a senate, as a second branch of the legislative assembly, distinct from and dividing the power with a first, must be in all cases a salutary check on the government. It doubles the security to the people by requiring the concurrence of two distinct bodies in schemes of usurpation or perfidy, where the ambition or corruption of one would otherwise be sufficient. This is a precaution founded on such clear principles, and now so well understood in the United States, that it would be more than superfluous to enlarge on it. I will barely remark, that as the improbability of sinister combinations will be in proportion to the dissimilarity in the genius of the two bodies, it must be politic to distinguish them from each other by every circumstance which will consist with a due harmony in all proper measures and with the genuine principles of republican government.

Secondly. The necessity of a senate is not less indicated by the propensity of all single and numerous assemblies to yield to the impulse of sudden and violent passions, and to be seduced by factious leaders into intemperate and pernicious resolutions. Examples on this subject might be cited without number; and from proceedings within the United States, as well as from the history of other nations. But a position that will not be contradicted need not be proved. All that need be remarked is, that a body which is to correct this infirmity ought itself to be free from it and consequently ought to be less numerous. It ought, moreover, to possess great firmness and consequently ought to hold its authority by a tenure of considerable duration.

Thirdly. Another defect to be supplied by a senate lies in a want of due acquaintance with the objects and principles of legislation. It is not possible that an assembly of men called for the most part from pursuits of a private nature, continued in appointment for a short time, and led by no permanent motive to devote the intervals of public occupation to a study of the laws, the affairs, and the comprehensive interests of their country, should, if left wholly to themselves, escape a variety of important errors in the exercise of their legislative trust. It may be affirmed on the best grounds that no small share of the present embarrassments of America is to be charged on the blunders of our governments; and that these have proceeded from the heads rather than the hearts of most of the authors of them. What indeed are all the repealing, explaining, and amending laws, which fill and disgrace our voluminous codes, but so many monuments of deficient wisdom; so many impeachments exhibited by each succeeding against each preceding session; so many admonitions to the people, of the value of those aids which may be expected from a well-constituted senate?

A good government implies two things: first, fidelity to the object of government, which is the happiness of the people; secondly, a knowledge of the means by which that object can be best attained. Some governments are deficient in both these qualities; most governments are deficient in the first. I scruple not to assert that in American governments too little attention has been paid to the last. The federal Constitution avoids this error; and what merits particular notice, it provides for the last in a mode which increases the security for the first.

Fourthly. The mutability in the public councils arising from a rapid succession of new members, however qualified they may be, points out, in the strongest manner, the necessity of some stable institution in the government. Every new election in the States is found to change one half of the representatives. From this change of men must proceed a change of opinions; and from a change of opinions, a change of measures. But a continual change even of good measures is inconsistent with every rule of prudence and every prospect of success. The remark is verified in private life, and becomes more just as well as more important, in national transactions.

To trace the mischievous effects of a mutable government, would fill a volume. I will hint a few only, each of which will be perceived to be a source of innumerable others.

In the first place, it forfeits the respect and confidence of other nations and all the advantages connected with national character. An individual who is observed to be inconstant to his plans, or perhaps to carry on his affairs without any plan at all, is marked at once . . . as a speedy victim to his own unsteadiness and folly. His more friendly neighbors may pity him, but all will decline to connect their fortunes with his; and not a few will seize the opportunity of making their fortunes out of his. One nation is to another what one individual is to another; with this melancholy distinction perhaps, that the former, with fewer of the benevolent emotions than the latter, are under fewer restraints also from taking undue advantage from the indiscretion of each other. Every nation, consequently, whose affairs betray a want of wisdom and stability, may calculate on every loss which can be sustained from the more systematic policy of their wiser neighbors. But the best instruction on this subject is unhappily conveyed to America by the example of her own situation. She finds that she is held in no respect by her friends; that she is the derision of her enemies; and that she is a prey to every nation which has an interest in speculating on her fluctuating councils and embarrassed affairs.

The internal effects of a mutable policy are still more calamitous. It poisons the blessing of liberty itself. It will be of little avail to the people that the laws are made by men of their own choice, if the laws be so voluminous that they cannot be read or so incoherent that they cannot be understood; if they be repealed or revised before they are promulgated or undergo such incessant changes that no man, who knows what the law is today, can guess what it will be tomorrow. Law is defined to be a rule of action; but how can that be a rule which is little known and less fixed?

Another effect of public instability is the unreasonable advantage it gives to the sagacious, the enterprising, and the moneyed few over the industrious and uninformed mass of the people. Every new regulation concerning commerce or revenue, or in any manner affecting the value of the different species of property, presents a new harvest to those who watch the change and can trace its consequences; a harvest, reared not by themselves but by the toils and cares of the great body of their fellow-citizens. This is a state of things in which it may be said with some truth that laws are made for the *few*, not for the *many*.

In another point of view, great injury results from an unstable government. The want of confidence in the public councils damps every useful undertaking, the success and profit of which may depend on a continuance of existing arrangements. What prudent merchant will hazard his fortunes in any new branch of commerce when he knows not but that his plans may be rendered unlawful before they can be executed? What farmer or manufacturer will lay himself out for the encouragement given to any particular cultivation or establishment when he can have no assurance that his preparatory labors and advances will not render him a victim to an inconstant government? In a word, no great improvement or laudable enterprise can go forward which requires the auspices of a steady system of national policy.

But the most deplorable effect of all is that diminution of attachment and reverence which steals into the hearts of the people towards a political system which betrays so many marks of infirmity, and disappoints so many of their flattering hopes. No government, any more than an individual, will long be respected without being truly respectable; nor be truly respectable, without possessing a certain portion of order and stability.   PUBLIUS

THE FEDERALIST NO. 64

(JAY)

To the People of the State of New York:

It is a just and not a new observation that enemies to particular persons and opponents to particular measures seldom confine their censures to such things only in either as are worthy of blame. Unless on this principle, it is difficult to explain the motives of their conduct, who condemn the proposed Constitution in the aggregate, and treat with severity some of the most unexceptionable articles in it.

The second section gives power to the President, *"by and with the advice and consent of the Senate, to make treaties,* PROVIDED TWO THIRDS OF THE SENATORS PRESENT CONCUR" [*sic*].[81]

The power of making treaties is an important one, especially as it relates to war, peace, and commerce; and it should not be delegated but in such a mode and with such precautions as will afford the highest security that it will be exercised by men the best qualified for the purpose, and in the manner most conducive to the public good. . . .

. . . It was wise, therefore, in the convention to provide, not only that the power of making treaties should be committed to able and honest men, but also that they should continue in place a sufficient time to become perfectly acquainted with our national concerns, and to form and introduce a system for the management of them. The duration prescribed is such as will give them an opportunity of greatly extending their political information, and of rendering their accumulating experience more and more beneficial to their country. Nor has the convention discovered less prudence in providing for the frequent elections of senators in such a way as to obviate the inconvenience of periodically transferring those great affairs entirely to new men; for by leaving a considerable residue of the old ones in place, uniformity and order, as well as a constant succession of official information, will be preserved.

There are a few who will not admit that the affairs of trade and navigation should be regulated by a system cautiously formed and steadily pursued; and that both our treaties and our laws should correspond with and be made to promote it. It is of much consequence that this correspondence and conformity be carefully maintained; and they who assent to the truth of this position will see and confess that it is well provided for by making concurrence of the Senate necessary both to treaties and to laws.

It seldom happens in the negotiation of treaties of whatever nature, but that perfect *secrecy* and immediate *despatch*

are sometimes requisite. There are cases where the most useful intelligence may be obtained, if the persons possessing it
can be relieved from apprehensions of discovery. Those apprehensions will operate on those persons whether they are actuated by mercenary or friendly motives; and there doubtless
are many of both descriptions, who would rely on the secrecy
of the President, but who would not confide in that of the
Senate and still less in that of a large popular Assembly. The
convention have done well, therefore, in so disposing of the
power of making treaties . . . although the President must in
forming them act by the advice and consent of the Senate,
yet he will be able to manage the business of intelligence in
such a manner as prudence may suggest.

They who have turned their attention to the affairs of men
must have perceived that there are tides in them; tides very
irregular in their duration, strength, and direction, and seldom found to run twice exactly in the same manner or measure. To discern and to profit by these tides in national affairs
is the business of those who preside over them; and they who
have had much experience on this head inform us, that there
frequently are occasions when days, nay, even when hours, are
precious.[82] The loss of a battle, the death of a prince, the
removal of a minister, or other circumstances intervening to
change the present posture and aspect of affairs, may turn the
most favorable tide into a course opposite to our wishes. As in
the field, so in the cabinet, there are moments to be seized
as they pass, and they who preside in either should be left in
capacity to improve them. So often and so essentially have
we heretofore suffered from the want of secrecy and despatch,
that the Constitution would have been inexcusably defective
if no attention had been paid to those objects. Those matters
which in negotiations usually require the most secrecy and
the most despatch, are those preparatory and auxiliary measures which are not otherwise important in a national view,
than as they tend to facilitate the attainment of the objects
of the negotiation. For these, the President will find no difficulty to provide; and should any circumstance occur which
requires the advice and consent of the Senate, he may at any
time convene them. Thus we see that the Constitution provides that our negotiations for treaties shall have every ad-

vantage which can be derived from talents, information, integrity, and deliberate investigations, on the one hand, and from secrecy and despatch on the other.

But to this plan, as to most others that have ever appeared, objections are contrived and urged.

Some are displeased with it, not on account of any errors or defects in it, but because, as the treaties . . . are to have the force of laws, they should be made only by men invested with legislative authority. These gentlemen seem not to consider that the judgments of our courts and the commissions constitutionally given by our governor, are as valid and as binding on all persons whom they concern as the laws passed by our legislature. All constitutional acts of power, whether in the executive or in the judicial department, have as much legal validity and obligation as if they proceeded from the legislature; and therefore, whatever name be given to the power of making treaties or however obligatory they may be when made, certain it is, that the people may with much propriety commit the power to a distinct body from the legislature, the executive, or the judicial. It surely does not follow that because they have given the power of making laws to the legislature, that therefore they should likewise give them power to do every other act of sovereignty by which the citizens are to be bound and affected.

Others, though content that treaties should be made in the mode proposed, are averse to their being the *supreme* laws of the land.[83] They insist . . . that treaties like acts of assembly should be repealable at pleasure. This idea seems to be new and peculiar to this country, but new errors as well as new truths often appear. These gentlemen would do well to reflect that a treaty is only another name for a bargain; and that it would be impossible to find a nation who would make any bargain with us, which should be binding on them *absolutely* but on us only so long and so far as we may think proper to be bound by it. They who make laws may, without doubt, amend or repeal them; and it will not be disputed that they who make treaties may alter or cancel them; but still let us not forget that treaties are made, not by only one of the contracting parties, but by both; and consequently, that as the consent of both was essential to their formation at first, so must it ever afterwards be to alter or cancel them. The proposed Constitution, therefore, has not in the least extended the obligation of treaties. They are just as binding, and just as far beyond the lawful reach of legislative acts now as they will be at any future period, or under any form of government.

However useful jealousy may be in republics, yet when . . . it abounds too much in the body politic, the eyes of both become very liable to be deceived by the delusive appearances which that malady casts on surrounding objects. From this cause, probably, proceed the fears and apprehensions of some that the President and Senate may make treaties without an equal eye to the interests of all the States. Others suspect that two thirds will oppress the remaining third, and ask whether those gentlemen are made sufficiently responsible for their conduct; whether, if they act corruptly, they can be punished; and if they make disadvantageous treaties, how are we to get rid of those treaties?[84]

As all the States are equally represented in the Senate, and by men the most able and the most willing to promote the interests of their constituents, they will all have an equal degree of influence in that body, especially while they continue to be careful in appointing proper persons, and to insist on their punctual attendance. In proportion as the United States assume a national form and a national character, so will the good of the whole be more and more an object of attention; and the government must be a weak one indeed if it should forget that the good of the whole can only be promoted by advancing the good of each of the parts or members which compose the whole. It will not be in the power of the President and Senate to make any treaties by which they and their families and estates will not be equally bound and affected with the rest of the community; and, having no private interests distinct from that of the nation, they will be under no temptations to neglect the latter.

As to corruption, the case is not supposable. He must either have been very unfortunate in his intercourse with the world, or possess a heart very susceptible of such impressions, who can think it probable that the President and two thirds of the Senate will ever be capable of such unworthy conduct. The idea is too gross and too invidious to be entertained. But in such a case if it should ever happen, the treaty so obtained from us would, like all other fraudulent contracts, be null and void by the law of nations.

With respect to their responsibility, it is difficult to conceive how it could be increased. Every consideration that can influence the human mind, such as honor, oaths, reputations, conscience, the love of country, and family affections and attachments, afford security for their fidelity. In short, as the Constitution has taken the utmost care that they shall be men of talents and integrity, we have reason to be persuaded that the treaties they make will be as advantageous as, all circumstances considered, could be made; and so far as the fear of punishment and disgrace can operate, that motive to good behavior is amply afforded by the article on the subject of impeachments.   PUBLIUS

THE FEDERALIST NO. 69

(HAMILTON)

To the People of the State of New York:

I proceed now to trace the real characters of the proposed Executive, as they are marked out in the plan of the convention. This will serve to place in a strong light the unfairness of the representations which have been made in regard to it.

The first thing which strikes our attention is, that the executive authority, with few exceptions, is to be bested in a single magistrate. This will scarcely, however, be considered as a point upon which any comparison can be grounded; for if, in this particular, there be a resemblance to the king of Great Britain, there is not less a resemblance to the Grand Seignior, to the khan of Tartary, to the Man of the Seven Mountains, or to the governor of New York.

That magistrate is to be elected for *four* years; and is to

be reëligible as often as the people of the United States shall
think him worthy of their confidence.[85] In these circumstances there is a total dissimilitude between *him* and a king
of Great Britain, who is an *hereditary* monarch, possessing
the crown as a patrimony descendible to his heirs forever; but
there is a close analogy between *him* and a governor of New
York, who is elected for *three* years, and is reëligible without
limitation or intermission.[86] If we consider how much less
time would be requisite for establishing a dangerous influence in a single State, than for establishing a like influence
throughout the United States, we must conclude that a duration of *four* years for the Chief Magistrate of the Union is a
degree of permanency far less to be dreaded in that office,
than a duration of *three* years for a corresponding office in a
single State.

The President of the United States would be liable to be
impeached, tried, and, upon conviction of treason, bribery,
or other high crimes or misdemeanors, removed from office;
and would afterwards be liable to prosecution and punishment in the ordinary course of law. The person of the king
of Great Britain is sacred and inviolable; there is no constitutional tribunal to which he is amenable; no punishment to
which he can be subjected without involving the crisis of a
national revolution. In this delicate and important circumstance of personal responsibility, the President of Confederated America would stand upon no better ground than a
governor of New York, and upon worse ground than the governors of Maryland and Delaware.

The President of the United States is to have power to
return a bill, which shall have passed the two branches of the
legislature, for reconsideration; and the bill so returned is to
become a law, if, upon that reconsideration, it be approved
by two thirds of both houses. The king of Great Britain . . .
has an absolute negative upon the acts of the two houses of
Parliament. The disuse of that power for a considerable time
past does not affect the reality of its existence; and is to be
ascribed wholly to the crown's having found the means of
substituting influence to authority, or the art of gaining a majority in one or the other of the two houses, to the necessity
of exerting a prerogative which could seldom be exerted

without hazarding some degree of national agitation. The qualified negative of the President differs widely from this absolute negative of the British sovereign; and tallies exactly with the revisionary authority of the council of revision of this State, of which the governor is a constituent part. In this respect the power of the President would exceed that of the governor of New York, because the former would possess, singly, what the latter shares with the chancellor and judges; but it would be precisely the same with that of the governor of Massachusetts, whose constitution, as to this article, seems to have been the original from which the convention have copied.

The President is to be the "Commander-in-Chief of the army and navy of the United States, and of the militia of the several States, when called into the actual service of the United States. He is to have power to grant reprieves and pardons for offences against the United States, *except in cases of impeachment;* to recommend to the consideration of Congress such measures as he shall judge necessary and expedient; to convene, on extraordinary occasions, both houses of the legislature, or either of them, and, in case of disagreement between them *with respect to the time of adjournment,* to adjourn them to such time as he shall think proper; to take care that the laws be faithfully executed; and to commission all officers of the United States."[87] In most of these particulars, the power of the President will resemble equally that of the king of Great Britain and of the governor of New York. The most material points of difference are . . .

The President is to have power, with the advice and consent of the Senate, to make treaties, provided two thirds of the senators present concur. The king of Great Britain is the sole and absolute representative of the nation in all foreign transactions. He can of his own accord make treaties of peace, commerce, alliance, and of every other description. It has been insinuated that his authority in this respect is not conclusive, and that his conventions with foreign powers are subject to the revision, and stand in need of the ratification, of Parliament. But I believe this doctrine was never heard of until it was broached upon the present occasion. Every jurist[88] of that kingdom and every other man acquainted with its Constitution knows . . . that the prerogative of making treaties exists in the crown in its utmost plentitude; and that the compacts entered into by the royal authority have the most complete legal validity and perfection, independent of any other sanction. The Parliament, it is true, is sometimes seen employing itself in altering the existing laws to conform them to the stipulations in a new treaty; and this may have possibly given birth to the imagination that its coöperation was necessary to the obligatory efficacy of the treaty. But this parliamentary interposition proceeds from a different cause: from the necessity of adjusting a most artificial and intricate system of revenue and commercial laws, to the changes made in them by the operation of the treaty; and of adapting new provisions and precautions to the new state of things, to keep the machine from running into disorder. In this respect, therefore, there is no comparison between the intended power of the President and the actual power of the British sovereign. The one can perform alone what the other can do only with the concurrence of a branch of the legislature. It must be admitted, that, in this instance, the power of the federal Executive would exceed that of any State Executive. But this arises naturally from the sovereign power which relates to treaties. If the Confederacy were to be dissolved, it would become a question whether the Executives of the several States were not solely invested with that delicate and important prerogative.

The President is also to be authorized to receive ambassadors and other public ministers. This, though it has been a rich theme of declamation, is more a matter of dignity than of authority. It is a circumstance which will be without consequence in the administration of the government; and it was far more convenient that it should be arranged in this manner, than that there should be a necessity of convening the legislature or one of its branches upon every arrival of a foreign minister, though it were merely to take the place of a departed predecessor.

The President is to nominate, and, *with the advice and consent of the Senate,* to appoint ambassadors and other public ministers, judges of the Supreme Court, and in general all officers of the United States established by law, and whose appointments are not otherwise provided for by the Constitution. The king of Great Britain is emphatically and truly styled the fountain of honor. He not only appoints to all offices, but can create offices. He can confer titles of nobility at pleasure; and has the disposal of an immense number of church preferments. There is evidently a great inferiority in the power of the President in this particular to that of the British king; nor is it equal to that of the governor of New York if we are to interpret the meaning of the constitution of the State by the practice which has obtained under it. The power of appointment is with us lodged in a council, composed of the governor and four members of the Senate, chosen by the Assembly. The governor *claims,* and has frequently *exercised,* the right of nomination, and is *entitled* to a casting vote in the appointment. If he really has the right of nominating, his authority is in this respect equal to that of the President and exceeds it in the article of the casting vote. In the national government, if the Senate should be divided, no appointment could be made; in the government of New York, if the council should be divided, the governor can turn the scale and confirm his own nomination. If we compare the publicity which must necessarily attend the mode of appointment by the President and an entire branch of the national legislature, with the privacy in the mode of appointment by the governor of New York, closeted in a secret apartment with at most four, and frequently with only two persons; and if we at the same time consider how much more easy it must be to influence the small number of which a council of appointment consists, than the considerable number of which the national Senate would consist, we cannot hesitate to pronounce that the power of the chief magistrate of this State, in the disposition of offices, must, in practice, be greatly superior to that of the Chief Magistrate of the Union.

Hence it appears that, except as to the concurrent authority of the President in the article of treaties, it would be difficult to determine whether that magistrate would in the aggregate possess more or less power than the governor of New York. And it appears yet more unequivocally that there is no pretence for the parallel which has been attempted between him and the king of Great Britain. But to render the contrast in this respect still more striking, it may be of use to throw the principal circumstances of dissimilitude into a closer group.

The President of the United States would be an officer elected by the people for *four* years; the king of Great Britain is a perpetual and *hereditary* prince. The one would be amenable to personal punishment and disgrace; the person of the other is sacred and inviolable. The one would have a *qualified* negative upon the acts of the legislative body; the other has an *absolute* negative. The one would have a right to command the military and naval forces of the nation; the other, in addition to this right, possesses that of *declaring* war and of *raising* and *regulating* fleets and armies by his own authority. The one would have a concurrent power with a branch of the legislature in the formation of treaties; the other is the *sole possessor* of the power of making treaties. The one would have a like concurrent authority in appointing to offices; the other is the sole author of all appointments. The one can confer no privileges whatever; the other can make denizens of aliens, noblemen of commoners, can erect corporations with all the rights incident to corporate bodies. The one can prescribe no rules concerning the commerce or currency of the nation; the other is in several respects the arbiter of commerce, and in this capacity can establish markets and fairs, can regulate weights and measures, can lay embargoes for a limited time, can coin money, can authorize or prohibit the circulation of foreign coin. The one has no particle of spiritual jurisdiction; the other is the supreme head and governor of the national church! What answer shall we give to those who would persuade us that things so unlike resemble each other? The same that ought to be given to those who tell us that a government, the whole power of which would be in the hands of the elective and periodical servants of the people, is an aristocracy, a monarchy, and a despotism.[89]   PUBLIUS

THE FEDERALIST NO. 70

(HAMILTON)

To the People of the State of New York:

There is an idea, which is not without its advocates, that a vigorous Executive is inconsistent with the genius of republican government. The enlightened well-wishers to this species of government must at least hope that the supposition is destitute of foundation, since they can never admit its truth without at the same time admitting the condemnation of their own principles. Energy in the Executive is a leading character in the definition of good government. It is essential to the protection of the community against foreign attacks; it is not less essential to the steady administration of the laws; to the protection of property against those irregular and high-handed combinations which sometimes interrupt the ordinary course of justice; to the security of liberty against the enterprises and assaults of ambition, of faction, and of anarchy. Every man the least conversant in Roman story, knows how often that republic was obliged to take refuge in the absolute power of a single man under the formidable title of Dictator —as well against the intrigues of ambitious individuals who aspired to the tyranny, and the seditions of whole classes of the community whose conduct threatened the existence of all government, as against the invasions of external enemies who menaced the conquest and destruction of Rome.

There can be no need, however, to multiply arguments or examples on this head. A feeble Executive implies a feeble execution of the government. A feeble execution is but another phrase for a bad execution; and a government ill executed, whatever it may be in theory, must be in practice a bad government.

Taking it for granted, therefore, that all men of sense will agree in the necessity of an energetic Executive, it will only remain to inquire what are the ingredients which constitute this energy? How far can they be combined with those other ingredients which constitute safety in the republican sense? And how far does this combination characterize the plan which has been reported by the convention?

The ingredients which constitute energy in the Executive are, first, unity; secondly, duration; thirdly, an adequate provision for its support; fourthly, competent powers.

The ingredients which constitute safety in the republican sense are, first, a due dependence on the people; secondly, a due responsibility.

Those politicians and statesmen who have been the most celebrated for the soundness of their principles and for the justice of their views have declared in favor of a single Executive and a numerous legislature. They have with great propriety considered energy as the most necessary qualification of the former, and have regarded this as most applicable to power in a single hand; while they have with equal propriety considered the latter as best adapted to deliberation and wisdom, and best calculated to conciliate the confidence of the people and to secure their privileges and interests.

That unity is conducive to energy will not be disputed. Decision, activity, secrecy, and despatch will generally characterize the proceedings of one man in a much more eminent degree than the proceedings of any greater number; and in proportion as the number is increased, these qualities will be diminished.

This unity may be destroyed in two ways: either by vesting the power in two or more magistrates of equal dignity and authority; or by vesting it ostensibly in one man, subject, in whole or in part, to the control and co-operation of others, in the capacity of counsellors to him. Of the first, the two Consuls of Rome may serve as an example; of the last, we shall find examples in the constitutions of several of the States. New York and New Jersey, if I recollect right, are the only States which have intrusted the executive authority wholly to single men. Both these methods of destroying the unity of the Executive have their partisans; but the votaries of an executive council are the most numerous. They are both liable, if not to equal, to similar objections, and may in most lights be examined in conjunction.

The experience of other nations will afford little instruction on this head. As far, however, as it teaches any thing, it teaches us not to be enamoured of plurality in the Executive. . . .

Wherever two or more persons are engaged in any common enterprise or pursuit, there is always danger of difference of opinion. If it be a public trust or office in which they are clothed with equal dignity and authority, there is peculiar danger of personal emulation and even animosity. From either, and especially from all these causes, the most bitter dissensions are apt to spring. Whenever these happen, they lessen the respectability, weaken the authority, and distract the plans and operations of those whom they divide. If they should unfortunately assail the supreme executive magistracy of a country, consisting of a plurality of persons, they might impede or frustrate the most important measures of the government in the most critical emergencies of the state. And what is still worse, they might split the community into the most violent and irreconcilable factions, adhering differently to the different individuals who composed the magistracy.

Men often oppose a thing, merely because they have had no agency in planning it, or because it may have been planned by those whom they dislike. But if they have been consulted and have happened to disapprove, opposition then becomes in their estimation an indispensable duty of self-love. They seem to think themselves bound in honor and by all the motives of personal infallibility, to defeat the success of what has been resolved upon contrary to their sentiments. Men of upright, benevolent tempers have too many opportunities of remarking with horror to what desperate lengths this disposition is sometimes carried, and how often the great interests of society are sacrificed to the vanity, to the conceit, and to the obstinacy of individuals, who have credit enough to make their passions and their caprices interesting to mankind. Perhaps the question now before the public may in its consequences afford melancholy proofs of the effects of this despicable frailty, or rather detestable vice, in the human character.

Upon the principles of a free government, inconveniences

from the source just mentioned must necessarily be submitted to in the formation of the legislature; but it is unnecessary, and therefore unwise, to introduce them into the constitution of the Executive. It is here too that they may be most pernicious. In the legislature promptitude of decision is oftener an evil than a benefit. The differences of opinion and the jarrings of parties in that department of the government, though they may sometimes obstruct salutary plans, yet often promote deliberation and circumspection, and serve to check excesses in the majority. When a resolution too is once taken, the opposition must be at an end. That resolution is a law, and resistance to it punishable. But no favorable circumstances palliate or atone for the disadvantages of dissension in the executive department. Here, they are pure and unmixed. There is no point at which they cease to operate. They serve to embarrass and weaken the execution of the plan or measure to which they relate, from the first step to the final conclusion of it. They constantly counteract those qualities in the Executive which are the most necessary ingredients in its composition,—vigor and expedition, and this without any counterbalancing good. In the conduct of war, in which the energy of the Executive is the bulwark of the national security, everything would be to be apprehended from its plurality.

It must be confessed that these observations apply with principal weight to the first case supposed that is, to a plurality of magistrates of equal dignity and authority, a scheme, the advocates for which are not likely to form a numerous sect; but they apply, though not with equal, yet with considerable weight to the project of a council, whose concurrence is made constitutionally necessary to the operations of the ostensible Executive. An artful cabal in that council would be able to distract and to enervate the whole system of administration. If no such cabal should exist, the mere diversity of views and opinions would alone be sufficient to tincture the exercise of the executive authority with a spirit of habitual feebleness and dilatoriness.

But one of the weightiest objections to a plurality in the Executive . . . is that it tends to conceal faults and destroy responsibility. Responsibility is of two kinds—to censure and to punishment. The first is the more important of the two, especially in an elective office. Man, in public trust, will much oftener act in such a manner as to render him unworthy of being any longer trusted, than in such a manner as to make him obnoxious to legal punishment. But the multiplication of the Executive adds to the difficulty of detection in either case. It often becomes impossible, amidst mutual accusations, to determine on whom the blame or the punishment of a pernicious measure, or series of pernicious measures, ought really to fall. It is shifted from one to another with so much dexterity and under such plausible appearances, that the public opinion is left in suspense about the real author. The circumstances which may have led to any national miscarriage of misfortune are sometimes so complicated that, where there are a number of actors who may have had different degrees and kinds of agency, though we may clearly see upon the whole that there has been mismanagement, yet it may be impracticable to pronounce to whose account the evil which may have been incurred is truly chargeable.

"I was overruled by my council. The council were so divided in their opinions that it was impossible to obtain any better resolution on the point." These and similar pretexts are constantly at hand, whether true or false. And who is there that will either take the trouble or incur the odium of a strict scrutiny into the secret springs of the transaction? Should there be found a citizen zealous enough to undertake the unpromising task, if there happen to be collusion between the parties concerned, how easy it is to clothe the circumstances with so much ambiguity as to render it uncertain what was the precise conduct of any of those parties?

In the single instance in which the governor of this State is coupled with a council—that is, in the appointment to offices, we have seen the mischiefs of it in the view now under consideration. Scandalous appointments to important offices have been made. Some cases, indeed, have been so flagrant that ALL PARTIES have agreed in the impropriety of the thing. When inquiry has been made, the blame has been laid by the governor on the members of the council, who, on their part, have charged it upon his nomination; while the people remain altogether at a loss to determine by whose influence their interests have been committed to hands so unqualified and so manifestly improper. In tenderness to individuals, I forbear to descend to particulars.

It is evident from these considerations, that the plurality of the Executive tends to deprive the people of the two greatest securities they can have for the faithful exercise of any delegated power: *first*, the restraints of public opinion, which lose their efficacy, as well on account of the division of the censure attendant on bad measures among a number, as on account of the uncertainty on whom it ought to fall; and, *secondly*, the opportunity of discovering with facility and clearness the misconduct of the persons they trust, in order either to effect their removal from office or . . . their actual punishment in cases which admit of it.

In England, the king is a perpetual magistrate; and it is a maxim which has obtained for the sake of the public peace, that he is unaccountable for his administration, and his person sacred. Nothing, therefore, can be wiser in that kingdom than to annex to the king a constitutional council who may be responsible to the nation for the advice they give. Without this, there would be no responsibility whatever in the executive department—an idea inadmissible in a free government. But even there the king is not bound by the resolutions of his council, though they are answerable for the advice they give. He is the absolute master of his own conduct in the exercise of his office, and may observe or disregard the counsel given to him at his sole discretion.

But in a republic, where every magistrate ought to be personally responsible for his behavior in office, the reason which in the British Constitution dictates the propriety of a council, not only ceases to apply, but turns against the institution. In the monarchy of Great Britain, it furnishes a substitute for the prohibited responsibility of the chief magistrate, which serves in some degree as a hostage to the national justice for his good behavior. In the American republic, it would serve to destroy or would greatly diminish, the intended and necessary responsibility of the Chief Magistrate himself.

The idea of a council to the Executive, which has so generally obtained in the State constitutions, has been derived from that maxim of republican jealousy which considers power as safer in the hands of a number of men than of a single man.

If the maxim should be admitted to be applicable to the case, I should contend that the advantage on that side would not counterbalance the numerous disadvantages on the opposite side. But I do not think the rule at all applicable to the executive power. I clearly concur in opinion . . . with a writer whom the celebrated Junius pronounces to be "deep, solid, and ingenious,"[90] that "the executive power is more easily confined when it is ONE";[91] that it is far more safe there should be a single object for the jealousy and watchfulness of the people; and, in a word, that all multiplication of the Executive is rather dangerous than friendly to liberty.

A little consideration will satisfy us that the species of security sought for in the multiplication of the Executive is unattainable. Numbers must be so great as to render combination difficult, or they are rather a source of danger than of security. The united credit and influence of several individuals must be more formidable to liberty than the credit and influence of either of them separately. When power, therefore, is placed in the hands of so small a number of men as to admit of their interests and views being easily combined in a common enterprise by an artful leader, it becomes more liable to abuse, and more dangerous when abused, than if it be lodged in the hands of one man; who, from the very circumstance of his being alone, will be more narrowly watched and more readily suspected, and who cannot unite so great a mass of influence as when he is associated with others. The Decemvirs of Rome, whose name denotes their number [10], were more to be dreaded in their usurpation than any ONE of them would have been. No person would think of proposing an Executive much more numerous than that body; from six to a dozen have been suggested for the number of the council. The extreme of these numbers is not too great for an easy combination; and from such a combination America would have more to fear than from the ambition of any single individual. A council to a magistrate, who is himself responsible for what he does, are generally nothing better than a clog upon his good intentions, are often the instruments and accomplices of his bad, and are almost always a cloak to his faults.

I forbear to dwell upon the subject of expense; though it

be evident that if the council should be numerous enough to answer the principal end aimed at by the institution, the salaries of the members, who must be drawn from their homes to reside at the seat of government, would form an item in the catalogue of public expenditures too serious to be incurred for an object of equivocal utility. I will only add that, prior to the appearance of the Constitution, I rarely met with an intelligent man from any of the States, who did not admit, as the result of experience, that the UNITY of the executive of this State was one of the best of the distinguishing features of our constitution. PUBLIUS

THE FEDERALIST NO. 71

(HAMILTON)

To the People of the State of New York:

Duration in office has been mentioned as the second requisite to the energy of the Executive authority. This has relation to two objects: to the personal firmness of the executive magistrate in the employment of his constitutional powers; and to the stability of the system of administration which may have been adopted under his auspices. With regard to the first, it must be evident that the longer the duration in office the greater will be the probability of obtaining so important an advantage. It is a general principle of human nature, that a man will be interested in whatever he possesses in proportion to the firmness or precariousness of the tenure by which he holds it; will be less attached to what he holds by a momentary or uncertain title than to what he enjoys by a durable or certain title; and, of course, will be willing to risk more for the sake of the one than for the sake of the other. This remark is not less applicable to a political privilege, or honor, or trust, than to any article of ordinary property. The inference from it is, that a man acting in the capacity of chief magistrate under a consciousness that in a very short time he *must* lay down his office, will be apt to feel himself too little interested in it to hazard any material censure or perplexity: from the independent exertion of his powers, or from encountering the ill-humors, however transient, which may happen to prevail, either in a considerable part of the society itself, or even in a predominant faction in the legislative body. If the case should only be that he *might* lay it down unless continued by a new choice, and if he should be desirous of being continued, his wishes, conspiring with his fears, would tend still more powerfully to corrupt his integrity or debase his fortitude. In either case, feebleness and irresolution must be the characteristics of the station.

There are some who would be inclined to regard the servile pliancy of the Executive to a prevailing current, either in the community or in the legislature, as its best recommendation. But such men entertain very crude notions, as well of the purposes for which government was instituted as of the true means by which the public happiness may be promoted. The republican principle demands that the deliberate sense of the community should govern the conduct of those to whom they intrust the management of their affairs; but it does not require an unqualified complaisance to every sudden breeze of passion, or to every transient impulse which the people may receive from the arts of men, who flatter their prejudices to betray their interests. It is a just observation that the people commonly *intend* the PUBLIC GOOD. This often applies to their very errors. But their good sense would despise the adulator who should pretend that they always *reason right* about the *means* of promoting it.[92] They know from experience that they sometimes err; and the wonder is that they so seldom err as they do, beset as they continually are by the wiles of parasites and sycophants, by the snares of the ambitious, the avaricious, the desperate, by the artifices of men who possess their confidence more than they deserve it, and of those who seek to possess rather than to deserve it. When occasions present themselves in which the interests of the people are at variance with their inclinations, it is the duty of the persons whom they have appointed to be the guardians of those interests, to withstand the temporary delusion in order to give them time and opportunity for more cool and sedate reflection. Instances might be cited in which a conduct of this kind has saved the people from very fatal consequences of their own mistakes, and has procured lasting monuments of their gratitude to the men who had courage and magnanimity enough to serve them at the peril of their displeasure.

But however inclined we might be to insist upon an unbounded complaisance in the Executive to the inclinations of the people, we can with no propriety contend for a like complaisance to the humors of the legislature. The latter may sometimes stand in opposition to the former, and at other times the people may be entirely neutral. In either supposition, it is certainly desirable that the Executive should be in a situation to dare to act his own opinion with vigor and decision.

The same rule which teaches the propriety of a partition between the various branches of power, teaches us likewise that this partition ought to be so contrived as to render the one independent of the other. To what purpose separate the executive or the judiciary from the legislative, if both the executive and the judiciary are so constituted as to be at the absolute devotion of the legislative? Such a separation must be merely nominal and incapable of producing the ends for which it was established. It is one thing to be subordinate to the laws and another to be dependent on the legislative body. The first comports with, the last violates, the fundamental principles of good government; and, whatever may be the forms of the Constitution, unites all power in the same hands. The tendency of the legislative authority to absorb every other has been fully displayed and illustrated by examples in some preceding numbers. In governments purely republican this tendency is almost irresistible. The representatives of the people in a popular assembly seem sometimes to fancy that they are the people themselves, and betray strong symptoms of impatience and disgust at the least sign of opposition from any other quarter; as if the exercise of its rights, by either the executive or judiciary, were a breach of their privilege and an outrage to their dignity. They often appear disposed to exert an imperious control over the other departments; and as they commonly have the people on their side, they always act with such momentum as to make it very difficult for the other members of the government to maintain the balance of the Constitution.

It may perhaps be asked how the shortness of the duration in office can affect the independence of the Executive on the legislature, unless the one were possessed of the power of appointing or displacing the other. One answer to this inquiry may be drawn from the principle already remarked—that is, from the slender interest a man is apt to take in a short-lived advantage, and the little inducement it affords him to expose himself, on account of it, to any considerable inconvenience or hazard. Another answer, perhaps more obvious though not more conclusive, will result from the consideration of the influence of the legislative body over the people; which might be employed to prevent the reëlection of a man who, by an upright resistance to any sinister project of that body, should have made himself obnoxious to its resentment.

It may be asked also whether a duration of four years would answer the end proposed; and if it would not, whether a less period, which would at least be recommended by greater security against ambitious designs, would not . . . be preferable to a longer period, which was . . . too short for the purpose of inspiring the desired firmness and independence of the magistrate.

It cannot be affirmed that a duration of four years, or any other limited duration, would completely answer the end proposed; but it would contribute towards it in a degree which would have a material influence upon the spirit and character of the government. Between the commencement and termination of such a period, there would always be a considerable interval, in which the prospect of annihilation would be sufficiently remote, not to have an improper effect upon the conduct of a man imbued with a tolerable portion of fortitude; and in which he might reasonably promise himself, that there would be time enough before it arrived, to make the community sensible of the propriety of the measures he might incline to pursue. Though it be probable that as he approached the moment when the public were by a new election to signify their sense of his conduct, his confidence, and with it his firmness, would decline; yet both the one and the other would derive support from the opportunities which his previous continuance in the station had afforded him, of establishing himself in the esteem and good-will of his constituents. He might, then, hazard with safety, in proportion to the proofs he had given of his wisdom and integrity, and to the title he had acquired to the respect and attachment of his fellow-citizens. As, on the one hand, a duration of four years will contribute to the firmness of the Executive in a sufficient degree to render it a very valuable ingredient in the composition; so, on the other, it is not enough to justify any alarm for the public liberty. If a British House of Commons, from the most feeble beginnings, *from the mere power of assenting or disagreeing to the imposition of a new tax,* have by rapid strides, reduced the prerogatives of the crown and the privileges of the nobility within the limits they conceived to be compatible with the principles of a free government, while they raised themselves to the rank and consequence of a coequal branch of the legislature; if they have been able, in one instance, to abolish both the royalty and the aristocracy, and to overturn all the ancient establishments, as well in the Church as State; . . . what would be . . . feared from an elective magistrate of four years' duration, with the confined authorities of a President of the United States? What, but that he might be unequal to the task which the Constitution assigns him? I shall only add that if his duration be such as to leave a doubt of his firmness, that doubt is inconsistent with a jealousy of his encroachments.　　　　PUBLIUS

THE FEDERALIST NO. 72

(HAMILTON)

To the People of the State of New York:
　　The administration of government in its largest sense comprehends all the operations of the body politic, whether

legislative, executive, or judiciary; but in its most usual and perhaps in its most precise signification, it is limited to executive details, and falls peculiarly within the province of the executive department. The actual conduct of foreign negotiations, the preparatory plans of finance, the application and disbursement of the public moneys in conformity to the general appropriations of the legislature, the arrangement of the army and navy, the direction of the operations of war,— these, and other matters of a like nature, constitute what seems to be most properly understood by the administration of government. The persons, therefore, to whose immediate management these different matters are committed, ought to be considered as the assistants or deputies of the chief magistrate, and on this account, they ought to derive their offices from his appointment, at least from his nomination, and ought to be subject to his superintendence. This view of the subject will at once suggest to us the intimate connection between the duration of the executive magistrate in office and the stability of the system of administration. To reverse and undo what has been done by a predecessor is very often considered by a successor as the best proof he can give of his own capacity and desert; and in addition to this propensity, where the alteration has been the result of public choice, the person substituted is warranted in supposing that the dismission of his predecessor has proceeded from a dislike to his measures; and that the less he resembles him, the more he will recommend himself to the favor of his constituents. These considerations and the influence of personal confidences and attachments would be likely to induce every new President to promote a change of men to fill the subordinate stations; and these causes together could not fail to occasion a disgraceful and ruinous mutability in the administration of the government.

With a positive duration of considerable extent, I connect the circumstance of reëligibility. The first is necessary to give to the officer himself the inclination and the resolution to act his part well, and to the community time and leisure to observe the tendency of his measures, and thence to form an experimental estimate of their merits. The last is necessary to enable the people, when they see reason to approve of his conduct, to continue him in his station in order to prolong the utility of his talents and virtues, and to secure to the government the advantage of permanency in a wise system of administration.

Nothing appears more plausible at first sight, nor more ill-founded upon close inspection than a scheme which in relation to the present point has had some respectable advocates, —I mean that of continuing the chief magistrate in office for a certain time, and then excluding him from it, either for a limited period or forever after. This exclusion, whether temporary or perpetual, would have nearly the same effects, and these effects would be for the most part rather pernicious than salutary.[93]

One ill effect of the exclusion would be a diminution of the inducements to good behavior. There are few men who would not feel much less zeal in the discharge of a duty, when they were conscious that the advantages of the station with which it was connected must be relinquished at a determinate period, than when they were permitted to entertain a hope of *obtaining*, by *meriting*, a continuance of them. This position will not be disputed so long as it is admitted that the desire of reward is one of the strongest incentives of human conduct; or that the best security for the fidelity of mankind is to make their interest coincide with their duty. Even the love of fame, the ruling passion of the noblest minds . . . would, on the contrary, deter him from the undertaking, when he foresaw that he must quit the scene before he could accomplish the work, and must commit that, together with his own reputation, to hands which might be unequal or unfriendly to the task. The most to be expected from the generality of men, in such a situation, is the negative merit of not doing harm, instead of the positive merit of doing good.

Another ill effect of the exclusion would be the temptation to sordid views, to peculation, and, in some instances, to usurpation. An avaricious man . . . looking forward to a time when he must at all events yield up the emoluments he enjoyed, would feel a propensity . . . to make the best use of the opportunity he enjoyed while it lasted, and might not scruple to have recourse to the most corrupt expedients to make the harvest as abundant as it was transitory; though the same man . . . with a different prospect before him might content himself with the regular perquisites of his situation, and might even be unwilling to risk the consequences of an abuse of his opportunities. His avarice might be a guard upon his avarice. Add to this that the same man might be vain or ambitious as well as avaricious. And if he could expect to prolong his honors by his good conduct, he might hesitate to sacrifice his appetite for them to his appetite for gain. But with the prospect before him of approaching an inevitable annihilation, his avarice would be likely to get the victory over his caution, his vanity, or his ambition.

An ambitious man, too, when he found himself seated on the summit of his country's honors, when he looked forward to the time at which he must descend from the exalted eminence for ever, and reflected that no exertion of merit on his part could save him from the unwelcome reverse; such a man in such a situation would be much more violently tempted to embrace a favorable conjuncture for attempting the prolongation of his power, at every personal hazard, than if he had the probability of answering the same end by doing his duty.

Would it promote the peace of the community or the stability of the government to have half a dozen men who had had credit enough to be raised to the seat of the supreme magistracy, wandering among the people like discontented ghosts, and sighing for a place which they were destined never more to possess?

A third ill effect of the exclusion would be the depriving the community of the advantage of the experience gained by the chief magistrate in the exercise of his office. That experience is the parent of wisdom is an adage the truth of which is recognized by the wisest as well as the simplest of mankind. What more desirable or more essential than this quality in the governors of nations? Where more desirable or more essential than in the first magistrate of a nation? Can it be wise to put this desirable and essential quality under the ban of the Constitution, and to declare that the moment it is acquired, its possessor shall be compelled to abandon the station in which it was acquired, and to which it is adapted? This, nevertheless, is the precise import of all those regulations which exclude men from serving their country, by the choice of their fellow-citizens, after they have by a course of service fitted themselves for doing it with a greater degree of utility.

A fourth ill effect of the exclusion would be the banishing men from stations in which, in certain emergencies of the state, their presence might be of the greatest moment to the public interest or safety. There is no nation which has not at one period or another experienced an absolute necessity of the services of particular men in particular situations; perhaps it would not be too strong to say, to the preservation of its political existence. How unwise, therefore, must be every such self-denying ordinance as serves to prohibit a nation from making use of its own citizens in the manner best suited to its exigencies and circumstances! Without supposing the personal essentiality of the man, it is evident that a change of the chief magistrate, at the breaking out of a war or at any similar crisis, for another, even of equal merit, would at all times be detrimental to the community inasmuch as it would substitute inexperience to experience, and would tend to unhinge and set afloat the already settled train of the administration.

A fifth ill effect of the exclusion would be, that it would operate as a constitutional interdiction of stability in the administration. By *necessitating* a change of men in the first office of the nation, it would necessitate a mutability of measures. It is not generally to be expected that men will vary and measures remain uniform. The contrary is the usual course of things. And we need not be apprehensive that there will be too much stability while there is even the option of changing; nor need we desire to prohibit the people from continuing their confidence where they think it may be safely placed, and where, by constancy on their part, they may obviate the fatal inconveniences of fluctuating councils and a variable policy.

These are some of the disadvantages which would flow from the principle of exclusion. They apply most forcibly to the scheme of a perpetual exclusion; but when we consider that even a partial exclusion would always render the readmission of the person a remote and precarious object, the observations which have been made will apply nearly as fully to one case as to the other.

What are the advantages promised to counterbalance these disadvantages? They are represented to be: 1st, greater independence in the magistrate; 2d, greater security to the people. Unless the exclusion be perpetual, there will be no pretence to infer the first advantage. But even in that case, may he have no object beyond his present station to which he may sacrifice his independence? May he have no connections, no friends, for whom he may sacrifice it? May he not be less willing, by a firm conduct, to make personal enemies, when he acts under the impression that a time is fast approaching, on the arrival of which he not only MAY, but MUST, be exposed to their resentments, upon an equal, perhaps upon an inferior, footing? It is not an easy point to determine whether his independence would be most promoted or impaired by such an arrangement.

As to the second supposed advantage, there is still greater reason to entertain doubts concerning it. If the exclusion were to be perpetual, a man of irregular ambition, of whom alone there could be reason in any case to entertain apprehension, would with infinite reluctance yield to the necessity of taking his leave forever of a post in which his passion for power and preëminence had acquired the force of habit. And if he had been fortunate or adroit enough to conciliate the good will of the people, he might induce them to consider as a very odious and unjustifiable restraint upon themselves, a provision which was calculated to debar them of the right of giving a fresh proof of their attachment to a favorite. There may be conceived circumstances in which this disgust of the people, seconding the thwarted ambition of such a favorite, might occasion greater danger to liberty, than could ever reasonably be dreaded from the possibility of a perpetuation in office, by the voluntary suffrages of the community, exercising a constitutional privilege.

There is an excess of refinement in the idea of disabling the people to continue in office men who had entitled themselves, in their opinion, to approbation and confidence; the advantages of which are at best speculative and equivocal, and are overbalanced by disadvantages far more certain and decisive. PUBLIUS

THE FEDERALIST NO. 73

(HAMILTON)

To the People of the State of New York:

The third ingredient towards constituting the vigor of the executive authority is an adequate provision for its support. It is evident that, without proper attention to this article, the separation of the executive from the legislative department would be merely nominal and nugatory. The legislature, with a discretionary power over the salary and emoluments of the Chief Magistrate, could render him as obsequious to their will as they might think proper to make him. They might . . . either reduce him by famine or tempt him by largesses, to surrender at discretion his judgment to their inclinations. These expressions, taken in all the latitude of the terms, would no doubt convey more than is intended. There are men who could neither be distressed nor won into a sacrifice of their duty; but this stern virtue is the growth of few soils; and in the main it will be found that a power over a man's support is a power over his will. If it were necessary to confirm so plain a truth by facts, examples would not be wanting, even in this country, of the intimidation or seduction of the Executive by the terrors or allurements of the pecuniary arrangements of the legislative body.

It is not easy, therefore, to commend too highly the judicious attention which has been paid to this subject in the proposed Constitution. It is there provided that "The President . . . shall, at stated times, receive for his services a compensation *which shall neither be increased nor diminished during the period for which he shall have been elected;* and he *shall not receive within that period any other emolument* from the United States, or any of them" [*sic*].[94] It is impossible to imagine any provision which would have been more eligible than this. The legislature, on the appointment of a President, is once for all to declare what shall be the compensation for his services during the time for which he shall have been elected. This done, they will have no power to alter it, either by increase or diminution, till a new period of service by a new election commences. They can neither weaken his fortitude by operating on his necessities nor corrupt his integrity by appealing to his avarice. Neither the Union nor any of its members will be at liberty to give, nor will he be at liberty to receive, any other emolument than that which may have been determined by the first act. He can, of course, have no pecuniary inducement to renounce or desert the independence intended for him by the Constitution.

The last of the requisites to energy, which have been enumerated, are competent powers. Let us proceed to consider those which are proposed to be vested in the President of the United States.

The first thing that offers itself to our observation is the qualified negative of the President upon the acts or resolutions of the two houses of the legislature; or, in other words, his power of returning all bills with objections, to have the effect of preventing their becoming laws, unless they should afterwards be ratified by two thirds of each of the component members of the legislative body.

The propensity of the legislative department to intrude upon the rights, and to absorb the powers, of the other departments, has been already suggested and repeated; the insufficiency of a mere parchment delineation of the boundaries of each, has also been remarked upon [*No. 48*]; and the necessity of furnishing each with constitutional arms for its own defence, has been inferred and proved. From these clear and indubitable principles results the propriety of a negative, either absolute or qualified, in the Executive, upon the acts of the legislative branches. Without the one or the other the former would be absolutely unable to defend himself against the depredations of the latter. He might gradually be stripped of his authorities by successive resolutions or annihilated by a single vote. And in the one mode or the other the legislative and executive powers might speedily come to be blended in the same hands. If even no propensity had ever discovered itself in the legislative body to invade the rights of the Executive, the rules of just reasoning and theoretic propriety would of themselves teach us that the one ought not to be left to the mercy of the other, but ought to possess a constitutional and effectual power of self-defence.[95]

But the power in question has a further use. It not only serves as a shield to the Executive, but it furnishes an additional security against the enaction of improper laws. It establishes a salutary check upon the legislative body, calculated to guard the community against the effects of faction, precipitancy, or of any impulse unfriendly to the public good, which may happen to influence a majority of that body.

The propriety of a negative has, upon some occasions, been combated by an observation that it was not to be presumed a single man would possess more virtue and wisdom than a number of men; and that unless this presumption should be entertained, it would be improper to give the executive magistrate any species of control over the legislative body.

But this observation, when examined, will appear rather specious than solid. The propriety of the thing does not turn upon the supposition of superior wisdom or virtue in the Executive, but upon the supposition that the legislature will not be infallible; that the love of power may sometimes betray it into a disposition to encroach upon the rights of other members of the government; that a spirit of faction may sometimes pervert its deliberations; that impressions of the moment may sometimes hurry it into measures which itself, on maturer reflection, would condemn. The primary inducement to conferring the power in question upon the Executive is to enable him to defend himself; the secondary one is to increase the chances in favor of the community against the passing of bad laws, through haste, inadvertence, or design. The oftener the measure is brought under examination, the greater the diversity in the situations of those who are to examine it, the less must be the danger of those errors which flow from want of due deliberation, or of those missteps which proceed from the contagion of some common passion or interest. It is far less probable that culpable views of any kind should infect all the parts of the government at the same moment and in relation to the same object, than that they should by turns govern and mislead every one of them.

It may perhaps be said that the power of preventing bad laws includes that of preventing good ones, and may be used to the one purpose as well as to the other. But this objection will have little weight with those who can properly estimate the mischiefs of that inconstancy and mutability in the laws, which form the greatest blemish in the character and genius of our governments. They will consider every institution calculated to restrain the excess of law-making, and to keep things in the same state in which they happen to be at any given period, as much more likely to do good than harm; because it is favorable to greater stability in the system of legislation. The injury which may possibly be done by defeating a few good laws, will be amply compensated by the advantage of preventing a number of bad ones.

Nor is this all. The superior weight and influence of the legislative body in a free government, and the hazard to the Executive in a trial of strength with that body, afford a satisfactory security that the negative would generally be employed with great caution; and there would oftener be room for a charge of timidity than of rashness in the exercise of it. A king of Great Britain, with all his train of sovereign attributes and with all the influence he draws from a thousand sources, would, at this day, hesitate to put a negative upon the joint resolutions of the two houses of Parliament. . . .

If a magistrate so powerful and so well fortified as a British monarch would have scruples about the exercise of the power under consideration, how much greater caution may be reasonably expected in a President of the United States, clothed for the short period of four years with the executive authority of a government wholly and purely republican?

It is evident that there would be greater danger of his not using his power when necessary than of his using it too often, or too much. An argument, indeed, against its expediency has been drawn from this very source. It has been represented . . . as a power odious in appearance, useless in practice. But it will not follow, that because it might be rarely exercised, it would never be exercised. In the case for which it is chiefly designed, that of an immediate attack upon the constitutional rights of the Executive or in a case in which the public good was evidently and palpably sacrificed, a man of tolerable firmness would avail himself of his constitutional means of defence, and would listen to the admonitions of duty and responsibility. In the former supposition, his fortitude would be stimulated by his immediate interest in the power of his office; in the latter, by the probability of the sanction of his constituents, who, though they would naturally incline to the legislative body in a doubtful case, would hardly suffer their partiality to delude them in a very plain case. I speak now with an eye to a magistrate possessing only a common share of firmness. There are men who, under any circumstances, will have the courage to do their duty at every hazard.

But the convention have pursued a mean in this business, which will both facilitate the exercise of the power vested in this respect in the executive magistrate, and make its efficacy to depend on the sense of a considerable part of the legislative body. Instead of an absolute negative, it is proposed to give the Executive the qualified negative already described. This is a power which would be much more readily exercised than the other. A man who might be afraid to defeat a law by his single VETO, might not scruple to return it for reconsideration; subject to being finally rejected only in the event of more than one third of each house concurring in the sufficiency of his objections. He would be encouraged by the reflection, that if his opposition should prevail, it would embark in it a very respectable proportion of the legislative body, whose influence would be united with his in supporting the propriety of his conduct in the public opinion. A direct and categorical negative has something in the appearance of it more harsh, and more apt to irritate, than the mere suggestion of argumentative objections to be approved or disapproved by those to whom they are addressed. In proportion as it would be less apt to offend, it would be more apt to be exercised; and for this very reason, it may in practice be found more effectual. It is to be hoped that it will not often happen that improper views will govern so large a proportion as two thirds of both branches of the legislature at the same time; and this, too, in spite of the counterposing weight of the Executive. It is at any rate far less probable that this should be the case, than that such views should taint the resolutions and conduct of a bare majority. A power of this nature in the Executive will often have a silent and unperceived, though forcible, operation. When men engaged in unjustifiable pursuits are aware that obstructions may come from a quarter which they cannot control, they will often be restrained by the bare apprehension of opposition, from doing what they would with eagerness rush into, if no such external impediments were to be feared.

This qualified negative . . . is in this State vested in a council, consisting of the governor, with the chancellor and judges of the Supreme Court, or any two of them. It has been freely employed upon a variety of occasions, and frequently with success. And its utility has become so apparent, that persons who, in compiling the Constitution, were violent opposers of it, have from experience become its declared admirers.[96]

I have in another place remarked, that the convention, in the formation of this part of their plan, had departed from the model of the constitution of this State, in favor of that of Massachusetts [*No. 69*]. Two strong reasons may be imagined for this preference. One is that the judges, who are to be the interpreters of the law, might receive an improper bias, from having given a previous opinion in their revisionary capacities; the other is that by being often associated with the Executive, they might be induced to embark too far in the political views of that magistrate, and thus a dangerous combination might by degrees be cemented between the executive and judiciary departments. It is impossible to keep the judges too distinct from every other avocation than that of expounding the laws. It is peculiarly dangerous to place them in a situation to be either corrupted or influenced by the Executive.

PUBLIUS

THE FEDERALIST NO. 75

(HAMILTON)

To the People of the State of New York:

The President is to have power, "by and with the advice and consent of the Senate, to make treaties, provided two thirds of the senators present concur."

Though this provision has been assailed, on different grounds, with no small degree of vehemence, I scruple not to declare my firm persuasion, that it is one of the best digested and most unexceptionable parts of the plan. One ground of objection is the trite topic of the intermixture of powers: some contending that the President ought alone to possess the power of making treaties; others, that it ought to have been exclusively deposited in the Senate. Another source of objection is derived from the small number of persons by whom a treaty may be made. Of those who espouse this objection, a part are of opinion that the House of Representatives ought to have been associated in the business, while another part seem to think that nothing more was necessary than to have substituted two thirds of *all* the members of the Senate, to two thirds of the members *present*. As I flatter myself the observations made in a preceding number [*No. 64*] upon this part of the plan must have sufficed to place it, to a discerning eye, in a very favorable light, I shall here content myself with offering only some supplementary remarks, principally with a view to the objections which have been just stated.

With regard to the intermixture of powers, I shall rely upon the explanations already given in other places [*Nos. 47–51*] of the true sense of the rule upon which that objection is founded; and shall take it for granted, as an inference from them, that the union of the Executive with the Senate, in the article of treaties is no infringement of that rule. I venture to add, that the particular nature of the power of making treaties indicates a peculiar propriety in that union. Though several writers on the subject of government place that power in the class of executive authorities, yet this is evidently an arbitrary disposition; for if we attend carefully to its operation, it will be found to partake more of the legislative than of the executive character, though it does not seem strictly to fall within the definition of either of them. The essence of the legislative authority is to enact laws, or, in other words, to prescribe rules for the regulation of the society; while the execution of the laws, and the employment of the common strength, either for this purpose or for the common defence, seem to comprise all the functions of the executive magistrate. The power of making treaties is, plainly, neither the one nor the other. It relates neither to the execution of the subsisting laws nor to the enaction of new ones; and still less to an exertion of the common strength. Its objects are CONTRACTS with foreign nations, which have the force of law but derive it from the obligations of good faith. They are not rules prescribed by the sovereign to the subject, but agreements between sovereign and sovereign. The power in question seems therefore to form a distinct department, and to belong, properly, neither to the legislative nor to the executive. The qualities elsewhere detailed as indispensable in the management of foreign negotiations, point out the Executive as the most fit agent in those transactions; while the vast importance of the trust, and the operation of treaties as laws, plead strongly for the participation of the whole or a portion of the legislative body in the office of making them.

However proper or safe it may be in governments where the executive magistrate is an hereditary monarch, to commit to him the entire power of making treaties, it would be utterly unsafe and improper to intrust that power to an elective magistrate of four years' duration. . . . An hereditary monarch, though often the oppressor of his people, has personally too much stake in the government to be in any material danger of being corrupted by foreign powers. But a man raised from the station of a private citizen to the rank of chief magistrate, possessed of a moderate or slender fortune, and looking forward to a period not very remote when he may probably be obliged to return to the station from which he was taken, might sometimes be under temptations to sacrifice his duty to his interest, which it would require superlative virtue to withstand. An avaricious man might be tempted to betray the interests of the state to the acquisition of wealth. An ambitious man might make his own aggrandizement, by the aid of a foreign power, the price of his treachery to his constituents. The history of human conduct does not warrant that exalted opinion of human virtue which would make it wise in a nation to commit interests of so delicate and momentous a kind, as those which concern its intercourse with the rest of the world, to the sole disposal of a magistrate created and circumstanced as would be a President of the United States.

To have intrusted the power of making treaties to the Senate alone, would have been to relinquish the benefits of the constitutional agency of the President in the conduct of foreign negotiations. It is true that the Senate would, in that case, have the option of employing him in this capacity, but they would also have the option of letting it alone, and pique or cabal might induce the latter rather than the former. Besides this, the ministerial servant of the Senate could not be expected to enjoy the confidence and respect of foreign powers in the same degree with the constitutional representatives of the nation, and, of course, would not be able to act with an equal degree of weight or efficacy. While the Union would, from this cause, lose a considerable advantage in the management of its external concerns, the people would lose the additional security which would result from the coöperation of the Executive. Though it would be imprudent to confide in him solely so important a trust, yet it cannot be doubted that his participation would materially add to the safety of the society. It must indeed be clear to a demonstration that the joint possession of the power in question, by the President and Senate, would afford a greater prospect of security than the separate possession of it by either of them. And whoever has maturely weighed the circumstances which must concur in the appointment of a President, will be satisfied that the office will always bid fair to be filled by men of such characters as to render their concurrence in the formation of treaties peculiarly desirable, as well on the score of wisdom as on that of integrity.

The remarks made in a former number [64] . . . will apply with conclusive force against the admission of the House of Representatives to a share in the formation of treaties. The fluctuating and . . . multitudinous composition of that body forbid us to expect in it those qualities which are essential to the proper execution of such a trust. Accurate and comprehensive knowledge of foreign politics; a steady and systematic adherence to the same views; a nice and uniform sensibility to national character; decision, *secrecy*, and despatch, are incompatible with the genius of a body so variable and so numerous. The very complication of the business, by introducing a necessity of the concurrence of so many different bodies, would of itself afford a solid objection. The greater frequency of the calls upon the House of Representatives and the greater length of time which it would often be necessary to keep them together when convened, to obtain their sanction in the progressive stages of a treaty, would be a source of so great inconvenience and expense as alone ought to condemn the project.

The only objection which remains to be canvassed is that which would substitute the proportion of two thirds of all the members composing the senatorial body, to that of two thirds of the members *present*. It has been shown . . . that all provisions which require more than the majority of any body to its resolutions have a direct tendency to embarrass the operations of the government, and an indirect one to subject the sense of the majority to that of the minority. This consideration seems sufficient to determine our opinion, that the convention have gone as far in the endeavor to secure the advantage of numbers in the formation of treaties as could have been reconciled either with the activity of the public councils or with a reasonable regard to the major sense of the community. If two thirds of the whole number of members had been required, it would, in many cases, from the non-attendance of a part, amount in practice to a necessity of unanimity. And the history of every political establishment in which this principle has prevailed, is a history of impotence, perplexity, and disorder. Proofs of this position might be adduced from the examples of the Roman Tribuneship, the Polish Diet, and the States-General of the Netherlands, did not an example at home render foreign precedents, unnecessary.

To require a fixed proportion of the whole body would not, in all probability, contribute to the advantages of a numerous agency, better than merely to require a proportion of the attending members. The former, by making a determinate number at all times requisite to a resolution, diminishes the motives to punctual attendance. The latter, by making the capacity of the body to depend on a *proportion* which may be varied by the absence or presence of a single member, has the contrary effect. And as, by promoting punctuality, it tends to keep the body complete, there is great likelihood that its resolutions would generally be dictated by as great a number in this case as in the other; while there would be much fewer occasions of delay. It ought not to be forgotten that under the existing Confederation, two members *may,* and usually *do,* represent a State; whence it happens that Congress, who now are solely invested with *all the powers* of the Union, rarely consist of a greater number of persons than would compose the intended Senate. If we add to this, that as the members vote by States and that where there is only a single member present from a State, his vote is lost, it will justify a supposition that the active voices in the Senate, where the members are to vote individually, would rarely fall short in number of the active voices in the existing Congress. When, in addition to these considerations, we take into view the coöperation of the President, we shall not hesitate to infer that the people of America would have greater security against an improper use of the power of making treaties under the new Constitution, than they now enjoy under the Confederation. And when we proceed still one step further, and look forward to the probable augmentation of the Senate by the erection of new States, we shall not only perceive ample ground of confidence in the sufficiency of the members to whose agency that power will be intrusted, but we shall probably be led to conclude that a body more numerous than the Senate would be likely to become, would be very little fit for the proper discharge of the trust. PUBLIUS

THE FEDERALIST NO. 78

(HAMILTON)

To the People of the State of New York:

We proceed now to an examination of the judiciary department of the proposed government.

In unfolding the defects of the existing Confederation, the utility and necessity of a federal judicature have been clearly pointed out. It is the less necessary to recapitulate the considerations there urged, as the propriety of the institution in the abstract is not disputed; the only questions which have been raised being relative to the manner of constituting it, and to its extent. To these points, therefore, our observations shall be confined.

The manner of constituting it seems to embrace these several objects: 1st. The mode of appointing the judges. 2d. The tenure by which they are to hold their places. 3d. The partition of the judiciary authority between different courts, and their relations to each other.

First. As to the mode of appointing the judges; this is the same with that of appointing the officers of the Union in general, and has been so fully discussed in the two last numbers, that nothing can be said here which would not be useless repetition.

Second. As to the tenure by which the judges are to hold their places: this chiefly concerns their duration in office; the provisions for their support; the precautions for their responsibility.

According to the plan of the convention, all judges who may be appointed by the United States are to hold their offices *during good behavior;* which is conformable to the most approved of the State constitutions, and among the rest, to that of this State. Its propriety having been drawn into question by the adversaries of that plan, is no light symptom of the rage for objection, which disorders their imaginations and judgments. The standard of good behavior for the continuance in office of the judicial magistracy is certainly one of the most valuable of the modern improvements in the practice of government. In a monarchy it is an excellent barrier to the despotism of the prince; in a republic it is a no less excellent barrier to the encroachments and oppressions of the representative body. And it is the best expedient which can be devised in any government to secure a steady, upright, and impartial administration of the laws.

Whoever attentively considers the different departments of power must perceive, that, in a government in which they are separated from each other, the judiciary, from the nature of its functions, will always be the least dangerous to the political rights of the Constitution; because it will be least in a capacity to annoy or injure them. The Executive not only dispenses the honors, but holds the sword of the community. The legislature not only commands the purse, but prescribes the rules by which the duties and rights of every citizen are to be regulated. The judiciary, on the contrary, has no influence over either the sword or the purse;[97] no direction either of the strength or of the wealth of the society; and can take no active resolution whatever. It may truly be said to have neither FORCE nor WILL, but merely judgment; and must ultimately depend upon the aid of the executive arm even for the efficacy of its judgments.

This simple view of the matter suggests several important consequences. It proves incontestably that the judiciary is beyond comparison the weakest of the three departments of power [*sic*];[98] that it can never attack with success either of the other two; and that all possible care is requisite to enable it to defend itself against their attacks. It equally proves that though individual oppression may now and then proceed from the courts of justice, the general liberty of the people can never be endangered from that quarter; I mean so long as the judiciary remains truly distinct from both the legislature and the Executive. For I agree, that "there is no liberty, if the power of judging be not separated from the legislative and executive powers."[99] And it proves, in the last place, that as liberty can have nothing to fear from the judiciary alone, but would have every thing to fear from its union with either of the other departments; that as all the effects of such a union must ensue from a dependence of the former on the latter, notwithstanding a nominal and apparent separation; that as, from the natural feebleness of the judiciary it is in continual jeopardy of being overpowered, awed, or influenced by its coördinate branches; and that as nothing can contribute so much to its firmness and independence as permanency in office, this quality may therefore be justly regarded as an indispensable ingredient in its constitution, and, in a great measure, as the citadel of the public justice and the public security.

The complete independence of the courts of justice is peculiarly essential in a limited Constitution. By a limited Constitution, I understand one which contains certain specified exceptions to the legislative authority; such, for instance, as that it shall pass no bills of attainder, no *ex-post-facto* laws, and the like. Limitations of this kind can be preserved in practice no other way than through the medium of courts of justice, whose duty it must be to declare all acts contrary to the manifest tenor of the Constitution void. Without this, all the reservations of particular rights or privileges would amount to nothing.

Some perplexity respecting the rights of the courts to pronounce legislative acts void, because contrary to the constitution, has arisen from an imagination that the doctrine would imply a superiority of the judiciary to the legislative power. It is urged that the authority which can declare the acts of another void must necessarily be superior to the one whose acts may be declared void. As this doctrine is of great importance in all the American constitutions, a brief discussion of the ground on which it rests cannot be unacceptable.[100]

There is no position which depends on clearer principles than that every act of a delegated authority, contrary to the tenor of the commission under which it is exercised, is void. No legislative act, therefore, contrary to the Constitution, can be valid. To deny this would be to affirm that the deputy is greater than his principal; that the servant is above his master; that the representatives of the people are superior to the people themselves; that men acting by virtue of powers may do not only what their powers do not authorize, but what they forbid.

If it be said that the legislative body are themselves the constitutional judges of their own powers, and that the construction they put upon them is conclusive upon the other departments, it may be answered that this cannot be the natural presumption where it is not to be collected from any particular provisions in the Constitution. It is not otherwise to be supposed that the Constitution could intend to enable the representatives of the people to substitute their *will* to that of their constituents. It is far more rational to suppose that the courts were designed to be an intermediate body between the people and the legislature, in order, among other things, to keep the latter within the limits assigned to their authority. The interpretation of the laws is the proper and peculiar province of the courts. A constitution is, in fact, and must be regarded by the judges, as a fundamental law. It therefore belongs to them to ascertain its meaning, as well as the meaning of any particular act proceeding from the legislative body. If there should happen to be an irreconcilable variance between the two, that which has the superior obligation and validity ought, of course, to be preferred; or, in other words, the Constitution ought to be preferred to the statute, the intention of the people to the intention of their agents.[101]

Nor does this conclusion by any means suppose a superiority of the judicial to the legislative power. It only supposes that the power of the people is superior to both; and that where the will of the legislature, declared in its statutes, stands in opposition to that of the people, declared in the Constitution, the judges ought to be governed by the latter rather than the former. They ought to regulate their decisions by the fundamental laws, rather than by those which are not fundamental.

This exercise of judicial discretion, in determining between two contradictory laws, is exemplified in a familiar instance. It not uncommonly happens that there are two statutes existing at one time, clashing in whole or in part with each other, and neither of them containing any repealing clause or expression. In such a case, it is the province of the courts to liquidate and fix their meaning and operation. So far as they can, by any fair construction, be reconciled to each other, reason and law conspire to dictate that this should be done; where this is impracticable, it becomes a matter of necessity to give effect to one in exclusion of the other. The rule which has obtained in the courts for determining their relative validity is, that the last in order of time shall be preferred to the first. But this is a mere rule of construction, not derived from any positive law but from the nature and reason of the thing. It is a rule not enjoined upon the courts by legislative provision but adopted by themselves, as consonant to truth and propriety for the direction of their conduct as interpreters of the law. They thought it reasonable, that between the interfering acts of an *equal* authority, that which was the last indication of its will should have the preference.

But in regard to the interfering acts of a superior and subordinate authority, of an original and derivative power, the nature and reason of the thing indicate the converse of that rule as proper to be followed. They teach us that the prior act of a superior ought to be preferred to the subsequent act of an inferior and subordinate authority; and that accordingly, whenever a particular statute contravenes the Constitution, it will be the duty of the judicial tribunals to adhere to the latter and disregard the former.

It can be of no weight to say that the courts, on the pretence of a repugnancy, may substitute their own pleasure to the constitutional intentions of the legislature. This might as well happen in the case of two contradictory statutes; or it might as well happen in every adjudication upon any single statute. The courts must declare the sense of the law; and if they should be disposed to exercise WILL instead of JUDGMENT, the consequence would equally be the substitution of their pleasure to that of the legislative body. The observation, if it prove any thing, would prove that there ought to be no judges distinct from that body.

If, then, the courts of justice are to be considered as the bulwarks of a limited Constitution against legislative encroachments, this consideration will afford a strong argument for the permanent tenure of judicial offices, since nothing will contribute so much as this to that independent spirit in the judges which must be essential to the faithful performance of so arduous a duty.

This independence of the judges is equally requisite to guard the Constitution and the rights of individuals from the effects of those ill humors, which the arts of designing men or the influence of particular conjunctures sometimes disseminate among the people themselves; and which, though they speedily give place to better information and more deliberate reflection, have a tendency, in the meantime, to occasion dangerous innovations in the government, and serious oppressions of the minor party in the community. Though I trust the friends of the proposed Constitution will never concur with its enemies[102] in questioning that fundamental principle of republican government, which admits the right of the people to alter or abolish the established Constitution whenever they find it inconsistent with their happiness; yet it is not to be inferred from this principle that the representatives of the people, whenever a momentary inclination happens to lay hold of a majority of their constituents, incompatible with the provisions in the existing Constitution, would, on that account, be justifiable in a violation of those provisions; or that the courts would be under a greater obligation to connive at infractions in this shape, than when they had proceeded wholly from the cabals of the representative body. Until the people have by some solemn and authoritative act annulled or changed the established form, it is binding upon themselves collectively, as well as individually; and no presumption, or even knowledge, of their sentiments, can warrant their representatives in a departure from it, prior to such an act. But it is easy to see that it would require an uncommon portion of fortitude in the judges to do their duty as faithful guardians of the Constitution, where legislative invasions of it had been instigated by the major voice of the community.

But it is not with a view to infractions of the Constitution only that the independence of the judges may be an essential safeguard against the effects of occasional ill humors in the society. These sometimes extend no farther than to the injury of the private rights of particular classes of citizens by unjust and partial laws. Here also the firmness of the judicial magistracy is of vast importance in mitigating the severity and confining the operation of such laws. It not only serves to moderate the immediate mischiefs of those which may have been passed, but it operates as a check upon the legislative body in passing them; who, perceiving that obstacles to the success of iniquitous intention are to be expected from the scruples of the courts, are in a manner compelled by the very motives of the injustice they meditate to qualify their attempts. This is a circumstance calculated to have more influence upon the character of our governments, than but few may be aware of. The benefits of the integrity and moderation of the judiciary have already been felt in more States than one; and though they may have displeased those whose sinister expectations they may have disappointed, they must have commanded the esteem and applause of all the virtuous and disinterested. Considerate men of every description ought to prize whatever will tend to beget or fortify that temper in the courts; as no man can be sure that he may not be tomorrow the victim of a spirit of injustice by which he may be a gainer today. And every man must now feel that the inevitable tendency of such a spirit is to sap the foundations of public and private confidence, and to introduce in its stead universal distrust and distress.

That inflexible and uniform adherence to the rights of the Constitution and of individuals, which we perceive to be indispensable in the courts of justice, can certainly not be expected from judges who hold their offices by a temporary commission. Periodical appointments, however regulated or by whomsoever made, would, in some way or other, be fatal to their necessary independence. If the power of making them was committed either to the Executive or legislature, there would be danger of an improper complaisance to the branch which possessed it; if to both, there would be an unwillingness to hazard the displeasure of either; if to the people or to persons chosen by them for the special purpose, there would be too great a disposition to consult popularity, to justify a reliance that nothing would be consulted but the Constitution and the laws.

There is yet a further and a weightier reason for the permanency of the judicial offices, which is deducible from the nature of the qualifications they require. It has been frequently remarked, with great propriety, that a voluminous code of laws is one of the inconveniences necessarily connected with the advantages of a free government. To avoid an arbitrary discretion in the courts, it is indispensable that they should be bound down by strict rules and precedents, which serve to define and point out their duty in every particular case that comes before them; and it will readily be conceived from the variety of controversies which grow out of the folly and wickedness of mankind, that the records of those precedents must unavoidably swell to a very considerable bulk, and must demand long and laborious study to acquire a competent knowledge of them. Hence it is, that there can be but few men in the society who will have sufficient skill in the laws to qualify them for the stations of judges. And making the proper deductions for the ordinary depravity of human nature, the number must be still smaller of those who unite the requisite integrity with the requisite knowledge. These considerations apprise us that the government can have no great option between fit character; and that a temporary duration in office, which would naturally discourage such characters from quitting a lucrative line of practice to accept a seat on the bench, would have a tendency to throw the administration of justice into hands less able, and less well qualified, to conduct it with utility and dignity. In the present circumstances of this country and in those in which it is likely to be for a long time to come, the disadvantages on this score would be greater than they may at first sight appear; but it must be confessed that they are far inferior to those which present themselves under the other aspects of the subject.

Upon the whole, there can be no room to doubt that the convention acted wisely in copying from the models of those constitutions which have established *good behavior* as the tenure of their judicial offices, in point of duration; and that so far from being blamable on this account, their plan would have been inexcusably defective if it had wanted this important feature of good government. The experience of Great Britain affords an illustrious comment on the excellence of the institution. PUBLIUS

THE FEDERALIST NO. 79

(HAMILTON)

To the People of the State of New York:
Next to permanency in office, nothing can contribute more to the independence of the judges than a fixed provision for their support. The remark made in relation to the President is equally applicable here. In the general course of human nature, *a power over a man's subsistence amounts to a power over his will.* And we can never hope to see realized in practice the complete separation of the judicial from the legislative power in any system which leaves the former dependent for pecuniary resources on the occasional grants of the latter. . . . The plan of the convention accordingly has provided that the judges of the United States "shall at *stated times* receive for their services a compensation which shall not be *diminished* during their continuance in office. . . ."[103]

This provision for the support of the judges bears every mark of prudence and efficacy; and it may be safely affirmed that, together with the permanent tenure of their offices, it affords a better prospect of their independence than is discoverable in the constitutions of any of the States in regard to their own judges.

The precautions for their responsibility are comprised in the article respecting impeachments. They are liable to be impeached for malconduct by the House of Representatives and tried by the Senate; and, if convicted, may be dismissed from office, and disqualified for holding any other. This is the only provision on the point which is consistent with the necessary independence of the judicial character, and is the only one which we find in our own Constitution in respect to our own judges.

The want of a provision for removing the judges on account of inability has been a subject of complaint. But all considerate men will be sensible that such a provision would either not be practised upon or would be more liable to abuse than calculated to answer any good purpose. The mensuration of the faculties of the mind has, I believe, no place in the catalogue of known arts. An attempt to fix the boundary between the regions of ability and inability would much oftener give scope to personal and party attachments and enmities than advance the interests of justice or the public good. The result, except in the case of insanity, must for the most part be arbitrary; and insanity, without any formal or express provision, may be safely pronounced to be a virtual disqualification.

The constitution of New York, to avoid investigations that must forever be vague and dangerous, has taken a particular age as the criterion of inability. No man can be a judge beyond sixty. I believe there are few at present who do not disapprove of this provision. There is no station in relation to which it is less proper than to that of a judge. The deliberating and comparing faculties generally preserve their strength much beyond that period in men who survive it; and when, in addition to this circumstance, we consider how few there are who outlive the season of intellectual vigor, and how improbable it is that any considerable portion of the bench, whether more or less numerous, should be in such a situation at the same time, we shall be ready to conclude that limitations of this sort have little to recommend them. In a republic, where fortunes are not affluent and pensions not expedient, the dismission of men from stations in which they have served their country long and usefully, on which they depend for subsistence, and from which it will be too late to resort to any other occupation for a livelihood, ought to have some better apology to humanity than is to be found in the imaginary danger of a superannuated bench.[104]   PUBLIUS

THE FEDERALIST NO. 80

(HAMILTON)

To the People of the State of New York:

To judge with accuracy of the proper extent of the federal judicature, it will be necessary to consider, in the first place, what are its proper objects.

It seems scarcely to admit of controversy that the judiciary authority of the Union ought to extend to these several descriptions of cases: 1st, to all those which arise out of the laws of the United States, passed in pursuance of their just and constitutional powers of legislation; 2d, to all those which concern the execution of the provisions expressly contained in the articles of Union; 3d, to all those in which the United States are a party; 4th, to all those which involve the PEACE of the CONFEDERACY, whether they relate to the intercourse between the United States and foreign nations, or to that between the States themselves; 5th, to all those which originate on the high seas, and are of admiralty or maritime jurisdiction; and, lastly, to all those in which the State tribunals cannot be supposed to be impartial and unbiased.

The first point depends upon this obvious consideration, that there ought always to be a constitutional method of giving efficacy to constitutional provisions. What, for instance, would avail restrictions on the authority of the State legislatures without some constitutional mode of enforcing the observance of them? The States, by the plan of the convention, are prohibited from doing a variety of things, some of which are incompatible with the interests of the Union, and others with the principles of good government. The imposition of duties on imported articles and the emission of paper money are specimens of each kind. No man of sense will believe that such prohibitions would be scrupulously regarded without some effectual power in the government to restrain or correct the

infractions of them. This power must either be a direct negative on the State laws or an authority in the federal courts to
overrule such as might be in manifest contravention of the
articles of Union. There is no third course that I can imagine.
The latter appears to have been thought by the convention
preferable to the former, and, I presume, will be most agreeable to the States.

As to the second point, it is impossible by any argument
or comment to make it clearer than it is in itself. If there are
such things as political axioms, the propriety of the judicial
power of a government being coextensive with its legislative
may be ranked among the number. The mere necessity of
uniformity in the interpretation of the national laws decides
the question. Thirteen independent courts of final jurisdiction
over the same causes, arising upon the same laws, is a hydra
in government from which nothing but contradiction and confusion can proceed.

Still less need be said in regard to the third point. Controversies between the nation and its members or citizens can
only be properly referred to the national tribunals. Any other
plan would be contrary to reason, to precedent, and to de-
corum.

The fourth point rests on this plain proposition, that the
peace of the WHOLE ought not to be left at the disposal of a
PART. The Union will undoubtedly be answerable to foreign
powers for the conduct of its members. And the responsibility
for an injury ought ever to be accompanied with the faculty
of preventing it. As the denial or perversion of justice by the
sentences of courts, as well as in any other manner, is with
reason classed among the just causes of war, it will follow
that the federal judiciary ought to have cognizance of all
causes in which the citizens of other countries are concerned.
This is not less essential to the preservation of the public faith
than to the security of the public tranquillity. . . .

The power of determining causes between two States, between one State and the citizens of another, and between the
citizens of different States, is perhaps not less essential to
the peace of the Union than that which has been just examined. . . .

A method of terminating territorial disputes between the

States, under the authority of the federal head, was not unattended to even in the imperfect system by which they have been hitherto held together. But there are many other sources, besides interfering claims of boundary, from which bickerings and animosities may spring up among the members of the Union. To some of these we have been witnesses in the course of our past experience. It will readily be conjectured that I allude to the fraudulent laws which have been passed in too many of the States. And though the proposed Constitution establishes particular guards against the repetition of those instances which have heretofore made their appearance, yet it is warrantable to apprehend that the spirit which produced them will assume new shapes that could not be foreseen nor specifically provided against. Whatever practices may have a tendency to disturb the harmony between the States are proper objects of federal superintendence and control.

It may be esteemed the basis of the Union, that "the citizens of each State shall be entitled to all . . . privileges and immunities of citizens of the several States."[105] And if it be a just principle that every government *ought to possess the means of executing its own provisions by its own authority,* it will follow, that in order to the inviolable maintenance of that equality of privileges and immunities to which the citizens of the Union will be entitled, the national judiciary ought to preside in all cases in which one State or its citizens are opposed to another State or its citizens. To secure the full effect of so fundamental a provision against all evasion and subterfuge, it is necessary that its construction should be committed to that tribunal which, having no local attachments, will be likely to be impartial between the different States and their citizens, and which, owing its official existence to the Union, will never be likely to feel any bias inauspicious to the principles on which it is founded.

The fifth point will demand little animadversion. The most bigoted idolizers of State authority have not thus far shown a disposition to deny the national judiciary the cognizances of maritime causes. These so generally depend on the laws of nations, and so commonly affect the rights of foreigners, that they fall within the considerations which are relative to the public peace. The most important part of them are, by the present Confederation, submitted to federal jurisdiction.

The reasonableness of the agency of the national courts in cases in which the State tribunals cannot be supposed to be impartial speaks for itself. No man ought certainly to be a judge in his own cause or in any cause in respect to which he has the least interest or bias. This principle has no inconsiderable weight in designating the federal courts as the proper tribunals for the determination of controversies between different States and their citizens. And it ought to have the same operation in regard to some cases between citizens of the same State. Claims to land under grants of different States, founded upon adverse pretensions of boundary, are of this description. The courts of neither of the granting States could be expected to be unbiased. The laws may have even prejudged the question, and tied the courts down to decisions in favor of the grants of the State to which they belonged. And even where this had not been done, it would be natural that the judges, as men, should feel a strong predilection to the claims of their own government.

Having thus laid down and discussed the principles which ought to regulate the constitution of the federal judiciary, we will proceed to test, by these principles, the particular powers of which, according to the plan of the convention, it is to be composed. It is to comprehend "all cases in law and equity arising under [this] Constitution, the laws of the United States, and treaties made, or which shall be made, under their authority; to all cases affecting ambassadors, other public ministers, and consuls; to all cases of admiralty and maritime jurisdiction; to controversies to which the United States shall be a party; to controversies between two or more States; between a State and citizens of another State; between citizens of different States; between citizens of the same State claiming lands [under] grants of different States; and between a State or the citizens thereof and foreign states, citizens [or] subjects."[106] This constitutes the entire mass of the judicial authority of the Union. Let us now review it in detail. It is, then, to extend:

First. To all cases in law and equity, *arising under the Constitution* and *the laws of the United States.* This corresponds with the two first classes of causes, which have been enumerated, as proper for the jurisdiction of the United States. It has been asked, what is meant by "cases arising under the Constitution," in contradistinction from those "arising under the laws of the United States"? The difference has been already explained. All the restrictions upon the authority of the State legislatures furnish examples of it. They are not, for instance, to emit paper money; but the interdiction results from the Constitution, and will have no connection with any law of the United States. Should paper money, notwithstanding, be emitted, the controversies concerning it would be cases arising under the Constitution and not the laws of the United States, in the ordinary signification of the terms. This may serve as a sample of the whole.

It has also been asked, what need of the word "equity"? What equitable causes can grow out of the Constitution and laws of the United States? There is hardly a subject of litigation between individuals, which may not involve those ingredients of *fraud, accident, trust,* or *hardship,* which would render the matter an object of equitable rather than of legal jurisdiction as the distinction is known and established in several of the States. It is the peculiar province, for instance, of a court of equity to relieve against what are called hard bargains; these are contracts in which, though there may have been no direct fraud or deceit sufficient to invalidate them in a court of law, yet there may have been some undue and unconscionable advantage taken of the necessities or misfortunes of one of the parties, which a court of equity would not tolerate. In such cases, where foreigners were concerned on either side, it would be impossible for the federal judicatories to do justice without an equitable as well as a legal jurisdiction. Agreements to convey lands claimed under the grants of different States may afford another example of the necessity of an equitable jurisdiction in the federal courts. This reasoning may not be so palpable in those States where the formal and technical distinction between LAW and EQUITY is not maintained, as in this State, where it is exemplified by every day's practice.

The judiciary authority of the Union is to extend:

Second. To treaties made, or which shall be made, under the authority of the United States, and to all cases affecting ambassadors, other public ministers, and consuls. These belong to the fourth class of the enumerated cases, as they have an evident connection with the preservation of the national peace.

Third. To cases of admiralty and maritime jurisdiction. These form, altogether, the fifth of the enumerated classes of causes proper for the cognizance of the national courts.

Fourth. To controversies to which the United States shall be a party. These constitute the third of those classes.

Fifth. To controversies between two or more States; between a State and citizens of another State; between citizens of different States. These belong to the fourth of those classes, and partake, in some measure, of the nature of the last.

Sixth. To cases between the citizens of the same State, *claiming lands under grants of different States.* These fall within the last class, and *are the only instances in which the proposed Constitution directly contemplates the cognizance of disputes between the citizens of the same State.*

Seventh. To cases between a State and the citizens thereof, and foreign States, citizens, or subjects. These have been already explained to belong to the fourth of the enumerated classes, and have been shown to be, in a peculiar manner, the proper subjects of the national judicature.

From this review of the particular powers of the federal judiciary as marked out in the Constitution, it appears that they are all conformable to the principles which ought to have governed the structure of that department, and which were necessary to the perfection of the system. If some partial inconveniences should appear to be connected with the incorporation of any of them into the plan, it ought to be recollected that the national legislature will have ample authority to make such *exceptions,* and to prescribe such regulations as will be calculated to obviate or remove these inconveniences. The possibility of particular mischiefs can never be viewed, by a well-informed mind, as a solid objection to a general principle, which is calculated to avoid general mischiefs and to obtain general advantages. Publius

THE FEDERALIST NO. 81

(HAMILTON)

To the People of the State of New York:

Let us now return to the partition of the judiciary authority between different courts, and their relations to each other.

"The judicial power of the United States . . . [shall] be vested in one Supreme Court, and in such inferior courts as the Congress may from time to time ordain and establish."[107]

That there ought to be one court of supreme and final jurisdiction, is a proposition which is not likely to be contested. The reasons for it have been assigned in another place, and are too obvious to need repetition. The only question that seems to have been raised concerning it, is, whether it ought to be a distinct body or a branch of the legislature. The same contradiction is observable in regard to this matter which has been remarked in several other cases. The very men who object to the Senate as a court of impeachments, on the ground of an improper intermixture of powers, advocate, by implication at least, the propriety of vesting the ultimate decision of all causes, in the whole or in a part of the legislative body.

The arguments, or rather suggestions, upon which this charge is founded, are to this effect: "The authority of the proposed Supreme Court of the United States, which is to be a separate and independent body, will be superior to that of the legislature. The power of construing the laws according to the *spirit* of the Constitution, will enable that court to mould them into whatever shape it may think proper; especially as its decisions will not be in any manner subject to the revision or correction of the legislative body. This is as unprecedented as it is dangerous. In Britain, the judicial power, in the last resort, resides in the House of Lords, which is a branch of the legislature; and this part of the British government has been imitated in the State constitutions in general. The Parliament of Great

Britain, and the legislatures of the several States, can at any time rectify, by law, the exceptionable decisions of their respective courts. But the errors and usurpations of the Supreme Court of the United States will be uncontrollable and remediless."[108] This, upon examination, will be found to be made up altogether of false reasoning upon misconceived fact.

In the first place, there is not a syllable in the plan under consideration which *directly* empowers the national courts to construe the laws according to the spirit of the Constitution, or which gives them any greater latitude in this respect than may be claimed by the courts of every State. I admit, however, that the Constitution ought to be the standard of construction for the laws, and that wherever there is an evident opposition, the laws ought to give place to the Constitution. But this doctrine is not deducible from any circumstance peculiar to the plan of the convention, but from the general theory of a limited Constitution; and as far as it is true, is equally applicable to most, if not to all the State governments. There can be no objection, therefore, on this account, to the federal judicature which will not lie against the local judicatures in general, and which will not serve to condemn every constitution that attempts to set bounds to legislative discretion.

But perhaps the force of the objection may be thought to consist in the particular organization of the Supreme Court; in its being composed of a distinct body of magistrates, instead of being one of the branches of the legislature, as in the government of Great Britain and that of the State. To insist upon this point, the authors of the objection must renounce the meaning they have labored to annex to the celebrated maxim, requiring a separation of the departments of power. It shall, nevertheless, be conceded to them, agreeably to the interpretation given to that maxim in the course of these papers, that it is not violated by vesting the ultimate power of judging in a *part* of the legislative body. But though this be not an absolute violation of that excellent rule, yet it verges so nearly upon it as on this account alone to be less eligible than the mode preferred by the convention. From a body which had even a partial agency in passing bad laws, we could rarely expect a disposition to temper and moderate them in the application. The same spirit which had operated in making them would be too apt in interpreting them; still less could it be expected that men who had infringed the Constitution in the character of legislators, would be disposed to repair the breach in the character of judges. Nor is this all. Every reason which recommends the tenure of good behavior for judicial offices militates against placing the judiciary power, in the last resort, in a body composed of men chosen for a limited period. There is an absurdity in referring the determination of causes, in the first instance, to judges of permanent standing; in the last, to those of a temporary and mutable constitution. And there is a still greater absurdity in subjecting the decisions of men, selected for their knowledge of the laws, acquired by long and laborious study, to the revision and control of men who, for want of the same advantage, cannot but be deficient in that knowledge. The members of the legislature will rarely be chosen with a view to those qualifications which fit men for the stations of judges; and as, on this account, there will be great reason to apprehend all the ill consequences of defective information, so, on account of the natural propensity of such bodies to party divisions, there will be no less reason to fear that the pestilential breath of faction may poison the fountains of justice. The habit of being continually marshalled on opposite sides will be too apt to stifle the voice both of law and of equity.

These considerations teach us to applaud the wisdom of those States who have committed the judicial power, in the last resort, not to a part of the legislature, but to distinct and independent bodies of men. Contrary to the supposition of those who have represented the plan of the convention, in this respect, as novel and unprecedented, it is but a copy of the constitutions of New Hampshire, Massachusetts, Pennsylvania, Delaware, Maryland, Virginia, North Carolina, South Carolina, and Georgia; and the preference which has been given to those models is highly to be commended.

It is not true, in the second place, that the Parliament of Great Britain or the legislatures of the particular States, can rectify the exceptionable decisions of their respective courts in any other sense than might be done by a future legislature of the United States. The theory, neither of the British, nor the State constitutions, authorizes the revisal of a judicial sentence by a legislative act. Nor is there anything in the proposed Constitution, more than in either of them, by which it is forbidden. In the former as well as in the latter, the impropriety of the thing on the general principles of law and reason is the sole obstacle. A legislature, without exceeding its province, cannot reverse a determination once made in a particular case; though it may prescribe a new rule for future cases. This is the principle, and it applies in all its consequences, exactly in the same manner and extent, to the State governments, as to the national government now under consideration. Not the least difference can be pointed out in any view of the subject.

It may in the last place be observed that the supposed danger of judiciary encroachments on the legislative authority, which has been upon many occasions reiterated, is in reality a phantom. Particular misconstructions and contraventions of the will of the legislature may now and then happen; but they can never be so extensive as to amount to an inconvenience, or in any sensible degree to affect the order of the political system. This may be inferred with certainty, from the general nature of the judicial power, from the objects to which it relates, from the manner in which it is exercised, from its comparative weakness, and from its total incapacity to support its usurpations by force. And the inference is greatly fortified by the consideration of the important constitutional check which the power of instituting impeachments in one part of the legislative body, and of determining upon them in the other, would give to that body upon the members of the judicial department. This is alone a complete security. There never can be danger that the judges, by a series of deliberate usurpations on the authority of the legislature, would hazard the united resentment of the body intrusted with it, while this body was possessed of the means of punishing their presumption, by degrading them from their stations. While this ought to remove all apprehensions on the subject, it affords, at the same time, a cogent argument for constituting the Senate a court for the trial of impeachments.

Having now examined . . . the distinct and independent organization of the Supreme Court, I proceed to consider the propriety of the power of constituting inferior courts and the relations which will subsist between these and the former.[109]

The power of constituting inferior courts is evidently calculated to obviate the necessity of having recourse to the Supreme Court in every case of federal cognizance. It is intended to enable the national government to institute or *authorize,* in each State or district of the United States, a tribunal competent to the determination of matters of national jurisdiction within its limits.

But why, it is asked, might not the same purpose have been accomplished by the instrumentality of the State courts? This admits of different answers. Though the fitness and competency of those courts should be allowed in the utmost latitude, yet the substance of the power in question may still be regarded as a necessary part of the plan, if it were only to empower the national legislature to commit to them the cognizance of causes arising out of the national Constitution. To confer the power of determining such causes upon the existing courts of the several States, would perhaps be as much "to constitute tribunals," as to create new courts with the like power. But ought not a more direct and explicit provision to have been made in favor of the State courts? There are, in my opinion, substantial reasons against such a provision: the most discerning cannot foresee how far the prevalency of a local spirit may be found to disqualify the local tribunals for the jurisdiction of national causes; whilst every man may discover, that courts constituted like those of some of the States would be improper channels of the judicial authority of the Union. State judges, holding their offices during pleasure or from year to year, will be too little independent to be relied upon for an inflexible execution of the national laws. And if there was a necessity for confiding the original cognizance of causes arising under those laws to them, there would be a correspondent necessity for leaving the door of appeal as wide as possible. In proportion to the grounds of confidence in, or distrust of, the subordinate tribunals, ought to be the facility or difficulty of appeals. And well satisfied as I am of the propriety of the appellate jurisdiction in the several classes of causes to which it is extended by the plan of the convention, I should consider everything calculated to give, in practice, an *unrestrained course* to appeals, as a source of public and private inconvenience.

I am not sure but that it will be found highly expedient and useful to divide the United States into four or five or half a dozen districts; and to institute a federal court in each district in lieu of one in every State. The judges of these courts with the aid of the State judges may hold circuits for the trial of causes in the several parts of the respective districts. Justice through them may be administered with ease and despatch; and appeals may be safely circumscribed within a narrow compass. This plan appears to me at present the most eligible of any that could be adopted; and in order to [effect] it, it is necessary that the power of constituting inferior courts should exist in the full extent in which it is to be found in the proposed Constitution.

These reasons seem sufficient to satisfy a candid mind, that the want of such a power would have been a great defect in the plan. Let us now examine in what manner the judicial authority is to be distributed between the supreme and the inferior courts of the Union.

The Supreme Court is to be invested with original jurisdiction . . . "in [all] cases affecting ambassadors, other public ministers, and consuls, and those in which A STATE shall be a party" [*sic*].[110] Public ministers of every class are the immediate representatives of their sovereigns. All questions in which they are concerned are so directly connected with the public peace, that, as well for the preservation of this, as out of respect to the sovereignties they represent, it is both expedient and proper that such questions should be submitted in the first instance to the highest judicatory of the nation. Though consuls have not in strictness a diplomatic character; yet as they are the public agents of the nations to which they belong, the same observation is in a great measure applicable to them. In cases in which a State might happen to be a party, it would ill suit its dignity to be turned over to an inferior tribunal.

Though it may rather be a digression from the immediate subject of this paper, I shall take occasion to mention here a supposition which has excited some alarm upon very mistaken grounds. It has been suggested that an assignment of the public securities of one State to the citizens of another would enable them to prosecute that State in the federal courts for the amount of those securities; a suggestion which the following considerations prove to be without foundation.

It is inherent in the nature of sovereignty not to be amenable to the suit of an individual *without its consent*. This is the general sense and the general practice of mankind; and the exemption, as one of the attributes of sovereignty, is now enjoyed by the government of every State in the Union. Unless, therefore, there is a surrender of this immunity in the plan of the convention, it will remain with the States, and the danger intimated must be merely ideal. The circumstances which are necessary to produce an alienation of State sovereignty were discussed in considering the article of taxation, and need not be repeated here. A recurrence to the principles there established will satisfy us that there is no color to pretend that the State governments would, by the adoption of that plan, be divested of the privilege of paying their own debts in their own way, free from every constraint but that which flows from the obligations of good faith. The contracts between a nation and individuals are only binding on the conscience of the sovereign, and have no pretensions to a compulsive force. They confer no right of action independent of the sovereign will. To what purpose would it be to authorize suits against States for the debts they owe? How could recoveries be enforced? It is evident, it could not be done without waging war against the contracting State; and to ascribe to the federal courts, by mere implication and in destruction of a pre-existing right of the State governments, a power which would involve such a consequence, would be altogether forced and unwarrantable.

Let us resume the train of our observations. We have seen that the original jurisdiction of the Supreme Court would be confined to two classes of causes, and those of a nature rarely to occur. In all other cases of federal cognizance the original jurisdiction would appertain to the inferior tribunals; and the Supreme Court would have nothing more than an appellate jurisdiction, "with such *exceptions* and under such *regulations* as the Congress shall make."[111]

The propriety of this appellate jurisdiction has been scarcely called in question in regard to matters of law; but the clamors have been loud against it as applied to matters of fact. Some well-intentioned men in this State, deriving their notions from the language and forms which obtain in our courts, have been induced to consider it as an implied supersedure of the trial by jury, in favor of the civil-law mode of trial, which prevails in our courts of admiralty, probate, and chancery. A technical sense has been affixed to the term "appellate," which, in our law parlance, is commonly used in reference to appeals in the course of the civil law. But if I am not misinformed, the same meaning would not be given to it in any part of New England. There, an appeal from one jury to another is familiar both in language and practice, and is even a matter of course until there have been two verdicts on one side. The word "appellate," therefore, will not be understood in the same sense in New England as in New York, which shows the impropriety of a technical interpretation derived from the jurisprudence of any particular State. The expression, taken in the abstract, denotes nothing more than the power of one tribunal to review the proceedings of another, either as to the law or fact, or both. The mode of doing it may depend on ancient custom or legislative provision (in a new government it must depend on the latter), and may be with or without the aid of a jury, as may be judged advisable. If, therefore, the reëxamination of a fact once determined by a jury should in any case be admitted under the proposed Constitution, it may be so regulated as to be done by a second jury, either by remanding the cause to the court below for a second trial of the fact, or by directing an issue immediately out of the Supreme Court.

But it does not follow that the reëxamination of a fact once ascertained by a jury will be permitted in the Supreme Court. Why may not it be said with the strictest propriety, when a writ of error is brought from an inferior to a superior court of law in this State, that the latter has jurisdiction of the fact as well as the law? It is true it cannot institute a new inquiry concerning the fact, but it takes cognizance of it as it appears upon the record and pronounces the law arising upon it.[112] This is jurisdiction of both fact and law; nor is it even possible to separate them. Though the common-law courts of this State ascertain disputed facts by a jury, yet they unquestionably have jurisdiction of both fact and law; and accordingly when the former is agreed in the pleadings, they have no recourse to a jury, but proceed at once to judgment. I contend, therefore, on this ground, that the expressions, "appellate jurisdiction, both as to law and fact," do not necessarily imply a reëxamination in the Supreme Court of facts decided by juries in the inferior courts.

The following train of ideas may well be imagined to have influenced the convention, in relation to this particular provision. The appellate jurisdiction of the Supreme Court (it may have been argued) will extend to causes determinable in different modes, some in the course of the COMMON LAW, others in the course of the CIVIL LAW. In the former, the revision of the law only will be, generally speaking, the proper province of the Supreme Court; in the latter, the reëxamination of the fact is agreeable to usage, and in some cases, of which prize cases are an example, might be essential to the preservation of the public peace. It is therefore necessary that the appellate jurisdiction should, in certain cases, extend in the broadest sense to matters of fact. It will not answer to make an express exception of cases which shall have been originally tried by a jury, because in the courts of some of the States *all causes* are tried in this mode;[113] and such an exception would preclude the revision of matters of fact, as well where it might be proper, as where it might be improper. To avoid all inconveniences, it will be safest to declare generally that the Supreme Court shall possess appellate jurisdiction both as to law and *fact*, and that this jurisdiction shall be subject to such *exceptions* and regulations as the national legislature may prescribe. This will enable the government to modify it in such a manner as will best answer the ends of public justice and security.

This view of the matter . . . puts it out of all doubt that the supposed *abolition* of the trial by jury by the operation of this provision is fallacious and untrue. The legislature of the United States would certainly have full power to provide that in appeals to the Supreme Court there should be no reëxamination of facts where they had been tried in the original causes by juries. This would certainly be an authorized exception; but if, for the reason already intimated, it should be thought too extensive, it might be qualified with a limitation to such causes only as are determinable at common law in that mode of trial.

The amount of the observations hitherto made on the authority of the judicial department is this: that it has been carefully restricted to those causes which are manifestly proper for the cognizance of the national judicature; that in the partition of this authority a very small portion of original jurisdiction has been preserved to the Supreme Court, and the rest consigned to the subordinate tribunals; that the Supreme Court will possess an appellate jurisdiction, both as to law and fact, in all cases referred to them, both subject to any *exceptions* and *regulations* which may be thought advisable; that this appellate jurisdiction does, in no case, *abolish* the trial by jury; and that an ordinary degree of prudence and integrity in the national councils will insure us solid advantages from the establishment of the proposed judiciary, without exposing us to any of the inconveniences which have been predicted from that source.   PUBLIUS

THE FEDERALIST NO. 82

(HAMILTON)

To the People of the State of New York:

The erection of a new government, whatever care or wisdom may distinguish the work, cannot fail to originate questions of intricacy and nicety; and these may, in a particular manner, be expected to flow from the establishment of a constitution founded upon the total or partial incorporation of a number of distinct sovereignties. 'Tis time only that can mature and perfect so compound a system, can liquidate the meaning of all the parts, and can adjust them to each other in a harmonious and consistent WHOLE.

Such questions, accordingly, have arisen upon the plan proposed by the convention, and particularly concerning the judiciary department. The principal of these respect the situation of the State courts in regard to those causes which are to be submitted to federal jurisdiction. Is this to be exclusive, or are those courts to possess a concurrent jurisdiction? If the latter, in what relation will they stand to the national tribunals? These are inquiries which we meet with in the mouths of men of sense, and which are certainly entitled to attention.

The principles established in a former paper [*No. 32*] teach us that the States will retain all *preëxisting* authorities which may not be exclusively delegated to the federal head; and that this exclusive delegation can only exist in one of three cases: where an exclusive authority is, in express terms, granted to the Union; or where a particular authority is granted to the Union, and the exercise of a like authority is prohibited to the States; or where an authority is granted to the Union, with which a similar authority in the States would be utterly incompatible. Though these principles may not apply with the same force to the judiciary as to the legislative power, yet I am inclined to think that they are, in the main, just with respect to the former as well as the latter. And under this impression, I shall lay it down as a rule that the State courts will *retain* the jurisdiction they now have unless it appears to be taken away in one of the enumerated modes.

The only thing in the proposed Constitution, which wears the appearance of confining the causes of federal cognizance to the federal courts, is contained in this passage:—"The JU-DICIAL POWER of the United States *shall be vested* in one Supreme Court, and in *such* inferior courts as the Congress . . . [may] from time to time ordain and establish."[114] This might either be construed to signify that the supreme and subordinate courts of the Union should alone have the power of deciding those causes to which their authority is to extend; or simply to denote, that the organs of the national judiciary should be one Supreme Court, and as many subordinate courts as Congress should think proper to appoint; or in other words, that the United States should exercise the judicial power with which they are to be invested, through one supreme tribunal, and a certain number of inferior ones, to be instituted by them. The first excludes, the last admits, the concurrent jurisdiction of the State tribunals; and as the first would amount to an alienation of State power by implication, the last appears to me the most natural and the most defensible construction.

But this doctrine of concurrent jurisdiction is only clearly applicable to those descriptions of causes of which the State courts have previous cognizance. It is not equally evident in relation to cases which may grow out of, and be *peculiar* to, the Constitution to be established; for not to allow the State courts a right of jurisdiction in such cases, can hardly be considered as the abridgement of a preëxisting authority. I mean not therefore to contend that the United States, in the course of legislation upon the objects intrusted to their direction, may not commit the decision of causes arising upon a particular regulation to the federal courts solely, if such a measure should be deemed expedient; but I hold that the State courts will be divested of no part of their primitive jurisdiction further than may relate to an appeal; and I am even of opinion that in every case in which they were not expressly excluded by the future acts of the national legislature, they will of course take cognizance of the causes to which those acts may give birth. This I infer from the nature of judiciary power and from the general genius of the system. The judiciary power of every government looks beyond its own local or municipal laws, and in civil cases lays hold of all subjects of litigation between parties within its jurisdiction, though the causes of dispute are relative to the laws of the most distant part of the globe. Those of Japan, not less than of New York, may furnish the objects of legal discussion to our courts. When in addition to this we consider the State governments and the national governments as they truly are, in the light of kindred systems and as parts of ONE WHOLE, the inference seems to be conclusive, that the State courts would have a concurrent jurisdiction in all cases arising under the laws of the Union where it was not expressly prohibited.

Here another question occurs: What relation would subsist between the national and State courts in these instances of concurrent jurisdiction? I answer, that an appeal would certainly lie from the latter, to the Supreme Court of the United States. The Constitution in direct terms gives an appellate jurisdiction to the Supreme Court in all the enumerated cases of federal cognizance in which it is not to have an original one, without a single expression to confine its operation to the inferior federal courts. The objects of appeal, not the tribunals from which it is to be made, are alone contemplated. From this circumstance and from the reason of the thing, it ought to be construed to extend to the State tribunals. Either this must be the case or the local courts must be excluded from a concurrent jurisdiction in matters of national concern, else the judiciary authority of the Union may be eluded at the pleasure of every plaintiff or prosecutor. Neither of these consequences ought, without evident necessity, to be involved; the latter would be entirely inadmissible, as it would defeat some of the most important and avowed purposes of the proposed government, and would essentially embarrass its measures. Nor do I perceive any foundation for such a supposition. Agreeably to the remark already made, the national and State systems are to be regarded as ONE WHOLE. The courts of the latter will of course be natural auxiliaries to the execution of the laws of the Union, and an appeal from them will as naturally lie to that tribunal which is destined to unite and assimilate the principles of national justice and the rules of national decisions. The evident aim of the plan of the convention is, that all the causes of the specified classes shall, for weighty public reasons, receive their original or final determination in the courts of the Union. To confine, therefore, the general expressions giving appellate jurisdiction to the Supreme Court to appeals from the subordinate federal courts, instead of allowing their extension to the State courts, would be to abridge the latitude of the terms, in subversion of the intent, contrary to every sound rule of interpretation.

But could an appeal be made to lie from the State courts to the subordinate federal judicatories? This is another of the questions which have been raised, and of greater difficulty than the former. The following considerations countenance the affirmative. The plan of the convention, in the first place, authorizes the national legislature "to constitute tribunals inferior to the Supreme Court." It declares, in the next place, that "the JUDICIAL POWER of the United States *shall be vested* in one Supreme Court, and in such inferior courts as [the] Congress . . . [may] . . . ordain and establish";[115] and it then proceeds to enumerate the cases to which this judicial power shall extend. It afterwards divides the jurisdiction of the Supreme Court into original and appellate, but gives no definition of that of the subordinate courts. The only outlines described for them, are that they shall be "inferior to the Supreme Court," and that they shall not exceed the specified limits of the federal judiciary. Whether their authority shall be original or appellate, or both, is not declared. All this seems to be left to the discretion of the legislature. And this being the case, I perceive at present no impediment to the establishment of an appeal from the State courts to the subordinate national tribunals; and many advantages attending the power of doing it may be imagined. It would diminish the motives to the multiplication of federal courts, and would admit of arrangements calculated to contract the appellate jurisdiction of the Supreme Court. The State tribunals may then be left with a more entire charge of federal causes; and appeals, in most cases in which they may be deemed proper, instead of being carried to the Supreme Court, may be made to lie from the State courts to district courts of the Union.   PUBLIUS

THE FEDERALIST NO. 83

(HAMILTON)

To the People of the State of New York:
    The objection to the plan of the convention, which has met with most success in this State, and perhaps in several of the other States, is *that relative to the want of a constitutional provision* for the trial by jury in civil cases.[116] The disingenuous form in which this objection is usually stated has been repeatedly adverted to and exposed, but continues to be pursued in all the conversations and writings of the opponents of the plan. The mere silence of the Constitution in regard to *civil causes* is represented as an abolition of the trial by jury, and the declamations to which it has afforded a pretext are artfully calculated to induce a persuasion that this pretended abolition is complete and universal, extending not

only to every species of civil, but even to *criminal, causes.* To argue with respect to the latter would, however, be as vain and fruitless as to attempt the serious proof of the *existence* of *matter,* or to demonstrate any of those propositions which, by their own internal evidence, force conviction when expressed in language adapted to convey their meaning.

With regard to civil causes, subtleties almost too contemptible for refutation have been employed to countenance the surmise that a thing which is only *not provided for,* is entirely *abolished.* Every man of discernment must at once perceive the wide difference between *silence* and *abolition.* But as the inventors of this fallacy have attempted to support it by certain *legal maxims* of interpretation, which they have perverted from their true meaning, it may not be wholly useless to explore the ground they have taken.

The maxims on which they rely are of this nature: "A specification of particulars is an exclusion of generals"; or, "The expression of one thing is the exclusion of another." Hence, say they, as the Constitution has established the trial by jury in criminal cases and is silent in respect to civil, this silence is an implied prohibition of trial by jury in regard to the latter.

The rules of legal interpretation are rules of *common-sense,* adopted by the courts in the construction of the laws. The true test, therefore, of a just application of them is its conformity to the source from which they are derived. This being the case, let me ask if it is consistent with common-sense to suppose that a provision obliging the legislative power to commit the trial of criminal causes to juries, is a privation of its right to authorize or permit that mode of trial in other cases? Is it natural to suppose that a command to do one thing is a prohibition to the doing of another, which there was a previous power to do, and which is not incompatible with the thing commanded to be done? If such a supposition would be unnatural and unreasonable, it cannot be rational to maintain that an injunction of the trial by jury in certain cases is an interdiction of it in others.

A power to constitute courts is a power to prescribe the mode of trial; and consequently, if nothing was said in the Constitution on the subject of juries, the legislature would be at liberty either to adopt that institution or to let it alone. This discretion in regard to criminal causes is abridged by the express injunction of trial by jury in all such cases; but it is, of course, left at large in relation to civil causes, there being a total silence on this head. The specification of an obligation to try all criminal causes in a particular mode excludes indeed the obligation or necessity of employing the same mode in civil causes, but does not abridge *the power* of the legislature to exercise that mode if it should be thought proper. The pretence, therefore, that the national legislature would not be at full liberty to submit all the civil causes of federal cognizance to the determination of juries, is a pretence destitute of all just foundation. . . .

From these observations it must appear unquestionably true that trial by jury is in no case abolished by the proposed Constitution; and it is equally true that in those controversies between individuals in which the great body of the people are likely to be interested, that institution will remain precisely in the same situation in which it is placed by the State constitutions. . . . The foundation of this assertion is, that the national judiciary will have no cognizance of them, and of course they will remain determinable as heretofore by the State courts only, and in the manner which the State constitutions and laws prescribe. All land causes, except where claims under the grants of different States come into question, and all other controversies between the citizens of the same State, unless where they depend upon positive violations of the articles of union, by acts of the State legislatures, will belong exclusively to the jursidiction of the State tribunals. Add to this, that admiralty causes, and almost all those which are of equity jurisdiction, are determinable under our own government without the intervention of a jury, and the inference from the whole will be, that this institution, as it exists with us at present, cannot possibly be affected to any great extent by the proposed alteration in our system of government.

The friends and adversaries of the plan of the convention, if they agree in nothing else, concur at least in the value they set upon the trial by jury; or if there is any difference between them it consists in this: the former regard it as a valuable safeguard to liberty; the latter represent it as the very palladium of free government. For my own part, the more the operation of the institution has fallen under my observation, the more reason I have discovered for holding it in high estimation; and it would be altogether superfluous to examine to what extent it deserves to be esteemed useful or essential in a representative republic; or how much more merit it may be entitled to as a defence against the oppressions of an hereditary monarch, than as a barrier to the tyranny of popular magistrates in a popular government. Discussions of this kind would be more curious than beneficial, as all are satisfied of the utility of the institution and of its friendly aspect to liberty. But I must acknowledge that I cannot readily discern the inseparable connection between the existence of liberty and the trial by jury in civil cases. Arbitrary impeachments, arbitrary methods of prosecuting pretended offences, and arbitrary punishments upon arbitrary convictions, have ever appeared to me to be the great engines of judicial despotism; and these have all relation to criminal proceedings. The trial by jury in criminal cases, aided by the *habeas-corpus* act, seems therefore to be alone concerned in the question. And both of these are provided for, in the most ample manner, in the plan of the convention. . . .

The excellence of the trial by jury in civil cases appears to depend on circumstances foreign to the preservation of liberty. The strongest argument in its favor is that it is a security against corruption. As there is always more time and better opportunity to tamper with a standing body of magistrates than with a jury summoned for the occasion, there is room to suppose that a corrupt influence would more easily find its way to the former than to the latter. . . . As matters now stand, it would be necessary to corrupt both court and jury; for where the jury have gone evidently wrong, the court will generally grant a new trial, and it would be in most cases of little use to practise upon the jury unless the court could be likewise gained. Here then is a double security; and it will readily be perceived that this complicated agency tends to preserve the purity of both institutions. By increasing the obstacles to success, it discourages attempts to seduce the integrity of either. The temptations to prostitution which the judges might have to surmount, must certainly be much fewer while the coöperation of a jury is necessary, than they might be if they had themselves the exclusive determination of all causes.

Notwithstanding, therefore, the doubts I have expressed, as to the essentiality of trial by jury in civil cases to liberty, I admit that it is in most cases, under proper regulations, an excellent method of determining questions of property; and that on this account alone it would be entitled to a constitutional provision in its favor if it were possible to fix the limits within which it ought to be comprehended. There is, however, in all cases, great difficulty in this; and men not blinded by enthusiasm must be sensible that in a federal government, which is a composition of societies whose ideas and institutions in relation to the matter materially vary from each other, that difficulty must be not a little augmented. For my own part, at every new view I take of the subject, I become more convinced of the reality of the obstacles which . . . prevented the insertion of a provision on this head in the plan of the convention. . . .   PUBLIUS

THE FEDERALIST NO. 84

(HAMILTON)

To the People of the State of New York:
        In the course of the foregoing review of the Constitution, I have taken notice of, and endeavored to answer most of the objections which have appeared against it. There, however, remain a few which either did not fall naturally under any particular head or were forgotten in their proper places. These shall now be discussed; but as the subject has been drawn into great length, I shall so far consult brevity as to compromise all my observations on these miscellaneous points in a single paper.
        The most considerable of the remaining objections is that

the plan of the convention contains no bill of rights. Among other answers given to this, it has been upon different occasions remarked that the constitutions of several of the States are in a similar predicament. I add that New York is of the number. And yet the opposers of the new system, in this State, who profess an unlimited admiration for its constitution, are among the most intemperate partisans of a bill of rights. To justify their zeal in this matter, they allege two things: one is that, though the constitution of New York has no bill of rights prefixed to it, yet it contains, in the body of it, various provisions in favor of particular privileges and rights, which, in substance, amount to the same thing; the other is, that the Constitution adopts, in their full extent, the common and statute law of Great Britain, by which many other rights, not expressed in it, are equally secured.

To the first I answer, that the Constitution proposed by the convention contains, as well as the constitution of this State, a number of such provisions.

Independent of those which relate to the structure of the government, we find the following: Article 1, section 3, clause 7—"Judgment in cases of impeachment shall not extend further than to removal from office, and disqualification to hold and enjoy any office of honor, trust, or profit under the United States; but the party convicted shall, nevertheless, be liable and subject to indictment, trial, judgment, and punishment according to law." Section 9, of the same article, clause 2—"The privilege of the writ of *habeas corpus* shall not be suspended, unless when in cases of rebellion or invasion the public safety may require it." Clause 3—"No bill of attainder or *ex-post-facto* law shall be passed." Clause 7—"No title of nobility shall be granted by the United States; and no person holding any office of profit or trust under them, shall, without the consent of the Congress, accept of any present, emolument, office, or title of any kind whatever, from any king, prince, or foreign state." Article 3, section 2, clause 3— "The trial of all crimes, except in cases of impeachment, shall be by jury; and such trial shall be held in the State where the said crimes shall have been committed; but when not committed within any State, the trial shall be at such place or places as the Congress may by law have directed." Section 3, of the same article—"Treason against the United States shall consist only in levying war against them, or in adhering to their enemies, giving them aid and comfort. No person shall be convicted of treason, unless on the testimony of two witnesses to the same overt act, or on confession in open court." And clause 3 [*sic*], of the same section—"The Congress shall have power to declare the punishment of treason; but no attainder of treason shall work corruption of blood, or forfeiture, except during the life of the person attainted."

It may well be a question whether these are not, upon the whole, of equal importance with any which are to be found in the constitution of this State. The establishment of the writ of *habeas corpus,* the prohibition of *ex-post-facto* laws, and of TITLES OF NOBILITY, *to which we have no corresponding provision in our Constitution,* are perhaps greater securities to liberty and republicanism than any it contains. The creation of crimes after the commission of the fact, or . . . the subjecting of men to punishment for things which, when they were done, were breaches of no law, and the practice of arbitrary imprisonments, have been, in all ages, the favorite and most formidable instruments of tyranny. The observations of the judicious Blackstone . . . are well worthy of recital: "To bereave a man of life . . . or by violence to confiscate his estate, without accusation or trial, would be so gross and notorious an act of despotism, as must at once convey the alarm of tyranny throughout the whole nation; but confinement of the person, by secretly hurrying him to jail, where his sufferings are unknown or forgotten, is a less public, a less striking, and therefore *a more dangerous engine* of arbitrary government." And as a remedy for this fatal evil he is everywhere peculiarly emphatical in his encomiums on the *habeas-corpus* act, which in one place he calls "the BULWARK of the British Constitution" [*sic*].[117]

Nothing need be said to illustrate the importance of the prohibition of titles of nobility. This may truly be denominated the corner-stone of republican government; for so long as they are excluded, there can never be serious danger that the government will be any other than that of the people.

To the second—that is, to the pretended establishment of the common and statute law by the Constitution, I answer, that they are expressly made subject "to such alterations and provisions as the legislature [of this State] shall from time to time make concerning the same."[118] They are therefore at any moment liable to repeal by the ordinary legislative power, and of course have no constitutional sanction. The only use of the declaration was to recognize the ancient law, and to remove doubts which might have been occasioned by the Revolution. This consequently can be considered as no part of a declaration of rights, which under our constitutions must be intended as limitations of the power of the government itself.

It has been several times truly remarked that bills of rights are, in their origin, stipulations between kings and their subjects, abridgments of prerogative in favor of privilege, reservations of rights not surrendered to the prince. Such was MAGNA CHARTA, obtained by the barons, sword in hand, from King John. Such were the subsequent confirmations of that charter by succeeding princes. Such was the *Petition of Right* assented to by Charles I, in the beginning of his reign. Such, also, was the Declaration of Right presented by the Lords and Commons to the Prince of Orange in 1688, and afterwards thrown into the form of an act of parliament called the Bill of Rights. It is evident, therefore, that, according to their primitive signification, they have no application to constitutions, professedly founded upon the power of the people, and executed by their immediate representatives and servants. Here, in strictness, the people surrender nothing; and as they retain every thing they have no need of particular reservations. "WE, THE PEOPLE of the United States, to secure the blessings of liberty to ourselves and our posterity, do *ordain* and *establish* this Constitution for the United States of America" [*sic*]. Here is a better recognition of popular rights than volumes of those aphorisms[119] which make the principal figure in several of our State bills of rights, and which would sound much better in a treatise of ethics than in a constitution of government.

But a minute detail of particular rights is certainly far less applicable to a Constitution like that under consideration, which is merely intended to regulate the general political interests of the nation, than to a constitution which has the regulation of every species of personal and private concerns.

If, therefore, the loud clamors against the plan of the convention, on this score, are well founded, no epithets of reprobation will be too strong for the constitution of this State. But the truth is, that both of them contain all which, in relation to their objects, is reasonably to be desired.

I go further, and affirm that bills of rights, in the sense and to the extent in which they are contended for, are not only unnecessary in the proposed Constitution, but would even be dangerous. They would contain various exceptions to powers not granted; and, on this very account, would afford a colorable pretext to claim more than were granted.[120] For why declare that things shall not be done which there is no power to do? Why, for instance, should it be said that the liberty of the press shall not be restrained, when no power is given by which restrictions may be imposed? I will not contend that such a provision would confer a regulating power; but it is evident that it would furnish, to men disposed to usurp, a plausible pretence for claiming that power. They might urge with a semblance of reason, that the Constitution ought not to be charged with the absurdity of providing against the abuse of an authority which was not given, and that the provision against restraining the liberty of the press afforded a clear implication, that a power to prescribe proper regulations concerning it was intended to be vested in the national government. This may serve as a specimen of the numerous handles which would be given to the doctrine of constructive powers by the indulgence of an injudicious zeal for bills of rights.

On the subject of the liberty of the press—as much as has been said, I cannot forbear adding a remark or two: in the first place, I observe that there is not a syllable concerning it in the constitution of this State; in the next, I contend that whatever has been said about it in that of any other State, amounts to nothing. What signifies a declaration, that "the liberty of the press shall be inviolably preserved"? What is the liberty of the press? Who can give it any definition which would not leave the utmost latitude for evasion? I hold it to be impracticable; and from this I infer that its security, whatever fine declarations may be inserted in any constitution respecting it, must altogether depend on public opinion, and on the general spirit of the people and of the government. And here, after all, as is intimated upon another occasion, must we seek for the only solid basis of all our rights.

There remains but one other view of this matter to conclude the point. The truth is, after all the declamations we have heard, that the Constitution is itself, in every rational sense and to every useful purpose, A BILL OF RIGHTS. The several bills of rights in Great Britain form its Constitution, and conversely the constitution of each State is its bill of rights. And the proposed Constitution, if adopted, will be the bill of rights of the Union. Is it one object of a bill of rights to declare and specify the political privileges of the citizens in the structure and administration of the government? This is done in the most ample and precise manner in the plan of the convention; comprehending various precautions for the public security, which are not to be found in any of the State constitutions. Is another object of a bill of rights to define certain immunities and modes of proceeding, which are relative to personal and private concerns? This we have seen has also been attended to, in a variety of cases, in the same plan. Adverting therefore to the substantial meaning of a bill of rights, it is absurd to allege that it is not to be found in the work of the convention. It may be said that it does not go far enough, though it will not be easy to make this appear; but it can with no propriety be contended that there is no such thing. It certainly must be immaterial what mode is observed as to the order of declaring the rights of the citizens, if they are to be found in any part of the instrument which establishes the government. And hence it must be apparent that much of what has been said on this subject rests merely on verbal and nominal distinctions, entirely foreign from the substance of the thing.

Another objection which has been made, and which, from the frequency of its repetition, it is to be presumed is relied on, is of this nature: "It is improper . . . to confer such large powers, as are proposed, upon the national government; because the seat of that government must of necessity be too remote from many of the States to admit of a proper knowledge on the part of the constituent, of the conduct of the representative body." This argument, if it proves anything, proves that there ought to be no general government whatever. For the powers which . . . ought to be vested in the Union, cannot be safely intrusted to a body which is not under every requisite control. But there are satisfactory reasons to show that the objection is in reality not well founded. There is in most of the arguments which relate to distance a palpable illusion of the imagination. What are the sources of information by which the people in Montgomery County [New York] must regulate their judgment of the conduct of their representatives in the State legislature? Of personal observation they can have no benefit. This is confined to the citizens on the spot. They must therefore depend on the information of intelligent men in whom they confide; and how must these men obtain their information? Evidently from the complexion of public measures, from the public prints, from correspondences with their representatives, and with other persons who reside at the place of their deliberations. This does not apply to Montgomery County only, but to all the counties at any considerable distance from the seat of government.

It is equally evident that the same sources of information would be open to the people in relation to the conduct of their representatives in the general government; and the impediments to a prompt communication which distance may be supposed to create, will be overbalanced by the effects of the vigilance of the State governments. The executive and legislative bodies of each State will be so many sentinels over the persons employed in every department of the national administration; and as it will be in their power to adopt and pursue a regular and effectual system of intelligence, they can never be at a loss to know the behavior of those who represent their constituents in the national councils, and can readily communicate the same knowledge to the people. Their disposition to apprise the community of whatever may prejudice its interests from another quarter, may be relied upon, if it were only from the rivalship of power. And we may conclude with the fullest assurance that the people, through that channel, will be better informed of the conduct of their national representatives, than they can be by any means they now possess of that of their State representatives.

It ought also to be remembered that the citizens who inhabit the country at and near the seat of government will, in all questions that affect the general liberty and prosperity, have the same interest with those who are at a distance, and that they will stand ready to sound the alarm when necessary, and to point out the actors in any pernicious project. The public papers will be expeditious messengers of intelligence to the most remote inhabitants of the Union.

Among the many curious objections which have appeared against the proposed Constitution, the most extraordinary and the least colorable is derived from the want of some provision respecting the debts due *to* the United States. This has been represented as a tacit relinquishment of those debts and as a wicked contrivance to screen public defaulters. The newspapers have teemed with the most inflammatory railings on this head; yet there is nothing clearer than that the suggestion is entirely void of foundation, the offspring of extreme ignorance or extreme dishonesty. In addition to the remarks I have made upon the subject in another place [*No. 43*], I shall only observe that as it is a plain dictate of common-sense, so it is also an established doctrine of political law, that *"states neither lose any of their rights, nor are discharged from any of their obligations, by a change in the form of their civil government"* [*sic*].[121]

The last objection of any consequence, which I at present recollect, turns upon the article of expense. If it were even true that the adoption of the proposed government would occasion a considerable increase of expense, it would be an objection that ought to have no weight against the plan.

The great bulk of the citizens of America are with reason convinced that Union is the basis of their political happiness. Men of sense of all parties now, with few exceptions, agree that it cannot be preserved under the present system nor without radical alterations; that new and extensive powers ought to be granted to the national head, and that these require a different organization of the federal government—a single body being an unsafe depositary of such ample authorities. In conceding all this, the question of expense must be given up; for it is impossible with any degree of safety to narrow the foundation upon which the system is to stand. The two branches of the legislature are, in the first instance, to consist of only sixty-five persons, which is the same number of which Congress, under the existing Confederation, may be composed. It is true that this number is intended to be increased; but this is to keep pace with the progress of the population and resources of the country. It is evident that a less number would, even in the first instance, have been unsafe, and that a continuance of the present number would, in a more advanced stage of population, be a very inadequate representation of the people.

Whence is the dreaded augmentation of expense to spring? One source indicated is the multiplication of offices under the new government. Let us examine this a little.

It is evident that the principal departments of the administration under the present government are the same which will be required under the new. There are now a Secretary of War, a Secretary of Foreign Affairs, a Secretary for Domestic Affairs, a Board of Treasury consisting of three persons, a Treasurer, assistants, clerks, etc. These officers are indispensable under any system, and will suffice under the new as well as the old. As to ambassadors and other ministers and agents in foreign countries, the proposed Constitution can make no other difference than to render their characters, where they reside, more respectable, and their services more useful. As to persons to be employed in the collection of the revenues, it is unquestionably true that these will form a very considerable addition to the number of federal officers; but it will not follow that this will occasion an increase of public expense. It will be in most cases nothing more than an exchange of State for national officers. In the collection of all duties, for instance, the persons employed will be wholly of the latter description. The States individually will stand in no need of any for this purpose. What difference can it make in point of expense to pay officers of the customs appointed by the State or by the United States?

Where then are we to seek for those additional articles of expense which are to swell the account to the enormous size that has been represented to us? The chief item which occurs to me respects the support of the judges of the United States. I do not add the President, because there is now a president of Congress, whose expenses may not be far, if any thing, short of those which will be incurred on account of the President of the United States. The support of the judges will clearly be an extra expense, but to what extent will depend on the particular plan which may be adopted in regard to this matter. But upon no reasonable plan can it amount to a sum which will be an object of material consequence.

Let us now see what there is to counterbalance any extra expense that may attend the establishment of the proposed government. The first thing which presents itself is that a great part of the business which now keeps Congress sitting through the year will be transacted by the President. Even the management of foreign negotiations will naturally devolve upon him, according to general principles concerted with the Senate, and subject to their final concurrence. Hence it is evident that a portion of the year will suffice for the session of both the Senate and the House of Representatives; we may suppose about a fourth for the latter and a third, or perhaps half, for the former. The extra business of treaties and appointments may give this extra occupation to the Senate. From this circumstance we may infer that, until the House of Representatives shall be increased greatly beyond its present number, there will be a considerable saving of expense from the difference between the constant session of the present and the temporary session of the future Congress.

But there is another circumstance of great importance in the view of economy. The business of the United States has hitherto occupied the State legislatures, as well as Congress. The latter has made requisitions which the former have had to provide for. Hence it has happened that the sessions of the State legislatures have been protracted greatly beyond what was necessary for the execution of the mere local business of the States. More than half their time has been frequently employed in matters which related to the United States. Now the members who compose the legislatures of the several States amount to two thousand and upwards, which number has hitherto performed what under the new system will be done in the first instance by sixty-five persons, and probably at no future period by above a fourth or a fifth of that number. The Congress under the proposed government will do all the business of the United States themselves, without the intervention of the State legislatures, who thenceforth will have only to attend to the affairs of their particular States, and will not have to sit in any proportion as long as they have heretofore done. This difference in the time of the sessions of the State legislatures will be clear gain, and will alone form an article of saving, which may be regarded as an equivalent for any additional objects of expense that may be occasioned by the adoption of the new system.

The result from these observations is that the sources of additional expense from the establishment of the proposed Constitution are much fewer than may have been imagined; that they are counterbalanced by considerable objects of saving; and that while it is questionable on which side the scale will preponderate, it is certain that a government less expensive would be incompetent to the purposes of the Union.

PUBLIUS

THE FEDERALIST NO. 85

(HAMILTON)

To the People of the State of New York:

According to the formal division of the subject of these papers, announced in my first number, there would appear still to remain for discussion two points: "the analogy of the proposed government to your own State constitution," and "the additional security which its adoption will afford to republican government, to liberty, and to property." But these heads have been so fully anticipated and exhausted in the progress of the work, that it would now scarcely be possible to do any thing more than repeat, in a more dilated form, what has been heretofore said . . .

It is remarkable, that the resemblance of the plan of the convention to the act which organizes the government of this State holds, not less with regard to many of the supposed defects, than to the real excellences of the former. Among the pretended defects are the reëligibility of the Executive, the want of a council, the omission of a formal bill of rights, the omission of a provision respecting the liberty of the press. These and several others which have been noted in the course of our inquiries are as much chargeable on the existing constitution of this State, as on the one proposed for the Union; and a man must have slender pretensions to consistency, who can rail at the latter for imperfections which he finds no difficulty in excusing in the former. Nor indeed can there be a better proof of the insincerity and affectation of some of the zealous adversaries of the plan of the convention among us, who profess to be the devoted admirers of the government under which they live, than the fury with which they have attacked that plan for matters in regard to which our own constitution is equally or perhaps more vulnerable.

The additional securities to republican government, to liberty, and to property, to be derived from the adoption of the plan under consideration, consist chiefly in the restraints which the preservation of the Union will impose on local factions and insurrections, and on the ambition of powerful individuals in single States who may acquire credit and influence enough from leaders and favorites to become the despots of the people; in the diminution of the opportunities to foreign intrigue, which the dissolution of the Confederacy would invite and facilitate; in the prevention of extensive military establishments, which could not fail to grow out of wars between the States in a disunited situation; in the express guaranty of a republican form of government to each; in the absolute and universal exclusion of titles of nobility; and in the precautions against the repetition of those practices on the part of the State governments which have undermined the foundations of property and credit, have planted mutual distrust in the breasts of all classes of citizens, and have occasioned an almost universal prostration of morals.

Thus have I, fellow-citizens, executed the task I had assigned to myself; with what success, your conduct must determine. I trust at least you will admit that I have not failed in the assurance I gave you respecting the spirit with which my endeavors should be conducted. I have addressed myself

purely to your judgments, and have studiously avoided those
asperities which are too apt to disgrace political disputants of
all parties, and which have been not a little provoked by the
language and conduct of the opponents of the Constitution.
The charge of a conspiracy against the liberties of the people,
which has been indiscriminately brought against the advocates
of the plan, has something in it too wanton and too malignant
not to excite the indignation of every man who feels in his
own bosom a refutation of the calumny. The perpetual
changes which have been rung upon the wealthy, the well-
born, and the great, have been such as to inspire the disgust
of all sensible men. And the unwarrantable concealments and
misrepresentations which have been in various ways practised
to keep the truth from the public eye, have been of a nature
to demand the reprobation of all honest men. It is not impossible that these circumstances may have occasionally betrayed me into intemperances of expression which I did not
intend; it is certain that I have frequently felt a struggle between sensibility and moderation; and if the former has in
some instances prevailed, it must be my excuse that it has
been neither often nor much.

Let us now pause and ask ourselves whether, in the course
of these papers, the proposed Constitution has not been satisfactorily vindicated from the aspersions thrown upon it; and
whether it has not been shown to be worthy of the public
approbation and necessary to the public safety and prosperity.
Every man is bound to answer these questions to himself according to the best of his conscience and understanding, and
to act agreeably to the genuine and sober dictates of his judgment. This is a duty from which nothing can give him a dis-
pensation. 'Tis one that he is called upon, nay, constrained
by all the obligations that form the bands of society, to discharge sincerely and honestly. No partial motive, no particular
interest, no pride of opinion, no temporary passion or prejudice, will justify to himself, to his country, or to his posterity,
an improper election of the part he is to act. Let him beware
of an obstinate adherence to party; let him reflect that the object upon which he is to decide is not a particular interest of
the community, but the very existence of the nation; and let

him remember that a majority of America has already given its sanction to the plan which he is to approve or reject.

I shall not dissemble that I feel an entire confidence in the arguments which recommend the proposed system to your adoption, and that I am unable to discern any real force in those by which it has been opposed. I am persuaded that it is the best which our political situation, habits, and opinions will admit, and superior to any the revolution has produced.

Concessions on the part of the friends of the plan, that it has not a claim to absolute perfection, have afforded matter of no small triumph to its enemies. "Why," say they, "should we adopt an imperfect thing? Why not amend it and make it perfect before it is irrevocably established?" This may be plausible enough, but it is only plausible. In the first place I remark, that the extent of these concessions has been greatly exaggerated. They have been stated as amounting to an admission that the plan is radically defective, and that without material alterations the rights and the interests of the community cannot be safely confided to it. This, as far as I have understood the meaning of those who make the concessions, is an entire perversion of their sense. No advocate of the measure can be found, who will not declare as his sentiment, that the system, though it may not be perfect in every part, is, upon the whole, a good one; is the best that the present views and circumstances of the country will permit; and is such an one as promises every species of security which a reasonable people can desire.

I answer in the next place, that I should esteem it the extreme of imprudence to prolong the precarious state of our national affairs, and to expose the Union to the jeopardy of successive experiments, in the chimerical pursuit of a perfect plan. I never expect to see a perfect work from imperfect man. The result of the deliberations of all collective bodies must necessarily be a compound, as well of the errors and prejudices as of the good sense and wisdom of the individuals of whom they are composed. The compacts which are to embrace thirteen distinct States in a common bond of amity and union, must as necessarily be a compromise of as many dissimilar interests and inclinations. How can perfection spring from such materials?

The reasons assigned in an excellent little pamphlet lately published in this city,[122] are unanswerable to show the utter improbability of assembling a new convention, under circumstances in any degree so favorable to a happy issue, as those in which the late convention met, deliberated, and concluded. I will not repeat the arguments there used, as I presume the production itself has had an extensive circulation. It is certainly well worthy the perusal of every friend to his country. There is, however, one point of light in which the subject of amendments still remains to be considered, and in which it has not yet been exhibited to public view. I cannot resolve to conclude without first taking a survey of it in this aspect.

It appears to me susceptible of absolute demonstration that it will be far more easy to obtain subsequent than previous amendments to the Constitution. The moment an alteration is made in the present plan, it becomes, to the purpose of adoption, a new one, and must undergo a new decision of each State. To its complete establishment throughout the Union, it will therefore require the concurrence of thirteen States. If, on the contrary, the Constitution proposed should once be ratified by all the States as it stands, alterations in it may at any time be effected by nine States. Here, then, the chances are as thirteen to nine[123] in favor of subsequent amendment, rather than of the original adoption of an entire system.

This is not all. Every Constitution for the United States must inevitably consist of a great variety of particulars, in which thirteen independent States are to be accommodated in their interests or opinions of interest. We may of course expect to see in any body of men charged with its original formation very different combinations of the parts upon different points. Many of those who form a majority on one question may become the minority on a second, and an association dissimilar to either may constitute the majority on a third. Hence the necessity of moulding and arranging all the particulars which are to compose the whole, in such a manner as to satisfy all the parties to the compact; and hence, also, an immense multiplication of difficulties and casualties in obtaining the collective assent to a final act. The degree of that multiplication must evidently be in a ratio to the number of particulars and the number of parties.

But every amendment to the Constitution . . . would be a single proposition, and might be brought forward singly. There would then be no necessity for management or compromise, in relation to any other point—no giving nor taking. The will of the requisite number would at once bring the matter to a decisive issue. And consequently, whenever nine, or rather ten States, were united in the desire of a particular amendment that amendment must infallibly take place. There can, therefore, be no comparison between the facility of affecting an amendment and that of establishing in the first instance a complete Constitution.

In opposition to the probability of subsequent amendments, it has been urged that the persons delegated to the administration of the national government will always be disinclined to yield up any portion of the authority of which they were once possessed. For my own part, I acknowledge a thorough conviction that any amendments which may, upon mature consideration, be thought useful, will be applicable to the organization of the government, not to the mass of its powers; and on this account alone, I think there is no weight in the observation just stated. I also think there is little weight in it on another account. The intrinsic difficulty of governing thirteen States at any rate, independent of calculations upon an ordinary degree of public spirit and integrity, will . . . constantly impose on the national rulers the necessity of a spirit of accommodation to the reasonable expectations of their constituents. But there is yet a further consideration, which proves beyond the possibility of a doubt that the observation is futile. It is this, that the national rulers, whenever nine States concur, will have no option upon the subject. By the fifth article of the plan, the Congress will be obliged "on the application of the legislatures of two thirds of the States . . . to call a convention for proposing amendments, which shall be valid, to all intents and purposes, as part of the Constitution, when ratified by the legislatures of three fourths of the States, or by conventions in three fourths thereof" [*sic*]. The words of this article are peremptory. The Congress "shall call a convention." Nothing in this particular is left to the discretion of that body. And of consequence, all the declamation about the disinclination to a change vanishes in air. Nor however difficult it may be supposed to unite two thirds or three fourths of the State legislatures, in amendments which may affect local interests, can there be any room to apprehend any such difficulty in a union on points which are merely relative to the general liberty or security of the people. We may safely rely on the disposition of the State legislatures to erect barriers against the encroachments of the national authority.

If the foregoing argument is a fallacy, certain it is that I am myself deceived by it, for it is . . . one of those rare instances in which a political truth can be brought to the test of a mathematical demonstration. Those who see the matter in the same light with me, however zealous they may be for amendments, must agree in the propriety of a previous adoption as the most direct road to their own object.

The zeal for attempts to amend, prior to the establishment of the Constitution, must abate in every man who is ready to accede to the truth of the following observations of a writer equally solid and ingenious: "To balance a large state or society . . . whether monarchical or republican, on general laws, is a work of so great difficulty, that no human genius, however comprehensive, is able, by the mere dint of reason and reflection, to effect it. The judgments of many must unite in the work; experience must guide their labor; time must bring it to perfection, and the feeling of inconveniences must correct the mistakes which they *inevitably* fall into in their first trials and experiments."[124] These judicious reflections contain a lesson of moderation to all the sincere lovers of the Union, and ought to put them upon their guard against hazarding anarchy, civil war, a perpetual alienation of the States from each other, and perhaps the military despotism of a victorious demagogue, in the pursuit of what they are not likely to obtain, but from time and experience. It may be in me a defect of political fortitude, but I acknowledge that I cannot entertain an equal tranquillity with those who affect to treat the dangers of a longer continuance in our present situation as imaginary. A nation without a national government is, in my view, an awful spectacle. The establishment of a Constitution in time of profound peace by the voluntary consent of a whole people is a prodigy, to the completion of which I look forward with trembling anxiety. I can reconcile it to no rules of prudence to let go the hold we now have, in so arduous an enterprise, upon seven out of the thirteen States, and after having passed over so considerable a part of the ground, to recommence the course. I dread the more the consequences of new attempts, because I know that powerful individuals, in this and in other States, are enemies to a general national government in every possible shape. PUBLIUS

ACKNOWLEDGMENTS

Acknowledging professional assistance is an inadequate process at best. Where does one draw the line between those providing background and those participating in the immediate result?

Professor Benjamin F. Wright provided the initial impetus for my interest in the *Federalist*. His lectures in political philosophy at Harvard invariably included references to or analysis of the great work.

In addition to those specifically cited in the annotation and bibliography, I wish to express appreciation to the following for the usual library courtesies: the staffs of Harvard Law School, Widener, Houghton, William L. Clements, New York Public, Congressional, Ohio State University, and Ohio University libraries. For the names of foreign scholars: the cultural-affairs officers of a large number of embassies in Washington. For particular insights regarding the Italian translation: Dr. Remsen Bird. For considerable routine research and clerical work: Anthony Cantagallo, Ronald Endrizal, Martha Goebel, Judith Hutchison, Phyllis Ihle, Larry Van Meter, Joseph Moore and Barbara Warner. For access to a representative group of high school textbooks: Edward Waterman and Philip Cosgrove of Uniondale High School, New York. For miscellaneous checking of "obscure data": Ellen P. Huddleson of G. P. Putnam's Sons, Professor Peter Waring, Margaret Carroll, and Melissa Moulton. For financial assistance in the early stages of the project: Professor Thomas Smith and the Ohio University Research Committee. For translation assistance and critical reading of various portions of the text: Ohio University students, Roger Moss and William Muller; my colleagues, Professors Richard Bald, Wallace

Cameron, Raymond H. Gusteson, Lewis Ondis, Harry R. Stevens, and Walter W. Wright; also, Professor Otto Krash of Yeshiva University. For duty and clerical work beyond the call of patience, my wife and my daughter, Maryllyn and Donna.

Acknowledgments Continued, 1966

To United States Information Service librarians around the world: for information pertaining to foreign editions and the circulation of the *Federalist* at their respective posts; special thanks to Anne M. Davis, Director of USIS librarians in East Africa, to Marilyn P. Johnson in Mali, and to those from whom data is cited in the preface. To Claire Murphy, for secretarial assistance. To Roger Moss and Gordon Keller for constructive suggestions.

ANNOTATIVE APPENDIX

Space limitations preclude technical documentation, but abbreviations should not seriously retard the reference process. Items which also appear in the bibliography have been simplified more drastically than the others.

A. *Notes on the Introduction*

1. Merrill Jensen, *The Articles of Confederation,* 3; John C. Ranney, "The Bases of American Federalism," *Wm. & Mary Quarterly* (Jan. 1946), 7; Harry Tarr, "Hamilton, Madison, and 'The Federalist,'" *Scholastic* (Nov. 25, 1940), 12, 16. George Washington used the term, "Disunited States," in a moment of despair during the Revolution.

2. Max Farrand, *The Records of the Federal Convention,* I, 304–11; John C. Miller, *Alexander Hamilton: Portrait in Paradox,* 49, 159–64.

3. Farrand, *op. cit.,* I, 48; this is Elbridge Gerry's phrase.

4. Paul L. Ford, ed., *Essays on the Constitution,* 285.

5. Alexander Hamilton, *Works,* IX, 425.

6. Henry Gilpin, ed., *The Papers of James Madison,* I, 648.

7. Other Federalist Party writers: Noah and Pelatiah Webster, John Dickinson, Tench Coxe, James Iredell, James Sullivan, Charles Pinckney, Roger Sherman, and James Wilson; anti-Federalists: Edmund Randolph, Richard Harry Lee, Samuel Chase, Abraham and Robert Yates, and Thomas Treadwell.

8. See Paul L. Ford, *op. cit.,* and Ford, ed., *Pamphlets on the Constitution.*

9. "Publius," adopted from the praenomen of a Roman patriot, Valerius Publicola; William C. Rives, *History of the Life and Times of James Madison,* II, 484.

10. William Duer wrote several numbers, but they were not included. Gouverneur Morris was "warmly pressed" to assist, but he refused. John McMaster, *A History of the People of the United States* (N.Y., 1885), I, 481–84; Gottfried Dietze, *The Federalist*, 101.

11. *Writings*, I, 361. Washington did attend to the republishing of some of the early numbers, but the project was discontinued. Matthew Carey also republished *Nos*. 1–5 in *The American Museum* (Phila.), Nov. 1787, II, 441–46, 523–34. But there is no public record of the reprinting of the *Federalist* papers during the crucial 1787–88 period. The compilation of such a list might assist us appreciably in measuring their influence.

12. Jonathan Elliot, *Debates*, V, 569; John T. Horton, *James Kent* (N.Y., 1939), 57.

13. Madison and Hamilton disclosed their authorship to Washington and Randolph. Brant, *James Madison*, III, 171; Madison, *Writings*, I, 361; Elliot, *op. cit.*, V, 569.

14. *Ibid.*

15. Though Madison returned to Virginia for the convention, his continued interest in the project is reflected in correspondence in which he makes suggestions about concurrent state-federal jurisdiction, points which Hamilton covered in *Nos*. 81–82. When the volumes came out, Hamilton sent Madison fifty-two copies for use in the ratifying debates. Rives, *op. cit.*, II, 503; Douglass Adair, "The Authorship of the Disputed Federalist Papers," *Wm. & Mary Quarterly* (July 1944), 235–36.

16. Quoted by Miller, *op. cit.*, 212.

17. *Ibid.*, 210–15; Andrew C. McLaughlin, *A Constitutional History of the U.S.* (N.Y., 1935), 208 ff; E. W. Spaulding, *His Excellency George Clinton*, 166–83.

18. For lists of amendments proposed at the state conventions, see Elliot, *op. cit.*, II–IV.

19. Quoted by Miller, *op. cit.*, 190.

20. Since some of the most controversial points in the Constitution were not discussed until most of the state conventions had been held, the probability is that the *Federalist* was not too influential. There is considerable variety of opinion on the matter. Some representative views: Benjamin

Andrews, *History of the U.S.* (N.Y., 1906), I, 239, says, "These discussions seemed to have much effect." Max Farrand remarks, ". . . it is doubtful how much immediate influence they had," *The Fathers of the Constitution*, 157. Harold U. Faulkner believes that the exact nature of the influence is "unknown," *American Political and Social History* (N.Y., 1937), 125. Carl Van Doren says that the book ". . . was too learned and reasonable to catch votes in the hustings," *The Great Rehearsal* (N.Y., 1948), 231. Since the majority in the N.H. and Va. conventions was only ten and that in N.Y. merely three, a shift of fourteen votes would have defeated ratification in those three states. Thus the margin of victory was thin. See Charles Beard, *An Economic Interpretation*, 217–91, and Robert E. Brown, *Charles Beard and the Constitution*, 138–56; Martin Diamond, "Democracy and *The Federalist* . . . ," *American Political Science Review* (Mar. 1959), 56.

21. McMaster, *op. cit.*, 484.

22. Paul L. Ford, *Pamphlets*, 395.

23. John McMaster and Frederick D. Stone, eds., *Pennsylvania and the Federal Constitution*, 635–36; John Fiske, *The Critical Period of American History*, 340.

24. Noah Webster, *American Magazine*, Mar. 1788; John Adams, *Works* (Boston, 1856), III, 20; Beard quotes Jefferson's remark in *The Enduring Federalist*, 17.

25. George Washington, *Writings*, ed., by J. C Fitzpatrick (Washington, 1939), XXX, 66.

26. Gibbons *v.* Ogden (1824).

27. See Bibliographical Appendix. Contemporary use abroad confirmed by personal correspondence with all U.S.I.A. libraries and about forty foreign scholars.

28. Quoted by Diamond, *op. cit.*, 53. After examining the political views of each Convention delegate, Beard concludes "that the authors of *The Federalist* generalized the political doctrines of the members of the Convention with a high degree of precision, in spite of the great diversity of opinion which prevailed on many matters," *op. cit.*, 216.

29. Cohens *v.* Virginia (1821); James Kent, *Commentaries on American Law* (N.Y., 1836), I, 241.

30. Benjamin F. Wright, "*The Federalist* on the Nature of

Political Man," *Ethics* (Jan. 1949), 26; William Rawle, *A View of the Constitution of the U.S.A.* (Phila., 1829), 37.

31. George W. Pierson, *Tocqueville and Beaumont in America* (N.Y., 1938), 602–7, 719–38; the [N.Y.] *Evening Post,* Apr. 6, 1864; Henry Maine, *Popular Government* (London, 1885), 202–53; Edward Freeman, *History of Federal Government in Greece and Italy* (London, 1893), 9, 10, 57, 74, 110–11, *passim.*; H. W. Torrey[?], *North American Review* (Apr. 1864), 586.

32. Henry Brackenridge, *Voyage to South America* (London, 1820), II, 141–42. For Canadian and Australian use, I made a thorough search of the *Canadian Parliamentary Debates* (Quebec, 1865), several Canadian histories, and many documents pertaining to the Australian Constitution-making period, including *Proceedings* of the 1891 and 1897 debates (London, 1891; Adelaide & Sydney, 1897); also, Howard Willoughby, *Australian Federation* (Melbourne, 1891); Robert Garran, *The Coming Commonwealth* (Sydney, 1897); H. S. Nicholas, *The Australian Constitution* (Sydney, 1952). For South African use, see Allan M. Hamilton, *The Intimate Life of Alexander Hamilton* (N.Y., 1910), 454–55.

33. Letter, Dr. Remsen Bird to Roy P. Fairfield (hereafter, RPF), May 24, 1959.

34. The New York *Times,* Oct. 26, 1955.

35. Bird, *op. cit.;* letter, R. G. Shephard of Crown Zellerbach to RPF, Oct. 24, 1958.

36. Letter, Gertrude S. Hooker, American Embassy, Rome, to RPF, Oct. 28, 1958.

37. Letter, Prof. Makoto Saito, Tokyo University, to RPF, Mar. 15, 1959; Dr. William Weld, American Embassy, Paris, to RPF, Oct. 15, 1958.

38. Letter, K. C. Wheare, Oxford University, to RPF, Jan. 21, 1959. Translation is currently progressing in several Asiatic languages. Letters, Bernard J. Lavin, U.S.I.A., Seoul, Korea, Oct. 31, 1959, Mar. 29, 1960; Dorothy Clark, U.S.I.A., Bombay, Nov. 7, 1958; Michael Weyl, U.S.I.A., Washington, Mar. 24 and Apr. 4, 1960.

39. For example: at an American studies seminar in Korea in the summer of 1959 a U.S.I.A. staff officer delivered a paper on the *Federalist* which aroused the interest of the Vice-

Minister of Education, Bernard Lavin, *op. cit.;* following the Italian translation, a symposium was held on the subject and subsequently the proceedings were published: Luciano Bolis, ed., *La Nascita degli Stati Uniti* (Milano, 1957); in the spring of 1958 a seminar at the University of Pavia used the *Federalist* as the basic text; Gertrude Hooker, *op. cit.*

40. Max Beloff, ed., *The Federalist,* viii. This and other quotations from Beloff by permission of Basil Blackwell & Mott.

41. William Crosskey, *Politics and the Constitution in the History of the U.S.* (Chicago, 1950), I, 8–9, 11. Quoted by permission of the University of Chicago Press.

42. Clinton Rossiter, *Review of Politics* (Apr. 1954), 240.

43. Examples: S. G. Goodrich, *The Young American or Book of Government and Law* (N.Y., 1847); George Bancroft, *History of the Formation of the Constitution* (N.Y., 1882); Edward E. Hale, *History of the U.S.* (N.Y., 1887); John Burgess, *Political Science and Comparative Constitutional Law* (Boston, 1886); James T. Adams, *History of the U.S.* (N.Y., 1933); Alan Nevins & Henry S. Commager, *America: The Story of a Free People* (Boston, 1943); Merle Curti, *The Growth of American Thought* (N.Y., 1943). For one report on the woeful state of student knowledge, see Roy P. Fairfield, "Progress by the Inch," *Ohio Schools* (Nov. 1959), 26–27. A check of seventeen "citizenship" textbooks used in American high schools revealed only three casual references to the *Federalist.* Of seventeen history and government texts, twelve made only minimal reference to the essays. Careful study of one or two of these texts, however, reveals that the authors continue to rely heavily upon outdated scholarship; see James Quillen and Edward Krug, *Living in Our America* (Chicago, 1956), 180, and Leon Canfield and Howard Wilder, *The Making of Modern America* (Cambridge, 1958), 137–38. School histories by John Fiske (1894), John McMaster (1903), and Channing (1906) contained no references to the "famous" papers! A survey of seventeen textbooks currently used for various elementary courses in American colleges and universities reveals minimal reference to the *Federalist's* place in history, wide use in comparative analysis, and one outright error regarding the authors' ano-

nymity (Cortez A. M. Ewing, *American National Government,* N.Y., 1958, 44 n). Of course, college professors make wide use of source materials, and the *Federalist* does appear in many anthologies, thus student contact with the book should not be judged solely upon its use in textbook materials.

44. Clarence Streit, *et al., The New Federalist,* intro. by John F. Dulles, xvi. Letter, Mrs. John F. Dulles to RPF, Dec. 1, 1959, indicates that the *Federalist* influenced his thinking. James Burnham uses the book similarly in *Congress and the American Tradition* (Chicago, 1959). Also, see the 1923 Henry C. Lodge edition, pp. liv–lix, in which Charles W. Pierson compiles a list of forty-five Supreme Court decisions, 1789–1923, in which the book is mentioned.

45. Clarence Streit, *op. cit.,* ix–x. This and the above quoted by permission of Harper & Brothers.

46. Streit, *Union Now* (N.Y., 1940) and *Union Now with Britain* (N.Y., 1941); Norman Cousins, ed., "For a Permanent United Nations," *Saturday Review of Literature* (June 12, 1943), 12; Cousins, "World Citizenship—When?" in Lyman Bryson, ed., *Approaches to World Peace* (N.Y., 1944); Cousins, *Modern Man Is Obsolete* (N.Y., 1945) and *'In God We Trust'* (N.Y., 1958). Rudolf Krämer-Badoni, reviewing the German edition of the *Federalist* for *Frankfurter Allgemeine,* Aug. 8, 1959, indicates that the book offers an excellent example for the Europeans at a time when unification is being pressed. After all, he points out, the Americans did develop a wonderfully functional Constitution despite the pressure under which they worked in 1787.

47. Letter, Edward W. McVitty to RPF, Sept. 16, 1958.

48. Douglass Adair, *op. cit.,* 97–122, 235–64.

49. Comparative lists: Hamilton's: Jay—*2, 3, 4, 5, 54;* Madison—*10, 14, 37–48;* Madison & Hamilton—*18–20;* Hamilton—the balance.

Adair's: same as above, except—Jay wrote *64* rather than *54;* Madison compiled most of *18–20,* obtaining only minor help from Hamilton; Madison also wrote *49–58* and *62–63.*

50. Gottfried Dietze, *The Political Theory of the Federalist,* 13.

51. Charles Merriam, *A History of American Political Theories* (N.Y., 1924), 119–20; Neal Riemer, "James Madi-

son and the Current Conservative Vogue," *Antioch Review* (Winter, 1954–55), 459; Sobei Mogi, *The Problem of Federalism* (London, 1931), I, 46.

52. For specific sources see the annotative notes on the text which follow. John C. Miller, *op. cit.*, 140, points out that ". . . Hamilton's reading was seldom a decisive force in establishing the convictions upon which he acted." For further details pertaining to the sources from which Hamilton and Madison drew, see Beloff, *op. cit.*, lvi–lxi; Theodore Dwight, "Harrington and His Influence . . . ," *Political Science Quarterly* (Mar. 1887), 1–44; E. P. Panagopoulos, *Classicism and the Framers of the Constitution;* E. G. Bourne, "The Use of History Made by the Framers of the Constitution," *American Historical Association Annual Report,* I (1896), 221–28; Dietze, *The Federalist,* 289–331.

53. From this point, numbers of specific essays will be included in the text to save space and to make for easy reference. In his Ph.D. dissertation, 188, Maynard Smith asks "whether the authors' philosophical orientation is not in itself a limitation upon the highest potentialities of reason, and hence upon the principles of freedom."

54. Panagopoulos, *op. cit.*, 212.

55. For further reference to axioms, see No. 23 and 44. Hamilton's discussion of geometrical, ethical, and political axioms is reminiscent of Spinoza's *Ethics*, though there is no necessary influence. Both Hamilton and Madison used such phrases and words as "precise demonstration," "momentum of civil power" (13), "eccentric tendency" (15), "equilibrium" (14), "commensurate" (50), "proportion" (10), and "probability" (60, 73) often enough to suggest the influence of science.

56. See *No. 38* for an excellent example of this technique.

57. See Mabel G. Benson's Ph.D. dissertation, *Some Rhetorical Characteristics of the "Federalist,"* 4: ". . . the rhetorical richness of the work lies in the skill with which many organizational patterns are interwoven into one complex whole."

58. Miller, *op. cit.*, 144. For a balanced view of Shays, see Walter Dyer, "Embattled Farmers," *New England Quarterly* (July 1931), 460–81.

59. Cecelia Kenyon, "Men of Little Faith: The Anti-Federalists . . . ," *Wm. & Mary Quarterly* (Jan. 1955), 15; Ford, *Pamphlets & Essays.* In *No.* 70 Hamilton said, "In tenderness to individuals I forbear to descend to particulars"; in *No. 85,* "I . . . have studiously avoided those asperities . . . too apt to disgrace political disputants of all parties . . ."

60. Diamond, *op. cit.,* 56. This and other quotes from the *American Political Science Review,* by permission of the *American Political Science Review.*

61. Ford, *Essays,* 288–89.

62. Wright, *op. cit.,* 1–31.

63. For full discussions of Madison's republicanism, see: E. M. Burns, *James Madison, Philosopher of the Constitution;* Dietze, *The Federalist;* Adrienne Koch, "James Madison and the Workshop of Liberty," *Review of Politics* (Apr. 1954), 175–93; and the several articles by Riemer listed in the bibliography.

64. Wright, *op. cit.,* 19; Riemer, *Antioch* article, 460.

65. A. T. Mason, "The Federalist—A Split Personality," *American Historical Review* (Apr. 1952), 625–43; Dietze, *The Federalist.* But even before Mason's and Dietze's work, Herbert Schneider, writing in *A History of American Philosophy* (N.Y., 1946), 94, perceptively remarked that Hamilton's "bold use of the terms 'national,' [*sic*] his references to 'the streams of national power' and 'fabric of American Empire,' required much clever explaining by his fellow author, Madison." (By permission of Columbia University Press.)

66. Beard, *op. cit.,* and Brown, *op. cit.,* disagree as to how democratic the ratification was.

67. In *No.* 37, for example, Hamilton says the convention "must have" done this, "must have" done that, as though he had never attended but was speculating upon the nature of the delegates' decision-making.

68. Mason points out, for example, that Madison's nationalism in *No. 14* was qualified in *39* and *40,* bolstered in *44;* Hamilton's nationalism in *Nos. 9, 15,* and *22* was toned down in *32. Op. cit.,* 641–42; also, see Panagopoulos, *op. cit.,* 28.

69. See annotative notes on the text, below.

70. Richard Morris, "The Confederation Period and the American Historian," *Wm. & Mary Quarterly* (Apr. 1956), 156, and Kenyon, *op. cit.*, 38, argue that the republican federalism which the *Federalist* proposed constituted a sharper break with the past than the colonists' severing of ties with England, thus "the Federalists and not the anti-Federalists were the radicals of the day." (Morris.)

71. Kenyon, *op. cit.*

(For *Notes on Preface to Second Edition*, see page 306.)

B. *Notes on the Text*

1. Those wishing to consult a modern text or two while studying the *Federalist's* deliberations will find Edwin S. Corwin's *The Constitution and What It Means Today*, 12th ed. (Princeton, 1958), most helpful as a clause-by-clause analysis. C. Herman Pritchett, in *The American Constitution* (N.Y., 1959), provides "an exposition of what the Supreme Court has said the American Constitution means" (p. ix). For a modern parallel to the *Federalist*, see Clarence Streit, *et al.*, *The New Federalist*.

2. Note overtones of the Age of Reason and an incipient concept of "Manifest Destiny."

3. For the impact of Scottish social science upon the founding fathers, see Douglass Adair, " 'That Politics May Be Reduced to a Science' . . . ," *The Huntington Library Quarterly* (Aug. 1957), 343–60. Prof. Adair argues, 345–46, that their use of history was for scientific reasons and "not mere rhetorical-historical window-dressing." Edward Freeman, *op. cit.*, 249, Henry Dawson, ed., *The Foederalist*, and others have pointed out, however, that Hamilton and Madison were not always accurate in their historical observations. Theodore Dwight suggests that the Constitution-makers borrowed liberally from old English statutes, the English Bill of Rights, etc. "In fact, they borrowed right and left, and so made up a splendid mosaic . . . ," *op. cit.*, 3.

4. Jay's rhetoric was better than his factual information. By 1775, for example, a quarter of the people were non-British; by the time of the first census, 17.9 per cent. Nor had each person enjoyed the same privileges; the Quakers in Massachusetts and minority groups in other colonies had suf-

fered various forms of discrimination. Nor was the religion
uniform. And, as Daniel Boorstin points out in *The Genius
of American Politics* (Chicago, 1953), 73, ". . . the American Revolution was *not* the product of a nationalist spirit."

5. Again, Jay's rhetorical flourish obscures the fact that no
group of colonists spoke "as with one voice," nor did the *people* form the Convention, as he claims five paragraphs later.
Rhode Island, for example, didn't even send any delegates.
Patrick Henry "smelled a rat," while George Clinton, Elbridge
Gerry, Robert Yates, Luther Martin, Robert Lansing, and
others questioned the procedure of calling the Convention
and the techniques of conducting it; see Ford, *Essays*, 14,
252–53, 300–1; Ford, *Pamphlets*, 18; Elliot's *Debates*, I,
358, 387–88; Farrand, *Records*, I, 336; also see *Federalist, No.
40*, for Madison's defense of Convention procedures.

6. Charles Beard's *Economic Interpretation* substantially
shattered the myth that the fathers had *only* "love for their
country."

7. William Shakespeare, *King Henry VIII*, III, ii.

8. Consideration of just and unjust causes of war, so seem-
ingly remote from contemporary deliberations, found their
definitive statement in Hugo Grotius' *The Rights of War and
Peace* (Paris, 1625), to which the founders had ample exposure. Just as Jay discusses proportions and weights of causes,
so did Grotius reduce international relationships to mathematics. For this and other influences of the scientific revolution upon political thought, see George Sabine, *A History of
Political Theory* (N.Y., 1937), 426 *passim*.

9. Beard cites this and other passages on the causes of war
as evidence that "the army and navy are considered . . . as
genuine economic instrumentalities." *Op. cit.*, 171. By permission of the Macmillan Company.

10. Almost neglected in the nineteenth century, this essay
has been analyzed repeatedly since Beard's controversial *Economic Interpretation* (1913). Most of the dispute emanated
from the varying interpretations of the seventh paragraph,
which *seems* like a Marxian interpretation. For Beard's retrospective views on this issue, see Richard Hofstadter, "Beard
and the Constitution: the History of an Idea," *American
Quarterly* (Fall, 1950), 209–10. Douglass Adair, whose several

essays on the *Federalist* afford keen insights for the serious student, has suggested that Madison's own "strict rules" regarding "pecuniary matters" serves as an antidote to the economic interpretation. Madison resolved "never to deal in public property, land, debts or money, whilst a member of a [political] body whose proceedings might influence these transactions." Adair, "James Madison's Autobiography," *Wm. & Mary Quarterly* (Apr. 1945), 195. Also, see Madison's remarks about "the moneyed few" and their "unreasonable advantage" (62). For cogent evidence tracing Madison's debt in *No. 10* to David Hume, see Adair, "That Politics . . . ," *op. cit.*, and Ralph Ketcham, "Notes on James Madison's Sources . . . ," *Midwest Journal of Political Science* (May 1957), 20–25.

11. Compare with Jefferson's *First Inaugural:* ". . . that though the will of the majority is in all cases to prevail, that will, to be rightful, must be reasonable . . ." See Herbert McClosky, "The Fallacy of Absolute Majority Rule," *Journal of Politics* (Nov. 1949), 637–54, and Wilmoore Kendall's response, *ibid.* (Nov. 1950), 694–713.

12. Both Federalists and anti-Federalists used "faction" and "party" synonymously. And, as J. Allen Smith pointed out, English conservatives had the same objections to factions; *The Spirit of American Government* (N.Y., 1912), 205.

13. Contrast with *Federalist, No. 9*, in which Hamilton, arguing for union, says that, "The utility of a Confederacy, as well to suppress faction and to guard the internal tranquillity of States . . . is in reality not a new idea."

14. Adair points to this sentence as a compression of "the greater part of Hume's essay on factions." Adair, "That Politics . . . ," *op. cit.*, 358.

15. Harold Laski, stressing Madison's economic determinism, misquoted this passage as follows: "the only durable source of faction is property." *The Grammar of Politics* (London, 1925), 162.

16. For Marxist comparisons other than Beard's, see Saul K. Padover, ed., *The Complete Madison*, 14–15, and Jacques Barzun, *Darwin, Marx, Wagner* (Garden City, 1958), 146. For scholarly evaluations of the Marxist interpretation, see Diamond, *op. cit.*, 65–66; Adair, "The Tenth Federalist Re-

visited," *Wm. & Mary Quarterly* (Jan. 1951), 48–67; Wright, *op. cit.*, 17; Riemer, "Republicanism . . . ," *op. cit.*, 50–51.

17. Democracy had a bad name from early times. Plato condemned it in *The Republic* (Book VIII), Aristotle in *Politics* (Book IV). In more recent times, Montesquieu, who had a great impact upon the fathers, attacked it in *Spirit of Laws* (I, Book VIII). For an account of the conservative-democratic controversy in the 1763–87 period, see Merrill Jensen, *The Articles of Confederation* and *The New Nation;* for a few typical eighteenth-century views of democracy, see Richard Hofstadter, *The American Political Tradition* (N.Y., 1948), 4. As Ralph Ketcham points out, *op. cit.*, 25, ". . . there was almost universal agreement in the eighteenth century that 'democracy' was a nasty word—it meant tumult, violence, instability, mob rule, and bloody revolution." (By permission of the Wayne State University Press.) For two other valuable historical and philosophical views, see Harold Laski's essay on the concept in the *Encyclopedia of the Social Sciences* (N.Y., 1931), V, 76–84, and Henry B. Mayo, *An Introduction to Democratic Theory* (N.Y., 1960).

18. A variation on a theme? Also, see Jay's reliance upon Providence in *No. 2.* Other "chosen people" concepts: Hebrew, England's Whig oligarchy, New England's theocratic oligarchy, etc. Suggested by B. C. Rodick, *American Constitutional Custom* (N.Y., 1953), 136.

19. It might be asked, Where does Madison acquire his faith in the magic of numbers? Does he come to grips with the problem of the demagogue? And does he discuss comprehensively the fact that the impediments eliminating the dire effects of faction might also prevent positive action? Is Louis Hartz correct when he claims that Madison did not solve the problem of faction as related to economic factors? *The Liberal Tradition in America* (N.Y., 1955), 84–85.

20. Aristotle said that "the size of a state . . . should be determined by the range of a man's voice," quoted by Cousins, "World Citizenship . . . ," *op. cit.*, 523. And such remained the thought and experience of the eighteenth century, that a republic was feasible only in a small geographic area. Thus it is not surprising to find the anti-Federalists attacking the concept of the extensive republic found in the Constitution

and *Federalist, No. 10;* Ford, *Essays,* 4, 74, 76, 91, 255–56. Adair, tracing the sources for *No. 10,* suggests that Madison may have been "electrified" by the following comments in Hume:

> *In a large government, which is modelled with masterly skill, there is compass and room enough to refine the democracy, from the lower people, who may be admitted into the first elections or first concoction of the commonwealth, to the higher magistrates, who direct all the movements. At the same time, the parts are so distant and remote, that it is very difficult, either by intrigue, prejudice, or passion, to hurry them into any measure against the public interest.* Op. cit., 351.

21. Diamond, *op. cit.,* 60, argues that the novelty "consisted in solving the problems of popular government by means which yet maintain the government 'wholly popular.' "

22. For a documentary outline of the steps leading to the Convention, 1781–87, see Elliot's *Debates,* I, 92–120. For an analysis similar to the one Madison made in *No. 15,* see Farrand, *Records,* I, 19. Jensen, *Articles,* 3 ff, points out that the Federalists began to propagandize about the weakness of the Articles of Confederation as early as May 1787. Washington referred to the Confederation as "a half-starved, limping government, that appears to be always moving upon crutches, and tottering at every step." *Writings, op. cit.,* XXVII, 305–6. For a preview of Madison's view of the defects, see his "Vices of the Political System of the United States," *Writings,* Hunt edition, II, 361 ff. Edward S. Corwin observes that for all the weaknesses of the Articles, they did keep the idea of union alive and give "formal recognition" to the fact that "war and foreign relations were intrinsically national in character." "The Progress of Constitutional Theory between the Declaration of Independence and the Meeting of the Philadelphia Convention," *American Historical Review* (Apr. 1925), 527.

23. It is doubtful that, dark as conditions were, things were as black as Madison depicts them here and in *No. 62* (Hamilton in *Nos. 30* and *81*). Beard warned in 1913, for example, that American history up to that point had been written by

Federalists; *Economic Interpretation,* 48. And John Fiske's analysis of the Confederation period in *The Critical Period of American History,* Chapter 4, exemplified Beard's view. Contemporary anti-Federalists such as Melanchthon Smith and Elbridge Gerry argued to the contrary, and John C. Miller, a modern scholar, observes that the economic crisis *was* easing, even if the political crisis was not; Ford, *Pamphlets;* Miller, *op. cit.,* 149. For a balanced view of conditions, see Richard B. Morris, "The Confederation Period and the American Historians," *Wm. & Mary Quarterly* (Apr. 1956), 139–56; also, Jensen, *The New Nation.*

24. William Riker observes that Madison and Hamilton were uncertain about the exact character of the new polity they had created. They knew it was unique, but "they could not state with adequate generality how their federalism improved others." He concludes that the uniqueness consisted of the centralizing of federalism; the "peripherized federalism" which they envisioned didn't develop. Rather, "American federalism allowed the central government to do almost all its business directly with persons—its taxing, its recruiting, its policing, its judging, etc." "The Senate and American Federalism," *American Political Science Review* (June 1955), 452–53.

25. There follows, here and in *Nos. 18, 19,* and *20,* a discussion of the strengths and weaknesses of ancient, medieval, and modern confederations. Regarding the value and validity of these numbers, omitted in this edition, Edward Freeman remarked, "Those chapters . . . show every disposition to make practical use of ancient precedents, but they show very little knowledge as to what those precedents really were. It is clear that Hamilton and Madison knew hardly anything more of Grecian history than what they picked up from the 'Observations' [*sur l'Histoire de Grèce*] of the Abbé [de] Mably. But it is no less clear that they were incomparably better qualified than their French guide to understand and apply what they did know." *Op. cit.,* 249. Also see Panagopoulos, *op. cit.,* 100 ff., for the historical sources which Hamilton and Madison used.

26. Hamilton's misquoting of the Articles of Confederation, as well as his and Madison's subsequent misquoting of

the Declaration, Constitution, and other sources (see notes which follow), raises questions about the method they used in writing the *Federalist*. Did they have the documents before them as they wrote, misquoting as a result of haste? Did they quote from memory? Or did they "slant" their quotes to suit their purpose? Obviously they were unfamiliar with German scholarly techniques!

For a discussion of the compact theory, as held at that time, see William S. Carpenter, *The Development of Political Thought* (Princeton, 1930), 1–37.

27. Jefferson admonished that the "Convention has been too much impressed by the insurrection in Massachusetts: and In the spur of the moment they are setting up a kite to keep the hen-yard in order." Letter to Colonel Smith, Paris, Nov. 13, 1787, *Documentary History of the Constitution*, IV, 378.

28. Charles Jenkinson (1727–1808). Max Beloff, ed., *The Federalist*, 479, observes that the bill in question was 28 George III. cap. 5, continuing the American Intercourse Act of 1783.

29. According to the 1790 Census, 2,050,933 persons lived in Va., Mass., Pa., and N.C., while 1,678,069 resided in the other nine states.

30. Supporters of the Constitution often referred to Rhode Island's non-co-operation with contempt; Elliot, *Debates*, V, 633–34; Ford, *Essays*, 423.

31. Hamilton's statement, along with *Federalist, No. 39*, provided grist for arguments about the states' sovereignty-perpetual union problem. See Alexander Stephens, *A Constitutional View*, I, 145; also, Mason and Leach, *In Quest of Freedom* (Englewood Cliffs, N.J., 1959), 309–49.

32. Presumably, if one disagreed with Hamilton's axiomatic approach to this problem, his mind would be prejudiced! Hamilton also used this argument later when discussing the constitutionality of the bank; Mason and Leach, *op. cit.*, 174–75. John Marshall gave it additional force in McCulloch *v.* Maryland (4 Wheat. 316, 421) when he remarked:

> *Let the end be legitimate, let it be within the scope of the Constitution, and all means which are appropriate, which are plainly adapted to that end, which are not pro-*

hibited, but consist with the letter and spirit of the Constitution, are constitutional.

Also, see Corwin, *The Constitution and What It Means,* 74–75.

33. R. H. Lee, Gerry, and Luther Martin were very critical of the indefinite power to raise armies; see Ford, *Pamphlets; Essays,* 358–59; Elliot, *Debates,* I, 371–72.

34. Compare these views with contemporary arguments about defense!

35. This appeared as *No. 30* in the original newspaper series. In the first edition, however, *No. 35* became *No. 29,* throwing off by one number those between 35 and 29. Most editions follow the numbering system of the first edition.

36. This seems to be Hamilton's summary, not an actual statement by an anti-Federalist. For specific arguments against the federal tax power, however, see comments by R. H. Lee, Gerry, Clinton, and Martin in Ford, *Essays.*

37. Felix Frankfurter observes that:

Marshall's use of the commerce clause greatly furthered the idea that though we are a federation of states we are also a nation, and gave momentum to the doctrine that state authority must be subject to such limitations as the Court finds necessary to apply for the protection of the national community. It was an audacious doctrine, which . . . could hardly have been publicly avowed in support of the Constitution. Indeed, The Federalist in effect denied it, by assuring that only express prohibition in the Constitution limited the taxing power of the states.

The Commerce Clause Under Marshall, Taney and Waite (Chapel Hill, 1937), 19; quoted by permission of the University of North Carolina Press.

38. Hamilton not only misquoted the clause, but also supplied the italics.

39. Hamilton provided the upper-case letters, also omitted "and uniform laws on the subject of bankruptcies" from this clause.

40. This sentence first appeared in the 1788 edition.

41. The reader may wish to consult these two sections of the Constitution to see how Hamilton altered them.

42. Compare Hamilton's axiomatic and rhetorical analysis (also used in *Nos. 23* and *31*) with Madison's approach to the same topic in *No. 44.*

43. Benjamin F. Wright, *op. cit.*, 14-15, points out that Hamilton's reliance upon the people at this point doesn't coincide with the concept of judicial review in *No. 78.* Also, see *No. 23.* Beloff, *op. cit.*, 480, says that Hamilton chose self-evident examples of power usurpation and thereby evaded the question of "who should interpret the constitutional division of powers between the Federal government and the States . . ."

44. Here, Hamilton quoted *No. 33,* but hardly with precision!

45. For specific examples of this criticism see Gerry's "Observations" and R. H. Lee's "Letters of a Federal Farmer" in Ford, *Pamphlets,* 12, 22; also, the arguments of Agrippa and George Clinton in Ford, *Essays,* 54, 268-69. Cecelia Kenyon, *op. cit.*, 10, says that this argument is the "chief component of the charge that the Constitution was not sufficiently democratic."

46. Although I would not charge Madison with coming "perilously close to falsehood," as Crosskey does, one may legitimately question Madison's sweeping generalization that *"all* the deputations" acceded or were accommodated [my italics]. It may be remembered that the citizens of New York did not have official representation at the Convention after July 5. Hamilton signed the Constitution as an individual, not an official. Crosskey, *op. cit.*, 8-9; Miller, *op. cit.*, 150-83.

47. Solon (c. 639-c. 559 B.C.) and Lycurgus (c. seventh cent. B.C.) were constitutional reformers of Athens and Sparta, the former effecting democratic and the latter military changes.

48. It is not difficult to relate this bill of particulars to specific anti-Federalist writers, but it is next to impossible to match each argument with the opponent whom Madison had in mind. Several opposed the Constitution under each of the arguments listed. But George Mason did use the phrase, "the shadow only of representation," almost the same words which Madison used; George Mason, "Objections," 3, in Ford, *Pamphlets.* Mason also thought the government would "vi-

brate" between monarchy and aristocracy; *ibid.*, 6. Lee was disturbed by the blending of power, while George Clinton thought that the consumer would pay the heavier portion of the taxes; Lee, *op. cit.*, 21; Ford, *Essays*, 271–72. Although Madison's list does not contain all the anti-Federalist arguments, it is the best summary in the *Federalist*.

49. Madison's use of "never" may be questioned. True, the anti-Federalists do not examine the Articles' weaknesses systematically; but, Clinton, for example, acknowledges their defects in his third "Cato" paper; Ford, *Essays*, 255.

50. Gottfried Dietze, Adrienne Koch, and Neal Riemer have analyzed Madison's republican principles carefully; see footnote 63, above.

51. Melanchthon Smith, Edmund Randolph, R. H. Lee, and Robert Yates all stressed this point in their writings. See Ford, *Pamphlets;* and *Essays*, 304–5, 314.

52. Contemporary Americans, disposed to identify "federal government" with the national government (in Washington), may need to remind themselves that "federation" and "confederation" were used synonymously in 1787. Also, a federal government is that in which the locus of political power is shared in varying degrees between the central and local governments. For further insights into federalism, see Beloff, *op. cit.*, 480–81; Duncan and Elizabeth Wilson, *Federation and World Order* (London, 1939), 61; Robert Bowie and Carl Friedrich, eds., *Studies in Federalism* (Boston, 1954); Arthur W. Macmahon, ed., *Federalism Mature and Emergent* (Garden City, 1955). For a study of both colonial and modern views, see Walter H. Bennett, "Early American Theories of Federalism," *Journal of Politics* (Aug. 1942), 383–95, and "Twentieth-Century Theories of the Nature of the Union," *ibid.* (May 1946), 160–73. Also, Rudolph Schlesinger makes some superbly provocative comparisons between European theories and those in the *Federalist* in *Federalism in Central and Eastern Europe* (London, 1945), 11–43.

53. Contrast Madison's view with Hamilton's argument (*No. 23*) that "The streams of national power ought to flow immediately from that pure, original fountain of all legitimate authority," the people. A. T. Mason regards Madison's viewpoint as "equivocal" and says that this provided the basis for

Southern secessionist doctrine; "The Nature of Our Federal Union Reconsidered," *Political Science Quarterly* (Dec. 1950), 512, 519. William Anderson not only suggests that Madison gave comfort to the states' righters in *No. 39*, but also argues that "he was somewhat confusing to his readers and ϟϑf-contradictory in what he said," *The Nation and States: Rivals or Partners* (Minneapolis, 1955), 119–20, quoted by permission of the University of Minnesota Press. Riemer disagrees in his several articles. Curious readers will want to see how John C. Calhoun and Alexander Stephens used Madison's views; Calhoun, *Works* (VI,II 1854), 150–62; Stephens, *op. cit.*, I, II; Stephens, *The Reviewers Reviewed* (N.Y., 1872), 5–29.

54 In view of U.S.-U.S.S.R. relations during the Cold War, many may be stimulated to compare the two federal systems. For a start, see Vernon V. Aspaturian, "The Theory and Practice of Soviet Federalism," *Journal of Politics* (Feb. 1950), 20–51.

55. Gottfried Dietze points out that "happiness" and "good" are identical in this passage. He also cites examples from *Nos. 37, 43, 57,* and *62* to illustrate. *The Federalist,* 116.

56. Hamilton's essential agreement with this view may be found in his famous *Report on the Subject of Manufactures,* Dec. 5, 1791, in Lodge edition of his *Works* (N.I., 1904), IV, 70–198.

57. Madison discussed the 2nd, 3rd, and 4th classes in *Nos. 42–43,* omitted here.

58. Those wishing to compare the U.S. and early state constitutions will find the latter in *The Federal and State Constitutions* (Washington, 1909), 7 vols.

59. Cecelia Kenyon, *op. cit.*, analyzes thoroughly the nature of this criticism.

60. Charles Louis de Secondat Montesquieu, *The Spirit of Laws* (1748); Benjamin F. Wright concludes that the concept of the separation of powers was popular as much because of our institutional history as reliance upon Montesquieu. *Op. cit.,* 7 ff.; also see Wright's penetrating discussion, "Origin of Separation of Powers in America," *Economica* (London, May 1933), 169–Or. Wright also observes that Polybius, Sydney, Locke, Blackstone, and Delolme had expressed such views and

were read widely in the Colonies. Then too, John Adams' three-volume *Defense of the Constitutions of Government of the United States of America* (London, 1786) was available to the fathers at Philadelphia.

61. Montesquieu actually said:

> When the legislative and executive powers are united in the same person or in the same body of magistrates, there can be no liberty, because apprehensions may arise, lest the same monarch or senate should enact tyrannical laws, to execute them in a tyrannical manner. Were it joined with the legislative, the life and liberty of the subject would be exposed to arbitrary control; for the judge would then be the legislator. Were it joined to the executive power, the judge might behave with violence and oppression.

Nugent translation (London, 1894), I, 163. Madison provided the italics.

62. See *The Federal and State Constitutions*, IV, 2457, for Article 37 of the N.H. Constitution, from which Madison quoted this passage. He added italics and the preliminary "that."

63. *Ibid.*, III, 1893. Madison added "that" and pluralized "department."

64. *Ibid.*, VII, 3815. Madison added "that," changed the punctuation, used lower-case form, and omitted the word indicated.

65. *Ibid.*, V, 2787.

66. *Ibid.*, II, 778. Madison added the "that."

67. *Nos.* 47–51 have been the subject of several illuminating discussions. In his *Ethics* article Neal Riemer points out that government is a competing power in a congeries of power struggles. Dietze, in *The Federalist*, contrasts Hamilton's view of separation with Madison's concept of blending; Wright, in his *Ethics* essay, observes that the authors placed more confidence in improving man's condition through institutions rather than through perfecting human nature. Francis G. Wilson, "Public Policy in Constitutional Reform," *Review of Politics* (Jan. 1945), 61–62, claims that the institutional ar-

rangement described in *Nos. 47–51* would be unworkable without the conditions prescribed in *No. 10.* Such blending of powers was a device to check and balance the various social and political forces. Serious readers, interested in comparing Madison's views of power with those of two provocative contemporary writers, may wish to read C. Wright Mills, *The Power Elite* (N.Y., 1956) and A. A. Berle, Jr., *The 20th Century Capitalistic Revolution* (N.Y., 1954) and *Power Without Property* (N.Y., 1960).

68. From Query XIII. Madison added italics.

69. *The Federal and State Constitutions,* V, 3091. Madison altered the spelling of "enquire" and changed the tense.

70. Note that Madison altered Jefferson's words, but didn't change his meaning. For copy of the Jefferson constitution, see Philip S. Foner, ed., *The Basic Writings of Thomas Jefferson* (N.Y., 1944), 190.

71. Professor Diamond observes that the founders were themselves "philosopher-founder[s]." *Op. cit.,* 68.

72. See footnote 69, above; here Madison is summarizing, not quoting.

73. Cecelia Kenyon observes that the anti-Federalists had essentially the same view of human nature; *op. cit.* For an interesting parallel in phraseology, see Pelatiah Webster's "The Weakness of Brutus . . . ," in which he remarked, ". . . 'tis the fate of human nature to *be imperfect and to err . . .* I have no expectation that they will make *a court of angels,* or be anything more than *men . . .*" Ford, *Pamphlets,* 7–8. For a most provocative critique of Madison's position and an interesting speculation about an angels' polity, see Ralph Ross and Ernest Van Den Haag, *The Fabric of Society* (N.Y., 1957), 628–30.

74. Compare this concept with Rousseau's "general will":

> *There is often a great deal of difference between the will of all and the general will; the latter regards only the common interest, while the former has regard to private interest, and is merely a sum of particular wills; but take away from these same wills the pluses and minuses which cancel one another, and the general will remains as the sum of the differences.*

(Bk. II, ch. 3), J. J. Rousseau, *The Social Contract*, ed. by Henry J. Tozer (London, 1912), 123.

75. Diamond observes that this passage, appearing only once in the book, is set in a context suggesting civil rights, "which in turn seems to refer primarily to the protection of economic interests," *op. cit.*, 62. I would disagree. Not only does the passage connote the traditional individual liberties; but, taken with Madison's discussion of factions in *No. 10*, makes Hamilton's statement "that the Constitution is itself . . . A BILL OF RIGHTS" (*No. 84*) almost plausible.

76. Although the Revolution had ended only four years before, Madison and Hamilton drew candidly and liberally from British institutions and experience. It is interesting to note, for example, that the ratio of 1 to 30,000, used to establish the membership of the House of Representatives, came almost directly from the 1 to 28,670 ratio for the House of Commons; see *No. 56*.

77. "1st clause, 4th section, of the 1st article.—PUBLIUS"

78. Melanchthon Smith, Robert Yates, Timothy Bloodworth, Patrick Henry, and others attacked this clause. See Ford *Pamphlets* and *Essays;* Elliot's *Debates*. And, as Kenyon observes, *op. cit.*, 15, the Massachusetts convention spent a day and a half debating the section. Possibly Noah Webster was the "gentleman" in question, for he remarked that the timing-and-altering clause was "needless and dangerous . . . I hope the states will reject it with decency, and adopt the whole system, without altering another syllable." "An Examination . . . ," 20, in Ford, *Pamphlets*.

79. For one of the best examples of this criticism, see R. H. Lee's "Letters from the Federal Farmer," *op. cit.*, 7, 20, 27, 39–40.

80. Note that an era ended in Sept. 1957, when Maine voted to "join the union" in 1960—by going to the polls in November rather than September to vote for national officials. The New York *Times*, Sept. 10, 1957.

81. Article II, Section 2. Jay provided the emphases.

82. Most prophetic: the Treaty of Ghent and Battle of New Orleans.

83. In his "Letter on the Federal Constitution," 17, in Ford, *Pamphlets*, Edmund Randolph listed eight items which

he hoped the states would adopt, among which was "abridging the power of the senate to make treaties supreme laws of the land." George Mason agreed; *op. cit.*, 5.

84. For a mature discussion of the problems which federal states face in making treaties, see James M. Hendry, *Treaties and Federal Constitutions* (Washington, 1955), 1–15. Also see Quincy Wright, *The Control of American Foreign Relations* (N.Y., 1922), Edwin S. Corwin, *The Constitution and What It Means*, 107–16. For a survey of the questions raised by the Bricker Amendment, see John T. Everett, Jr., "The Bricker Amendment . . . ," *University of Cincinnati Law Review* (Spring 1954), 173–98.

85. Modified, of course, by Amendment XXII, adopted in 1951.

86. Beloff observes, *op. cit.*, 482, that the comparison with the New York governor was especially apt, not only because of Clinton's opposition, but also in view of the fact that the N.Y. governor was the only one not elected by a legislature.

87. Indeed, the President has these powers; but this is a summary, not an exact quote from the Constitution.

88. "*Vide* Blackstone's 'Commentaries,' vol. i., p. 257.— PUBLIUS"

89. For a contemporary analysis of the American presidency, see Corwin, *The President* (N.Y., 1957).

90. Junius was an English political controversialist whose letters, signed "Junius," reflected the Whig viewpoint and appeared in the London *Public Advertiser* between 1769 and 1772.

91. This statement appeared as an italicized heading of Bk. II, ch. 2, of Jean Louis Delolme's *The Constitution of England* (London, 1775), 191.

92. Hamilton may not have borrowed directly from the *Social Contract,* but note the similarity of this passage with Rousseau's: "Of themselves, the people always desire what is good, but do not always discern it. The general will is always right, but the judgment which guides it is not always enlightened." *Op. cit.*, 133.

93. See Amendment XXII.

94. Article II, Section 1. Italics and extra words, omitted here, supplied by Hamilton.

95. Thomas Cooley points out that the *Federalist* seems to assume that the veto power was to protect the Executive from legislative encroachments, not much being said about the fact that the Executive could veto a bill for any reason whatever; *The General Principles of Constitutional Law in the United States* (Boston, 1880), 161–62.

96. In a footnote Hamilton identified Abraham Yates as one of this persuasion. Abraham, 1724–1796, was a cousin of Robert, who bolted the Convention; both opposed the Constitution.

97. Hamilton's judgment seemed to be borne out a half century later when Andrew Jackson, disagreeing with the court in Worcester *v.* Georgia (1832), allegedly remarked, "John Marshall has made his decision, now let him enforce it." Mason and Leach, *op. cit.*, 262. The 1954–55 desegregation decisions and their subsequent application continue to raise questions about the relationships between the Executive and judiciary.

98. At this point in the text Hamilton ran a footnote: "The celebrated Montesquieu, speaking of them, says: 'Of the three powers above mentioned, the judiciary is next to nothing.' 'Spirit of Laws,' vol. i., page 186.—PUBLIUS" A close check of the Nugent text, which Hamilton used, reveals that Montesquieu actually said, "Of the three powers above mentioned, the judiciary is *in some measure* next to nothing." (Edinburgh edition, 1772; I, 193.) I have provided the italics to indicate that Montesquieu made a *qualified* judgment about the power of the judiciary, not an unqualified one, as Hamilton indicated. A few pages later Montesquieu did say that "the national judges are no more than the mouth that pronounces the words of the law, mere passive beings, incapable of moderating either its force or rigour" (197). He seemed to regard the power of judging with some awe, referring to it as ". . . a power so terrible to mankind . . ." (166).

99. This quote is accurate. *Ibid.*, 165.

100. Next to *No. 10*, this essay has probably been studied more than any other because it sets forth a systematic argument for the doctrine of judicial review. Marshall gave it living force in Marbury *v.* Madison (1803) and other precedent-forming decisions, and it remains today among the most dis-

cussed American judicial practices. Even the Europeans, long skeptical of the doctrine, seem to be considering it more seriously; see Arnold J. Zurcher, ed., *Constitutions and Constitutional Trends since World War II* (N.Y., 1951), 20–22, 216. Although it is generally agreed that Sir Edward Coke probably originated the doctrine in the *Dr. Bonham Case* (1610), there is controversy as to whether or not the founding fathers intended to include judicial review in the new system of government. Serious students of this question, as well as other problems pertaining to judicial review, will not only wish to consult the bibliography in Beloff's ed. of the *Federalist,* 483, but they will also find the following helpful: Robert K. Carr, *The Supreme Court and Judicial Review* (N.Y., 1942), 54–55; Gottfried Dietze, *The Federalist;* Farrand, *Records,* II, 73–80; Crosskey, *op. cit.,* II, 941–45; Miller, *op. cit.,* 204; Robert J. Harris, "The Decline of Judicial Review," *Journal of Politics* (Feb. 1948), 1–19, Corwin's survey in *Encyclopedia of the Social Sciences,* VIII, 456, and Corwin, *Court over Constitution* (Princeton, 1938). Also see "Luther Martin's Letter," Elliot, *Debates,* I, 380, in which Martin said, "Whether . . . any laws or *regulations* of the Congress, any acts of *its President or other officers,* are contrary to, or not warranted by, the Constitution, rests only with the judges, who are appointed by Congress, to determine; by whose determinations every state must *be bound."*

101. For Justice David Brewer's famous statement indicating the way in which the court employs the Constitution as a higher law, see Ralph Gabriel, *The Course of American Democratic Thought* (N.Y., 1940), 233.

102. Hamilton's footnote: "*Vide* 'Protest of the Minority of the Convention of Pennsylvania,' Martin's Speech, etc.– PUBLIUS" The former may be found in McMaster and Stone, *op. cit.,* 454–82; the latter, Elliot's *Debates,* I, 344–89.

103. Article III, Section 1. Hamilton's italics.

104. This viewpoint invites comparison with Franklin D. Roosevelt's in the now famous court-packing plan of 1937, when the need for change was seen as a function of superannuation. See Alfred H. Cope and Fred Krinsky, *Franklin D. Roosevelt and the Supreme Court* (Boston, 1952).

105. Article IV, Section 2. Hamilton provided the extra word, here omitted.

106. Article III, Section 2. Hamilton's errors corrected here.

107. Article III, Section 1. Hamilton's misquoting corrected.

108. Probably a composite quotation. But for anti-Federalist essays with strikingly parallel passages (e.g., "superior to that of the legislature" and "spirit of the Constitution"), see Robert Yates' "Brutus" letters, reprinted in Corwin, *Court over Constitution*, 231–62.

109. Hamilton's footnote: "This power has been absurdly represented as intended to abolish all the county courts in the several States, which are commonly called inferior courts. But the expressions of the Constitution are, to constitute 'tribunals INFERIOR TO THE SUPREME COURT' [(*sic*), Article I, Section 8]; and the evident design of the provision is to enable the institution of local courts, subordinate to the Supreme, either in States or larger districts. It is ridiculous to imagine that county courts were in contemplation.—PUBLIUS"

110. Article III, Section 2. Hamilton used upper-case letters, probably to convince states-minded objectors.

111. *Ibid.* Hamilton's italics.

112. Hamilton's note: "This word is composed of JUS and DICTIO, *juris dictio*, or a speaking and pronouncing of the law. —PUBLIUS"

113. Hamilton's note: "I hold that the States will have concurrent jurisdiction with the subordinate federal judicatories, in many cases of federal cognizance, as will be explained in my next paper.—PUBLIUS"

114. Article III, Section 1. Hamilton's misquoting corrected.

115. Article I, Section 8; Article III, Section 1. Hamilton's italics.

116. E. Gerry, L. Martin, P. Henry, and many other anti-Federalists used the argument which Hamilton reviewed. For examples, see Elliot, *Debates*, I, 381; II, 109–11; III, 167.

117. Hamilton modified Blackstone interestingly, not only providing the italics for emphasis but also substituting the word "nation" for "kingdom" and "jail" for "gaol." In the lat-

ter statement Blackstone actually said, "by that great bulwark of our constitution, the *habeas corpus* act." William Blackstone, *Commentaries on the Laws of England* (London & Oxford, 1787), 136, 438.

118. Article XXXV, New York Constitution (1777); *The Federal and State Constitutions*, V, 2635.

119. C. E. Merriam feels that the use of this word reflects the attitudinal distance between 1776 and 1788. "In 1776, to have referred to the declaration of rights as 'aphorisms' which properly belong only to the domain of ethics, would have been almost equivalent to high treason . . ." *American Political Theories*, 118.

120. Note that Amendments IX and X tend to do just this. Alexander Hanson in "Remarks on the Proposed Plan . . . ," 24, in Ford, *Pamphlets*, defended the fathers for omitting a bill of rights. "An omission of a single article," he said, "would have caused more discontent, than is either felt or pretended, on the present occasion. A multitude of articles might be the source of infinite controversy. . . . To be full and certain, a bill of rights might have cost the convention more time, than was expended on their other work."

121. Hamilton changed Rutherford's statement from singular to plural and italicized it. Thomas Rutherford, *Institutes of Natural Law* (Cambridge, 1754–56), II, 673.

122. The "excellent little pamphlet" to which Hamilton referred was John Jay's "An Address to the People of the State of New York," published about April 15, 1788. Included in Ford's *Pamphlets*.

123. Hamilton's footnote: "It may rather be said TEN, for though two thirds may set foot the measure, three fourths must ratify.—PUBLIUS"

124. Again, Hamilton italicized the word he wished to stress in quoting David Hume's "Of the Rise and Progress of the Arts and Sciences," *Essays and Treatises on Several Subjects* (London, 1768), I, 134. As both Adair and Robert MacIver point out, Hamilton was attracted to Hume's "tempered skepticism." MacIver also observes that Hamilton read Adam Smith's *Wealth of Nations* as soon as the first copies crossed the Atlantic; see Conyers Read, ed., *The Constitution Reconsidered* (N.Y., 1938), 59–60.

C. *Notes on Preface to Second Edition*

1. Jacob Cooke's essay, "Alexander Hamilton's Authorship of the 'Caesar' Letters," came to my attention after the first edition went to press. If Professor Cooke is correct in his contention that Hamilton could not have written the Caesar letters, I have certainly overdrawn the conflict between Clinton and Hamilton on pages vii–viii above. See *William & Mary Quarterly* (Jan. 1960), 78–85.

2. Frederick Mosteller & David L. Wallace, *Inference and Disputed Authorship* (Reading, Mass., 1964).

3. Jacob E. Cooke, ed., *The Federalist* (Middletown, Conn., 1961).

4. Benjamin F. Wright, ed., *The Federalist* (Cambridge, 1961).

5. Adrienne Koch, "Return of 'Publius'," *Nation* (Sept. 2, 1961), 125.

6. Willmoore Kendall, "On the 'Federalist': The State of Our Understanding," *National Review* (Dec. 3, 1965), 494.

7. Holmes Moss Alexander, *How to Read the Federalist* (Boston, 1961), especially pages 7 and 43, but the entire text is "shot through" with ambiguity, sloppy scholarship and gross misreading of American history.

8. See page 322.

9. Letters to RPF from Margaret V. Taylor, Helsinki, Jan. 7, 1966; Preston E. Amos, Damascus, Oct. 23, 1965; Nicholas E. Conduras, Saigon, Oct. 18, 1965; Alice E. Kopp, Rio de Janeiro, Feb. 14, 1966; Peter E. Bock, Nairobi, Jan. 11, 1966; Mary Smeaton, Johannesburg, Jan. 17, 1966; William C. Petty, Abidjan, Oct. 25, 1965; Eunice El-Kadhimi, Baghdad, Nov. 8, 1965; Howard E. Stingle, Singapore, Oct. 15, 1965; Gregory Gay, Yaoundé, Oct. 13, 1965; Jeanne M. Pryor, Fort-Lamy, Oct. 9, 1965; Warren Brown, Salisbury, Oct. 11, 1965; Elizabeth Randles, Karachi, Oct. 13, 1965; Margaret F. MacKellar, Cairo, Oct. 18, 1965; C. Kenneth Snyder, Kampala, Uganda, Jan. 18, 1966; C. Joan Addiscott, Hong Kong, Oct. 8, 1965.

10. Karl Schriftgiesser, "Constitutional Triumvirate," *Saturday Review* (May 6, 1961), 24.

BIBLIOGRAPHICAL APPENDIX

FIRST EDITION

Since 1788 many bibliographies of the *Federalist* have appeared, almost every editor having prepared one. Since there have been no extensive bibliographies in this century, however, possibly it is time for a new summing up, one which will not only include the latest editions but also afford the opportunity to correct omissions in previous lists.

Between the Civil War and 1900 at least three men endeavored to track down the editions which had appeared earlier in the century. Henry B. Dawson prepared the first such comprehensive list for his controversial 1863 edition. A generation later Paul L. Ford compiled *A List of Editions of 'The Federalist'* (Brooklyn, 1886); fifty copies were published. By this time Joseph Sabin had begun his renowned *Dictionary of Books Relating to America*, thus Ford's annotated list contained comparative references to both Dawson's and Sabin's work. Meanwhile, Henry Cabot Lodge was working on a similar bibliography. When his 1888 edition appeared, he remarked, "Protracted and minute search, supplemented by widespread advertisements, and by the obliging aid of many kind correspondents, has enabled me to add only two editions to the list of the editions of the *Federalist* already given by Mr. Dawson" (p. xxxv). Strangely enough, Lodge did not include three of the items which Ford had listed two years before. In 1898 Ford updated the 1886 listing; but since then bibliographies have been sketchy.

The essays originally appeared in the following newspapers:

Nos. 1–85, The Independent Journal or *The General Advertiser* (semiweeklies: Wed. & Sat.), Oct. 27, 1787–Apr. 2, 1788, June 14–Aug. 16, 1788.

Nos. 1–76, The New York Packet (semiweekly: Tues. & Fri.), Oct. 30, 1787–Apr. 4, 1788.

Nos. 1–50, The Daily Advertiser, Oct. 30, 1787–Feb. 11, 1788.

Nos. 23–38, The New York Journal and Daily Patriotic Register, Dec. 18, 1787–Jan. 13, 1788.

J. M'Lean & Company, owner of the *Independent Journal and General Advertiser,* published Volume One of the first edition on March 22, 1788. Two weeks later, after the appearance of *No. 77,* the newspapers suspended publication of the articles while compiling Volume Two. This appeared on May 28 and contained the last eight essays, which were subsequently reprinted in the newspapers the following summer.

I

After a transcription of the title pages of the first two editions, the following annotated list is simplified for functional use:

1788   [Alexander Hamilton, James Madison, and John Jay], *The Federalist: A Collection of Essays, written in Favour of the New Constitution, as agreed upon by the Federal Convention, September 17, 1787.* In Two Volumes. Vol. I. New York: Printed and Sold by J. & A. M'Lean, No. 41, Hanover-Square. M, DCC, LXXXVIII.

1792   [Trudaine de la Sablière, ed.], *Le Fédéraliste, ou Collection de quelques Écrits en faveur de la Constitution proposée aux États-Unis de l'Amérique par la Convention convoquée en 1787; Publiés dans les États-Unis de l'Amérique par MM. Hamilton, Madisson et Gay* [sic], *Citoyens de État de New-York.* Tome Premier. A Paris, Chez Buisson, Libraire, rue Hautefeuille, No. 20. 1792. 2 vols.

There were two Paris editions in 1792 and a reissue in 1795.

1799   New York: John Tiebout. 2 vols.

1802   John Wells, ed. New York: George F. Hopkins. 2 vols.

1810   John Wells, ed. New York: Williams & Whiting. 2 vols. Volumes Two and Three of the *Works of Hamilton.*

First American edition with names of authors inside the respective numbers.

1817 Philadelphia: Benjamin Warner.
Reissued in 1818.

1818 Washington, D.C.: Jacob Gideon.
The first of several "Gideon" editions, this volume contained Madison's first public comment upon his contributions to the *Federalist*. In a sense, however, the authorship dispute had begun officially a year or two before, when Joseph Delaplaine published *Repository of the Lives and Portraits of Distinguished Americans* (Phila., 1813–18). Hamilton's followers made claims to which Madison's friends objected. As Adair points out, by 1818 Madison's political vulnerability was minimal, but even at that, his corrections were careful.
Reissued in 1821.

1826 Hallowell, Maine: Glazier & Co.

1826 Philadelphia: M'Carty & Davis.
Probably a reissue of the Hallowell edition, since Glazier & Co. printed it and the copyrights are identical. Not included in the nineteenth-century bibliographies.

1831 Hallowell: Glazier, Masters & Co.

1831 Washington: Thompson & Homans.
Contained the first index, one used in many subsequent editions.

1837 Hallowell: Glazier, Masters & Smith.

1840 *O Federalista*. Rio de Janeiro: J. Villeneuve e comp.
Although there may have been an 1835 and/or 1836 Portuguese translation, evidence pertaining to its existence is not conclusive. (See Gustavo R. Velasco, ed., *El Federalista*, Mexico City, 1943, xv; letter, Prof. Americo Lacombe to RPF, Nov. 8, 1958.)

1842 Hallowell: Glazier, Masters & Smith.

1845 Washington: J. & G. S. Gideon.

1847 Philadelphia: R. Wilson Desilver.

1852 Hallowell: Masters, Smith & Co.
Reissued in 1857.

1863 Henry B. Dawson, ed. *The Foederalist*. New York: Charles Scribner; London: Samson Low, Son & Co.
Dawson was so biased in his introduction that critics

accused him of using the book as a "vehicle for enforcing the principles of state sovereignty." George T. Curtis in Justin Winsor, *Narrative and Critical History of America*. Boston & New York, 1888. VII, 260. He was so critical of Hamilton and Jay that he gave offense to the authors' descendants. Most reissues of the Dawson edition omitted the introduction. Despite professional criticism he returned to the original spelling of the title of the essays and the newspaper text. See *North American Review*, XCVIII Apr. 1864, 589.

1864   Henry B. Dawson, ed. New York: Charles Scribner & Co.

1864   Henry B. Dawson, ed. Morrisania, N.Y.

1864   Henry B. Dawson, ed. New York: Charles Scribner & Co. The first of several university editions reprinted from the Dawson text. Others: 1865, 1867, 1873, 1876, 1881, 1888, 1891, and some with no date.

1864   John C. Hamilton, ed. Philadelphia: J. B. Lippincott & Co. This edition opened a new era in the interpretation of Hamilton's part in the project. Until recently, most editors followed John Hamilton's designations of the disputed essays. Reissued many times with a change of date only. Others: 1866, 1868, 1871, 1882, 1885, 1888, 1904.

1864   Wilhelm Kiesselbach, *Der Amerikanische Federalist*. Bremen: Verlag von J. Kühtmann's Buchhandlung; London: Longman & Co.; New York: Westermann & Co. A two-volume work, the second volume features the *Federalist* in condensed form. Reissued in 1868 and 1871.

1865   John C. Hamilton, ed. Philadelphia: J. B. Lippincott & Co. 2 vols. From the same plates as the 1864 edition, but in two volumes; printed on finer and larger paper in a limited edition of one hundred.

1868   J. M. Cantilo, ed., *El Federalista*. Buenos Aires: Imprenta del Siglo.

1887   D. Ildefonso Isla, ed., *El Federalista*. Buenos Aires: Establecimiento Tipográfico de La Pampa.

1888   Henry Cabot Lodge, ed. New York & London: G. P. Putnam's Sons.
Reissued many times with a change of date only. Others: 1889, 1891, 1894, 1900, 1902, 1904, 1907, 1908, 1911.

1894   E. H. Scott, ed. Chicago: Albert, Scott & Co.

1896   *The Federalist, Nos. 1 & 2*. Boston: Directors of the Old South Work.

1896   *O Federalista*. State of Minas, Brazil: Imprensa Oficial Do Estado De Minas.

1898   Paul L. Ford, ed. New York: Henry Holt & Co.

1898   E. H. Scott, ed. Chicago: Scott, Foresman & Co.

1901   Goldwin Smith, ed. New York: The Colonial Press.

1901   Edward G. Bourne, ed. Washington & London: M. Walter Dunne. 2 vols.
Part of the Universal Classics Library, Volume One is devoted to the *Federalist*, while Volume Two contains the latter numbers and "The English Constitution."

1902   Gaston Jèze and A. Esmein, eds., *Le Fédéraliste*. Paris: V. Giard & E. Brière.

1911   W. J. Ashley, ed. London: J. M. Dent & Sons; New York: E. P. Dutton & Co.
This, the Everyman, was the first British-initiated edition. Reissued in 1926, 1929, 1942.

1914   Henry C. Lodge, ed. London & Leipsic: F. Fisher Unwin.

1914   William B. Monro, ed. Cambridge, Mass.: Harvard University Press.
A student edition, this contains about one third of the numbers.

1914   Edward G. Bourne, ed. St. Louis: The Central Law Journal Co.

1921   John S. Bassett, ed. New York: Charles Scribner's Sons.
Part of the Modern Student's Library, this includes two thirds of the numbers.

1923   Henry C. Lodge, ed., with an introduction by Charles W. Pierson. New York: G. P. Putnam's Sons.
Most interesting for the list of forty-five Supreme Court decisions citing the *Federalist*.

1937   Edward G. Bourne, ed. New York: Tudor Publishing Co.
Reissued in 1947.

1938   Edward M. Earle, ed. Washington: National Home Library Foundation.
Printed both as a paperback (fifty cents) and as a clothbound book (seventy-five cents and one dollar); The New York *Times*, Feb. 22, 1938, the sesquicentennial edition Now available in college paperback text.

1941   Edward M. Earle, ed. New York: The Modern Library.

1943   Gustavo R. Velasco, ed., *El Federalista*. Mexico City: Fondo de Cultura Economica, Panuco, 63.
Reissued in 1957.

1945   Carl Van Doren, ed. New York: Heritage Press.
A "Heritage" book, designed and decorated by Bruce Rogers and printed "For the Members of the Limited Editions Club."

1947   Ann Arbor, Michigan: J. W. Edwards.
Published as a discussion source book for the Great Books Foundation, this contains *Nos. 1–10, 15, 31, 47, 51, 68–71.*

1948   Charles A. Beard, ed., *The Enduring Federalist*. Garden City, N.Y.: Doubleday & Co., Inc.
Includes all or parts of seventy-four numbers, of about half the text.

1948   Max Beloff, ed. Oxford, England: Basil Blackwell; New York: The Macmillan Co.

1948   Chicago: Henry Regnery Co.
Also published for the Great Books program; includes same essays as the 1947 Edwards edition.

1949   Henry S. Commager, ed. New York: Appleton-Century-Crofts, Inc.
A Crofts Classic, containing about a third of the original text.

1951   *Za Federalisto*. Tokyo: Iwanami Shoten.

Prof. Makoto Saito of Tokyo University, in a letter to RPF, Mar. 15, 1959, indicated that this is part of the Institute of American Studies edition, *Genten Amerika Shi* (*Documentary History of the American People*), II, 349–94, and includes *Nos. 1, 4, 10, 39, 47, 48, 51, 70, 71, 78,* and *84.*

1952   Robert M. Hutchins and Mortimer J. Adler, eds. Chicago, London, and Toronto: Encyclopædia Britannica, Inc.
Volume No. 43 in the fifty-fourth volume, Great Books publication; also includes three works by John Stuart Mill. Reissued in 1955.

1954   Ralph H. Gabriel, ed. New York: The Liberal Arts Press, Inc.
Volume No. 7 of the American Heritage Series, the text includes about half the numbers.

1955   Chicago: The Great Books Foundation.
Part of Volume No. 6 in the Foundation's First Year Readings; contains *Nos. 1, 10, 15,* and *51.*

1955   Gaspare Ambrosini, ed., *Il Federalista.* Pisa, Italy: Nistri-Lischi.

1957   *El Derecho De Gobenar: Cartas Federalistas.* Buenos Aires: Editorial Agora.
Spanish translation of the 1954 Gabriel edition.

1957   M. André Tunc, ed., *Le Fédéralisto.* Paris: R. Pichon & R. Durand-Auzias.

1957   Milton Mayer, ed., *The Tradition of Freedom.* New York: Oceana Publications.
Compiled for the Fund for the Republic, this volume includes a little less than a third of the *Federalist* text; also, portions of John Locke's *Second Treatise of Civil Government* and Adam Smith's *Wealth of Nations.*

1958   Felix Ermacora, ed., *Der Föderalist.* Vienna: Manzsche Verlagsund Universitätsbuchhandlung.

1959   Charles A. and William Beard, eds., *The Enduring Federalist.* New York: Frederick Ungar Publishing Co.

1959   H. E. Jamal M. Ahmed, ed., *The Federalist* [in Arabic]. Beirut: Dar Maktabat Al-Hayat; New York: Franklin Publications, Inc.
In a letter to RPF, Sept. 2, 1958, Mr. Ahmed pointed

out that translating the *Federalist* was especially difficult because of difference in nuance between English and Arabic, nonexistence of terms like "federation" and "confederation" in Arabic, the essential economy of modern Arabic and the lengthy paragraphs which the *Federalist* authors used.

1959 *O Federalista.* Rio de Janeiro: Editora Nacional de Direito.

1959 Saigon, Vietnam: Nhu Nguyen Publishing Company. Vietnamese translation of the 1954 Gabriel edition.

1960 Rekha Bandopadhyay, translator, into Bengali. Calcutta: Sribhumi Publishing Co.

1960 Mahendra Bora, translator, into Assamese. Calcutta: Sribhumi Publishing Co.

1960 Kim Sung-bok, translator, into Korean. Seoul: Eul-yoo Publishing Company. Translation of the 1954 Gabriel edition.

(For later editions, see page 321.)

II

The following articles, dissertations, and books comprise the major body of *Federalist* scholarship.

Periodicals

Adair, Douglass, "The Authorship of the Disputed Federalist Papers," *Wm. & Mary Quarterly*, Third Series, I, No. 2 (Apr. 1944), 97–122; *ibid.*, No. 3 (July 1944), 235–64; "James Madison's Autobiography," *ibid.*, II, No. 2 (Apr. 1945), 191–209; "The Tenth Federalist Revisited," *ibid.*, VIII, No. 1 (Jan. 1951), 48–67; " 'That Politics May Be Reduced to a Science': David Hume, James Madison, and the Tenth *Federalist*," *The Huntington Library Quarterly*, XX, No. 4 (Aug. 1957), 343–60.

Anderson, William, Book Review of Max Beloff edition of the *Federalist*, *American Historical Review*, LIV, No. 1 (Oct. 1948), 151–52.

Bourne, E. G., "The Use of History Made by the Framers of the Constitution," *American Historical Association Annual Report*, I (1896), 221–28.

Cousins, Norman, ed., "For a Permanent United Nations," *Saturday Review of Literature*, XXVI, No. 24 (June 12, 1943), 12.

Diamond, Martin, "Democracy and *The Federalist*: A Reconsideration of the Framers' Intent," *American Political Science Review*, LIII, No. 1 (Mar. 1959), 52–68.

Dietze, Gottfried, "Hamilton's Federalist—Treatise for Free Government," *Cornell Law Quarterly*, XLII, No. 3 (Spring 1957), 307–28; *ibid.*, XLII, No. 4 (Summer 1957), 501–18; "Madison's Federalist—A Treatise on Free Government," *Georgetown Law Journal*, XLVI (1957), 21–51; "Jay's Federalist—Treatise for Free Government," *Maryland Law Review*, XVII, No. 3 (Summer 1957), 217–30; "Der Federalist und die Friedensfunktion des Föderalismus," *Jahrbuch des Offentlichen Rechts*, VII (N.F.) (1958), 1–47.

Ford, Paul L. and Bourne, E. G., "The Authorship of the Federalist," *American Historical Review*, II, No. 4 (July 1897), 675–87.

Hopkins, Frederick M., "Rare Book Notes," *The Publishers' Weekly*, CXXX, No. 16 (Oct. 17, 1936), 1629–30.

Kenyon, Cecelia, "Men of Little Faith: The Anti-Federalists on the Nature of Representative Government," *Wm. & Mary Quarterly*, Third Series, XII, No. 1 (Jan. 1955), 3–43.

Ketcham, Ralph L., "Notes on James Madison's Sources for the Tenth Federalist Paper," *Midwest Journal of Political Science*, I, No. 1 (May 1957), 20–25.

Koch, Adrienne, "James Madison and the Workshop of Liberty," *Review of Politics*, XVI, No. 2 (Apr. 1954), 175–93.

Lodge, Henry C., "The Authorship of the Federalist," *Proceedings of the American Antiquarian Society*, New Series, III (Oct. 1883–Apr. 1885), 409–20.

Mason, A. T., "The Federalist—A Split Personality," *American Historical Review*, LVII, No. 3 (Apr. 1952), 625–43.

Nadelmann, Kurt H., "Apropos of Translations (Federalist, Kent, Story)," *American Journal of Comparative Law*, VIII (1959), 204–14.

Riemer, Neal, "The Republicanism of James Madison," *Political Science Quarterly*, LXIX, No. 1 (Mar. 1954), 45–64;

"James Madison's Theory of the Self-Destructive Features of Republican Government," *Ethics*, LXV, No. 1 (Oct. 1954), 34–43; "James Madison and the Current Conservative Vogue," *Antioch Review*, XIV, No. 4 (Winter 1954–55), 458–70; "Two Conceptions of the Genius of American Politics," *Journal of Politics*, XX, No. 4 (Nov. 1958), 695–717.

Scanlan, James P., "The Federalist and Human Nature," *Review of Politics*, XXI (1959), 657–77.

Tarr, Harry A., "Hamilton, Madison, and 'The Federalist,'" *Scholastic*, XXXVII, No. 11 (Nov. 25, 1940), 12, 16.

The New York *Times*, Feb. 6, 1938, IV, 8; Feb. 22, 1938, 17; Dec. 10, 1947, 30; Oct. 26, 1955, 28; Nov. 19, 1959, 1; Dec. 4, 1959, 30.

Torrey, H. W. [?], Book Review of Henry Dawson's ed., *North American Review*, XCVIII, No. 203 (Apr. 1864), 586–92.

Tuckerman, Henry T., "Dawson's 'Federalist,'" *Harper's Weekly*, VIII, No. 400 (Aug. 27, 1864), 546.

Wright, Benjamin F., "*The Federalist* on the Nature of Political Man," *Ethics*, LIX, No. 2, Part II (Jan. 1949), 1–31.

Dissertations and Books

Beard, Charles, *An Economic Interpretation of the Constitution of the United States.* New York, 1941, 152–88.

Benson, Mabel G., *Some Rhetorical Characteristics of the "Federalist."* Univ. of Chicago Ph.D. dissertation, Mar. 1945.

Bourne, E. G., *Essays in Historical Criticism.* New York, 1901, 113–62.

Dietze, Gottfried, *The Political Theory of the Federalist.* Princeton Ph.D. dissertation, 1952.

——, *The Federalist.* Baltimore, 1960.

Ford, Paul L., *A List of Editions of 'The Federalist.'* Brooklyn, 1886.

Garosci, Aldo, *Il Pensiero Politico Degli Autori Del "Federalist."* Milan, 1954.

Grimes, Alan P., *American Political Thought.* New York, 1955, 119–27.

Mason, A. T., and Leach, Richard H., *In Quest of Freedom*. Englewood Cliffs, N.J., 1959, 145–66.

Merriam, Charles E., *A History of American Political Theories*. New York, 1924, 100–22.

Panagopoulos, Epaminondas P., *Classicism and the Framers of the Constitution*. Univ. of Chicago Ph.D. dissertation, 1952.

Parrington, Vernon L., *Main Currents in American Thought*. New York, 1927, I, 284–91.

Roberts, Owen J., Schmidt, John, and Streit, Clarence K., *The New Federalist*. New York, 1950.

Scanlan, James P., *The Concept of Interest in the Federalist*. Univ. of Chicago Ph.D. dissertation, 1956.

Smith, Maynard, *The Principles of Republican Government in "The Federalist."* New School for Social Research dissertation, 1951.

Story, Joseph, *Commentaries on the Constitution of the United States*. Boston, 1858. 2 vols.

Weaver, Irvin W., *The Social Philosophy of the Federalist*. Boston Univ. Ph.D. dissertation, 1953.

(For further Periodicals and Books, see page 322.)

III

The selected list of articles and books which follows includes the biographies and writings of the *Federalist*'s authors, also documentary, historical, and critical works on the Constitution-making period.

Periodicals

Anderson, William, "The Intentions of the Framers," *American Political Science Review*, XLIX, No. 2 (June 1955), 340–52.

Bishop, Hillman, "Why Rhode Island Opposed the Federal Constitution," *Rhode Island History*, VIII, No. 1 (Jan. 1949), 1–10; No. 2 (Apr. 1949), 33–44; No. 3 (July 1949), 85–95; No. 4 (Oct. 1949), 115–26.

Corwin, E. S., "The Progress of Constitutional Theory Between the Declaration of Independence and the Meeting of the Philadelphia Convention," *American Historical Review*, XXX, No. 3 (Apr. 1925), 511–36.

Crowl, P. A., "Anti-Federalism in Maryland, 1787–1788," *Wm. & Mary Quarterly*, Third Series, IV, No. 4 (Oct. 1947), 446–69.

Dwight, Theodore W., "Harrington and His Influence Upon American Political Institutions and Political Thought," *Political Science Quarterly*, II, No. 1 (Mar. 1887), 1–44.

Fairfield, Roy P., "Progress by the Inch," *Ohio Schools*, XXXVIII, No. 8 (Nov. 1959), 26–27.

Hofstadter, Richard, "Beard and the Constitution: the History of an Idea," *American Quarterly*, II, No. 3 (Fall 1950), 195–213.

Mason, A. T., "The Nature of Our Federal Union Reconsidered," *Political Science Quarterly*, LXV, No. 4 (Dec. 1950), 502–21.

Robinson, James H., "The Original and Derived Features of the Constitution," *Annals of the American Academy of Political and Social Science*. Phila., 1890, I, 203–43.

Steiner, B. C., "Maryland's Adoption of the Federal Constitution," *American Historical Review*, V, No. 1 (Oct. 1899), 22–44.

Wright, Benjamin F., "Origins of the Separation of Powers in America," *Economica*, XIII, No. 40 (May 1933), 169–85.

Books

Aly, Bower, *The Rhetoric of Alexander Hamilton*. New York, 1941.

Bloom, Sol, *The Story of the Constitution*. Washington, 1937.

——, *History of the Formation of the Union Under the Constitution*. Washington, 1941.

Bowers, Claude, *Jefferson and Hamilton*. Boston and New York, 1925.

Brant, Irving, *James Madison*. Indianapolis, 1941–56. 5 vols.

Brown, Robert E., *Charles Beard and the Constitution*. Princeton, 1956.

Burns, Edward M., *James Madison, Philosopher of the Constitution*. New Brunswick, N.J., 1938.

Butzner, Jane, *Constitutional Chaff*. New York, 1941.

Cousins, Norman, "World Citizenship—When?" in Lyman Bryson, ed., *Approaches to World Peace*. New York, 1944.

Documentary History of the Constitution of the United States of America, 1786–1870. Washington, 1894–1905. 5 vols.

Elliot, Jonathan, *Debates in the Several State Conventions on the Adoption of the Federal Constitution*. Phila., 1876. 5 vols.

Farrand, Max, ed., *The Records of the Federal Convention of 1787*. New Haven, 1911. 3 vols. (1937, revised edition, 4 vols.)

——, *The Fathers of the Constitution*. New Haven, 1921.

Fiske, John, *The Critical Period of American History*. Boston and New York, 1888.

Ford, Paul L., ed., *Essays on the Constitution of the United States*. Brooklyn, 1892.

——, ed., *Pamphlets on the Constitution of the United States*. Brooklyn, 1888.

Hacker, Louis M., *Alexander Hamilton in the American Tradition*. New York, 1957.

Hamilton, Alexander, *Works* (Henry C. Lodge, ed.), New York, 1904. 12 vols.

Hill, Roscoe, ed., *Journals of the Continental Congress, 1774–1789*. Washington, 1937.

Jensen, Merrill, *The Articles of Confederation*. Madison, Wis., 1940.

——, *The New Nation*. New York, 1950.

Kent, James, *Commentaries on American Law*. New York, 1836. 2 vols.

Koch, Adrienne, *Jefferson and Madison: the Great Collaboration*. New York, 1950.

McMaster, John, and Stone, Frederick, eds., *Pennsylvania and the Federal Constitution, 1787–1788*. Lancaster, Pa., 1888.

Madison, James, *The Debates in the Federal Convention* (Gaillard Hunt and James B. Scott, eds.). New York, 1920.

——, *The Writings of James Madison* (Gaillard Hunt, ed.). New York, 1900–10. 9 vols.

Miller, John C., *Alexander Hamilton, Portrait in Paradox*. New York, 1959.

Miner, C. E., *Ratification of the Federal Constitution in New York*. New York, 1921.

Mitchell, Broadus, *Alexander Hamilton*. New York, 1957.

——, *Heritage from Hamilton*. New York, 1957.

Monaghan, Frank, *John Jay*. New York and Indianapolis, 1935.

Padover, Saul K., ed., *The Complete Madison*. New York, 1953.

——, ed., *The Mind of Alexander Hamilton*. New York, 1958.

Rives, William C., *History of the Life and Times of James Madison*. Boston, 1886. 3 vols.

Smith, Abbot E., *James Madison: Builder*. New York, 1937.

Spaulding, E. W., *His Excellency George Clinton*. New York, 1938.

Stephens, Alexander H., *A Constitutional View of the Late War between the States*. Phila., 1868–70. 2 vols.

Tansill, Charles C., ed., *Documents Illustrative of the Formation of the Union of the American States*. Washington, 1927.

Trenholme, Louise I., *The Ratification of the Federal Constitution in North Carolina*. New York, 1932.

Van Doren, Carl, *The Great Rehearsal*. New York, 1948.

Walsh, James, *Education of the Founding Fathers of the Republic*. New York, 1935.

Whitelaw, W. Menzies, "American Influence on British Federal Systems," in Conyers Read, ed., *The Constitution Reconsidered*. New York, 1938, 297–313.

BIBLIOGRAPHICAL APPENDIX

SECOND EDITION

I

Editions of *Federalist* (continued from page 314)

1954 Nouveaux Horizons Edition, *Le Federaliste, Extraits des Articles Rediges par A. Hamilton, J. Madison, et J. Jay en Defense du Projet de Constitution des Etats-Unis.* Paris: Les Editions Inter-Nationales.

1961 Brock, W. R., ed. New York & London: E. P. Dutton.
Reissue of Everyman, with new introduction.

1961 Cooke, Jacob E., ed. Middletown, Conn.: Wesleyan University Press.

1961 Fairfield, Roy P., ed. Garden City, N.Y.: Doubleday & Co.
Includes all or parts of fifty-one numbers, about half the text.

1961 Rossiter, Clinton, ed. New York: Mentor.
Most inclusive paperback; has excellent index.

1961 Wright, Benjamin F., ed. Cambridge: The Belknap Press of Harvard University Press.

1962 Longaker, Richard P., *Moulding A Republic: The Federalist Papers.* Washington, D.C.: United States Information Service.
A USIS publication, consists of key quotes, commentary on theory found in *Federalist* and *No. 78* complete. Designed as an introduction for overseas use.

1964 Hacker, Andrew, ed. New York: Washington Square Press.
Includes twenty-six numbers, about one quarter of the text.

II

Periodicals

Adair, Douglass, "The Federalist Papers: A Review Article," *William & Mary Quarterly*, Third Series, XXI, No. 1 (Jan. 1965), 131–39.

Brant, Irving, "Settling the Authorship of *The Federalist*," *American Historical Review*, LXVII, No. 1 (Oct. 1961), 71–75.

Cooke, Jacob E., "Alexander Hamilton's Authorship of the 'Caesar' Letters," *William & Mary Quarterly*, Third Series, XVII, No. 1 (Jan. 1960), 78–85.

Crane, Elaine P., "Publius in the Provinces: Where Was *The Federalist* Reprinted Outside New York City?" *William & Mary Quarterly*, Third Series, No. 4 (Oct. 1964), 589–92.

Kendall, Willmoore, "On the 'Federalist': The State of Our Understanding," *National Review*, XV, No. 22 (Dec. 3, 1965), 491–94.

Koch, Adrienne, "Return of 'Publius'," *Nation*, CXCIII, No. 6 (Sept. 2, 1961), 125–28.

Riemer, Neal, "Political Theory as a Guide to Action: Madison and the Prudential Component in Politics," *Social Science*, XXXV, No. 1 (Jan. 1960), 17–25.

Swindler, William F., "The Letters of Publius," *American Heritage*, XII, No. 4 (June 1961), 4–7, 92–97.

Books

Alexander, Holmes Moss, *How To Read the Federalist*. Boston, 1961.

Mosteller, Frederick, and Wallace, David L., *Inference and Disputed Authorship*. Reading, Mass., 1964.

SELECTED BIBLIOGRAPHY
1981

Editions of *Federalist* (continued from pages 314 and 321)

1966   Kendall, Wilmoore, and Carey, George W., eds. New Rochelle, N.Y.: Arlington House.

In the introduction to this Heirloom Edition, published for the Conservative Book Club, the editors disagree that the essays were "propaganda"; although they were a polemic, they were not "schoolteacherish," but refined the Constitution "so daringly" as to make them "a further and drastic step in constitution-building." The editors exhort conservatives to "steep" themselves in the papers for the rationale to oppose liberal egalitarianism, and they stress "self-government with justice" through elected representatives.

Periodicals and Books

No serious student of federalism can neglect *The Federalist Papers,* hence:

De Pauw, Linda G. *The Eleventh Pillar.* Ithaca, 1966.

De Pauw's one-chapter overview is a succinct analysis of the origins, nature, and impact of the *Papers* upon the times; there is "no evidence" that they "converted a single antifederalist." Remarkably concise.

Mace, George. *Locke, Hobbes, and "The Federalist Papers": An Essay on the Genesis of the American Political Heritage.* Carbondale, Ill., 1979.

A cogent comparison of the three bodies of writing, turning most scholarship on its head to argue that "the birthrights in our heritage are Hobbesian, not Lockean."

Ostrom, Vincent. *The Political Theory of a Compound Republic: A Reconstruction of the Logical Foundations of American Democracy as Presented in "The Federalist."* Blacksburg, Va., 1971.

  Fascinating and well-sustained contention that "a theory of concurrent regimes" or a "compound republic" is a much needed paradigm to deal with the current problems of our diverse society.

Riker, William. *Federalism: Origin, Operation, Significance.* Boston, 1964.

  Cautions readers to avoid the ideological fallacy that federalism is related to freedom.

Rokeach, M.; Homant, R.; and Penner, L. "A Value Analysis of the Disputed *Federalist Papers." Journal of Personality Social Psychology,* XII, No. 2 (Oct. 1970), 245–50.

  This report on a study to determine whether values in the disputed twelve papers could contribute to determination of authorship concludes that the correlation is significantly higher with the papers of Madison than with those of Hamilton or Jay.

Smith, M. "Reason, Passion, and Political Freedom in *The Federalist." Journal of Politics,* XXII, No. 3 (Aug. 1960), 525–44.

  This study of the classical conflict between passion and reason which is a major theme in the *Papers* concludes that a rational government protects the commonweal against excessive passion.

Stockton, C. N. "Are There Natural Rights in *The Federalist?" Ethics,* LXXXII, No. 1 (Oct. 1971), 72–82.

  Although the Lockean philosophy of natural rights inspired the American Revolution, Stockton finds few clear appeals to natural rights except for the right of private property; hence, the work appears to be based more on empirical than metaphysical premises.

INDEX*

Agriculture, 11, 42, 90, 97, 124, 175, 187
Ambassadors. *See* Foreign Affairs, 195
Amending Constitution, 117, 151, 155–58, 273–76
American Genius, 38, 98
American Indian, 12, 64, 65, 68
American Revolution, 6, 28, 51–52, 69, 70, 71, 91, 111, 134, 150, 272
Anarchy, Danger of, 36, 54, 71, 162, 198
Anti-Federalists, 7, 12, 27–28, 57, 62, 78–79, 106–11, 122, 126, 131, 197, 221, 231, 276
Aristocracy, Fear of, 107, 197
Army, Standing. *See* Militia
    danger of, 120–22, 177
    organization, function, and importance of, 15, 33, 36–39, 51, 59–75, 109, 119, 136, 194
Articles of Confederation
    defects of, 1, 4, 7, 12–13, 29–41, 45–49, 50–58, 59, 66, 99, 105, 108–11, 132, 134, 225, 270
Axioms of Government, 76–77, 130, 243

Bill of Attainder, 126, 128, 228, 260
Bill of Rights, 106, 259–64, 270
Blackstone, William, 261
Britain
    bill of rights, 71, 261, 262, 264
    competition with, 11, 13, 14, 15, 64–65, 68
    Constitution and laws, 101, 139–41, 203, 260
    executive, 193–96, 203, 218
    geographical advantage, 120, 123
    government, general, 112
    judiciary, 233, 242–43, 244
    Parliament, 140, 166, 209, 242–43, 244
    treaty with, 12
    wars, 90, 121–22

Capitol, Location of, 264
Checks and Balances. *See* Power, Powers, 109, 131, 133, 138–63, 167–81, 173, 183–84, 203–4, 215–20, 226, 231–32, 242–45, 265, 274
China, 14
Chosen People, Americans as, 1, 6–7

* For a more descriptive index, one comparing concepts in the *Federalist* with those in other great books, see the Syntopicon volumes indexing the 1952 Great Books edition.

Citizens, Impact of Government upon. *See* People, 38–44, 60–61, 93–94, 100, 117, 171, 187, 237

Civil Liberties. *See* Bill of Rights, Bill of Attainder, *Ex-Post-Facto* Laws, *Habeas Corpus*, Liberty, 6–7, 38–41, 84, 100, 106, 128, 138, 161–64, 166, 180, 257, 259–64, 270

Civil Rebellion
danger of, 36–38, 40–41, 75, 89, 99, 173, 275

Class Interests, 2, 6, 7–9, 11, 18, 19, 93–94, 96–98, 136, 154, 172–78, 186, 271

Commerce, Domestic and Foreign, 9, 11, 14, 15, 30, 50, 55, 60, 65–66, 80–81, 89, 93–97, 119, 124, 137, 175–76, 186–88, 236, 241

Common Defence. *See* Security, Union, 58–75, 77, 89–90, 119–26, 137

Common Sense, 27, 28, 52, 76, 77, 198–99, 206, 256, 266

Commonweal, 1, 3, 4, 5–9, 16–23, 28, 35, 54, 60, 73–74, 77, 104, 118, 134, 137, 188, 192, 206, 213, 219, 266, 271

Communication and Transportation. *See* Commerce, 6, 24, 64

Community. *See* Commonweal, 206

Concurrent Jurisdiction. *See* Power, national vs. state, 76–98, 234–38

Confederacy, as Alternative to Federal Union, 4, 5, 9, 11, 12, 15, 62, 114, 122, 162, 171

Congress. *See* House, Senate, 21, 22, 81, 82, 215–20, 241, 267–69

Connecticut, 47, 142

Consent of Governed. *See* Democracy, People, Representative Gov't, Republican Gov't, Social Contract, 5–6, 57–58, 100, 112, 114–15, 151–52, 159, 160, 165–67, 197, 228–29, 231, 275

Conspiracy. *See* Faction, Treason, 74–75

Continental Congress, 8–9, 35–36, 53–54, 57, 60, 110–11, 126

Contracts, 126, 128, 222

Convention, Constitutional
problems of, 99–104
general, 7, 9, 12, 28, 62, 83, 85, 87, 92, 105, 108, 114, 130, 131

Corruption in Government. *See* Faction, Parties, 258

Cost of Government. *See* Taxation, 38, 69, 90–93, 106–7, 266–69

Courts. *See* Judiciary

Credit, Public. *See* Cost of Gov't, Debt, Fiscal Policy, 30

Council of Censors, Pennsylvania, 156–58

Coup d'etat. See Civil Rebellion, 177

Debt. *See* Fiscal Policy, 91, 110

Debtors, Attitude of, 23

Delaware, 113, 143, 193, 244

Democracy. *See* Consent of Governed, People, Representative Gov't, Republican Gov't, Social Contract
direct, 16, 20, 24–25, 47

Democracy (*cont'd*)
representative, 20–23, 147, 197
Despotism. *See* Tyranny, 3, 197
Disunion. *See* Union, 9

Economic Conditions, 6, 8, 9, 29–31
Economy in Government. *See* Cost of Gov't
Elections. *See* House, President, Senate, 100, 165–81
Empire, American, 1, 2, 41, 58
Equality, Political. *See* Civil Liberties, Democracy, Elections, Suffrage, 20–21
Executive. *See* President, States
Experience as Teacher, 8, 28, 32, 34, 67, 69, 70, 96, 101, 128, 146, 148, 160, 165, 200, 212, 275
Ex-Post-Facto Laws, 126, 128, 228, 261
Exports. *See* Commerce, Tariffs, 80, 81, 124

Faction
defined, 17
general, 6, 8, 11, 16–23, 34, 40, 46, 47, 54, 73–74, 96–98, 102, 103, 154–55, 156–58, 162, 170, 171, 173, 179, 184, 198, 200, 201, 206, 217, 244, 271
Farmer. *See* Agriculture
Federalism. *See* Republican Gov't
defined, 114–18
general, 21–23, 26–27, 39, 42–43, 134–38, 163, 169–70, 182–84, 251–55
Federalist, The
object of, 4, 99
Fiscal Policy. *See* Cost of Gov't,

15, 30, 73–75, 76–98, 110, 119, 121, 124, 126–28, 148, 266–69
Fishing, as Industry, 14
Foreign Affairs. *See* Common Defence, Treaties
negotiations, 50–51, 137, 182, 190, 195, 221–25, 236, 237, 240, 267
security problems, 10–13, 14, 27, 30, 33, 55, 69, 89, 99, 172, 186, 198
Founding Fathers, 147
France, 14, 15, 47, 90
Free Government. *See* Consent of Governed, Democracy, Representative Gov't, Republican Gov't

Geography, as Related to Union. *See* Sectional Interests, 4, 6, 21–22, 24–28, 63, 163, 173, 179–80
Georgia, 145, 244
Germany. *See* Prussia, 47
Glorious Revolution, England, 71
God, 6, 103
Government
accidental, 1
bad, inefficient, 57, 185–86, 198
good, efficient, energetic, 1, 3, 4, 7, 11, 54–55, 58–63, 99, 129–31, 134, 160, 185, 198, 207
municipal, 116
national, value of (*see* Federation, Power, Republican Gov't, Union), 7, 10–13, 14–15, 43, 58–59, 68, 114–18
number employees, 136, 266–69

Government (cont'd)
　objectives of, 17–18, 34, 58–
　　63, 118, 119, 134, 162, 185
Greece, Ancient, 25, 104–5

Habeas Corpus, 258, 260
Happiness of People. See Com-
　monweal
History, Use of, 3, 90, 101, 103–
　5
Holland. See Netherlands
Homer, 139
House of Representatives
　election of, 113, 115, 133,
　　135, 167–81
　general function, 116, 164–
　　67, 194, 221, 224, 234
　membership, 95–98, 106, 107
　qualifications for, 181
　tenure, 113
Hudson River, 123
Human Nature. See Passion . . . ,
　Self-interest, Reason, 2–4,
　5–9, 10, 13, 14, 18, 34, 43,
　103, 152–53, 155, 160, 200,
　205–6, 211–12, 231, 233,
　235, 272
Humors. See Human Nature,
　206, 231

Impeachment, 107, 192–94, 234,
　260
Imports. See Commerce, 80, 81,
　124
Industry, 18, 19, 90, 93–94, 96,
　97, 124, 174–75, 187
Injustice. See Faction, 12, 14,
　16–23, 52–53, 60, 161, 231,
　232
International Relations. See For-
　eign Affairs
Italy, 25

Japan, 253

Jefferson, Thomas, 148, 151
Jenkinson, Charles, 50
Judicial Review, 156–58, 228–33
Judiciary
　appointment of, 113, 159, 226
　compensation of, 234
　cost of, 267
　divisions of, 242–51
　function of, 39–41, 101–2,
　　117, 190, 226–33, 234, 236–
　　41, 242–55
　miscellaneous problems, 11,
　　55–56, 242
　qualifications for, 244
　tenure, 113, 159, 226–35, 244
Jury Trial, 125, 248–51, 255–59,
　260
Justice, 16, 18–19, 39, 42, 43, 52,
　127, 162, 228–33

Landlords. See Class Interests,
　96–97
Land Values, 30, 47, 49
Language, 6
Law. See Judiciary, Justice
　civil, 69, 126, 128, 185, 186,
　　217, 228, 249, 250, 256,
　　258, 259, 262
　common, 249–50, 260, 262
　Constitution as Supreme Law
　　of the Land, 40, 55, 78, 84,
　　87, 109, 131–32, 190
　criminal, 256, 258
　defined, 186
　international (see Treaties),
　　11–13, 190
　interpretation of (see Judici-
　　ary), 101, 226–33
　miscellaneous, 12, 190
Law Enforcement. See Militia,
　Security, 33, 39–41, 42–43,
　45–46
Leadership. See President, State,
　executives in, 19, 23

Legislature of the United States. *See* House, Senate

Legislatures, Function of, 18, 57, 84, 201, 207

Letters of Marque, 126

Liberty. *See* Civil Liberties, 3–5, 8, 17, 28, 42, 43, 46, 69, 70, 104, 109, 120–26, 154, 186, 266

Loyalty, 42–44, 67

Lycurgus, 105, 108

Magna Charta, 262

Majority Rule, Minority Rights. *See* Civil Liberties, 16, 17, 19, 52, 117, 161, 201

Manifest Destiny, 1, 6, 103

Manners and Customs, 6

Manufacturing. *See* Industry

Maryland, 47, 105, 113, 123, 144, 193, 244

Massachusetts, 46, 142, 193, 220, 244

Means and Ends in Government. *See* Necessary and Proper Clause, 39, 59, 76–79, 92, 118, 130

Mechanics. *See* Class Interests, 97

Merchants. *See* Class Interests, Commerce, 96, 97, 187

Military. *See* Army, Militia, 30

Militia. *See* Army, Military, 15, 65, 119, 124, 136, 194

Mississippi River, 15, 30

Monarchy, Advantages and Disadvantages, 55, 107, 147, 197, 222

Money. *See* Cost of Gov't, Fiscal Policy, Taxation, 38, 126–28

Montesquieu, 139–41

National Character, 99

Natural Resources, 6, 15, 98, 110, 267

Natural Rights, 5, 6–7

Navigation Rights, 30

Navy. *See* Army, 66, 89, 119, 123, 194

Necessary and Proper Clause. *See* Means and Ends in Gov't, 83–86, 129–31

Negative Pregnant, 82

Netherlands, The, 47, 103, 112, 225

New England, 249

New Hampshire, 141, 244

New Jersey, 47, 105, 143, 199

New York
constitution, 142–43, 235, 260, 263, 269–70
executive, 192, 193, 194–97, 202, 205, 220
judiciary, 194, 249
legislature, 97, 113, 253, 265
miscellaneous, 47, 95, 123

Nobility, Titles of, 114, 126, 129, 260, 261

North Carolina, 47, 70, 144, 244

Oath to Constitution, 132–33

Office-holding, 11, 98, 165, 176, 181–82, 244

Pardon and Reprieve, 194

Parties, Political. *See* Faction, 3, 22–23, 73–74, 103, 156–58, 235, 266, 271

Passion and Immediate Interest. *See* Faction, Human Nature, Self-interest, 1–2, 12, 18, 20, 34, 37, 56, 153, 155, 157, 184, 205

Patriotism. *See* Loyalty, 7, 8, 9, 21

Peace. *See* Foreign Affairs, Treaties, 10–11, 90, 137, 188, 240–41

Pennsylvania, 47, 70, 143, 149–50, 244
People. *See* Consent of Governed, Democracy, Social Contract, 4–9, 62, 67, 71, 74, 99–100, 111, 112, 131, 165–67, 206, 228–29
Plato, 153
Poland, 112, 225
Politicians, 6, 134
Population, 47
Portugal, 11
Power. *See* Federalism, Republican Gov't, States
   abuse of, 34, 67, 166–72
   classes of, 118–33
   defined, 84
   duration, ideal, 166–67
   of judiciary, national, 138–63, 227–28, 236–52
   of legislature, national, 63–75, 122, 125, 138–63, 215–16, 229, 256–57
   of national gov't, 5, 21–23, 31, 38, 42, 45–49, 50, 57–63, 70, 77–78, 114–18, 129–31, 137, 167–81, 273–76
   national vs. state, 26, 42–44, 46–47, 63–98, 131–33, 251–55, 272–76
   of people (*see* Consent of Governed), 57–58, 100
   of president, 41, 63, 64, 68, 71–72, 73, 75, 107, 109, 115, 138–63, 187–225
   of states, 2, 42–44, 45, 52–53, 56–58, 117, 126–29, 131, 134–38, 167–81, 252
Powers
   blending of, 109, 146, 158–63, 221–25
   separation of, 100–1, 107, 118, 138–63, 207, 215–20, 226–34, 243–51

Preamble to Constitution, 262
President of the United States
   appointive power, 107, 195
   cabinet, 210, 267, 268
   commander-in-chief of the military, 194
   compensation, 215–16
   election, 113, 133, 135, 210–15
   execution of law, 100
   power, general, 11, 115, 192–225
   qualifications for, 198, 199, 208–9, 219
   tenure, 113, 192–94, 205–9
   treaty-making, 109, 187–92, 221–25
   unity of, 199–205
   veto power, 161, 193–94, 216–20
Press, 8, 125, 263
Privileges and Immunities, 238
Professions. *See* Class . . . , 96, 97
Progress. *See* Manifest Destiny, 27–28, 267
Property. *See* Land Values, 4, 17, 18, 20, 21, 23, 43, 69, 70, 174–77, 186, 198, 241
Prussia. *See* Germany, 11
Public Good. *See* Commonweal
Public Opinion, as Restraint. *See* People, 203

Ratification of Constitution, 114–15
Reason and Permanent Interest. *See* Human Nature, Passion . . . , Self-interest, 5, 7, 8, 9, 10, 13, 17, 155, 157
Rebellion. *See* Civil Rebellion
Referendum, 151–56
Religion, 6, 23, 161
Reparations, 13

Representative Government. *See* Federalism, Republican Gov't, 8–9, 20–21, 25, 52, 61, 95–100, 131, 165, 182–84, 228–29

Republican Government. *See* Federalism, Representative Gov't, 3, 19, 20–23, 24–25, 55, 100, 111–18, 147, 153, 160, 163, 198, 199, 206, 235, 257–58, 261

Revolution. *See* Civil Rebellion

Rhode Island, 142, 163

Right of Revolution, 58, 231

Rivers, 9, 15

Roman Government, 225

Rotation in Office, 100, 165, 170, 180

Rural Influence. *See* Agriculture

Russia, 47

Sectional Interests, 21, 102, 163, 173, 179–80

Security. *See* Army, Common Defence, Commonweal, 10, 11, 12, 14–15, 59, 99, 120, 179, 182–87, 214, 223, 225

Self-interest. *See* Faction, Human Nature, Passions . . . , 1–2, 10, 17–23, 35–36, 96–98, 160, 162, 205, 211–12, 223

Senate
appointive power, 107
election, 113, 115, 135, 167–81
general function of, 181–92, 194, 234, 242
membership, 183–84
qualifications for, 181–82, 185
quorum, 170
tenure, 113, 170, 183–86, 188
treaty-making, 109, 187–92, 194, 221–25

Shays' Rebellion, 46

Slavery, 109

Social Compact, 45, 58, 128, 272, 273

Sovereignty. *See* Power, States, 6, 30, 31, 35–36, 76–98, 100–2, 222, 248

South Carolina, 113, 144–45, 244

Spain, 11, 13, 15, 30, 64–65, 68

Speculators, 128

Spoils System, 210

St. Lawrence River, 15

States. *See* Federalism, Power, Union
constitutions, 16, 63, 111, 128, 131, 132, 141–45, 153, 161, 164–65, 203, 260, 262, 264
employees, 136
executives in, 11, 113, 195
factions in, 23
fiscal policy, 91, 248
government, general, 11–12, 14, 28, 66, 100
judiciary, 11, 56, 61, 113, 114, 136, 236, 237, 238, 243–55, 257–58
legislatures, 11, 22, 39–41, 70–73, 113, 115, 128, 131, 135, 167–81, 182, 185, 236, 240, 244–45, 268, 274
national-state relations, 5, 11–12, 45–46, 52–58, 78–80, 85, 265
raising Revolutionary army, 51–52, 60
ratifying processes, 105, 114–15
small state-large state conflict, 52–53, 102, 106, 182–84
sovereignty, 11, 12–13, 15, 35, 113, 114–15, 116–17, 132, 134–38, 251–55, 272–76

States (*cont'd*)
    taxation, 47, 76–98
    territorial disputes, 110, 238, 241
    voting qualifications set by, 165
Suffrage, 21–22, 164–65, 177, 178–79
Supreme Court. *See* Judiciary

Tariff, 14, 51, 93–95, 124
Taxation, 19, 47–49, 76–98, 107, 109, 121, 124, 136–38, 186
Town Influence, 11
Treason, 261
Treaties. *See* President, Senate, 7, 10, 11, 12–13, 30, 32–33, 56, 109, 126, 131, 187–92, 194–95, 221–25, 239, 240
Tyranny. *See* Despotism, 40, 46–47, 57, 139

Unconstitutional Action, 39–40
Uniformity of Interests, 17, 20
Union, Advantages of. *See* Gov't, efficient, 1–23, 45–46, 52– 53, 56, 58–63, 75, 110–11, 120–26, 133–34, 172, 237, 266, 270, 275
Utopia, 272

Venice, 112
Veto Power, General, 53–55
Virginia, 47, 113, 123, 144, 148, 166, 244

War. *See* American Revolution
    causes of, 11, 12, 14, 90, 237
    civil (*see* Civil Rebellion), 36–38, 40–41
    cost of, 90
    dangers of, 10, 90
    declaration of, 68, 119, 197
    general problems of, 7, 69, 137, 188
    Indian, 12
    prevention of, 89–90
Washington, George, 150
Wealth, National, 48
West Indies, 64
Western Territory, 26, 30, 64, 65–66, 110

Roy P. Fairfield is professor of humanistic studies at the Union Graduate School, Union for Experimenting Colleges and Universities, in Cincinnati. He is a former Fulbright Professor of History at Athens College in Greece and has had numerous articles, fables, poems, and book reviews published in the *New York Times*, the *Christian Science Monitor*, *American Literature*, the *New England Quarterly*, the *Journal of Politics*, the *Humanist*, and other periodicals. He is the author of *Sand, Spindles, and Steeples: A History of Saco, Maine* and *Person-Centered Graduate Education*. He is also the editor of *Humanistic Frontiers in American Education* and *Humanizing the Workplace*.